The Institutional Evolution of China

ADVANCES IN NEW INSTITUTIONAL ANALYSIS

Series Editor: Claude Ménard, *Professor of Economics and Director, ATOM (Center for Analytical Theory of Organizations and Markets), University of Paris Panthéon-Sorbonne, France*

Understanding the nature and role of institutions in the dynamics and failures of modern economies is an increasing concern among scholars and policy makers. Substantial progress has been made in economics as well as in other social sciences, particularly political science, history, sociology and the managerial sciences. New institutional scholars have been, and remain, at the forefront of this movement. Alternative views have also been proposed that deserve consideration. This series intends to promote the development and diffusion of these analyses with books from leading contributors as well as younger up-and-coming scholars.

The series will include topics such as:

- Institutions and growth
- Transaction cost economics
- The role of formal rules and legal institutions
- Regulation and deregulation
- Political institutions and the state
- Institutions and modes of governance
- Contracting issues
- Customs, beliefs and institutional changes.

The series will be essential reading for researchers in economics, the social and managerial sciences, as well as policymakers.

Titles in the series include:

Institutions and Development
Mary M. Shirley

Regulation, Deregulation, Reregulation
Institutional Perspectives
Edited by Claude Ménard and Michel Ghertman

Managing Transaction Costs in the Era of Globalization
Frank A.G. den Butter

Law and Development
An Institutional Critique
Frank H. Stephen

The Institutional Evolution of China
Government vs Market
Fan Zhang

The Institutional Evolution of China

Government vs Market

Fan Zhang

National School of Development, Peking University, China

ADVANCES IN NEW INSTITUTIONAL ANALYSIS

Edward Elgar
PUBLISHING

Cheltenham, UK • Northampton, MA, USA

Published by
Edward Elgar Publishing Limited
The Lypiatts
15 Lansdown Road
Cheltenham
Glos GL50 2JA
UK

Edward Elgar Publishing, Inc.
William Pratt House
9 Dewey Court
Northampton
Massachusetts 01060
USA

A catalogue record for this book
is available from the British Library

Library of Congress Control Number: 2018943997

This book is available electronically in the **Elgar**online
Economics subject collection
DOI 10.4337/9781784716912

MIX
Paper from responsible sources
FSC® C013056

ISBN 978 1 78471 690 5 (cased)
ISBN 978 1 78471 691 2 (eBook)

Typeset by Servis Filmsetting Ltd, Stockport, Cheshire
Printed and bound in Great Britain by TJ International Ltd, Padstow

Contents

Figures

Tables

Acknowledgements

I would like to thank many researchers in the field with whom I discussed relevant topics, including Dr Wen Guanzhong, Dr Zheng Yongnian, Dr Li Lixing, Dr Xi Tianyang, Dr Tao Ran, Mr Fan Dongsheng, Dr Yin Hongbiao, Dr Zhang Weiying, and anonymous reviewers. I would like to thank Alex Pettifer, who invited me to write this book three years ago when we walked together at the campus of Peking University, and Professor Claude Ménard for his time and effort in editing the manuscript of this book. I would also like to thank Mr Edward Elgar, under whose support I finished my first book in English, *China's Urbanization and the World Economy*. Thanks to Tori Nicols, Emily Mew, Rachel Downie, Harry Fabian, David Adams, Kaitlin Gray, and Ellen Pearce, all from Edward Elgar Publishing, for helping me finish the process of editing and improving the text.

I would like to thank Lisa Zhang, who did a close-read edit of the drafts of this book during the hot summer days of 2017. I would also like to thank my research assistants at Peking University, Liu Jiajia, Zheng Yawen, Bi Jiachuan, Dong Ye, Huang Tianyu, and Lv Kaichen, for their excellent work. Finally, I owe a great debt to my wife, Li Yuping, for her continued support of my work.

Introduction to *The Institutional Evolution of China*

China's experience over the past four decades is not just a story of economic growth, but also one of institutional change. The most impressive event of economic reform in the past four decades has been the creation of private enterprises and the market from nowhere, through the joint efforts of the Chinese government and society in a period of one generation. This is a tremendous achievement, which has created a miracle of economic growth and brought benefits to Chinese people. This rich experience of institutional change in China needs to be explored. The reform since the late 1970s has not finished. As a result, the current political-economic system in China is a dual system, a bureaucratic-market system in which the government and the market both coexist and conflict with each other. China's economic growth in the past 40 years can be explained within the framework of this bureaucratic-market system. China matters economically and politically to the rest of the world, and understanding institutional changes in China is important for policy makers, business people, students, and researchers. In this book, I give a detailed description of the institutional evolution in China during its recent economic reform, using a large number of documents and cases. The book also provides an index to measure the scale of China's marketisation.

The central issue of China's institutional changes in the past 40 years is the relationship between government and market. Different from many existing researches which emphasise inputs of production, this book argues that institutional changes have been the most fundamental causes of China's recent economic growth. The institutional rearrangement of government and market has been crucial in this process. The government's gradual relaxation of control of the market played an extremely important role in the process of reform. The market has been the fundamental source of the economic growth in China, as the government has cleared the obstacles to the development of the market. This has resulted in rapid growth, but at the same time it has created problems of income inequality and corruption in a system without many checks and balances.

This book describes China's economic reform from 1978 to the 2010s following two theoretical frameworks: (i) Douglass North's theory of path dependence in institutional evolution, which explains the sequence of institutional changes in China, and (ii) a theory of political economy (developed in section 1.2), which explains an authoritarian government's decision-making in a bureaucratic-market economy like the one in China.

Path dependence exists in the process of China's institutional evolution. The reform in China experienced a circuitous path, from the creation and development of the market to stagnation and redirection of the reform. Historically, China's economic reform came from the rock bottom of the Cultural Revolution, which hurt every group in Chinese society, including government officials. This built the whole society's consensus on the need for change and resulted in the government-led reform. In the early years of reform, the government reduced its control of the society and increased incentives to the lower level of government and the society. However, such a consensus on reform has been diluted incredibly in the process of change when the expansion of the market hurts the interests of different groups of people. The nature of the bureaucratic-market system fostered corruption among government officials and business executives, and this has damaged social equity and justice. The last 15 years of reform have experienced stagnation and readjustments of government policies. This was fundamentally a result of the changing priorities of government decisions, which in turn was caused, ironically, by the improving economic situation and the loosening of government control.

This book provides a framework of a theory of political economy explaining the origin of China's reform, the political and economic forces driving the reform, and the reasoning behind the stagnation of the reform. The government has multiple targets, and political stability and economic performance have become restrictions on its behaviour. Economic performance has been an important source of legitimacy of the rule of the government. Social stability, meanwhile, has been the main target and the foundation of the existence of the government. There are two basic policy options, economic policy and social stability policy, for the government to choose. Economic policy promotes economic growth and marketisation, whereas social stability policy maintains social stability and the government's own existence. The two policies are sometimes contradictory, so the leadership has to make trade-offs. The weight of the two policies changes over time, based on the political and economic environment. The book tries to draw a theoretical boundary between the government and the market, according to two rules: (i) following the economic theory of government intervention, intervention is appropriate only if several conditions exist, including asymmetric information, externalities, natural monopoly, non-existence of markets, and absence of property rights; (ii) considering the institutional background, certain government interventions will be reasonable if the market is less developed and imperfect.

The economic and political reform that started in the late 1970s created a market economy, but reforms in many fields still need to be achieved. The unfinished reforms contain several serious flaws: (i) the administrative branch of the government has not been not effectively restricted; (ii) the market reform has not been completed, with upstream resource-intensified sectors still controlled by the state; (iii) large state-owned enterprises (SOEs) still dominate some key sectors, whereas private firms face high tax burdens and overregulation; (iv) farmers do not have full property rights of the land, and local government monopolises the transfer of rural land to urban uses, which causes soaring urban housing prices; (v) the nature of the bureaucratic-market system fostered corruption among government officials and business executives. The main risk in China today is the government's unrestricted power to further squeeze out the private market.

This kind of government-led economic reform using a gradual approach reduced the difficulty of reform but at the same time left the bureaucratic system largely untouched, and this has become a perennial risk to the continuation of the reform. The most recent adjustments of the ruling strategy focus on the restructuring of power within the government and restraining the behaviour of government officials. These adjustments follow the logic of government rule, rather than that of market expansion. One of the key targets of the adjustments is corruption, the main concern of Chinese society today. To fight corruption, the government took back power and used more administrative means. This move indicates a major change in the strategy of governance that has been in place since the late 1970s.

To sum up, the government-led and non-balanced political counterpart nature of the reform created a bureaucratic-market system, which fostered corruption and to some extent lost control of both the society and the supervision of government officials. A radical response of the government to corruption and a decree barrier using administrative means, may have further centralised the system. This solved some urgent problems but might hurt the long-term vitality of the Chinese economy.

In the near future it is quite possible that, in China, a strong, impersonal, and efficient government will coexist with an under-control market in the short term. This system will have the large mobilisation forces needed to reach many of its targets, such as building large public projects or developing high-tech industries by mobilising large numbers of workers, technicians, and resources. Yet the enthusiasm of the market may be more restricted, and that may have effects on the creativity of the Chinese economy. In the long run, the bureaucratic-market system is unstable and further political and economic reforms are needed. The role of government should further retreat from many areas; government power must be restricted, and the initiative and creativity of the market should be brought into full play. These are the many issues this book deals with.

1. Analytical framework

China began its transition to a market economy nearly thirty years ago under an authoritarian and hierarchical political system . . . the dramatic change in transition strategy . . . gives insight into the achievements, limitations, and future prospects of reform under authoritarian auspices.
Barry Naughton (2008, p. 91)

In this book, I will illuminate features of institutional changes in China since the late 1970s, focusing on the relationship between the government and the market during the economic reform. Douglass North defines institutions as 'humanly devised constraints that structure political, economic and social interactions' (North 1991, p. 97). Constraints, as North describes them, are devised as formal rules (constitutions, laws, property rights) and informal restraints (sanctions, taboos, customs, traditions, codes of conduct), which usually contribute to the perpetuation of order and safety within a market or society. Institutions work as structures or mechanisms of social order (e.g. the rules and organisations), the background upon which economic and political activities perform. The book highlights the institutional bases of the economic growth in China in the process of economic reform in the past four decades.

China has experienced dramatic changes in economic performance in the past 40 years, but not enough attention has been paid to the background of this progress: the institutional changes. China's success over the past several decades is a story of not only economic growth but also institutional changes. These changes in economic performance and the difference between the planned economy of the past and the market economy today are rooted in the evolutions of China's political and economic institutions. Furthermore, to perform an international comparison, the differences between the economies in Western industrial countries and in China are also based on the differences between their institutions.

In the planned period from 1949 to 1977, the Chinese government played a near-omnipotent role in China, owning most of the resources, infrastructure, and enterprises.[1] It made the decisions of what to produce, for whom to produce, and how to produce. Only a small market existed in the area of consumer goods, and government rationing interfered with this. The tight control created incentive problems for workers, and per capita income was at a very low level. The poverty and the political conflict hurt every citizen and helped to form a consensus, among the leadership and the ordinary people, that this controlled-economy system should be abandoned, and the reform began in 1978. The economic reform from 1978 to the 2010s introduced market principles and opened up the Chinese economy to the world.[2] In the process of reform, the government deliberately and gradually relaxed its control over the economy, letting the market play a more important role. The government gave the peasants rights to use the land, and lifted price controls on most consumer goods and some producer goods, letting the price mechanism work freely in these sectors. There was a silent privatisation in 1990s, in which the government sold most of the small and medium-sized state-owned enterprises (SOEs) to the public. More and more development zones were established, opening to the outside world. These institutional changes resulted in unprecedented growth. Many institutional innovations were created in the process of reform. While the government changed its role to some extent during the reform, the basic political system did not change much.

As a result of this unfinished reform, the current political-economic system in China is a dual system – a bureaucratic-market system in which the government and the market coexist and conflict with each other. The government is in a dominant position, whereas the market has occupied a corner of Chinese society and become part of the existing hierarchical system.[3] The government makes major macroeconomic decisions and intervenes in the market to a certain extent, whereas enterprises maximise their profits under government regulation. As a result of reforms to the economic system, for example the relaxing of government control of pricing and the selling of small state-owned firms to the public, private firms have grown significantly and now play an indispensable role in the economy. On the political side, however, after nearly 40 years of economic reform, to some extent the political system is moving back towards its historical and tradition form. Many of the changes in the reform process can be explained by this dual political-economic system. As noted by Barry Naughton, 'new economic powers have grown up alongside authoritarian hierarchy' (Naughton 2008, p.130). All solutions to socioeconomic problems need to address the roles of both the government and the markets, and the system is still in a process of change and far from equilibrium.

The most incredible event of the economic reform in the past 40 years has been the creation of private enterprises and the market from the institutional rubble of the Cultural Revolution. China's institutional reform created a miracle of economic performance, in which both the government and the market played an extremely important role. The increased productivity comes from two sources: (i) creativity from the bottom of the society made possible by relaxation of government regulations; and (ii) strong leadership by the government, especially local government, in economic development as a product of the competition between local governments.

The institutional change in China is a long-term process from a planned economy to a market economy or, politically, a change from a totalitarian to an authoritarian system. A market economy has large numbers of economic agents making their decisions independently, reacting to the signals of the price mechanism. Therefore, decentralisation of authority and incentive creation[4] are the central issues of transition. Since the beginning of the reform, the government has reduced its control on society, and it has increased the incentives of the lower level of government and the society to work. The public domain is still controlled by the government, whereas the private sphere has been freed to some degree. Strong economic performance has become the primary measure of political legitimacy in China. In the transition process, where the existing system lacks a number of institutional features, the government has played an important role and served as an alternative to the formal legal system in providing security and stability to non-state-owned firms.

The central issue of the institutional changes in China over the past 40 years has been, and continues to be, the relationship between the government and the market. This book develops a framework of a political-economy theory of government and market in a bureaucratic-market economy like China. The government is rational and has multiple targets, including maintaining social stability and improving the living standards of its citizens, under certain restrictions. Economic performance and social stability become two major restrictions on political power, whereas firms maximise their profits under the supervision of the government. The government is the designer, controller, and supervisor of society, and the firms and citizens choose to follow the rules or disobey them in different ways. As for the relationship with the different levels of government, the central government sets the rules, while the local government changes its behaviour given the rules set by the central government. A principal–deputy relationship is involved. Supervision and incentive become two major issues in this dual political-economic system, a major trade-off policy makers must face.

Path dependence matters a lot in the process of China's institutional evolution. The reform experienced a circuitous path, from the creation and development of the market to stagnation and redirection of the reform. Historical connections can be seen before and after reform. China's economic reform came from the depths of the Cultural Revolution, which hurt every group in society, including government officials, shaking Chinese society to its foundations. This built the consensus on the need for change in the whole society and resulted in the government-led reform, which was supported by all walks of society. The reform was initiated from the bottom of the society, while the government later accepted the reform and relaxed the relevant regulations. As the reform went on, government took over leadership and initiated follow-up reforms from the top. Since the majority of government officials were seriously damaged by the Cultural Revolution, they became leaders of the reform, which determined its government-led nature. The reform has been an economic one without a balanced political counterpart following the events of Tiananmen Square in 1989. The bureaucracy–market combination is a result of the planned economy and gradual reform. The nature of the bureaucratic-market system fostered corruption among government officials and business executives, many of whom acquired their initial wealth by using their connections with political power. This kind of systematic corruption damaged social equity and justice, and resulted in stagnation of the reform. The market itself proved to be a double-edged sword, hurting some individuals and institutions in the society during the reform process and finally helping to alter its path. The consensus on economic reform has been gradually lost in the process of change when the newly created market hurts the interests of some social groups. A new consensus on the need to stamp out corruption now exists in today's Chinese society. Because the extreme case of the Cultural Revolution is not easy to duplicate, China's economic reform was a black swan event, which cannot be repeated on a similar scale in the near future. Reform is a process involving progress, adjustments, and readjustments. To make adjustments, the government has occasionally changed policy back towards the old system, because of the lack of means of checks and balances.

From the dynamics perspective, the institutional changes have alternately followed bureaucratic logic and market evolution logic and created conflicts. The current situation in China can be considered as an unstable equilibrium in the short run. The long-run equilibrium depends on the balance of government power and market vitality. The future path of China's institutional evolution depends on the trade-off between political stability and economic development by the elites and general society. Compared with the risks of market flaws, the main risk in China is the government's unrestricted power to further squeeze out the private market. Even after 40 years of marketisation reform, the government is still much stronger than the private firms in the market and dominates most aspects of social life. To balance government control and market vitality, further reforms need to be made and government power should be restricted. Economic reform without a balanced political counterpart and the government-led nature of the reform eased economic reform in its early years but left the bureaucratic system largely untouched, and this became a source of stagnation.

This book is unique in several respects. First, I use many documents and cases to give a detailed description of the institutional changes in the past 40 years in China, focused on the government–market relationship, covering changes in formal and informal rules, in political and economic organisations, and in attitudes of government officials, business people, and ordinary citizens. Second, I provide a historical perspective to explain the origin and reasons for China's economic reform, the political and economic forces driving economic reform, and the causes that led to the stagnation of the reform. Third, I present a framework of a theoretical model of political economy, based on existing literature, to explain the targets and incentives of government and business firms in a dual political-economy society. Finally, I offer an index of marketisation in China since 1978, which shows that, overall, market expansion has continued but with diminishing marginal gains, and government control has been enhanced.

Throughout the volume, Chinese names are given in the Chinese official style that is used in mainland China today: the family name without a comma followed by the given name (i.e. Deng Xiaoping). Commas are used only in the Reference list for the first author, following the family name (i.e. Deng, Xiaoping). For the names after the first author in the Reference list, the given name is followed by the family name. The author's name on the cover follows the Western style, the given name (Fan) without a comma followed by the family name (Zhang). All information used in this book is from open sources. Values of RMB are converted to US dollars using official annual average exchange rates. In the period before 1994, the official rates were overvalued compared to market rates, which may distort comparisons between different years (National Bureau of Statistics 2009a and 2015).

I belong to the generation born at the beginning of the planned economy, who were children when the Great Leap Forward resulted in the Great Famine in the late 1950s, who could not finish their middle school when the Cultural Revolution began, who entered colleges when they were in their mid-twenties, and who experienced the whole process of economic reform. I believe that it is our responsibility to rethink the changes in China over the past 40 years and explore reasons behind these changes.

1.1 LITERATURE REVIEW

A tremendous amount of literature exists in the fields related to this book, of which I can only review the most closely related ones due to limited space. These literatures are divided into two groups: (i) the relationship between the government and the market; and (ii) institutional changes in general and those specific to China.

The Relationship between the Government and the Market

Many studies focus on the relationship between the government and the market. Karl Polanyi's *The Great Transformation* (1957 [1944]) analyses the power and limits of the free market, the role of government in economic governance, and the boundaries of the two. One of the functions of the government is to provide a safety net to reduce the damage of the free market on ordinary people. Stiglitz (2016) discusses the advances in understanding of the role of the state in the developmental process over the past 30 years, and the contribution to those advances played by changes in economics, changes in the world, and key experiences, in particular the successes in East Asia and the failures for the countries pursuing Washington Consensus policies. Przeworski (2003) offers a highly readable account of the main ideas around the relationship between the government and the market. The author emphasises that the operation of the economic system depends on the relationship between the state and the private agents, and that the institutional design of this relationship is critical for the development of a society. Other researches on this topic include Datta-Chaudhuri (1990), Bai and Wang (2013), Zhang Jun (2014), Zheng Lixin (2013), Cheng (2013), and Du (2006).

The literature on regulation is closely related to that on the relationship between the government and the market. Stigler (1971) focused on how regulation benefits producers more than consumers, which is a phenomenon termed 'regulatory capture'. Peltzman (1976) improved on Stigler's model and rebalanced Stigler's explanation by showing that the political actors ultimately responsible for regulatory agencies have significant interests that may conflict with those of producers. Legislators seek an equilibrium solution between the interests and campaign contributions of producers and the votes and contributions of citizens on whom they depend for their re-election.

Some literatures are related to the experience in East Asia. Stiglitz (1996 and 2003) offers a list of the ingredients that contributed to the success in East Asia and argues that it is the combination of these ingredients, many of which involve government interventions acting together, that accounts for this success. Robert Wade (1990) provides an analytical account of East Asia's economic miracle in the second half of the 20th century in his book *Governing the Market*. He rejects the claims of both those who see it as the result of the free market and those who see it as the result of government intervention. He argues that what needs attention is the way allocation decisions were divided between markets and the public administration. Aoki et al. (1996) discuss two competing views which have shaped inquiries into the source of the rapid growth of Asian economies:

the market-friendly view, according to which government intervenes little in the market, and the developmental state view, in which it governs the market. The authors suggest a third view: the market-enhancing view. Instead of viewing government and the market as mutually exclusive substitutes, it examines the capacity of government policy to facilitate or complement private-sector coordination. Page (1994) has also conducted research on the topic.

Many researchers have studied the transition in East European countries. Shleifer and Vishny (1994) present a model of bargaining between politicians and managers that explains many stylised facts about the behaviour of state firms, their commercialisation, and privatisation. The model was used to understand why commercialisation and privatisation might work, and what forces contribute to the effective restructuring of public enterprises.

A large number of studies focus on the relationship between the government and the market in the economic reform in China. Wu and Ma's *Restarting the Reform Agenda* (2013) raises the question of where China is going, and points out that the only way out is to restart the economic and political reform. The current system, which consists of both the new market economy and the old controlled economy, could either move forward to a more improved market economy through reform or move back to the planned economy by increasing the government's control. To push forward the reform, China needs to adhere to the direction of marketisation and promote the institutionalisation of socialist democracy.

Justin Yifu Lin and Zhang Weiying had famous debates on the relationship of the government and the market as early as in 1995, which aroused a lot of attention from economists and political scientists in China. They recently had another debate on the industrial policy of the government. Lin insisted that an industrial policy is necessary for developing countries and the government needs to support enterprises, while Zhang argued that all industrial policies fail due to the lack of information and the biased incentives of governments (Lin and Zhang 2017). Zhang Weiying's *Market vs. Government: The Key Game of China's Reform* (2014) points out that effectively restraining the government's destruction of the market is the central issue of every market economy. Tian Guoqiang and Chen Xudong (2015) argue that the slowdown of the Chinese economy in recent years is due to institutional problems, including the halfway marketisation and the unclear boundary between the government and the market. The focus point of marketisation should include allowing private companies to become the main part of the economy, freedom of the financial market, and marketisation of the land. Zhang Jun (2014) reviews the process of economic reform and discusses in detail the relationship between the government and the market.

Zhang Qianfan (2012) discusses, from a legal perspective, the division of power between the central government and the local governments in China. This book argues that without legalisation on the central–local relationship, the centralisation and decentralisation of government power cannot solve China's problems of central–local government relations. The book discusses the meaning of Constitutionalism in dealing with the relationship between central government and local governments in China, and offers suggestions on how this relationship could be dealt with.

Some researchers have tried to find the advantages of a bureaucratic-market economy. Daniel A. Bell's *The China Model: Political Meritocracy and the Limits of Democracy* (2016) defines the Chinese system of political meritocracy, which has a long history and is widely used today in China. Bell argues that the system is a good alternative to the democratic system in Western countries. The system is able to select leaders who have long-term vision and overall consciousness, through examination and evaluation. Ian Bremmer describes state capitalism as a challenge to the free market economies of the developed world. In this system, governments use various kinds of state-owned companies to manage the exploitation of resources. They use selected privately owned companies to dominate certain economic sectors and sovereign wealth funds to invest their extra cash in ways that maximise the state's profits. The ultimate motive of the state is not economic (maximising growth) but political (maximising the state's power and the leadership's chances of survival). This is a form of capitalism but one in which the state acts as the dominant economic player and uses markets primarily for political gain (Bremmer 2010).

Du and Xu (2005) find that the contemporary economic system of China represents a state capitalist system as opposed to a market socialist system. One reason for this categorisation is the existence of financial markets in the Chinese economic system, which are absent in the market socialist literature and in the classic models of market socialism; another is that state profits are retained by enterprises rather than being equitably distributed among the population. Vladimir Popov (2007) asked why many transition economies succeeded by pursuing policies that are so different from radical economic liberalisation. His answer is that optimal policies are context dependent. They are specific for each stage of development and what worked in Slovenia cannot be expected to work in Mongolia. Growth will be different depending on the history and on the path chosen going forward. The reduction of government expenditure as a share of gross domestic product (GDP) did not significantly undermine the institutional capacity of the state in China, but in Russia it turned out to be ruinous. He suggests that the art of the policy maker is to create markets without causing the government's failure.

Theoretical and empirical analyses on the central–local relationship have been done based on China's experience. Qian and Xu (1993) and Qian et al. (1999) create a theory of China's fiscal federalism from the perspective of organisation theory, arguing that China developed an M-form government structure to improve the incentives and efficiency of the local officials. Zhou (2008) builds a championship theory of local government competition and a theory of administrative subcontracting and promotion competition to model the relationships between central and local governments and among local governments. Zheng Yongnian's *De Facto Federalism in China* (2013) points out that the relationship between central and local governments in China is actually de facto federalism, which provides an institutional foundation for the power of local government. The central government uses selective re-centralisation to adjust the central–local relationship, from which a new institutional framework is emerging. Zhang and Gong (2005) empirically test the relationship between fiscal decentralisation and economic development in China between 1986 and 2002 and find that the improvement of coordination between government agencies after the tax-sharing reform was one important factor promoting fiscal decentralisation. Other literatures in this field include Berkowitz and Li (2000) and Li and Hu (2010).

Many empirical studies have been carried out in related fields. Csanadi's paper 'A Comparative Model of Party-States' draws up an empirically based comparative analytical model and details the elements, the principles of connection of these elements, and the principle of operation of the whole party-state construct. The model reveals the structural reasons for power distribution and different patterns of communications in this party-state structure. It also defines the specific principles of operation based on the characteristics of the structure, the specific motivations, and behaviour deriving from those (Csanadi 2004). Li and Zhou (2005) discuss the relationship between political turnover and economic performance, focusing on the incentive role of personnel control in China. Other researches about politically connected firms include Claessens et al. (2008), Faccio (2006), and Fisman (2001).

A large amount of research focuses on the role of the Chinese government and the relationship between government and firms in the rapid growth of the Chinese economy. Li and Zhou (2005) find that the likelihood of promotion of provincial leaders increases with their local economic performance, while the likelihood of termination of provincial leaders decreases with their economic performance; that is, if a provincial leader cannot achieve good economic performance, he or she has a higher probability of being fired. The authors interpret these empirical findings as evidence that China uses personnel control to induce desirable economic outcomes. Cai et al. (2011) present the results of an investigation of corruption involving entertainment and travel costs of Chinese firms. Huang et al. (2015) examine the reasons for the Chinese government's decision to decentralise SOEs, finding empirical evidence that a greater distance between the government and the enterprise should lead to a higher likelihood of decentralisation, since the government located closer to an enterprise has more information on that enterprise. Other researches on this topic include Li (1998) and Megginson and Netter (2001).

Other studies discussed the strategy of the political and economic reform in China. Xiao Gongqin's *Beyond Left and Right Radicalism* (2012) argues that, to promote the economic and political transition, China needs to fight against challenges from both left and right radicalism and follow a middle-of-the-road strategy. Yang Xiaokai (2004) discusses the 'curse to the latecomer', arguing that developing countries can imitate technology already developed by developed countries without undergoing large-scale institutional reform, which will generate problems in the later stages of development in these countries. Yao Zhongqiu (2013) provides a detailed description and analysis of the development of the Chinese political system. Many institutional designs of the government in Chinese history are useful for understanding the design of the political-economic system today in China. For example, the joint governance system of the emperor and scholar-officials during the Han Dynasty and the checks and balances system between the emperor and the officials in the Song Dynasty are good references for the design of the political system today.

Institutional Changes in China

A large number of prior studies have examined institutional changes generally.

Douglass North's *Structure and Change in Economic History* (1981) creates a theory to explain economic development. He emphasises the role of property rights and the role of law in long-term economic growth. Property rights have been the precondition for market transaction, and the efficiency of the property structure has determined the development or backward movement of the economy in history. North et al.'s *Violence and Social Orders* (2009) integrates the problem of violence into a larger social and historical framework, showing how economic and political behaviour are closely linked. The authors provide a framework for understanding two types of social orders, natural states and modern societies, which deal with violence in different ways. North (1991, p. 97) points out that institutions 'evolve incrementally, connecting the past with the present and the future . . . Institutions provide the incentive structure of an economy; as that structure evolves, it shapes the direction of economic change towards growth, stagnation, or decline.'

Francis Fukuyama's *The Origins of Political Order* (2011) provides a sweeping account of how today's political institutions developed in world history, with a lengthy discussion on the growth of the first modern state in China. The author points out that China created the first modern state in the Weberian sense in history, but this state was not restrained by rule of law or by institutions of accountability to limit the power of the sovereign. A modern political system should consist of three components: a strong state, a rule of law, and accountability. Without these key components, economic development cannot be sustainable (Fukuyama 2011). Alston et al. (1996) provide a group of empirical analyses of institutional changes in various countries.

Acemoglu and Robinson's *Why Nations Fail: The Origins of Power, Prosperity and Poverty* (2012) gives an answer to the question of why nations fail. The political and economic institutions of a country determine the economic performance of that country. It is not the geography, culture, weather, or the choice of wrong policies that make countries rich or poor but the institutions. Institutions, defined as the rules that govern and shape economic and political life, are of two types: inclusive and extractive. Institutions are 'inclusive' when many people have a say in political decision-making. Inclusive institutions promote economic prosperity because they provide an incentive structure that allows talents and creative ideas to be rewarded. In contrast, 'extractive' institutions are ones that permit the elite to rule over and exploit others, extracting wealth from those who are not in the elite. Nations with a history of extractive institutions have not prospered, because entrepreneurs and citizens have less incentive to invest and innovate. Seymour Martin Lipset's book *Political Man: The Social Bases of Politics* (1960) asserts that there is a direct relationship between economic development and democracy, and this was subjected to extensive quantitative and qualitative empirical examination. The evidence shows a strong causal relationship between economic development and democracy.

Many studies focus on the institutional changes in China. By using property rights theory, Steven N.S. Chuang produced many works on economic institutions (e.g. Chuang 1968). Xu (2011) points out that China's institution is a regionally decentralised authoritarian system. The central government has control over personnel, whereas subnational governments run the bulk of the economy. China's reform trajectories have been shaped by regional decentralisation. Spectacular performances on the one hand and grave problems on the other are all determined by this governance structure. Kang (2002) describes the structural changes in China since the Cultural Revolution and points out that the totalitarian state in China has changed to an authoritarian state. The paper identifies the economic reform as a counteraction movement to the Cultural Revolution. A coalition between the political and economic elite was formed in the 1990s, which stabilised the social structure in China. A market economy does not necessarily require political freedom and can coexist with an authoritarian government. He concluded that democracy may not be a good solution for China in the short term and an administrative political system is the direction of the political reform in China.

China's Great Economic Transformation, edited by Loren Brandt and Thomas Rawski, is a collection of studies on China's economic development and reform from the late 1970s to the first decade of the 21st century. The authors of the book combine deep Chinese experience with broad disciplinary knowledge to explain China's mixture of high-speed growth and deeply flawed institutions (Brandt and Rawski 2008). Barry Naughton's *The Chinese Economy: Transitions and Growth* (2007) provides a comprehensive overview of the modern Chinese economy since 1949 based on his extensive research. Xiao and Sui (2011) provide a history of the Chinese economy, covering different periods before and after the economic reform. Wu Xiaobo (2014a, 2014b) provide a complete history of Chinese enterprises from the late 1970s to the early 21st century, covering the stories of a large number of enterprises. Zhou (2004) summarises the experience of China's economic reform and explains it by using the theory of institutional changes. Li et al. (2009) give a detailed review on the changes in China's financial system since 1949, covering banking, the securities market, and many other fields. Li Youhuan (2010) gives a detailed review of the underground financial institutions in China during the period of reform. Sun (2015) discusses the deep structure of the Chinese culture and explores the behavioural foundation of Chinese institutions. The first edition of this book was published in 1983 in the United States, and the book was first published in mainland China in 2015.

Shambaugh (2016) points out that, having enjoyed unprecedented levels of growth, China is at a critical juncture in the development of its economy, society, polity, national security, and international relations. Andrew Browne (2016) reviews the process of the Cultural Revolution and finds that Mao's legacy has formed a part of current government policy.

Many works focus specifically on property rights and institutions in China, including Che and Qian (1998), Long (2010), and Cull and Xu (2005). Li (1996) proposes a theory of ambiguous property rights, which argues that ambiguous property rights arise due to an imperfect market environment and shows that China's highly successful non-state sector is an example of ambiguous property rights. A large number of empirical studies have been conducted on the institutions during the transition of China's economy. Nee (1992) studies the hybrid forms in the current market transitions in state socialism through an examination of the emergence of marketised firms and cadre-entrepreneurs in China. Wen (2006) performed an economic geographical analysis on the reasons why China was trapped as an agrarian society for such a long time. A group of researchers from China Unirule Research Institute performed a large number of researches on institutional changes in China (e.g. Sheng 2017). Other related researches include Yang (2006), Zhang et al. (2008), and Li and Han (2009).

Fan et al. (2017) create an index for marketisation for China and its 31 provinces, using information on 23 variables reflecting the relationship between the government and the market, the development of non-SOEs, the development of product markets and factor markets, and the growth of market intermediary organisations.

These studies are very helpful for my studies of China's institutional changes in this book. These researches cover the broad field of China's development and reform from different perspectives. My book adds value to these contributions by focusing specifically on institutional changes in the economic reform, such as the reforms of enterprises and governments, the creation of the market and regulations governing the market, and the logics behind these changes.

1.2 A THEORY OF THE RELATIONSHIP BETWEEN THE GOVERNMENT AND THE MARKET

The existing literature studies China's economic development and reform from different perspectives, some of which have provided the theoretical and empirical basis for this book. However, most of the existing researches on China's economic development do not focus on institutional changes, while most of the researches on institutional changes do not specifically focus on China. To explain the institutional changes in China in the past 40 years, especially the bureaucratic-market nature of the Chinese economy, one needs to develop a theoretical framework of analysis. This section provides such a framework for a theory of the government-led market system.

Conditions for Government Intervention Set by Economic Theory

One economic theory to explain government regulation is called 'normative analysis as a positive theory', or 'the public interest theory' by Joskow and Noll (1981) and Viscusi et al. (2005). In the rest of this book, I will call this theory the 'economic theory of government intervention' for short.

The theory is based on microeconomic theory of the requirements of competition. According to the economic theory of government intervention, a government is allowed to intervene in economic activity when unrestrained competition does not function well. According to economic theory, the market fails to reach efficiency when several conditions exist, including (i) asymmetric information, (ii) externalities, (iii) natural monopoly, (iv) absences of markets, and (v) poorly defined property rights. Under these situations, the market cannot operate efficiently. When these market failures occur, there is a potential rationale for government intervention. This book refers these conditions as 'conditions for government intervention set by economic theory'. These areas should be the basic areas of government intervention. In China, the degree of government intervention has been much bigger than that in a standard market economy. Some of the interventions have been detrimental; others have benefited economic development. These positive interventions include China's development mode in the 1990s and 2000s, in which the local governments worked as organisers of the local economy by designing industrial structures and attracting investments, while the central government used a performance evaluation system to control the local officials. These positive interventions were based on the institutional foundation in China during that period in which the government played a much larger role, and the market and society were less developed than that of a fully developed market economy. These interventions are necessary and should be considered as reasonable intervention. However, other government interventions might have negative effects on economic development; for example, overregulation makes it difficult for private firms to enter certain sectors. Such interventions should be eliminated. Economic theory sets a boundary for government intervention but does not explain why the government sometimes goes beyond this boundary. This book develops a theory of political economy to explain these phenomena along the following lines.

A Political-Economic Model of Government Decision-Making in a Bureaucratic-Market Economy

A bureaucratic-market political-economic system prevails in contemporary Chinese society and has two major institutional components: the government and the market. The two components form a dual political-economic system, a bureaucratic-market system. In this system, government is the dominant force, but it cannot completely control society without the support of the market. The private sector has grown, but it is still subject to a number of political and economic constraints. The government makes policies to permit the existence and guide the development of the private sector. The changes of the institutions in this society can be summarised by the relative degree of government control or, equivalently, the relative freedom of firms in the market. As a result of the changes in China over the past 40 years, the market has grown to a relatively large size and become an important force in the society, but it is still far from dominant.

The target of the authoritarian government can be described by a benefit function (or utility function) with two basic components – stability of the society and economic growth – assuming complete information. Stability of the society means safety of the rule of the regime. Economic performance has been an important source of legitimacy of the rule of the government and the primary measure of political legitimacy since the end of the Cultural Revolution in the late 1970s. The government's reputation rises and falls with GDP, yet stability of the society has been the main target and the foundation of the existence of the government. The two components are correlated with each other. Economic performance has been a critical condition for social stability, whereas social stability provides an environment for the growth of the market. The government's benefit function is a weighted sum of social stability and economic development.

There are two basic policy options – economic policy and social stability policy – from which the government may choose. Economic policy promotes economic growth and marketisation, whereas social stability policy maintains the stability of society and the existence of the government itself. The government has to choose the correct combination of the two policies. Although favourable to economic growth, the economic policy may create political instability and inequality in the society, which may damage government control of the society. Meanwhile, social stability policy focuses on the control of society but could be unfavourable to economic development. The government makes choices regarding these two contradictory policies. The weight of the two policies changes over time and is determined by political and economic environments. For example, in the economic turmoil of the late 1970s, the leaders greatly increased the weight of economic performance in their benefit function, which resulted in economic reform and rapid economic growth.

The game being played between firms and the government is basically a Stackelberg's game[5] in which government first maximises its net benefit knowing the firm's strategy then the firm maximises its profit given the government's policy.[6] The government's preference problem is to maximise its gross benefit subtracted by costs, which includes costs of government control. A firm's profit is its total revenue subtracted by costs, which includes transaction costs. Private firms use strategies to maximise their profits legally or offer bribes to capture government officials to gain their benefits illegally. This practice is consistent with the reality in China, where a much stronger intervention by the government has been experienced than that in most market economies. The private sector has to follow government interventions and take the risk of being hurt by them. The government might have its own enterprises, which would also follow the government's instructions to maximise the net benefit of the government.

The government's behaviour in the system is under two major constraints: social instability and economic decline. The leadership has to work hard to avoid these situations. The critical policy decisions are made by the national leadership when acting in the context of an authoritarian political system, as reactions to the political-economic environment (Naughton 2008, p.91). The checks and balances mechanism between three branches of the Chinese government is weak. The officials are selected through an examination system and competition for promotion. The lower-level officials are supervised by higher-level government, and the local officials are mainly supervised by central government. At the highest level of leadership, the shift to the next generation of leadership is determined by the old generation of leadership or by members of the current leadership. The process needs to be more transparent.

A political-economic equilibrium of the system can be reached under some reasonable assumptions, when the government chooses its social and economic policies given the firm's behaviour and assuming no change in other conditions, while the representing firm maximises its profits by choosing its effort level given the government's policy. Equilibrium will be derived by maximising government's net benefits, which equals the weighted sum of social stability and the firm's profits in the society. The authoritarian government's benefit maximisation may deviate from the maximisation of social welfare if government's weights on social stability and economic development deviate from that of the society. The government's optimal policy mix is reached when the ratio between marginal benefits and marginal costs of the social stability policy equals that of the economic policy, given the weight of the two policies. These weights between social stability and economic growth are determined by the existing political and economic conditions and change over time when national and global political and economic conditions change. Under some extreme assumptions, no equilibrium exists.

In a large country with a multilevel government such as China, the relationship between the central and local government is crucial to the political system. The problem is actually one of distribution and redistribution of power in the bureaucratic hierarchy. It is basically a principal–agent relationship. The central government uses (i) a performance appraisal and accountability system and (ii) an incentive mechanism such as a fiscal revenue-sharing system to control the local government. During the reform process in China, the central government mainly used the incentive mechanism to mobilise the enthusiasm of the local government during the early stages of the reform, and then it changed to the performance appraisal and accountability system as the main tool to control the local government. Under the performance appraisal system, the local officials have competed against each other like in a championship.

The relatively classical approach above does not conflict with the institutional approach if one makes some revisions of the concept of costs. Transaction costs can be used to explain the evolution of the relationship between the government and the market. Transaction costs include the costs of arranging a contract and costs of monitoring and enforcing it. Here, I include the government's costs of operation as a special type of transaction cost, which North (1990) identified as the transaction costs of politics. Transaction costs determine the boundary between a planned economy and the market. Economic reform has reduced transaction costs for each transaction and encouraged the use of the market as a major approach to solve economic problems. Decision-making in the process of reform can be viewed as a series of choices between the logic of the government and the logic of the market.

The relationship between the government and the market in a bureaucratic-market economy could be viewed as a dynamic game, from the perspective of the time, in which the government and the firms have strategies to play with each other. The government's priority between control and economic development is represented by the weights of social stability and economic development in its benefit function. In a repeated game, these weights could be endogenously created in the model and negatively depend on the economic situation in the previous period. That means if the economic situation was improved, the weight of economic performance would be reduced. This can explain why government changes its priority (by reducing the importance of economic development in its list of priorities) when the economic situation improves, as has happened in recent years in China.

The above theory provides a framework for us to understand a bureaucratic-market economy such as the one in China over the past 40 or so years. The economics theory of government intervention argues that market failure provides a rationale for, and presents conditions for, government intervention, including (i) asymmetric information, (ii) externalities, (iii) natural monopoly, (iv) absences of markets, and (v) poorly defined property rights. A framework of a theory of authoritarian government's decision-making in a bureaucratic-market economy has been developed in this section to explain the behaviour of the Chinese government in the process of economic reform. The government changed its priorities on stability of society and economic development when the economic and institutional environment changed. When the economic situation was not good, the Chinese government placed marketisation high on its priority list, as in the late 1970s. When the economic situation improved, it focused more on stability of the society, as in the early 21st century.

This analytical framework is not inconsistent with the institutional theory which emphasises the roles of path dependence, transaction costs, and property rights in the development process. I incorporate transaction cost into the government decision-making model, and path dependence is one of the main clues of analysis of the transition of the Chinese economic and political system. Using the theory of path dependence, I will show how violence during the Cultural Revolution formed the consensus on reform, how the development of the market created the need to set up a social network, and how the bureaucratic system in the planned economy determined the nature of government-led reform. I will use path dependence and the model of government decision-making in a bureaucratic-market economy as two major hidden clues to explain the institutional changes in China in the past 40 years.

NOTES

1. Traditionally, Chinese society is composed of nucleus cells (Sun 2015). Different levels of government, units, and families have a similar structure, with a leader at the centre and a group of followers surrounding.
2. Hereafter, if there is no particular indication, 'reform' refers to the economic reform from 1978 to the 2010s.
3. The system can be further divided into market capitalism at the bottom of the society and crony capitalism at the top, according to Zheng (2016).
4. In the planned economy in China, workers and managers did not have enough incentive to finish their jobs, because their compensation was not related to their work. The economic reform needed to create incentives by connecting workers' contributions with their payments.
5. Stackelberg's game is a leader–follower game in which the leader moves first and the follower moves second following the rules set by the leader.
6. The government knows the firm's strategy completely, or with certain probability.

2. From command-and-control to reform: 1949–1978

Modern China has been moving between a free market and strong government since the end of the Qing Dynasty in 1911. A much stronger government replaced the incumbent government in 1949 and then completely wiped out the market.

The government in China controlled and operated the economy under the Soviet-style planned system from 1949 to 1978. The leadership tried to adopt the Soviet-type planned system at the begging of the People's Republic. This system was inefficient, because the political power and the economy were unbalanced. It was the starting point from which the economic reform was carried out in the late 1970s and explains the political and economic forces driving the economic reform later.

Based on China's development in the late 20th century, this planned economy was the status quo of the economic reform from the 1970s to the 2010s.[1] Path dependence explains the rationale and nature of the institutional changes in China. The strong bureaucratic system built in this period resulted in the government-led nature of reform in the following period.

Using the theoretical framework of the political economy of government decision-making in a bureaucratic-market system developed in section 1.2, this planned system can be considered as the initial status of the model, when the government put a lot of weight on controlling the society and ignored economic development to a large extent. This unbalanced policy led to the demand for reform in the late 1970s.

This chapter will introduce (i) the political system and government in China during the planned period; (ii) the development strategy and economic planning; (iii) the economic organisations – including collective farms, urban enterprises, and households – and the financial system; and (iv) the problems with the planned system and the formation of consensus on the reform.

2.1 THE POLITICAL SYSTEM AND GOVERNMENT

The People's Republic of China was founded in 1949 by the Communist Party of China (CCP), which is the sole governing party of China, although it coexists alongside eight other parties which comprise the United Front. The highest body of the CCP is the National Congress, but the power is controlled by the Politburo Standing Committee and the chairman of the party. Mao Zedong was the chairman of the CCP from the 1940s to 1976, when he passed away. The CCP was founded in 1921 by a group of young Marxists supported by the Russian Communist Party. The CCP drove the Nationalist government from mainland China to Taiwan, after more than 20 years of civil war, and established the People's Republic of China in 1949.

The supreme political authority of the People's Republic of China is the CCP. It controls the state, which is run by the central government through its various branches: the legislative branch – the National People's Congress; the executive branch – the State Council; and the judicial branch – the Supreme People's Court and the Supreme People's Procuratorate. The Congress and the Court are relatively weak compared with the State Council. The People's Liberation Army is directly led by the Party.

From the early 1950s to late 1970s, China adopted a 'centrally planned economic system' or 'a command economic system'. Most of the resources were owned and controlled by the government. The system was operated like a big company, in which the government, like a board of directors, made all the important decisions on production and distribution. The market was restricted and played a limited role, operating only in less important areas such as personal consumption. The government attempted to close all markets down several times in history. During the Great Leap Forward[2] in the late 1950s, the government tried to establish 'public dining halls' to replace family dining as a part of an effort to diminish the consumer goods market. The planned system originally came from the Soviet Union, which provided a ready-to-use tool for the CCP to control the economy in the early 1950s. At the beginning, all important administrative decisions were made by the central government, and all powers came from it. The fiscal system was highly concentrated. All fiscal revenue, including taxes and agricultural tax paid in grain, was handed over to the central government, except very limited local tax revenue and local surcharges of agricultural tax, which were left to the local governments. All tax rules and rates were decided by the central government.[3] Local expenditure needed to be approved by the central government, which controlled the personnel of the two lower-level governments.[4] The central government controlled the nomination and promotion of provincial and prefectural main officials, as well as the revenue and expenditure of the lower-level governments at the beginning of the 1950s.

The system worked through 'lines and blocks' (Figure 2.1). 'Lines' refers to government departments, with a command line that goes vertically from the department at the central level to the same department at the local level, which is independent from the control of local government. 'Blocks' refers to the local government, which has branches of government that operate horizontally, similar to the central government but smaller in size. The 'lines and blocks' compose a matrix or system of government, where administrative powers can be distributed at any level of the bureaucratic structure. The leadership needs to balance the lines and blocks when distributing power within the system. The lines were supposed to be the main control tools in the traditional Soviet-type command economy. However, in China, due to the government's limited resources, and hence its more limited ability to control, blocks were used more often than in the Soviet Union. Power distribution within the bureaucratic system is correlated with the distribution of incentives to officials. When the lines dominated the blocks, the lower-level officials lost incentives to provide public services. When the block was relatively strong, on the other hand, the central government lost control of the bureaucratic system. The relationship between the lines and the blocks is the key to understanding the institutional changes in the past 60 years in China, in both the planned period and the reform years.

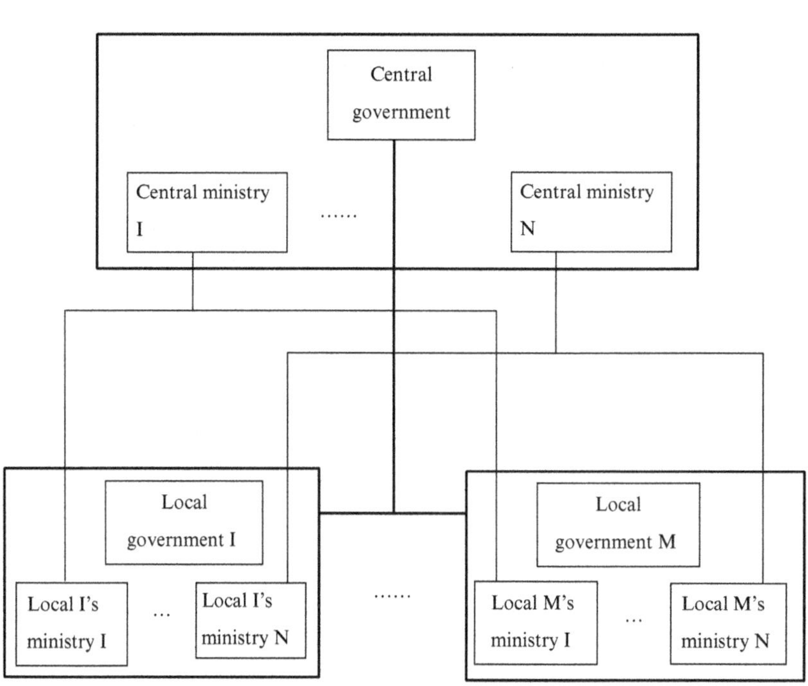

Figure 2.1 'Lines and blocks'

The central government of the People's Republic was established in October 1949. In the early 1950s, under the Committee of Economics and Finance, a number of government ministries were established, including the Ministry of Finance, the Ministry of Trade, the Ministry of Heavy Industries, the Ministry of Fuel Industries, the Ministry of Textile Industries, the Ministry of Food Processing Industries, the Ministry of Light Industries, the Ministry of Railways, the Ministry of Posts and Telecommunications, the Ministry of Transportation, the Ministry of Agriculture, the Ministry of Forest and Land Reclamation, the Ministry of Water Resources, the Ministry of Labour, the People's Bank, and the General Administration of Customs (Xiao and Sui 2011, p.44). The number of ministries increased as the government grew in size. Each of the ministries worked as a commander of a group of enterprises owned by the central government, to realise the output target of the industry set out by the national economic plan. This formed the management system of the economy, where resource distribution, price setting, and labour allocation were controlled by the central government through its departments or 'lines'.

The 'lines' were supposed to include all the economic activities in the fields they were in charge of. However, the instructions could not go all the way to the lowest level of this bureaucratic structure. In reality, lack of information and other factors restrained the role of the 'lines'. Where the 'lines' ended, the 'blocks' began to play a role, and the local governments were in charge. The 'blocks' refer to the lower level of government (the provincial governments, the prefectural governments, or the county governments), which have a similar structure to the central government but are smaller in size. In China, they played a larger role than that in the Soviet Union. When the 'lines' system did not work, the leadership used the 'blocks' as an alternative. Specifically, the main task of the county governments was to rule the countryside, which accounted for more than 80 per cent of the population in China in the 1950s and 1960s.

The responsibilities of local governments, except in defence and foreign relations, largely overlapped that of the central government. The division of the responsibility between central and local governments was not based on functions but on locality. Usually, the local branches of the departments, the lower ends of the 'lines', were managed by the local government with respect to personnel, finance, and materials. The central departments were only responsible for 'operational guidance'.

The central government controlled the local officials through a system of official appointment, under which officials of provincial and prefectural governments were appointed by the central government and those at the county level were appointed by the provincial government. Within a certain level of government, a single core power structure existed, and the leader of the government made all the important decisions.

Administrative powers shifted up and down the bureaucratic structure. This became a major game played by the leadership, not only in the planned period but also in the reform years. In 1958, during the Great Leap Forward, Mao initiated a movement shifting the power downwards. Of the 1,165 central government-owned and managed industrial enterprises, 885 were transferred to the local government. The transfer was badly planned and was carried out in only half a month. The central government also transferred large amounts of power to the local governments, including the powers of planning, infrastructure approval, material distribution, fiscal expenditure and tax revenue, and personnel management. The power transfer meant that the local governments had to make large infrastructure investments. It increased employment within the local governments and broke the balance of the planned economy. In March 1959, less than one year later, the central government took all the transferred powers back. In 1970, during the Cultural Revolution, another central to local power transfer was implemented, wherein 98.6 per cent of 10,533 central government-owned enterprises were transferred to the local government (Zhou 2008, pp.124–127). The central government also transferred powers controlling revenue and expenditure, infrastructure, planning, and material distribution to the local government. This kind of power-shifting game was played several times during the planned period, because decision makers in the central government had no experience in dealing with the central–local relations and swung between giving incentives to local leaders and enhancing control. Although the power shifted up and down, the trend was for the downwards shifting of powers, which represented a move from the Soviet-type planned economy to a more traditionally Chinese type of government structure.

2.2 DEVELOPMENT STRATEGY AND PLANNING

From the early 1950s to the late 1970s, China followed a development strategy with an emphasis on the development of heavy industries. The planning agency allocated nearly all investment funds to heavy industries, while neglecting agriculture, light industries, and the service industries, prioritising low interest rates and low wages to reduce the costs of developing heavy industries. The price of agricultural product was lowered for urban workers to enable them to survive on their low wages. The exchange rate was minimised to lower the cost of imported machinery. To minimise the cost of developing heavy industries, enormous distortions were introduced

(Lin et al. 2003). The low price of agricultural products damaged food production, and food consumption was rationed by the government from the late 1950s to the 1980s. At the same time, factories were focused on producing aeroplanes and nuclear weapons with the aid of the Soviet Union, despite the lack of food.

The planned economy was actually a command economy, which operated in a centralised and hierarchical manner where directives were issued from the National Planning Committee to lower-level government organisations. The directives were enforced through inducements in a vertical power structure, the 'lines'. A highly centralised financial system was established in the early 1950s and included the People's Bank of China and several policy banks. The People's Bank of China, owned by the state, was both a government agency and an operating depositary institute, which was the main provider of liquidity to the enterprises. The financial system was operated under a consolidated credit plan. Interest rates and exchange rates were set by the state, and all foreign exchange was state controlled.

2.3 COLLECTIVE FARMING IN THE COUNTRYSIDE

Through the collectivisation in the countryside and the socialisation of private ownership, the government completed the building of a so-called socialist economy in the late 1950s. In the countryside, the government redistributed the land more equitably to the peasants. From 1950 to 1953, land and various means of production were redistributed among hundreds of millions of peasants who had been landless before. The peasants were then organised into mutual aid teams, which involved the temporary sharing of labour and capital. Mutual aid teams were organised into agricultural producers' cooperatives, in which tools, draft animals, and labour were shared on a permanent basis. In 1956, the agricultural cooperatives were moved to advanced producers' cooperatives, in which the profits were distributed to members based on labour contributions. The size of the cooperatives increased to several hundreds of people and most of the land was owned collectively by the cooperative. In 1958, during the Great Leap Forward, the collectives[5] were organised into People's Communes, or much larger units with an average of 5,400 households and a total of 20,000–30,000 members. The 'People's Commune' (*renmin gongshe*), a combination of collectives, was the highest administrative level in rural areas from 1958 to 1983 under the county government. The communes were further divided into brigades and production teams. Animals originally owned by the households were contributed to the commune. All farming activities were assigned by the village officials and were no longer planned based on the farmers' own volition. Every morning, all members of the production team got together and walked to the fields under the direction of team leaders. The grains were distributed according to labour contribution. At the beginning, the accounting unit was at the commune level, which meant that the income and expenditure of all production teams were calculated at the commune level, and everybody wanted to take a free ride. For a limited period in 1958, everything in private kitchens, such as tables, chairs, cooking utensils, and pans, was 'contributed' to the commune's kitchen. Private cooking was banned and replaced by communal dining. After a short time, all the available food had been eaten, and the Great Famine came. To meet the problem, the leadership closed the public kitchens and changed the accounting unit back to the production team level, and from the early 1960s to the early 1980s, this commune production team system dominated in rural China.

After paying the agricultural tax, usually paid in products, the peasants had to sell most of their remaining products to the state. During the planned period, purchases of agricultural products were monopolised by the government. The government separated the acquisition into several categories:

1. Procurement. In November 1953, the State Council decided to monopolise the purchase and sale of grain and edible oil. Starting in September 1954, cotton procurement was implemented, and the procurement of tobacco and timber was implemented in 1957. These products were referred as Category One.
2. Apportion. Apportion was first applied to pigs in 1955, and then extended to major staple foodstuffs and major industrial raw materials (e.g. cattle, sheep, eggs, vegetables, fruit, hemp, sugar, tea, silkworm cocoons, wool, and hides). These products were referred to as Category Two. The purchase prices of (1) and (2) were set by the government, and were usually much lower than the market price. Higher prices were set for the over-purchases of products.
3. Purchase on negotiation. This category, referred to as Category Three, covered other agricultural products with less importance. Peasants were allowed to sell some of the extra products on free markets.

2.4 URBAN ENTERPRISES

In urban areas, during the planned period in China, most of the enterprises were owned by the state and subordinated to the government. All large enterprises were run by government-appointed managers and financed from the government budget. The People's Republic first seized the large enterprises originally owned by the Nationalist government and then transferred the private firms into state-owned enterprises (SOEs). In the early 1950s, the preliminary socialist transformation of capitalist industry and commerce was accomplished through placing state orders with private firms, having private shops market the products of SOEs, and instituting a state monopoly on the purchase and marketing of the products of private firms. Starting in 1953, efforts were concentrated on developing joint state–private enterprises, in which management was exercised jointly by representatives of the state and of the original owners, with the former as leaders. The original owners were entitled to about one-quarter of the profits while the rest went to the state. In 1955, the Central Committee decided to transfer all private enterprises into joint state–private ownership, which was completed by the end of 1956. Most of the capitalists left their management positions in a couple of years and lost their shares during the Cultural Revolution.

From the late 1950s to the early 1980s, most of the enterprises in China, except a small number of proprietors, were SOEs. These SOEs were actually owned by different levels of government. The central government owned the largest enterprises in each industry. The provincial governments and city governments had their own SOEs, called 'local state-owned' enterprises. The central government had five-year plans and annual plans, produced by the planning committee, which gave a rough guide for the country. The economic committee was the director of production during most of the years of the planned period. Under the economic committee were the industrial ministries, each of them in charge of the production of a particular sector, leading thousands of SOEs. The SOEs owned by the central government usually produced goods on larger scales, had better equipment, larger numbers of workers, and higher wages and benefits. These enterprises usually had their own residential buildings for their employees, dining halls, kindergartens, primary schools, and theatres. Some of these large SOEs were set up with the aid of the Soviet Union or East Germany in the 1950s. The status of a worker in a SOE was hereditary in the 1970s and still in the 1980s, which meant when a worker retired, his or her son or daughter could inherit the position.

Joint Factory 718 was an example of a large SOE that produced electronic parts and components during the planned period. The factory complex was an extension of the military–industry cooperation between China and the Soviet Union at the beginning of the 1950s. The Russians suggested that the Chinese work with East Germany, and the project started in 1952. The architectural plans for the factory were produced by the Germans, and a Bauhaus-influenced design was chosen over the

Soviet style. The location of the project was a 640,000 square metre site in Dashanzi, north-east of Beijing. The initial budget was 9 million rubles, or $17 million at today's rate, fully funded by the Chinese government. Construction started in 1954, with over a hundred East German experts working on the project. When production began in 1957, the first director was Li Rui. Products covered a wide variety of military and civilian equipment, including acoustic equipment for the Great Hall of the People, where Congress meet annually, and all the loudspeakers on Tiananmen Square. The workers attended training frequently in cooperation with East Germany. The factory offered good benefits to its 10,000–20,000 workers, including fully furnished housing for less than a thirtieth of a worker's income, a hospital with German equipment, diverse extracurricular activities, and many other things. The factory was visited by leaders of the government, including Liu Shaoqi, Zhu De, Deng Xiaoping, Jiang Zemin, and Kim Il-Sung of North Korea. I used to visit part of the complex for business purposes in the 1970s, going through tight security checks to enter. Joint Factory 718 was split into more manageable components, such as sub-factory 798, in the 1960s. The government reduced its support for large SOEs after the reform in the 1980s, and the complex underwent a gradual decline in the late 1980s and early 1990s. Most of the sub-factories ceased production, 60 per cent of the workers were laid off, and the remains of the management were constituted as a real-estate operation, charged with overseeing the industrial park. Part of the complex became the famous 798 Art Zone (Culture.Pl n.d.).

Like the central government, other levels of government had their own enterprises. This was even the case for the lowest level of government in urban areas, community or sub-district offices of the local government. For example, in 1958, during the Great Leap Forward, a group of housewives organised a rotary wood-cutting factory and produced shovel handles and rolling pins. The factory was incorporated by the Xuanwu district government in Beijing. The factory became the Xuanwu Capacitors Factory in the late 1960s, owned by the Xuanwu district government.[6] The factory produced a variety of electric capacitors, used in radio, TV, and electronic equipment. Seventy workers worked in the factory in 1967, and 80 per cent of them were women. A couple of college graduates and about 60 high school students were sent to the factory[7] in the late 1960s, doubling the size of the factory. As more students and young people were sent to the factory, it grew to about 300 employees in the mid-1970s. The factory was located in a south-west suburb of the city of Beijing, near the city moat. Since it was an 'urban collective enterprise', workers' wages were lower than at the SOEs. For example, a grade three worker[8] in an urban collective enterprise earned RMB34 ($19.9) per month, compared with RMB36 ($21.1) per month for the same grade in an SOE. Major production decisions were made by the district government's industrial bureau, which also appointed the party secretary and the manager of the factory. The Xuanwu district industrial bureau had 20–30 similar factories, producing diodes, transistors, resistors, and adaptors. This kind of local government-owned enterprise had significant effects on urban employment and provided about one-quarter of employment in urban areas in China during the planned period.

2.5 URBAN AND RURAL HOUSEHOLDS

In urban areas, households were divided into two groups, the cadres and the workers, operating at both 'unit' and resident community level. The two groups were managed separately, with the cadres being managed by the Department of Organisation and the workers being managed by the Labour Departments. The cadres came from college graduates, officers transferred from the military, and promotion from workers, although the last one was very limited. The two groups of urban residents were treated differently in terms of compensation, benefits, housing, retirement, and health insurance. The cadres had 30 pay scales, while the workers had 8. The actual payment also depended on the area of living. The highest pay for cadres was 28 times the lowest pay in area #1.[9] The highest pay for workers was 3.8 times the lowest pay. The highest pay for workers equalled the 18th pay scale for cadres (the smaller the number the higher the pay scale) (Wang 2013). A worker just completing his or her apprenticeship in a central government-owned factory would earn RMB36 ($21.1) per month, and he or she might expect to earn the same in the next ten years without any promotions.

Household income mainly came from wages. The state set the standard pay scale for cadres and workers. A relatively small share of income came from rents, interests, and shares of stock before 1966. After 1966, when the Cultural Revolution began, people were not allowed to receive income from their assets. During the planned period, the average wage was lowered by the government, in order to lower the costs of industrial production. At the same time the prices of consumer goods were lowered to allow households to afford a minimum level of living. Important consumer goods were rationed in cities, including rice, flour, edible oil, sugar, eggs, and cotton material. Meat, poultry, bicycles, and sewing machines were also rationed during certain periods. Ration Cards were issued to families by the community authorities in cities in the late 1950s. The average monthly ration of grain was under 15 kilograms in the early 1960s. A person had to register as a customer in a particular shop near his or her home, and could not use his or her card elsewhere. The card could not be replaced easily if you lost it, which means you risked starvation. Exclusive stores existed for high-rank officials. In Beijing, where the supply of consumer goods was managed under the guidance of the central government and was the best in China, peanuts, a luxury good at the time, were only supplied during the Chinese New Year, with each person receiving about a half pound (0.2 kilograms). Housing was supplied by a person's 'unit' (*dawei*, the office or factory a worker belonged to), and depended on whether the 'unit' had enough funds to build residential buildings for its employees. The rent was very low compared to income. Health insurance was also provided by the state through the 'units' in urban areas. People spent over half of their income on food, and other expenses were very limited.

Rural–urban migration was strictly controlled from the late 1950s to the early 1980s, and it partially remains controlled. The most important institutional tool used by the government was the *hukou* system, a resident registration system. Under the *hukou* system, established in 1958, a household registration record officially identified a person as a resident of an area, and included information on residency, temporary residency, birth, death, and moves to and from an address. A rural resident cannot change his or her residency status except through joining the army or becoming a college student. A rural resident was excluded from the social benefits, such as food rationing, which were enjoyed by an urban resident.

In rural areas, a peasant family lived in a much worse situation. Peasants worked in the production team and earned points. At year-end, they received their payment (most of them in the form of grain) according to the points they had earned in the year. Most of the agricultural products had to be turned over to the government or sold to the state commercial companies, with a low price set by the government. The state lowered the prices of agricultural products to promote the development of the industries and raised the prices of industrial products. The farmers had to sell their products at a low price and buy industrial products (e.g. chemical fertilizers) at a high price. The rationing system did not cover rural areas. Without a rationing book, a peasant was not able to live or work in the cities. The state controlled the agricultural product purchase system through the state-owned purchasing firms.

A Soviet-style social security system was set up under the planned economy in the early 1950s. The Labour Insurance Regulation was considered the starting point of the social security system in the People's Republic of China (Law Library 1951). The funding mode of the system was 'pay as you go',[10] which involved inter-generation transfer payments. The system only covered the workers in the state sector, the government and SOEs; most of them were in urban areas. In the countryside, the main insurance came from family savings, without much support from the government. At the beginning, social security was provided as extra salary. The premiums paid by the companies were allocated to the labour insurance fund of the labour union. From the end of the 1960s, since salaries were insufficient to pay social security, all pensions, medical expenditure, and other types of social security were managed by enterprises on their own. Since social security was paid by the 'unit' from its budget, the benefit a worker received depended on the ability of the 'unit' to pay, which in turn depended on the financial situation of the 'unit'. The benefit of social security heavily depended on the rank of a person in the bureaucratic system, which treated people differently (Sha 2010).

2.6 FINANCIAL SYSTEM

The financial system was a subordinate of the planned economic system during the planned period. A centralised financial system was set up in the early 1950s, and banks became the sole important financial institution. All public–private joint managed banks were merged into the People's Bank of China. The old management of private financial firms handed over the control of operations, finance, and personnel, and received a dividend. The People's Bank of China became both a government institute managing national finance activities and a financial operations agency. Branches of the People's Bank covered most areas in the country.

The People's Bank established a centralised deposit and loan system. All branches of the People's Bank were required to prepare credit plans and to hand the plans to the upper level of the bank. The head office approved the plans and issued them to the branches. All deposits attracted by the branches had to be transferred to the head office and all loans issued by branches needed to be approved by the head office. Commercial credit was abolished and all credit was concentrated in the national bank, the People's Bank of China. All deposit and loan interests were controlled by the People's Bank of China. Foreign exchange management was controlled by the Ministry of Foreign Trade, the Ministry of Finance, and the People's Bank of China. The use of foreign exchange had to be consistent with the plan and all foreign currencies had to be sold to the Bank of China.

From 1953 to 1957, a vertical unified credit management, a centralised savings and loans management and a cash plan, a unified interest management, and a centralised foreign exchange management constituted the highly concentrated financial management system in China. The Great Leap Forward in 1958 and the Great Famine from 1959 to 1962 had an enormous impact on China's financial system. Most management of credit and loans was shifted from the head office of the People's Bank to local offices, resulting in problems of loose management, credit expansion, and bubbles. From 1961 to 1965, the central government took back all powers and returned to a vertical management structure. The Cultural Revolution paralysed the financial system and removed some of the financial institutions. The People's Bank of China was merged with the Ministry of Finance.

The Chinese economy under the planned system was actually a barter economy, with a very limited financial sector. Financial institutions were of little importance, financial products were very limited, and no monetary policy existed. The People's Bank of China monopolised the market, with several poorly organised special banks. All bank branches were government institutes that carried out the plan and made loans. In 1977, after the Cultural Revolution, the State Council decided to treat the People's Bank as a ministry-level institution separated from the Ministry of Finance. Under the planned system, banks were the only financial institution in China, deposit and cash were the only financial means. In this closed economy, resources came only from the savings of residents.

2.7 AN INSTITUTION CHART OF THE ECONOMIC SYSTEM UNDER THE PLANNED ECONOMY

To sum up the section, a chart of the economic system in the planned economy in China has been drawn (see Figure 2.2). The chart shows the main institutions (enterprises, households, and government) in the system and the flows between them. The enterprises were owned by the

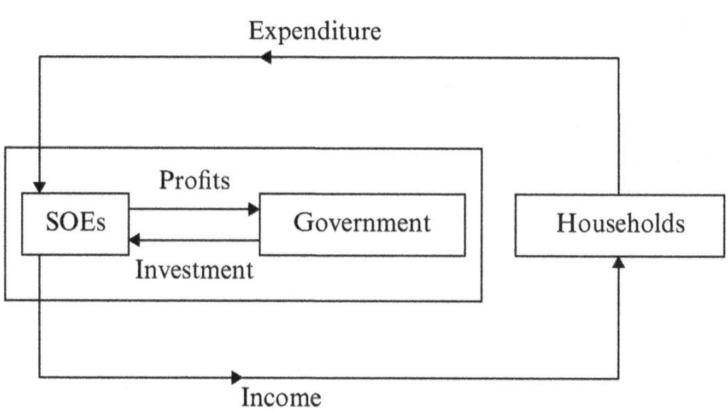

Figure 2.2 Institution chart of a planned economy

government, and the two institutions formed the inner circle of state ownership. The government invested in these SOEs and rural 'collectives', and in return received profits (instead of taxes) from them. Most of the products produced by the enterprises were used by other enterprises, while a small portion of products (consumer goods) were sold outside of the inner circle to households through the market. The whole inner circle worked like a big firm, with no market mechanism existing within the inner circle. The market existed only between the inner circle and the households. Money and price mechanisms still worked when households exchange money for consumer goods, even though the market was restricted and the prices were set by the government.

This chart is an abstract illustration of the Chinese economy during the planned period. The households in the chart include both urban and rural households. The enterprises include both urban SOEs and rural 'collectives'. 'Government' includes both central government and local governments. The chart can be understood as a revised version of the circulation flow chart of an economy.

2.8 PROBLEMS OF THE PLANNED SYSTEM

The planned system in China from the 1950s to the 1970s did not work well, partly because of the shortcomings of an all-planned economy, and partly because of non-economic factors (e.g. political turmoil).

General Problems of a Planned System

The planned system has certain inherent problems. The first is the information problem. In a planned economy, all the important decisions, such as the allocation of resources, are made at the centre by the government. This contrasts to a market economy, where all economic actors make their decisions independently and the market coordinates these activities through a price mechanism. Given current technology, it is impossible for the government to make all important decisions properly. If the decisions taken by the government prove wrong, it would be difficult to change the decisions already made. Therefore, a planned economy cannot adapt to a change as rapidly as that of a market economy. The planning practice in the former Soviet Union and China showed how difficult it was for the central government to balance the different parts of the economy. One approach to reduce the problem was to delegate the decision-making to the lower-level government. In many cases, Mao Zedong, the chairman of the Communist Party and the chairman of the People's Republic, was in favour of giving certain powers to provincial and local authorities in the late 1950s and 1960s.

The second problem of a planned system is the incentives problem. When all decisions are made by the central government, all other actors in the economy – the local government officials, the managers of enterprises, and workers – must follow the instructions made by the central government without large deviation. In reality, local government officials, managers, and workers had their own interests and concerns (e.g. promotion and wage increase). This command economy largely ignored these personal interests, which resulted in lost incentives to work hard and creatively. The primary central–local government relationship problem could also be extended to the SOEs, if we consider them as an extension of the government. The central government had to design a mechanism for delegating jobs to everyone else in the economy. This mechanism should have given every economic actor proper incentives to follow the decision made by the central government. The design of this mechanism was more important than the plan itself. It was a tough task, if not an impossible one. The Soviet Union tried some reforms to improve the incentives of factory managers and workers in the 1960s. China also had tremendous problems in this second task of a planned economy. As soon as the Soviet-type planned system, in which the lines dominated, was set up in China in the 1950s, reform had started to change the system to place more emphasis on the role of the blocks. Mao pointed this out as early as 1956 (Mao 1956). Similar reforms or downward shifting of powers continued during the planned years. This pointed back to the historical Chinese government system before the 20th century, which emphasised the role of self-governance of local governments.

A bureaucratic government system was established in China during the Qin Dynasty (221–207 BC), as a multilevel system including a central government and several levels of local government. Zhou Li'an points out two distinguishing features of this traditional governance system: subcontracting and territorial management (Zhou 2008, pp.57–66). He is one of the first researchers to have concerns about the relationship between central and local government. All powers were concentrated in the hands of the central government, but the implementation of the policies was the responsibility of the local government. Based on the technology and resources available, the central government usually franchised/subcontracted the power of governance and the power to collect financial resources to the local officials, who were appointed by the central government. Although only limited resources (and low salaries) were given to the local officials to realise the tasks of local governance, the central government gave the local leaders the power to collect resources by themselves. This approach was a way of dealing with the principle–agent problem, which reduced the cost of delegation. Another feature of the traditional governance system was 'territorial management', which meant a citizen was under the control of the government located in his or her own locality. He or she could not be taken to court in another locality. There were fewer correlations between local governments at the same bureaucratic level. The problem of this traditional Chinese governance was that it was not easy for the central government to control the local officials and standardise the public goods provided by different localities. The administrative discretion of the local officials and their low salary was also a source of corruption. The history of modern China shows that this traditional system was so attractive that any modern system set up in China will always, sooner or later, change back to this traditional Chinese system. These changes happened both before the reform initiated in 1978 and after it. Therefore, the bureaucratic system in China was never a purely modern bureaucratic system with clearly defined responsibilities for each position and the necessary resources for taking on these responsibilities. Besides these common problems for all centrally planned economies, China had special problems which led to the failure of the planned economy in the late 1970s. Among these problems, the shock from the turmoil of the political system was an important one.

Shocks from the Political Turmoil

In the early 1950s, the members of the CCP were a group of revolutionaries; most of them were peasants before they joined the Revolution. They were not experts in running an economy. Very few of the Communist leaders had any practical experience of governing. The political struggle was more intense after the CCP became the ruling party of China. Starting from the 1950s, Mao cleared out dissidents from outside and inside of the Party. These purges adopted the form of mass political movements. The movements leaped like a flame, one after another, in the 1950s and 1960s, included land reform against landlords, elimination of counterrevolutionaries, the Three-anti and Five-anti campaigns against the capitalists,[11] ideology education movement against intellectuals, the Great Leap Forward, the 'Four Clean-ups' movement,[12] and many others. These movements were against the enemies outside the Communist Party. Inside the Party, there were campaigns against the Gao Gang/Rao Shushi anti-party group[13] in 1954 and a purge of the Peng Dehuai anti-party group[14] in 1959, among many smaller purges.

When a political movement erupted, everything including production activities had to give way to the movement. Production was always the first to be sacrificed. Political movements, such as the Great Leap Forward and the Cultural Revolution, further disrupted the economy.

Great Leap Forward

The Great Leap Forward was an economic and social campaign aimed at rapidly transforming China from an agrarian economy to a socialist society through rapid industrialisation and collectivisation in the late 1950s and early 1960s. Mao encouraged the establishment of small backyard steel furnaces in every village, school, government agency, and urban neighbourhood to meet the targeted increase in steel production. Pots, pans, and other metal items were requisitioned to supply the 'scrap' for the furnaces. In rural areas, People's Communes were set up as a combination of smaller farm collectives and consisted of 4,000–5,000 households. The communes had governmental, political, and economic functions and were divided into production brigades and production teams. Private plots were entirely abolished and communal kitchens were introduced in the countryside for a short period of time before the Great Famine. The Great Leap Forward is widely considered to have caused the Great Famine[15] that immediately followed.

The Cultural Revolution

The Cultural Revolution, or the Great Proletarian Cultural Revolution, was a socio-political movement led by Mao Zedong, then chairman of the CCP, in China from 1966 to 1976.[16] The stated goal of the Cultural Revolution was to preserve 'true' Communist ideology by purging capitalist and traditional elements from Chinese society. Different from the preceding 17 years, the Cultural Revolution adopted a form of mass movement never seen before in Chinese history, to purge the entire government-official class in the first three years. In the 17 years from 1949 to 1966, Mao used the government officials and party members to attack the elites of the old society, using a mass movement controlled by government officials. It was a top-down movement, where the stability of the society was maintained. After the Great Leap Forward and the readjustment during the Great Famine by other leaders of the Party, Liu Shaoqi and Deng Xiaoping, Mao was worried that the whole official class and party members wanted to restore the capitalist society, and he wanted to use extraordinary means, mass movements, to purge the whole party. It was a campaign in which Mao made an alliance with ordinary people against the whole official class.

The Revolution was launched in May 1966, when Mao accused the 'representatives of the bourgeoisie' of infiltrating every corner of the Party in a vast conspiracy to restore the old capitalist society. He insisted that these 'revisionists' be removed through violent class struggle. Liu Shaoqi, the president of the Republic, and Deng Xiaoping, who was in charge of party administration, were at the top of Mao's target list.

An 'expanded session' of the Politburo was held in May 1966. According to the 'May 16 Notification', which summarised Mao's ideological justification for the Cultural Revolution, 'those representatives of the bourgeoisie who have sneaked into the Party, the government, the army, and various spheres of culture are a bunch of counter-revolutionary revisionists'. 'Once conditions are ripe, they will seize political power and turn the dictatorship of the proletariat into a dictatorship of the bourgeoisie' (MacFarquhar and Schoenhals 2006, p. 47) and restore the old capitalist society. The conference criticised some recently ousted leaders such as Peng Zhen, the party secretary of Beijing, and Luo Ruiqing, chief of staff of the army. Nie Yuanzi, a philosophy lecturer at Peking University, wrote and posted a big-character poster publicly attacking the university's party administration. Following Nie's example, students began to revolt against their respective party leaders and teachers. Classes were suspended nationwide in June 1966. The first Red Guard group was formed by middle school students in Beijing, and soon spread nationwide. In August 1966, the Party's Central Committee passed its 'Decision Concerning the Great Proletarian Cultural Revolution', elevating the student movement to a nationwide mass campaign, encouraging workers, farmers, and soldiers to rise up and challenge authority. At the 11th Plenary Session of the 8th Central Committee of the CCP in August 1966, Mao criticised Liu Shaoqi and Deng Xiaoping. Liu and Deng were sidelined from day-to-day party affairs and then removed from the leadership in late 1966. Lin Biao[17] became the number-two figure in the Party. Mao responded to a letter from the Red Guards in August 1966, rallying people to target the 'headquarters of the counterrevolution'. Mao met a million Red Guards in Tiananmen Square in Beijing on 18 August 1966. Eight similar mass rallies were held in which over 12 million people from all over the country participated. Millions of party leaders, professors, teachers, and elites of the old society were persecuted in the violent struggles and suffered a wide range of abuse (e.g. public humiliation, arbitrary imprisonment, and torture). Many houses were searched by the Red Guards and the properties of these households were confiscated. A lot of people could not bear the humiliation and committed suicide in the first few months of the Revolution (Browne 2016).

The Cultural Revolution proceeded in two stages. During the first three years, Mao made an alliance with the ordinary people in the society, including college students, and fought against the government officials, who belonged to the middle tier of the society. When it finally spun into near civil war, Mao called in the army and released the government officials who were removed by the masses during the first stage of the Revolution, in order to restore control. This fundamental change in Mao's strategy hurt all major groups in Chinese society. The Cultural Revolution officially ended with Mao's death in 1976.

The fundamental reason for the Cultural Revolution was the unrestrained political power of the highest leadership. The Cultural Revolution hurt every person or group of persons in Chinese society. The old generations of elites and their families, the officials of the Nationalist government, landlords, capitalists, and intellectuals had been, for a while, overthrown. The Communist Party and government officials were criticised and replaced by more radical younger revolutionaries. These radical younger revolutionaries were purged later when the Cultural Revolution was close to the end, and replaced by the older officials who had been overthrown at the beginning of the Revolution. Everybody and every political group was hurt. These experiences made people rethink why the Cultural Revolution happened.

Mao knew well that he was battling against the whole society and expected that the right-wing in the Party would gain power after his death, but he thought that the right-wing would not hold on to power for long. These words were not widely quoted after Mao's death (Mao 1966).

2.9 THE FORMATION OF CONSENSUS ON REFORM

The Cultural Revolution was a socio-political campaign against 'the representatives of the bourgeoisie in the Communist Party', the entire class of government officials, by mass movement. Since everybody in the society was hurt one way or another, everybody wanted some kind of change. They thought something had to be done. This hope for reform existed at the apex of the pyramid as well as at the base.

A consensus on reform that had been formed by the late 1970s was shared by most groups of Chinese society. Mao reinstated Deng Xiaoping in 1973 and Deng ran the government for a short period of time in 1974 and 1975 when Zhou Enlai was seriously sick. After Zhou died in January 1976, the massive public outpouring of grief in Beijing turned to anger towards the Gang of Four[18] and Mao, leading to the Tiananmen incident in 1976.[19] Deng was thereafter purged by Mao for the second time. I was travelling on a train in February 1976. Everybody on the train, strangers from different places, was discussing Deng's second dismissal when the loudspeaker announced the Central Committee's decision to dismiss Deng, and everybody supported Deng. This was unprecedented during the Cultural Revolution, because anybody could report this type of behaviour to the authorities and the person who expressed this opinion would have got into trouble. It seemed that all the passengers in the train had similar ideas, which were against Mao's decision.

In the 1960s and 1970s, workers had group meetings before or after work. In these group meetings, Chairman Mao's works and party documents were read and discussed. The workshop directors and group leaders always supported the existing government policies. If they had different opinions from the official statement, they might talk with each other, but would not express their real opinions in front of ordinary workers. However, in late 1975 and early 1976, the atmosphere in these group meetings changed completely. Everybody, including a lot of cadres, made political jokes and gossiped during the group meetings. Nobody reported this to the authorities. Political jokes were widespread in every group of the society.

Zhou Enlai, the prime minister whom people believed would protect them against Mao's persecution, died in January 1976. The government imposed a set of restrictions on public displays of mourning for Zhou. Years of resentment over the Cultural Revolution led to popular discontent against Mao, and Zhou was seen as a symbol of anti-Cultural Revolution policy. Hundreds of thousands of people gathered in Tiananmen Square during the Tomb Sweeping Days in April to remember Zhou and express their feelings against the Cultural Revolution. Everyone in the society had formed a consensus that the leader of the country should not initiate a political movement, like the Cultural Revolution, again and again, and something had to be done to change the entire political and economic situation. This was the starting point of the economic reform over the next 40 years.

NOTES

1. At the beginning of the reform in 1978, the economy was controlled by the government and most enterprises were owned by the government. This planned economy was the starting point and the target of the reform.
2. See section 2.8 for details.
3. This Soviet-type system created high administrative costs and was soon reformed to a system of 'division of revenue and expenditure classification management' in the early 1950s.
4. It changed to a system in which the upper-level government controlled the personnel of just one lower-level government after the economic reform in the 1980s.
5. Throughout this book, collectives (villages) refers to the lowest level of local government as well as community of rural residents.
6. District government-owned firms in urban areas are called 'urban collective enterprises'.
7. I was one of these students.
8. Grade three was for young workers who had just completed their three-year apprenticeship. During the Cultural Revolution, salaries were frozen and a large number of

workers had grade three wages for a long time without promotion; the period depending on when you were hired. The salaries of all workers were raised after the reform.

9. The country was divided into several areas by the government with different wage levels, based on living costs in different areas.
10. This is a social security system used in many countries. Under this system, today's workers pay social security taxes into the programme and money flows back out to beneficiaries.
11. The Three-anti/Five-anti campaigns were launched in the early 1950s, designed to target the capitalist class. The three antis imposed were corruption, waste, and bureaucracy. The five antis imposed were bribery, theft of state property, tax evasion, cheating on government contracts, and stealing state economic information.
12. The 'Four Clean-ups' campaign, or the Socialist Education Movement, sought to cleanse the cadres in rural and urban areas, particularly in political, economic, organisational, and ideological fields.
13. Gao Gang was a CCP leader during the Chinese Civil War and the early years of the People's Republic of China. Rao Shushi was a military figure who had his power based in East China.
14. Peng Dehuai was a prominent CCP military leader and served as China's Defence Minister from 1954 to 1959.
15. The Great Famine from 1959 to 1961 was a widespread famine in China. Policies that focused on rapid industrialisation and overlooked the importance of food production and poor weather contributed to the famine. Estimates of deaths due to starvation range in the tens of millions.
16. Some researchers think that the critical part of the Revolution was from 1966 to 1969, when the target of the Revolution was 'the people in authority who took the capitalist road'.
17. Lin Biao (1907–1971) was a Marshal of the People's Republic of China. He was named Mao's designated successor, as the sole vice-chairman of the Communist Party of China from 1966 to 1971. He died on 13 September 1971, when an aeroplane he was aboard crashed in Öndörkhaan, Mongolia.
18. The Gang of Four was a political faction composed of four CCP officials, including Mao's wife Jiang Qing, Zhang Chunqiao, Yao Wenyuan, and Wang Hongwen. They came to power during the Cultural Revolution and were later charged with a series of crimes.
19. People gathered at Tiananmen Square in April 1976 to commemorate Zhou Enlai and were cracked down later by the police.

3. Reform 1979–1989: building market institutions

The Cultural Revolution and the experience of the planned economy in China from the 1950s to the 1970s wiped out almost all the institutions and mechanisms a market economy needed. There was no stock market, no market for commodities, almost no private ownership, and no free market prices. In terms of market infrastructure, China was a blank canvas for reformers to draw on at the end of the 1970s. To be efficient and sustainable in the long run, strong political power needs to work with a market economy. The task of reform was to rebuild all these institutions of a market economy from nothing and to start the process of economic reform from nowhere. An American businessman told me that when he first went to China in the early 1980s there were no production standards, no sales channels, and no transportation facilities. To start your business you had to do everything yourself. It was quite different from the current Chinese market in the 21st century, in which an entire business system is there, and for a foreign business person, the process has been much simplified.

Path dependence determined the anti-Cultural Revolution and government-led nature of the reform. The political turmoil during the Cultural Revolution played an important role in the economic and political reform that followed. According to Kang Xiaoguang, 'The reform, at the beginning stage, was a backward movement of the Cultural Revolution' (Kang 2002, p. 31). The Cultural Revolution hurt everyone, especially the top leaders in the Communist Party of China (CCP). Most CCP leaders thought reform was necessary and a market economy was one possible target of the reform. The reform was motivated by a wish to avoid a repeat of the Cultural Revolution.

The reform focused on the development of a market economy. This can be explained by the political economy model developed in section 1.2, which surmises that a government in a bureaucratic-market society will put more weight on economic development when it faces a deteriorating economy. In some cases, markets were created by the government, supported by the majority of social groups in Chinese society, and complied with the popular wishes of the people. In other cases, markets were created by ordinary people in society, and the government authorised these markets ex post. An institutional landscape was formed in which unprecedented amounts of private capital and enthusiasm could flow into economic development.

At the same time, within the government system, power was shifted down the bureaucratic structure. The user rights of farmland were given to the peasants, the state-owned enterprises (SOEs) were franchised to the managers, and the central government 'franchised' the localities to the local leaders. Informal institutions were developed to carry out functions not provided by formal institutions in this early stage of reform.

Since government officials were the main target under attack in the Cultural Revolution, most of the officials supported and actually led the reform. This was important for the success of the reform. At the same time, controlled by the government officials, the reform could not go beyond a given political baseline. A prerequisite of reform was that the rule of the CCP must remain.

The reform in the countryside and the decentralisation of government were generally successful, while the franchising of SOEs failed because property rights were not clearly defined and effectively implemented. A market mainly controlled by the government was created by the end of the 1980s. The political reform then stopped when a restriction on such reform was put in place by the CCP leadership after the failure of the political movement for democracy in 1989. This slowed down the economic reform for a short period.

3.1 THE STRATEGY AND LIMIT OF THE REFORM

For most of the leaders of the Communist Party, the target of reform was to introduce market mechanisms into the existing socio-political system. The purpose of the reform was to improve the efficiency of the economy, not its equality. Most officials and economists agreed at the end of the 1970s that the existing system was not as efficient as the so-called capitalist system or the market economy. The performance of the Chinese economy from the early 1950s to the late 1970s proved this. Based on the facts of the Chinese economy after the Cultural Revolution, anyone making a judgement would reach the same conclusion: if the efficiency of the economy did not improve, the Party would be destroyed and the nation would be subjugated. Economic development became the most important source of legitimacy for the CCP. Most people agreed that inequality was not the biggest problem in Chinese society.

In the 1970s, after 20 years of closing the door to the outside world, most of the factory equipment and infrastructure was old and shabby, representing the technology of the 1930s or the 1950s. A group of Chinese journalists were invited to visit the United States after President Nixon's visit to China in 1972. They found themselves in a world that was so strange, like an ancient suddenly transported to the 21st century. The Chinese economy needed to be modernised through reform.

A dual-track approach was used during the reform. Under this approach, a free market was allowed to emerge, while the old planned system continued to exist. This protected the people who enjoyed the low prices of consumer goods in the planned system. The price margin between the two systems created an opportunity for speculation, and government officials and their children, who were able to access the planned products, earned profits through their political power.

There was no detailed plan for reform. When an agreement could not be reached, Deng Xiaoping let his followers, mainly party secretaries at the provincial level, conduct policy experiments in their provinces. The well-known examples were the agricultural reforms led by Zhao Ziyang and Wan Li in Sichuan province and Anhui province, respectively. If the results were positive, Deng would activate the policy across the whole country. This reform strategy was called 'crossing the river by touching the stones'. The sequence of the reform was 'starting from the easiest and ending with the hardest' and 'following circuitous tactics'. It has been summarised as a 'gradual reform strategy' rather than 'shock therapy'.

The group of leaders of the CCP, who were beaten down during the Cultural Revolution, not only had to undergo a power struggle in the Party, but also needed to meet the challenge of governing the country. If they could not solve the problem of rural poverty and the inefficiency of SOEs, China would suffer a serious social and economic crisis. While the leadership shared the view that reform of the economic system was necessary, they disagreed on the direction and the strategy of the reform. Some of the provincial leaders held an opportunist attitude to reform. The leaders did not have enough information with which to judge how best to reform and how fast to reform. The leadership undertook various actions to promote the reform. In January 1984, Deng visited Shenzhen and Zhuhai, the cities created by economic reform and through opening up, to show his support for the recently created special economic zones and the economic reform in general.

Different groups of people in Chinese society had different expectations of the reform. The peasants and workers wanted an improved life, enough food, and housing. The young people who were sent to the countryside wanted to return to the cities and find a job. The intellectuals wanted freedom in their professional work, freedom of speech, and a more democratic political system.

In the Communist Party, most of the leaders supported some kind of reform. A small group, represented by Chen Yun, thought the economy should be returned to a normally functioning planned economy, political power should not interfere with the economy too much, and the reform should not go beyond a certain point. Most of the leaders, represented by Deng, wanted to introduce a market mechanism into the system and improve the efficiency of production, but did not want to change the political system too much. A small group of leaders, represented by Zhao Ziyang, wanted some political reform and had open minds towards new ideas coming from the outside world.

Differences in the expectations of reform existed, but these expectations did not vary significantly, partly because Deng wanted to delay the political debate about the distinction of what is socialism and what is capitalism. Some of the ideologists in the Communist Party insisted that a market economy meant a return of capitalism, which was viewed as politically incorrect. To avoid holding up the creation of a market economy, Deng tried to delay this kind of debate with an ideology claiming that 'whether it is a black cat or a white cat, a cat that can catch mice is a good cat'.

3.2 HOUSEHOLD RESPONSIBILITY SYSTEM IN THE COUNTRYSIDE

Agriculture was sacrificed during the planned period in China in order to support the industrialisation of the country. This was a decision made by Mao and his team. The prices of agricultural products were lowered by the planning authority, while that of the agricultural input, including machinery, chemical fertiliser, and other industrial products, were raised. The countryside was completely impoverished. Since the peasants had no incentive to produce agricultural products due to collectivisation, the urban food supply was in chronic shortage. The situation was getting worse in the late 1970s as a result of the Cultural Revolution. The leadership worried about the risk of another famine, like the one from 1958 to 1962.

It was no secret to rural families that the source of low productivity and poverty was collective farming. Production team members worked together every day and collections were distributed at the end of harvest according to their gender and the time they worked. People had no incentives to work hard. The solution to this problem was to divide the collective farmland among families and for them to work separately. During the planned period, besides the collective farmland, a small portion of the plots were left to the households. The households put much more effort into these 'household plots', which produced large amounts of product which were sold in the country fair.

During the planned period, in East and Southeast China, lots of attempts were made by the lower level of authority, and by the peasants themselves, to distribute the collective land to the peasants. Some government officials supported these attempts, but it was banned by the central government again and again. In 1956, Yongjia county in Wenzhou district, Zhejiang province first split land into plots. It spread to 1,000 production teams and was banned soon after (Baidu Baike n.d.-a). After Mao's death, the political atmosphere changed, and the peasants and the lower-level cadres in various places tried to distribute land again.

In the late 1970s, attempts to distribute plots to households started in poor provinces. The direct purpose was to solve the problem of hunger and to maintain stability in the countryside. The party secretaries in Anhui province and Sichuan province, Wan Li and Zhao Ziyang, respectively, supported these activities. The official documents banned the distributions of land at first, but later the practice was allowed in poor areas.

Xiaogang and Other Villages

A severe drought struck Anhui province in 1978. To prevent famine, some brigade and production teams tried to distribute plots to households. The party secretary of Feixi county imposed 'responsibility of output to households' across the whole county. This was seriously criticised but was later supported by Wan Li, the party secretary of Anhui province (Chen 1985, p.33).

The most famous example of plot distribution was that in Xiaogang village, Fengyang county, Anhui province, where 18 households signed a contract with local cadres. Xiaogang was a famously poor village that could not hand in any grain to the state, and 79 per cent of the grain the villagers ate had been purchased from the state over the 13 years before 1978 (Chen 1985, p.39). During the Great Famine from 1959 to 1961, 67 villagers died of starvation out of a population of 120. The villagers were worried that another famine might come after a bad harvest in 1978.

In December 1978, 18 peasants in the village, led by Yan Hongchang, met in a peasant's house in the village (Chen and Chun 2009). They agreed to sign a secret contract to divide the land owned by the People's Commune into family plots. This was illegal at that time, and the peasants risked severe punishment. According to the contract, each plot was to be worked by an individual family who could keep the surplus after turning over a portion of their product to the government and the collective. They agreed that should one of them be caught by the government and sentenced to death, the other villagers would raise their children until the children were 18 years old.

After this secret change, Xiaogang village had a 'bumper harvest'[1] the following year, with an output larger than the previous five years combined. Per capita income in Xiaogang village increased from RMB22 ($12.9) per year to RMB400 ($234.6) per year in 1979. This attracted the attention of surrounding villages and the government. After serious debate, the central government authorised the provincial governments to experiment with similar policies, in order to see the result. In a couple of years it turned out that the reform was a big success. The secret signing of the contract in Xiaogang is widely regarded as the beginning of the economic reform of the countryside.

Xiaogang village was not the only example of 'distributing plots to households' in the late 1970s. A large number of villages, in different provinces, adopted similar approaches. The Research Group of Rural Development did a field survey in Anhui province, visiting 15 counties, 127 government units, 103 production brigades and production teams, and 304 peasants in 1980. (Chen 1985). The number of production teams (villages) that adopted 'distributing plots to households' increased to 23 per cent of all production teams in May 1980, from 0.4 per cent at the end of 1978. In five counties, more than 50 per cent of production teams had adopted the reform by May 1980.

Before the reform, households were organised into production teams. Each production team had several groups of families. In the initial stage of the reform, the responsibility system had several forms:

1. Output responsibility to groups. A group usually had seven or eight households with more than ten labourers. The group signed a contract to pay the production team a certain amount of product at the end of the year and the means of production and land were distributed to groups. Payments were based on output, while keeping the production team's functions of planning, accounting, and distribution.
2. Quotas to group. Peasants worked in groups under the lead of the production team. The production team owned the means of production, which were used by the groups. Each group had quotas in terms of the production plan, grain turn-in to the state, and team accumulations. After meeting the quota, each group distributed any excesses among themselves.
3. Output responsibility directly to households. Each household signed a contract with the production team and paid a certain amount of product to the production team at the end of the year. In return, the production team distributed land and the means of production to households.

Table 3.1 Growth in grain production, Chuxian district, 1979 compared with 1978, %

	Quanjiao county	Chuxian county	Laian county	Jiashan county
County sum	+12.4	+12.5	+0.7	+0.3
No responsibility	+6.0	+4.3	–6.7	–6.3
Production responsibility to group	+12.7	+16.3	+3.4	+4.0
Production responsibility to household	+35.7	+68.9	+37.1	+31.0

Note: Only 40 per cent of production team was included in Jiashan county's data.

Source: Chen (1985, p.37).

The reform had different effects on different households in different villages. The supporters included the veterans of farm work, who were more productive if working independently than as a part of a production team. Some of the team cadres and poor households, who had less labour and knowledge to work independently, were against the reform. After seeing the results of the reform, most of the team cadres changed their minds. The reformers tried various forms of responsibility system at the beginning: responsibility to households, responsibility to groups, and so on. Responsibility to household led to the highest growth in production (Table 3.1).

Table 3.2 shows the economic effects of the reform in four very poor production teams in Fengyang county, Anhui province. Xiaogang, located in East Huai River Plain, was a village famous in Anhui province because of its poverty. Xiaxiaozhuang, located in the mid-Anhui Plain, with per capita farmland of less than 2 Mu,[2] adopted 'responsibility to household' at the end of 1978. Qiandong, located in North Anhui Plain, with per capita farmland of about 4 Mu, adopted 'responsibility to household' in 1977. Songshushan, located in the East Anhui area near the Yangtze River, with per capita farmland of less than 3 Mu, adopted 'responsibility to household' in 1978.

The responsibility system raised productivity for the following reasons: (i) it gave the peasants the autonomy to make their own decisions on what to produce under the state plans,[3] and how to distribute their products, and (ii) it solved the problem of the 'big pot'[4] and gave the peasants incentives to increase production. Teamwork could not solve the incentive problem because there was always someone who wanted to take a free ride. Since

Table 3.2 Effects of responsibility to household in four poor villages

	Per capita grain production (Jin)		Per capita grain peasants' retained (Jin)		Per capita grain hand-in and sold to state (Jin)		Per capita income (RMB yuan ($))	
	1979	1979/78, %	1979	1979/78, %	1979	1979/78, %	1979	1979/78, %
China	776	+4.3	465	+5.2	155	+7.6	83.4 (48.9)	+12.7
Xiaogang	1,147	+187	720	+306	199	–	110.8 (65.0)	+280
Xiaxiaozhuang	1,270	+98	520	+44	246	+151	75.7 (44.4)	+95.5
Qiandong	2,136	+196	650	+62	1,000	+1,308	122.7 (72.0)	+43.5
Songshushan	1,978	+129	819	+72	665	–	134.0 (78.6)	+55.9

Note: 1 Jin equals 0.5 kilograms. Xiaxiaozhuang and Qiandong's comparisons were data for 1979 compared with 1977.

Source: Chen (1985, p.40).

the cost of evaluating a team member's work precisely through measuring his or her contributions would be high, most of the teams recorded members' points approximately. According to transaction cost theory, the boundary between an enterprise and the market is determined by transaction costs. Ronald Coase set out his transaction cost theory of the firm in 1937, making it one of the first attempts to define the firm theoretically in relation to the market (Coase 1937). According to Coase, people begin to organise their production in firms when the transaction cost of coordinating production through the market exchange is greater than within the firm. This theory can be applied to the analysis of the boundary between the planned economy and the market. In the planned economy, government regulation made the use of the market extremely costly. The responsibility system greatly reduced the transaction costs of the market, including both agency costs and information costs, and greatly increased the role of the market in the economy.

Contracts were widely used during this period, partly because the peasants did not believe that the governments would keep their promises. A contract usually stated that the responsibilities of Party A (the production team) include providing Party B (the household) with land, cattle, and equipment, while Party B's responsibilities were to fulfil the production plan set by Party A, the state purchase quota, public accumulation, and withdraw and retain by Party A. The contracts were usually signed for one year.

The CCP Central Committee did not make the decision whether to adopt the system nationally for a couple of years, letting local authorities and peasants make their own choices. It turned out that the new approach was much better, and it spread throughout the country in a few years.

The system of household plots is officially called the 'household responsibility system'. It was created by the peasants and supported by local governments and the central government. By 1983, more than 93 per cent of production teams had adopted the system. The system allowed households to make decisions independently as to how to use land and other facilities optimally in production, while preserving the collective land ownership. Theoretically, the ownership of the land and the user rights of the land were split, and only the user rights of the land were delegated to the peasants. The contract covered only a few years at first, then was extended again and again by the government. Households could freely dispose of the surplus products above the national and collective (or the village government)[5] quotas. The system was successful nationwide. Agricultural production increased dramatically, and the food shortage disappeared within four to five years. The gross outputs of farming, forestry, animal husbandry, and fishery increased from RMB139.7 billion ($81.9 billion) in 1978 to RMB321.4 billion ($138.1 billion) in 1984 (National

Bureau of Statistics 1999). No one knew at the beginning that the system would be so successful. So it was a surprise when in 1984 so much grain had been harvested that some of the peasants could not even sell it. The success of the agricultural reform, as pointed out by Zhao Ziyang, was just like magic (Zhao 2009, p.114).

At first the contract between the village and the households covered a short period, which caused households' short-term behaviour. Since the contracts were signed for very short periods, the peasants tried to squeeze as much value as possible out of the soil without investment. For example, the peasants used large amounts of chemical fertilisers to raise the short-run output and ignored the practice of letting land lie fallow. In some cases, the villagers deserted public housing and sold equipment, because this public infrastructure and means of production were not useful for their household production in the short term. To change this, the government tried to improve the households' expectations. In China, the CCP published documents about important issues, functioning as law. The 'Number 1' document of the Communist Party Central Committee was the first document issued at the beginning of each year. Between 1982 and 1986 and between 2004 and 2017, the Central Committee issued 19 'Number 1' documents which talk about agriculture. In 1982, the Central Committee issued the first 'Number 1' document about agriculture, which affirmed the use of the production responsibility system in the countryside. The 'Number 1' document in the following years tried hard to reassure households that the responsibility system would not change and there would be no new collectivisation.

As the population changed in a village, the household plots had to be re-divided. In the past 30 years, a lot of peasants have left the countryside and moved to the cities. When someone leaves, should the village redistribute the land? The practical question that village governments need to consider is how often to adjust the plots and using what standards.

Based on the experiment of Guanghan county, Sichuan province, the CCP and the State Council decided to end the People's Commune system and set up township governments in October 1983 (CCP Central Committee and State Council 1983). The document also prevised that with the establishment of the village government at the lower administrative level, a village-level financial and budget system would need to be established. This required the reorganisation of the lower-level government in rural areas, with the village government replacing the brigade or production team which existed under the People's Commune. The document also defined the villagers' committee as the grass-roots mass self-government organisation. The director and members of the villagers' committee should be elected by villagers.

Table 3.3 Succession of reforms in agriculture

Time	Reform
1978–1984	Land ownership reform: user rights of land were franchised to peasants
1984–late 1980s	Changing purchase channels of agricultural products and reform in pricing system and purchases system of agricultural products

The reform of redistributing farmland to households changed the mode of agricultural production fundamentally, from collective production to individual family production. This land ownership reform split user rights from ownership rights and gave the former to the peasants, which changed the incentive structure fundamentally. This basic change in China's rural society raised, or recovered, productivity dramatically, and set the tone of rural life in China over the following years.

The government reduced the number of products under procurement and apportion from 117 under the administration of the Ministry of Commerce and Federation of Supply and Marketing Cooperatives in 1978 to 38 in 1984 (Chen Lifen n.d.). Peasants were allowed to sell and purchase products in 1983 (CCP Central Committee 1983). The demand for trading extra products was created (Cai et al. 2008, p.39).

Tremendous problems arose when the purchase channels changed. Most of the problems related to the second category of agricultural products, such as pigs and edible oil. This was because these products were no longer bought by the state-owned wholesale companies under the plan. When the government agencies were not able or had no incentive to purchase agricultural products, peasants were unable to sell such products. The government purchasing agencies were not flexible enough to change the price when market supply and demand changed, which resulted in products becoming overstocked and unsaleable. More reforms to the pricing system and the purchases system were adopted in the mid-1980s after the reform in agricultural production (Table 3.3).

Township and Village Enterprises (TVEs)

Township and Village Enterprises (TVEs) were built up entirely on the basis of local governments in towns and villages in the countryside during the planned period. The predecessor of TVEs, the commune- and brigade-run enterprises, prevailed under the planning system. At the beginning of the reform, the government tried to use TVEs as a means of industrial development. The State Council issued the Provisions on Several Issues of the Development of Commune and Brigade Run Enterprises in July 1979, which promoted the development of commune- and brigade-run enterprises, but emphasised the direction of socialism (State Council 1979a). Since the commune ceased to exist in the early 1980s, these enterprises changed their name to TVEs.

As the price of agricultural products was very low in the planned period, agriculture was not profitable. Some peasants tried to move to other businesses. When the restrictions were relaxed, a large number of TVEs emerged. They can be traced back to the 'commune and brigade enterprises' in the 1950s to 1970s, which were restricted and played a limited role.

TVEs were market-oriented public enterprises under the purview of local governments based in townships and villages. The ownership structures of TVEs had various forms; they were not only enterprises owned by townships and villages. TVEs underwent great development in the 1980s. When the household responsibility system developed in the countryside, productivity increased, and a large number of peasants became surplus labour. TVEs absorbed these surplus labourers when the urban–rural residential policy did not allow peasants to move to the cities. The total value of outputs of TVEs increased from RMB49.3 billion ($28.9 billion) in 1978 to RMB101.7 billion ($51.5 billion) in 1983, increasing by 15.6 per cent annually, and they employed 32 million workers (Ministry of Agriculture Bureau of Policy and Law 1999, p.144). At the end of 1986, the number of TVEs reached 15.2 million, the total value of outputs was RMB330 billion ($95.6 billion), and the total number of workers was 80 million (Wu Xiaobo 2014a, p.202).

3.3 URBAN ENTERPRISES

At the beginning of the reform, local governments were the effective owners of all but the largest central government-owned enterprises in urban areas. The separation of ownership and control caused an incentive problem for the managers of SOEs. Instead of adopting a strategy of rapid privatisation as in many transition countries, China took an alternative approach in the 1980s to give managers of SOEs incentives to pursue efficiency.

In 1984, the Central Committee of the CCP decided to set the economic reform in full motion in urban areas. The main idea of urban reform was to delegate more power to the local governments and the SOEs.

SOEs: Expansion of Enterprise Autonomy and Contract Responsibility System

There was a widely shared consensus at the end of the 1970s on the need to reform SOEs by expanding enterprise autonomy. The reformers applied a version of the rural reform to the urban industrial sector. Since most of the large and medium-sized enterprises were owned by the government at that time, this policy was targeting SOEs. Sichuan province started experiments on six SOEs in October 1978, and the National Economic Committee picked eight SOEs to conduct similar experiments. To increase the incentives of the management of the SOEs, enterprises were allowed to retain a portion of the profits. In these experimental SOEs, the government delegated more powers to enterprises, including those over production, sales, use of funds, employment, and worker reward and punishment systems. A director responsibility system under the leadership of party committees and a workers' congress system were implemented. The workers' congress was designed to represent the interests of the workers and had limited powers of checks and balances. These experiments were extended rapidly to many industries. The number of experimental enterprises increased to 6,600, which accounted for 60 per cent of SOEs supported by the state budget in China in 1980 (Xiao and Sui 2011, p.192). It soon turned out that expanding enterprises' autonomy gave enterprises incentives to expand production, but not to increase efficiency. This was because the enterprises were still under the control of the plan, and the plan still emphasised the scale of production rather than efficiency.

In December 1980, the leadership of the CCP decided to implement an 'economic responsibility' policy in enterprises. It outlined the division of benefits and responsibilities between the government and the enterprises. The enterprises were allowed to retain a portion of the profit if they met the profit quotas. In April 1983, the State Council decided to replace the SOEs' profit delivery with tax payments. All large and medium-sized SOEs with positive profits should pay income tax amounting to 55 per cent of these profits. The enterprises received a portion of the remaining profits as retained earnings after delivering after-tax profits to the state. At the same time, government appropriations were replaced by loans issued by the state-owned banks.

Urban reform started officially in 1984. The reform of the SOEs was one of the main components of urban reform. The main strategy was to give SOEs more operational autonomy, a replication of rural responsibility reform applied to urban SOEs. Because of the success of rural reform, the leadership believed that franchising and contracting was the best approach to solving all the problems, but this turned out to be wrong.[6]

Government intervention was reduced, and the management was given more operational autonomy, in an adaption of rural responsibility reform. In September 1985, the State Council approved the Interim Provision on Strengthening the Vitality of Large and Medium-Sized SOEs (State Council 1985), which proposed 14 measures to improve the vitality of SOEs. In April 1988, the People's Congress passed the Law on Industrial Enterprises Owned by the Whole People, which confirmed that the SOEs were socialist commodity producers and business units that were legally autonomous and self-financing, and conducted independent accounting (National People's Congress 1988b).

The management contract responsibility system was expanded to SOEs nationwide from 1984 to 1988, promoted by the government. Under this system the management of an SOE signs a contract with the government promising to turn in a certain percentage of minimum profits, and the government allowed the management to control the remaining profits. The approach was based on the theory that ownership and the right of operation could be separated. Its purpose was to incentivise the management to increase production while ensuring the government received enough revenue. The responsibility system was adopted in various forms, including contracts on growth in profits, minimum profits, lump sum profit, and deficit reduction. The system had some defects, including difficulty in drawing a clear line between ownership and operation rights, and the government's over-intervention. The State Council issued the Provisional Regulations on SOEs' Contract Responsibility System (State Council 1988a) in February 1988 to implement the contract responsibility system, which standardised the approach of the contract responsibility system for various SOEs.

While the large SOEs adopted the contract responsibility system, the smaller SOEs were leased to individuals. By December 1986, about 60,000 small state-owned stores had been leased to individuals. Most of them increased their profitability (Xiao and Sui 2011, p.210).

Another bold attempt of SOE reform was to experiment with the shareholding system. According to CCP's Resolution on Economic Reform in 1984, public ownership is the dominant force of the socialist economy, but the restriction of other ownership forms is never a precondition of the development of the public economy (CCP 1984). In November 1984, Shanghai Feile Audio issued shares, becoming the first shareholding company in China since 1949. The Bank of Communications became the first shareholding bank in 1986 (Bank of Communications n.d.). In December 1986, the State Council issued the Regulations on Deepening the Enterprises Reform and Enhancing the Vitality of Enterprises (State Council 1986a), which stated that local governments could pick some large and medium-sized SOEs to carry out experiments on changing the SOEs to shareholding companies. By the end of 1986, about 6,000 shareholding companies had been set up nationwide.

These reforms of the SOEs in 1980s were not totally successful in terms of increasing efficiency. Part of the reform was concerned with income distribution and redistribution between SOEs and their owner, the government. The responsibility system gave part of the control to the managers. The government retained ownership and held power over personnel and management. This resulted in a situation of 'insider control' and increased the conflict of interest between the managers and the government. The managers tried to maximise their benefits by reducing the benefits of the government. To maximise their benefits during the period of contracting, the managers also ignored long-term investment. The reform of SOEs became an unresolved headache.

Some of the contracted SOEs expanded rapidly, but the managers ignored possible improvements to the management of these companies because they wanted to optimise their own benefits within the contract period, which was usually short. Ma Shengli was not the first SOE contractor, but he was the first contractor who aroused the concern of the whole nation thanks to the propaganda of the media. Mr Ma, the business section chief of Shijiazhuang Paper Mill, a SOE with 800 workers, signed a contract with the local government and became director of the factory in 1984. The factory had experienced a deficit for three years. Ma changed the size and colour of the toilet paper they produced and gave bonuses to sales people. As a result, the factory made RMB1.4 million ($0.6 million) in profits during the first year of the contract. The government-held media reported the story nationwide and Mr Ma became a star of economic reform. He set up a paper mill group under his name and became a contractor of tens of paper mill factories. He was welcomed by local government officials and SOE managers wherever he travelled. Since most of the factories that joined Ma's group were money-losers, and no improvements were made to their management, his group failed in a couple of years (Zhou 2014).

The failure of the contract and responsibility system was partly due to the complicated relationship between SOEs and local governments. This relationship is much more complicated than that between farmers and village government in rural areas. The urban SOEs were more tightly controlled by the government before the reform. The contract system franchised part of the control to the managers without changing the ownership of the enterprises. This created conflicts of interest between the managers and government and affected the short-term behaviour of the managers. Since the profits of SOEs made up a large part of the government's revenue, the government continued to interfere with the SOEs' operations after they were contracted to managers or other individuals.

The Birth and Growth of Non-State-Owned Enterprises

While the reform of SOEs stagnated, various forms of non-state-owned enterprises were born in this spring of political and economic reform. The leadership changed the focus of reform to some degree from the SOEs to non-state-owned enterprises, taking a 'roundabout' strategy.

Different forms of enterprises

Millions of young people, who were sent to the countryside by the government during the Cultural Revolution, returned to the cities without jobs. To solve this problem, the State Council decided to allow these 'returned youth' to set up proprietorships in 1979 (CASS Institute of Law 1980, p.102). In 1981, the CCP's 'On a Number of Historical Issues since the Founding of the People's Republic' pointed out that the individual economy is a supplement to the public ownership (CCP 1981b). In December 1982, the new amended constitution provided that the individual economy is supplementary to the socialist public ownership and the state should protect the legal rights and benefits of the individual economy (National People's Congress 1982a). In January 1987, the CCP issued a document on how to deepen the rural reform (CCP 1987a) and pointed out that in the primary stage of a socialist society it is inevitable that individual economy and private economy will coexist with the public economy. This was the first time since the socialist transformation of capitalist business enterprises in 1956 that the CCP clearly allowed the existence of private enterprises. One of the amendments of the Constitution the National People's Congress passed in April 1988 was that 'the State allows private economy to exist and the private economy is a complement to the socialist public economy'. According to this document, 'the State protects the lawful rights and interests of the private economy, and provides guidance, supervision and management to the private economy'.

A large number of individual proprietorships started during these years; many of them were owned by young people without jobs. Some of the private companies today in China were started by 'wheelers and dealers' in the 1980s. The number of registered individual household businesses reached 14.5 million and the number of people employed by individual household businesses increased from 0.3 million in 1979 to 23.0 million in 1988 (Xiao and Sui 2011, p.213).

Nian Guangjiu was 42 years old in 1979. He was illiterate and had been imprisoned for illicit trading in 1963. After being released, he began to roast watermelon seeds, which were delicious. People called him a 'fool' and his seeds 'Fool Melon Seeds'. After the economic reform, his business increased, and he hired 12 workers. This became an emotive issue, because Karl Marx had said that when a person hires more than 8 workers, he becomes a capitalist and the activity becomes exploitation (Marx, *Capital*, Vol. 1, Ch 9, 1867). Deng talked about the issue and 'Fool Melon Seeds' in a meeting of the Political Bureau and allowed the private business to exist as an experiment. Nian hired 105 workers in 1982 and produced 9,000 kilograms of seeds per day (Fenghua 2012).

Wenzhou is a coastal area in Zhejiang province that lacks farmland and had no railway during the planned period and the early years of the reform. The people in Wenzhou have a tradition of engaging in trade. At the end of the 1970s, smuggling grew on a large scale in Wenzhou. Small home appliances and clothing from Hong Kong and Taiwan were smuggled in by fishing boats. The trade of these smuggled goods created the first free markets in Wenzhou. The sole proprietors in the area reached 3,000 around 1980, and large-scale producers were called 'Kings', such as the 'King of Electric Appliances', 'King of Screws', and 'King of Lamps' (Wu Xiaobo 2014a, p.74).

In China, foreign-invested enterprises (FIEs) refers to enterprises set up either jointly by domestic investors and foreign investors or by foreign investors alone. FIEs have various legal forms. Any one of a number of legal entities can be considered FIEs, including equity joint ventures, cooperative joint ventures, wholly owned foreign enterprises, and foreign-invested partnerships. In early years of the reform, foreign-invested firms tended to engage more in exporting and innovation, and often had substantially higher export-to-sales ratios than domestic firms or a higher percentage of sales made up of new products (Hale and Long 2012, p.13).

The first group of foreign firms entering the Chinese market was a group of Japanese firms. Panasonic set up an office in Beijing in 1979 after Deng Xiaoping visited Panasonic in Japan in 1978. Coca-Cola signed a contract on 2 January 1979 with China National Cereals, Oils and Foodstuffs Corporation to sell Coca-Cola in China, one day after the restoration of diplomatic relations at the ambassadorial level between China and the United States. According to the agreement, Coca-Cola was allowed to sell its products in Chinese cities and certain recreational areas, including foreign tourist hotels and travel shops, through compensation trade,[7] and to set up factories in China (Cendrowski 2014). American Motors Corporation (AMC) signed an agreement with Beijing Automobile Production Company in 1984, which was the largest joint venture in auto production in China in the 1980s.[8] The first Beijing jeep rolled off the production line in 1985. Tremendous problems emerged in the early years of the joint venture, including cultural conflict between American and Chinese managers and conflicts about the shares of investment. This joint venture between AMC and the Beijing Automobile Production Company was an example of a failed foreign-invested project (Mann 1997).

Hong Kong- and Taiwan-invested enterprises were an important part of the investment coming from the outside world. These investors knew China well and first discovered the business opportunities in mainland China after the Cultural Revolution. Henry Fok (Fok Ying-tung), a Hong Kong businessman, contacted the Guangdong provincial government and built the White Swan Hotel in February 1983. The White Swan Hotel is a 28-storey luxury hotel in Guangzhou, located on Shamian Island, overlooking the Pearl River. The hotel is reached by its own private 635 metre causeway (Newsgd 2014).

Where does the first group of entrepreneurs come from?

Some of the earliest companies were initiated by old capitalists, whose assets were stripped by the government after the 1949 Revolution. They were supported by the government. Rong Yiren was a businessman in Shanghai who lost all his enterprises during the Revolution. After the beginning of the reform, he suggested that the government should set up a state-supported trust company to absorb foreign investment. Deng supported the suggestion personally, and Rong became the founder of China International Trust and Investment Corporation (CITIC). The first large business project CITIC had was to issue bonds for Yizheng Chemical Fiber, a large SOE on the verge of closing due to lack of funds (Landai Gongzhu 2012).

A group of companies was set up by scientists and technicians from state-owned research institutes and universities. Chen Chunxian, a major scientist of nuclear fusion and a research fellow of the Chinese Academy of Sciences, suggested to the government that China needed to build its own Silicon Valley after visiting the United States. The Beijing Association for Science and Technology accepted his suggestion and gave him RMB200 ($117.3). Mr Chen set up the first private science and technology entity, Beijing Plasma Society Advanced Technology Development Services, in 1980, with 15 employees (Chen Chunxian Studio n.d.). The company made some progress in providing technical support to other small factories, but it was not so successful in competing with other high-tech companies set up later.

Liu Chuanzhi, an engineer in the Chinese Academy of Science's Institute of Computing Technology in Beijing, was appointed in 1984 as the associate manager of the New Technology Development Company, which was funded by the Institute of Computing Technology. The company was the predecessor of Lenovo. Eleven employees worked in the small reception room of the Institute. The company was an SOE and its initial capital was RMB200,000 ($85,947.5) given by the Institute. The first big deal the company did involved checking, maintaining, and providing training for 500 IBM computers imported by the Chinese Academy of Science in 1985. Later Liu developed his own computer, and established Lenovo (Yu Donghui 2015).

Some of the entrepreneurs used their connections with government officials to start their businesses. Wang Shi, a young man in Shenzhen originally from North China, found out that corn from Northeast China was transported to Shenzhen through Hong Kong. Northeast China was a region that produced large amounts of corn while the south (where Shenzhen is located) was a major region of corn consumption. The corn was usually transported from the Northeast to Southern China by rail, which was expensive. Wang Shi used *Guanxi* (relations) to find ships to transport corn from Northeast China directly to Guangdong and made RMB3 million ($1.3 million, Fenghuang 2012). Wang used the money to set up a modern science and education equipment exhibition centre in 1984 (Wu Xiaobo 2014a, p.156, 252).

Other companies came out of SOEs. For some reason, the government relaxed the control of these companies, which gave entrepreneurs the chance to develop their own businesses. Zhang Ruimin, a 35-year-old worker, was assigned to head an electrical appliance factory on the verge of bankruptcy. On his first day as director, 53 employees applied to quit their jobs. Zhang thereafter set up 13 rules to tighten worker discipline. He then introduced technology and equipment from Liebherr, a refrigerator producer in Germany, and changed the company's name to Haier, which is the largest refrigerator producer in China today (Lingnanhui Laowang n.d.).

In the mid-1980s, with the prosperity of the market economy, many people became dissatisfied with the status quo, in favour of businesses, and quit their jobs in government or SOEs to 'jump into the sea' and embrace the market by setting up their own businesses. Some of them later became the richest entrepreneurs in China.

Other entrepreneurs emerged from the bottom of Chinese society. Mu Qizhong was a boiler worker in Wanzhou, Chongqing. He wrote several political articles in 1974 and was arrested and sentenced to death. He was released in 1979 and set up a trade shop in 1982. He was put into prison again for speculation in 1983, but was released in 1984 and upgraded his business to a company. After borrowing RMB2.5 million ($0.9 million) from the Bank of Agriculture, he started a company that imported sugar from the United States and refrigerators from South Korea. He bought four aeroplanes made by the Soviet Union and sold them to Sichuan Airlines in 1991, which made him an overnight star. He understood the importance of media and used it as a support to his business. He was arrested in 1999 for fraud and was sentenced to life imprisonment in 2000. He was released in 2016 after spending 16 years in prison (Zhang 2016). This is an example of an entrepreneur who emerged from the bottom of Chinese society and was brave enough to break existing rules without knowing much about the modern ways of doing business.

Four brothers of the Liu family in Xinjin, Sichuan province – Liu Yongyan, Liu Yongxing, Liu Yonghao, and Liu Yongmei – set up a poultry breeding station by raising RMB1,000 ($586.5). Using the earnings from the breeding station, they set up a feed mill in 1982, which became a feed group with capital of RMB10 million ($2.7 million) in 1987. Today the group provides a large range of products and services, with 70,000 employees and annual sales of RMB100 billion ($16.1 billion) (New Hope Group n.d.).

3.4 CREATION OF MARKETS: FREEING PRICES

As soon as the market players were created, the authorities needed to create the market itself, which included the creation of market facilities and a pricing mechanism. Price reform is a key issue of economic reform. If the prices are controlled by the government and cannot be freely determined by supply and demand, producers and consumers cannot correctly value products and make the right decisions to buy and sell. A large price distortion existed during the planned period. The prices of consumer goods were deliberately reduced and those of industrial products raised. Correcting these price distortions may have caused serious social instabilities.

Dual Pricing System and Price Reform

In the late 1970s and early 1980s, the pricing system was reformed gradually by introducing a dual pricing system. In this system, some commodity prices were still under state planning and control, while other commodity prices were determined by the market. For example, to protect the urban consumers who enjoyed the benefits of low prices of rationed rice and flour during the planned period, the prices for rationed consumer goods were still under state control. At the same time, if extra amounts of rice and flour were needed, one had to buy them in the free market at market prices. This was better than the situation in the planned period, because if you needed more rice and flour, you could find them in the market, although the prices could be higher. This pricing system also created positive incentives for peasants to produce more farm products than that required by the state plan.

There were problems with the dual pricing system. Some people took advantage of dual pricing to speculate, hoarding the low-cost products in the national plan, and then selling them in the market at high prices, causing market instability and price volatility. Price subsidies were financially costly for the government and producers had no incentives to fulfil their quotas as set by the central plan.

To correct the distortion in the price system created in the planned period, the government adjusted the relative prices in the late 1970s and 1980s. In 1979, the government raised the agricultural product procurement prices. The grain and oil prices increased by 20 per cent, and the prices of cotton, pork, beef, and eggs increased by 15 per cent, 26 per cent, 40 per cent, and 26 per cent, respectively. On the consumer price side, the retail prices of pork, beef, mutton, eggs, poultry, fish, vegetables, and milk were raised by an average of 30 per cent, with price subsidies given to urban consumers for certain products.[9] In 1985, the government removed the state monopoly of grain purchases and implemented contract purchases; the price was calculated as the average of the prices of state purchases and the extra purchases. The extra purchase price was negotiated between the government and the peasants. Government control of the retail prices of pork, beef, mutton, poultry, eggs, fish, and vegetables was relaxed in 1985, with price subsidies given to urban consumers.

The price reform of industrial products started in the mid-1980s. The State Council issued Interim Provisions on the Further Expansion of the Autonomy of State-Owned Industrial Enterprises (State Council 1984b) in May 1984, which stated that industrial products, after meeting the national plan, could be sold in the free market. Management could set the price independently according to market supply and demand, within a margin of 20 per cent. Relevant ministries of the State Council removed the 20 per cent margin seven months later. Starting in 1985, the prices of industrial products for consumers were adjusted. The prices of cotton, aluminium cookware, bicycles, cigarettes, and wine were raised, while those of chemical fibre cloth, watches, and radio were lowered (Xiao and Sui 2011, pp.214, 216).

In 1988, the government introduced a project named 'Price Breaking through the Barrier' (*Jia Ge Chuang Guan*), which tried to raise the prices of most commodities to solve the problems caused by the dual pricing system. In May 1988, Zhao Ziyang presented a plan to rationalise the relative prices and solve the problem of irrational salaries, or salaries lower than the market level due to government regulation. He showed his proposal to Deng Xiaoping, who agreed to it. In August 1988, the CCP Political Bureau adopted the 'preliminary program on prices and wages reform', which pointed out what the general direction of price reform is that 'a small number of key commodities and services prices will be administered by the state, while most commodity prices will be open . . . to convert the price formation mechanism' and gradually realised the principle that 'the state regulates the market and the market guides enterprises'.

The 'Price Breaking through the Barrier' project started in March 1988 in Shanghai. The retail prices of 280 items, most of them necessities, were raised by 20–30 per cent by the government. In April, the retail prices of non-staple foods were raised in all cities and subsidies were given to workers. In May, the retail prices of meat in central cities increased by 70 per cent. The price increase caused panic. The municipal government in Shanghai issued coupons for salt and matches. Retail prices increased by 18.5 per cent in 1988 compared to the previous year (Wu Wei 2014b).

Price reform was a major reform in 1988. The government tried to raise the prices of numerous consumer goods to end the dual pricing system within a short period. This approach was quite different from the gradual approach China adopted in most of its reforms, and was more like the 'shock therapy' approach adopted in the Soviet Union. The Chinese media widely reported the price reform before its implementation, which caused a bank run and panic.

Because of severe inflation and panic, Zhao Ziyang decided to postpone price reforms in September 1988. Zhao believed that the economic environment was not ready for a quick price reform. The 'Price Breaking through the Barrier' reform of 1988 was not successful, mainly because the leaders tried to solve all the problems with the pricing system within a short period. Zhao later said that he would bear the main responsibility for this failure. Zhao lost his job as the party secretary during the Tiananmen Square crisis in 1989. Even so, price reform resumed gradually in the 1990s, and by the end of the 1990s the government's control of most of the prices of consumer goods had been relaxed, although price control on raw materials and producer goods would continue for decades.

As a by-product of the development of private business, fake products raged all over the country. The Secretary of Commerce bought a shoe when doing a field investigation in Wuhan city. The next day, after going back home to Beijing, part of the heel dropped off (Chen 1990). Liushi, a small town in Wenzhou, became a national centre of production and trade of low electrical voltage apparatus (e.g. switches and contactors). One thousand workshops repaired disassembled used contactors, bought from SOEs all over the country. These workshops used cheap materials to reduce costs, replacing silver with iron and using rice chaff rather than quartz sand. Housewives washed the products in a river and dried them on the farm fields. Only 0.1 per cent of the products had licences, and all the products without licences were below grade. Fake trademark labels, bought from SOEs in large cities, were stuck on the products to deceive buyers. The central government sent an investigation group to Liushi and closed all 1,267 low voltage apparatus salesrooms in 1990. One year after the crackdown, 25 producers got licences and integrated thousands of small workshops. By 2000, 60 per cent of low voltage apparatus in China was produced in Liushi (Wu Xiaobo 2014a, p.293).

The problems of private businesses raised the question of whether the market should be developed further. The government's crackdown on fake products caused the owners of private businesses to worry that the government would take over their businesses again, like in the 1950s.

Building Market Facilities

In the late 1970s and early 1980s, the reform expanded from the production area to the area of market distribution. In the planned period, the state's commercial companies were the only companies that bought agricultural products from the peasants and sold inputs for farm production to the peasants. This monopoly was broken, and the peasants were allowed, after selling the stipulated quota to the state and paying taxes, to sell their products on the market. The government reduced the quantity and scope of the quotas of agricultural products the peasants must sell to the state at prices set by the government. The peddlers' markets were promoted and agricultural product wholesale markets were set up in the early 1980s. Peasants were allowed to transport agricultural products for sale over long distances. Peasants from Shandong province, which was hundreds of miles away from Beijing, transported vegetables to Beijing. Peasants were also allowed to set up and operate their businesses, selling and purchasing agricultural products. The government partially relaxed price controls on agricultural products in the early 1980s (Chen Lifen n.d.).

In the mid-1980s, the state-owned consumer goods wholesale system was streamlined by merging national-level state-owned wholesale stations with city-level wholesale stations and setting up urban wholesale markets. An open, multi-channel, multi-ownership wholesale system gradually took shape.

On 19 July 1984, the State Council approved the *Report on Further Improving Rural Commodity Circulation*, a report by the Committee of Economic Reform, the Ministry of Commerce, and the Ministry of Agriculture pointing out that the rural commodity distribution system must be further reformed. According to the report, multi-channel operations, including state-owned, collective, and individual-owned businesses, needed to be developed and the peasants needed to be encouraged to enter the commodity distribution process, and measures should not be used to restrict peasants' business activities (State Council 1984a). The report also ordered that planning purchases should be reduced, and the 21 categories of agricultural products controlled by the Ministry of Commerce should be reduced to 12. State-monopolised purchases included only three categories: grain (rice, wheat, and corn), oil, and cotton. In cities, merchandise distribution centres, agricultural trade centres, and wholesale markets should be established gradually. Free pricing of agricultural products remaining after state purchases would be implemented in the market. The reform of the traditional state-controlled Supply and Marketing Cooperatives and the rural commerce system in the planned period should be speeded up. State procurement and apportioned state purchases of grain were actually ended by 1985, except for cotton and a small number of other products (Zhao 2009, p.139).

CASE 3.1: DAZHONG AGRICULTURAL PRODUCTS WHOLESALE MARKET[10]

The Beijing Dazhong agricultural products wholesale market was set up by Bell Temple Village, Haidian district, Dongsheng township in 1986, as a Ministry of Agriculture designated wholesale market. It was highly regarded by the international community, and customers came from Japan, South Korea, the United States, Britain, Belgium, the Netherlands, Canada, Singapore, Thailand, and many other countries. The market sold 600 million kilograms of products daily and the annual turnover was more than RMB50 million ($8.0 million). More than 60 varieties of vegetables were sold in the market. The market covered 60,400 square metres, within which was a construction area of 54,300 square metres, with more than 1,600 fixed stalls, more than 1,000 sellers in booths, and 20,000 people trading daily. The market consisted of six departments, selling fresh vegetables, fruits, dried vegetables, non-staple food seasoning, fish, seafood, cereals, oil, meat, eggs, and other thousands of varieties of agricultural products. Besides Beijing, the market supplied more than 600 counties nationwide in 28 provinces (Baidu Baike n.d.-b). Thousands of retailers in north-west Beijing went to the Dazhong market every morning before dawn to buy fresh vegetables and fruits for re-sale to customers in the community.

The central government also encouraged local governments and private investors to set up market facilities in the urban areas to help transaction activities. Local government played an important role in this area.

CASE 3.2: YIWU SMALL COMMODITIES WHOLESALE MARKET

Yiwu Small Commodity Market (also known as 'China Commodity City') is located in Yiwu city, Zhejiang province. Founded in 1982 by local government, it is one of the earliest founded professional markets for small commodities. Xie Gaohua, the party secretary of Yiwu county, made the decision to open a small commodities market in November 1982. Yiwu county government invested RMB580,000 ($293,566.8) to build a booth-type market in 1983. At the end of 1983, there were 1,050 sellers and 600 buyers, most of them from outside of Yiwu. Over 3,000 products were traded at that time (Wu Xiaobo 2014a, p.133).

For over 30 years, after experiencing several relocations and expansions, Yiwu Small Commodity Market now covers more than 260 million square metres and has 200,000 employees. More than 20,000 customers from all over the world visit the market daily. In 2013, the total market turnover was RMB68.302 billion ($11.029 billion). It has become an international commodity distribution, research, and exhibition centre.

The market covers 43 industries, 1,900 categories of products, and 1.7 million types of commodities, including crafts, jewellery, hardware, general merchandise, rain gear, electronic appliances, toys, chemical cosmetics, fashion, hosiery, food, watches and clocks, cable and knitting cotton, textiles, ties, clothing, and all other everyday industrial products. Among them, jewellery, socks, and toys sales accounted for one-third of the national market. Yiwu Small Commodity Market connects to more than 200 countries and regions and annual exports account for more than 60 per cent of total turnover. Currently, more than 8,000 overseas business people stay permanently in Yiwu.

Land and Labour Market

Urban development created a large demand for land. Land became a scarce resource, and a price mechanism was introduced to solve the land distribution problem. In 1982, Shenzhen first changed the policy of free allocation by the government, charging the land users (developers) a land-use fee. Many cities followed Shenzhen. In November 1987 the State Council approved experiments of land-use reform in Shenzhen, Shanghai, Tianjin, Guangzhou, Xiamen, and Fuzhou. In December 1987 the Shenzhen municipal government transferred the usage rights of 8,588 square metres of land for 50 years, through open auctions. This was the first time since 1949 that usage rights for state-owned land were sold as assets. The National Congress revised the Constitution in 1988, deleted the terms saying that land cannot be leased, and added terms stating that land-use rights can be transferred (National People's Congress 1988a). The State Council published a regulation in 1990 stating that municipal and county governments are responsible for the transfer of land-use rights, the maximum term of transfer for residential land is 70 years (for industry it is 50 years), and the land-use rights can be obtained through agreement, tender, or auction (State Council 1990, Articles 9, 12, 13).

While SOE reform was going on, the welfare-housing distribution reform started in the late 1980s. In the planned economy, workers gave all of the surplus value of their production to the government, which used part of the surplus value, through enterprises and offices, to provide housing. Housing was distributed according to employees' rank, length of service, and age. Rents actually paid by residents living in the house were far below the cost of construction and maintenance. Therefore, the allocation of housing was considered a benefit. Experiments of housing reform started in 1986. In 1988, the government decided to speed up the reform and realise commercialisation of housing in three years.

Large amounts of surplus labour were created under the planned system. Since peasants did not own the land, they had less incentive to work hard. The number of labourers was much greater than was actually needed in rural areas. This surplus labour could not move out of the agriculture sector due to the residence registration (*hukou*) system. After the rural reform started, peasants began to move to places where labour productivity was higher. First, they moved to nearby villages and joined the TVEs. Then large numbers of them began to move longer distances to coastal areas. In 1984, peasants were allowed to move to small towns, but they had to secure their own food since they did not have the rations allotted to urban residents (CCP 1984).

In urban areas, a lifetime employment system was adopted in SOEs during the planned period. Under this system, managers could not choose who they wanted to hire and workers could not choose who they wanted to work for. The lack of incentives resulted in low productivity. In 1981, the CCP pointed out that future employment policy should focus on the combination of assignment through the government labour department, self-searching for jobs by individuals, and self-employment, as well as on implementing an employment system with a combination of contract workers, temporary workers, and permanent workers (CCP 1981a). This was a fundamental change in labour policy. Under the planned system, most of the employees in SOEs were permanent employees who did not have to worry about losing their jobs if they did not work hard. The reform allowed firms to hire contract workers and temporary workers in order to change the incentives of the workers by implementing a punishment mechanism. The State Council issued four notification provisions on the reform of the employment system in 1986, including the Interim Provisions on Implementation of the Labour Contract System in SOEs, the Interim

Provisions on Recruiting Workers in SOEs, the Provisional Regulations on Laying Off Workers and Discipline in SOEs, and the Provisional Regulations on Unemployment Insurance in SOEs. These provisions promoted labour contracts nationwide and set up unemployment insurance.

3.5 CREATION OF THE FINANCIAL SYSTEM

The evolution of the production system needed financial support and led to an unexpected development of the financial system during the reform period. The importance of the financial system to a market economy was not foreseen by the reformers. The reform of production created the need for reform in other sectors, and hence for reforms in all supporting areas. The reform occurred horizontally, at least for a while. The financial sector was the weakest compared with either domestic manufacturing or financial sectors in other countries. The centralised financial system was divided into a complicated financial system, consisting of banks and non-banking institutions. Different from the reform in many other fields, most of the new financial institutions created in the reform came from old institutions of the planned system. For example, the central bank and four major commercial banks were all originally part of the People's Bank of China.

The financing sources for firms' fixed investments included bank loans, self-fund-raising, the state budget, foreign direct investment (FDI), and underground financial sources. Private firms relied more on self-fund-raising[11] and underground financial resources. Even for SOEs and quasi-state-owned firms, self-fund-raising was important. After the economic reform, the state budget now only contributed to a small portion of SOEs' total funding (Allen et al. 2008, p.515).

Banks

During the planned period, there was only one bank in mainland China, the People's Bank of China. All banking institutions were actually branches of the People's Bank. The People's Bank of China was both a government institute and an operating entity, which was inconsistent with the need for economic reform. The strategy of the reformists was to separate the government institute from the operating entity.

In July 1982, the State Council decided that the People's Bank of China would become the central bank, while the operating part of the People's Bank would become the Industrial and Commercial Bank of China, a state-owned commercial bank operating in industrial and commercial loans and the deposits of urban residents. Some branches of the People's Bank were separated from the bank and became independent commercial banks, such as the Bank of China. In September 1983, the State Council defined the function of the People's Bank as a government institute in charge of financial activities nationwide, including macro-finance decision-making, administrating credit and loans, and maintaining monetary stability. The People's Bank of China officially began to operate as China's central bank in January 1984. The operational part of the People's Bank of China officially became the Industrial and Commercial Bank of China in the same month. The Bank of China performed the functions of the State Administration of Foreign Exchange (SAFE) until 1982, when the SAFE became an independent agency under the People's Bank of China.

The government started to build a commercial banking system in the late 1970s. The Agriculture Bank of China was restored in February 1979 as one of the state-owned commercial special banks. The responsibility of the Agriculture Bank includes managing funds for supporting agriculture, issuing loans in the countryside, and leading Credit Cooperatives, which is a credit union in the rural areas of China. The Bank of China was separated from the People's Bank of China in 1979, as one of the largest state-owned commercial banks in China, with the largest network of branches overseas. In 1982, the State Council defined the Bank of China as a national foreign exchange special bank responsible for organising, using, cumulating, and managing foreign exchange funds, operating foreign exchange business, dealing with international financial activities, and handling credit operations delegated by the state (State Council 1982). The Construction Bank of China, which was originally set up in 1954 as the People's Construction Bank of China, was officially changed to the Construction Bank of China in 1996, another state-owned commercial bank, in charge of fixed-investment loans and residential deposits. The Industrial and Commercial Bank of China, the Bank of China, the Construction Bank of China, and the Agricultural Bank of China became the four largest state-owned commercial banks in China. The four large special banks operated in separate fields and obtained monopoly positions.

Besides the state-owned commercial banks, a number of shareholding banks were set up by the government in the late 1980s, including China CITIC Bank and the Bank of Communications. The Bank of Communications was reorganised by the State Council as a state-owned entity in July 1986. The People's Bank of China held RMB1 billion ($0.3 billion) of the RMB2.9 billion ($0.8 billion) registered capital; other shares are held by local governments, central government departments, and enterprises. The bank operates nationwide and is not restricted to any special domain. China CITIC Bank, another national shareholding bank, was established in April 1987. It is a commercial bank wholly owned by CITIC Group, a large SOE directly under the control of the State Council. China Merchants Bank, a shareholding bank completely held by business entities, was also set up in April 1987. A group of local shareholding banks was established after 1986, including Shenzhen Development Bank, China Guangdong Development Bank, and Fujian Industrial Bank. The founding of China Everbright Bank and Hua Xia Bank in 1992 brought the total number of shareholding banks to 12. These shareholding banks set the foundations for creating competition in the banking area.

In the countryside, rural credit cooperatives were defined by the State Council as a collective financial organisation and the grass-roots unit of the national bank (State Council 1977). In 1979, the State Council stipulated that the Agriculture Bank of China was responsible for managing the government fund for supporting agriculture and loans for rural development. The rural credit cooperatives became both collective financial institutes and the grass-roots unit of the Agriculture Bank. This established the monopoly position of the Agriculture Bank in rural finance. The credit cooperative became both a grass-roots branch of the government department and a collective financial organisation. The local credit cooperative was both the lowest-level institute of the National Rural Credit Cooperative (a government department) and a financial institute which attracted deposits and issued loans in rural areas. At the end of 1995, 50,219 credit cooperatives existed in China, with RMB986 billion ($118.1 billion) in total assets, RMB620 billion ($74.2 billion) in saving deposits, and RMB518 billion ($62.0 billion) loans, accounting for 80 per cent of loans to rural households and 70 per cent of loans to TVEs (Li et al. 2009, p.110).

The economic reform opened up China to foreign banks. The strategy of opening up the banking sector was to provide financial support for FIEs. The government allowed foreign banks to set up operating institutes in special economic zones in 1981. The Export-Import Bank of Japan established an office in Beijing in 1980. Nanyang Commercial Bank set up a branch in Shenzhen in 1982, which was the first operating institute of a foreign bank set up after the economic reform (Baidu Baike n.d.-d). By the end of 1993, foreign banks had established 73 operating institutes in 13 cities, dealing with foreign currency business for foreign-invested firms and foreign citizens, with total assets of $8.9 billion. These foreign banks were not allowed to do RMB business for Chinese citizens.

During this period, cash was widely used and people held their wealth in wasteful forms, since wealth accumulation was not secure and people did not trust the government. Anonymous banking played an important role in solving the problem of unsecure private financial assets (Clarke et al. 2008, p.417).

The reformers created a system of commercial banks from the state-monopolised planned banking system immediately after the reform of urban enterprises. A system of commercial banks had begun to take shape as early as in the 1980s, although the largest banks were all state owned.

Non-Banking Financial Institutions

Non-banking financial institutions, including trust companies, security companies, and insurance companies, which had disappeared during the planned period, developed rapidly in the 1980s.

The trust companies experienced a dramatic growth due to the huge expansion of responsibilities of the local government when the central government shifted financial power down to local governments and the lower level in the bureaucratic structure. The original purpose of setting up trust companies was to explore channels other than banking to introduce foreign investment and circulate funds. The first trust company, CITIC, was established in October 1979 as a window for introducing foreign investments. As a matter of fact, all trust companies adopted a business model in which banking was the main business and financial–industrial mixed operation was their business strategy. The trust companies were used by banks to circumnavigate the credit plan restrictions and by local governments to finance local developments. The trust companies caused an increase of credit and illegal funds operations, which resulted in an overheated economy. The central government used drastic measures on four occasions to clean up the trust companies – in 1982, 1985, 1988, and 1993. The last clean-up followed the principle of segregating management and cutting off the relationship between banks and trust companies completely.

For insurance companies, China Life Insurance Company's domestic operations were restored in 1979. In the next two years, over 400 insurance institutions were set up in China. Xinjiang Corps Agricultural and Animal Husbandry Insurance Company was set up in 1986 and changed its name to Xinjiang Corps Insurance Company in 1992. A local insurance company set up in Shenzhen in 1985 changed its name to China Ping An Insurance Company in 1992. Separated from the Bank of Communications, the China Pacific Insurance Company (CPIC) became another insurance company operating nationwide.

The first securities company, Shenzhen Securities Company, was set up in 1987. The State Council permitted some cities to experiment in Treasury bill transfers in 1988, and the People's Bank approved 33 securities companies thereafter. In 1993, with approval from the People's Bank, the Industrial and Commercial Bank of China, the Construction Bank of China, and the Agriculture Bank of China led the formation of Hua Xia Securities, Guotai Securities, and Southern Securities, respectively, in 1992.

Financial leasing services were started in the early 1980s, when China Orient Leasing Co., Ltd (COLC) was set up by CITIC, Beijing Mechanical and Electrical Equipment Company, and Japan Oriental Leasing Company in 1981. China Leasing Company was established by CITIC and the State Administration of Materials and Equipment afterwards. After that, the People's Bank, Ministry of Foreign Trade and Economic Cooperation, and local governments approved large numbers of leasing companies.

Financial Market

Under the centralised credit fund management system, the surplus or deficiency of funds between banks could only be adjusted vertically by administrative means. Horizontal adjustment between banks was not allowed. As soon as the state-owned banks were allowed to do credit business independently after the economic reform, short-term fund accommodation among banks was needed. The People's Bank of China became the central bank in 1984 and required the commercial banks to make deposits of legal reserves in the central bank. This in turn created commercial banks' need for short-term borrowing and lending of funds. The People's Bank of China allowed banks to borrow and lend with each other as early as 1984. The National Institutional Reform Committee and the People's Bank of China set up the target of creating an inter-bank money market in 1986, as a major component of the reform in the financial area. In the same year, the State Council issued the Provisional Regulations of the People's Republic of China on the Control of Banks, allowing banks to borrow and lend with each other (State Council 1986b). Therefore, the inter-bank money market was developed with the original purpose of short-term fund swapping among financial institutes. The inter-bank money market was unofficially started in 1986, when Wuhan set up a borrowing and lending market for city credit cooperatives. Many other cities followed. By 1987, all provinces had set up an inter-bank money market, forming a network of inter-bank money markets nationwide. The new inter-bank market had tremendous problems. The main purpose of the borrowing and lending activities was to avoid the control of the monetary authority, in order to invest in long-term projects. Therefore, the inter-bank money market in China was not intended to provide short-term fund swapping, but was effectively the capital market for companies to borrow. This led to a chaotic market and soaring interest rates. The People's Bank tried to control the situation by changing the institutional arrangements, taking all inter-bank money markets under its control. In 1990, the People's Bank regulated the inter-bank money market, through setting standards and limits for inter-bank borrowing, and the number of transactions went down. In 1992, as the macro-economy recovered, the demand for funds, especially for long-term investment, jumped. The inter-bank money market boomed again and the monetary authority enhanced its control again.

As part of the inter-bank money market, the repo market started in the early 1990s. Bond repurchase is a financing activity where the funds receiver receives funds by pledging bonds to the funds provider. On a certain date in the future, the funds receiver shall refund the funds to the funds provider at the amount calculated on the basis of the stipulated interest for the repurchase. The repurchase market is a means for banks' liquidity management and for the central bank's open market operation. The repurchase of Treasury bonds first occurred in 1988, but the reaction of the market was not warm. The national Security Traders Automatic Quotations (STAQ) system started operating in 1991, making the trade of Treasury bills active. The Wuhan Stock Exchange introduced its Treasury bond repo operation in 1992. The Shanghai Stock Exchange, Shenzhen Stock Exchange, and Tianjin Stock Exchange all started the repo operations in the early 1990s.

The commercial paper market was developed at the same time. Instances of acceptance of commercial bills and discount of bills first appeared in the early 1980s. Commercial paper markets were set up nationwide in 1985, and the central bank started rediscounting activities with commercial banks in 1986.

The People's Republic issued its first Treasury bond in 1949. From 1949 to 1958, the government issued Treasury bonds six times. Thereafter, no Treasury bonds were issued until 1981. The original purpose of the 1981 bond issuance was not to develop the bonds market, but to solve the budget deficit. In the early 1980s, Treasury bonds were administratively distributed among offices and factories, which distributed the bonds among their workers. The bonds could not be transferred. Since there was no bond market, the amount of bonds issued was less than RMB80 billion ($46.9 billion). Experimental bond markets were set up in some large cities, such as Shenyang, in 1986. By 1988, more than 60 cities had experimented with a bond market. In 1990, the administrative distribution of Treasury bonds to individuals was changed to selling at banks' counters. The underwriting of Treasury bonds was adopted. In 1990, the government allowed Treasury bonds to be traded in the secondary market, which includes both securities exchanges and banks as well as other intermediaries. The amount of issuance in 1991, 1992, and 1993 reached RMB19.9 billion ($3.7 billion), RMB39.6 billion ($7.2 billion), and RMB31.5 billion ($5.5 billion), respectively, more than the total amount issued in the previous decade.

The issuance of corporate bonds started in 1984, when some local enterprises issued bonds publicly or to their own employees. The enterprises needed resources to develop their businesses and corporate bonds developed rapidly. There were some default events, so the government started regulating the corporate bond market. In 1987, the State Council issued the Corporate Bond Management Regulations, which were revised in 1993 (State Council 1993a). According to these regulations, only SOEs were allowed to issue corporate bonds, the fixed investment project must be approved by the government and included in the bond issuance plan, and the interest rate should not be higher than 140 per cent of the bank deposit interest rate. Even with these regulations, the amount of corporate debt issued in 1990 reached RMB4.9 billion ($1.0 billion).

Financial activities created the need for more financial tools. In 1986, the Shenyang branch of the People's Bank allowed Shenyang Trust and Investment Corporation to start a bond transfer counter service, which was the first case of legal Treasury bond transfer in China since 1949. In 1988, Shenyang and six other cities were allowed to carry out Treasury bond transfer experiments. The Treasury bond market opened nationwide, and all Treasury bonds held by individuals were allowed to enter the transfer market. The issuance process of Treasury bonds also changed from administrative distribution to market operations.

Stocks were issued first in Shenzhen in 1983. As some SOEs changed to shareholding companies, they sold their stocks to the public. A stock trading brokerage house was set up in Shanghai in 1989, and the Shanghai Stock Exchange was established in 1990. Shenzhen Stock Exchange was set up the next year.

Informal Financial Sector

The growth of small private enterprises needed financial support, but the large state-owned banks were not willing to provide financial support to these small companies. The job was fulfilled by an illegal underground private financial system.

An informal financial sector has existed in China for hundreds of years. During the Ming and Qing Dynasties, private lending activities were thriving. More than 4,000 pawnbrokers existed in Shanxi province during the years of Emperor Kangxi (ruled 1662–1722), accounting for one-fifth of pawnbrokers nationwide (Li Youhuan 2010, p.5). Money exchange shops in Shanxi province underwent great development in the 19th century, and eventually reached 400 head offices and branches throughout China. The government banned private financial institutions during the planned economy from 1949 to 1978. During the planned economy, the informal financial sector, most participants of which violated the formal institutional rules, was cracked down on by the government, but still existed in some areas, especially in the eastern coastal area.

After the beginning of the economic reform in 1978, informal financial institutes emerged in the countryside and on the rural–urban fringe, especially in eastern coastal areas like Zhejiang province, becoming an important component of the support system for private industries.

CASE 3.3: THE FIRST UNDERGROUND BANK

The first group of underground banks was created in Wenzhou, Zhejiang province, an eastern coastal city with a tradition of capitalism. Fang Peilin, a doorman who worked in a hospital, established the first private bank since 1949 on 28 September 1984. Fang was an urban youth sent to the countryside during the Cultural Revolution and had just returned to the city. Fang observed the rapid development of small private firms and read a CCP document which said farmers' joint stock businesses will be encouraged. He did a survey and found that in the area surrounding the city, private businesses needed RMB10 million ($4.3 million), with a shortage of RMB2 million ($0.9 million), and that large amounts of idle funds were available. Mr Fang wrote a report to the district leaders applying to open a bank, and this was approved. The bank's board of directors was elected by the stockholders. The manager, who was in charge of daily operations, was appointed by the chairman of the board. When his bank opened for business, Mr Fang stuck a list of lending and deposit rates on the door of the bank, which were more favourable to depositors than the state-owned banks. The monthly interest rate was 1.2 per cent for deposits of longer than three months, 1 per cent for current deposit, and 2 per cent for loans. Fang's bank was banned the next day by the Agriculture Bank of China. The bank went underground thereafter, and business boomed, with 2,400 depositors and lenders and a turnover of RMB5 million ($2.1 million). Two reporters from the *Wenzhou Daily* interviewed Mr Fang and wrote a report, which was not published but became an internal reference for government officials (Huang 2012).

Because it was very difficult for the small private enterprises to get loans from the large state-owned banks, informal financial institutions became a necessary precondition for these small firms to operate. Usually the borrower invited the potential lenders to attend a meeting, most of whom were the borrower's relatives and friends. The meeting raised a certain amount of money and gave it to the highest bidder. The borrower would use the fund, paying interest, and returned the fund according to the contract. Some of these temporary organisations became underground banks managed by specialists.

Tai Hui was an underground financial cooperation popular in Wenzhou in the 1980s. Each member paid RMB11,600 ($4,984.9) when joining the group. The owner paid RMB9,000 ($3,867.6) back to the member each month starting from the second month for 12 months, for a total of RMB108,000 ($46,411.7). The member then paid RMB3,000 ($1,289.2) per month for 88 months, for a total of RMB264,000 ($113,450.8), and the owner paid RMB9,000 ($3,867.6) per month back to the member during the same period. One membership period was 100 months. To keep the cash flowing, the membership needed to increase quickly. In Leqing county in the Wenzhou district, over 1,300 Tai Hui existed in the 1980s. The largest Tai Hui had more than 12,000 members. Over 300,000 people in Wenzhou were involved in various Tai Hui from 1985 to 1987. Tai Huis were cracked down on by the government in 2000 (Wu Xiaobo 2014a, p.212).

Most members of the underground banks were relatives and friends. The banks were operated by family members, with a fixed place of trading, usually in a store or a residence. The underground banks usually had a stable source of funds and customers. New customers were introduced by old customers. The managers of underground banks communicated with customers using the telephone or telex. Domestic money transactions were usually conducted through banks, while international transactions went through account transfers. An underground bank often had representatives outside of China who dealt with international transactions. In order to avoid police raids, the transactions usually had no written contract. The interest rates charged by underground banks were flexible, and changed with supply and demand, in contrast to the fixed (and low) rates at the state-owned banks. Their business hours were unlimited, with services available at any time.

The underground banks adopted four major forms:

1. Underground banks that dealt with illegal deposits and lending, which were widespread nationwide, especially in eastern coastal areas such as Zhejiang, Jiangsu, Guangdong, and Fujian, in the forms of 'Biao Hui', 'Tai Hui', and Rotating Savings and Credit Associations. These underground financial institutions collected funds from relatives and friends. The funds went to the member who bid on the highest interest rates during auctions. In Huangqiao, a town in Jiangsu province with 100,000 people, 50 per cent of the families attended the 'Biao Hui',

which was able to collect RMB1 billion ($0.4 billion) in ten minutes. The terms of the loans ranged from six months to five years. Members of the 'Biao Hui' usually met at the home of the head at 12 o'clock for an auction where each of them would write a return rate on a piece of paper and the highest bidder would get the fund. The monthly interest rate was generally 30 per cent. The winner would present his or her business plan to a committee for evaluation. Some risks were avoided since the members knew each other well, and personal relationships replaced legal rules as a source of trust for lending activities over a long period.

2. Underground banks that illegally bought and sold foreign exchange, mainly in Guangdong, Fujian, and Shandong. A foreign-owned processing firm needed to transfer foreign exchange into China, to pay the cost of production. Because of the huge gap between the official exchange rate and the market rate in the 1980s, foreign firms did not want to use formal banking. Currency smuggling through the underground banking system prevailed.
3. Pawnshop and usury lenders, which prevailed in inland provinces such as Hunan and Jiangxi. While many pawnshops were recognised by the government, a large number of underground pawnshops existed under the name of other businesses. In Jiangmen, Guangdong province, over 100 pawnshops collected houses and cars and did business as a pawnshop under the name of 'service shops'.
4. Privately offered funds and other private fund-raising. Privately offered funds raised money from investors with no public disclosure. Most of the raised funds were invested in the stock market. Some of the foreign-based private funds established branches in China and collected funds. Until recently, there was no law that applied to the privately offered

CASE 3.4: PAWNSHOPS IN GUANGDONG PROVINCE

A large number of underground pawnshops operated under the titles of consignment line, service line, or intermediary. Many underground pawnshops have been operating without licence. In Zhongshan city, Guangdong province, about 20 illegal pawnshops operated under the name of consignment line. In Jiangmen city, Guangdong province, about 100 pawnshops operated under the titles of real-estate agent or service department (Ma 2001).

Usury has a long history in China and has been widespread in modern China. The usurers included business people with some savings, government officials, and private financial institutions. The monthly interest rates are usually between 3 and 20 per cent for the loans from ordinary business people.

CASE 3.5: WAN'S UNDERGROUND BUSINESS

Wan Yongnian was a businessman in Ordos city, Inner Mongolia. His lending firm was located in a residential apartment. He collected funds from acquaintances at 1 to 2 per cent per month and lent them at 3 to 5 per cent interest rates. He operated the business for two years, with RMB5 million ($0.6million) circulating funds, which was smaller than many underground banks doing similar business. At the beginning, Wan borrowed RMB3 million ($0.366 million) from his relatives and friends, and lent it to a mine owner, a distant relative. In half a year, his RMB3 million ($0.366 million) became RMB3.6 million ($0.439 million). After two years of operation, he wound up his business and left the city (Yang 2009).

funds. Other forms of fund-raising were widespread in China during the economic reform, when large amounts of extra funds existed in the society and there was a high demand from firms for funds. These activities were not protected by law and often became the target of government crackdowns (Li Youhuan 2010, pp.39–40, 48–51).

The development of underground banks in China during the period of economic reform occurred for the following reasons:

1. Due to the commercialisation of the operations, the large state-owned banks were more concerned with the profitability and safety of the loans. To improve the safety of their loans, these large banks shifted the loan decision-making power from local branches up to their respective provincial branches. A large number of branches of the four large state-owned banks under the county level ceased operations when the loan decisions moved upwards. This created some space for the operation of small underground banks.
2. The state-owned banks had good relations with large SOEs and the government had special policies to support large SOEs rather than small enterprises.
3. Foreign exchange controls blocked the free floating of foreign exchange.
4. Rapid economic growth brought a large amount of wealth to residents, but the investment channels were limited and the real interest rates of deposit in state-owned banks were negative for a long period. A large number of residents, therefore, deposited their savings at underground banks, which provided returns higher than the state-owned banks.
5. Financial supervision lagged behind the development of the underground banks and smuggling, tax evasion, and money laundering prevailed.

The underground financial institutions provided irreplaceable support for small private enterprises during the economic reform but created huge risks at the same time. To reduce risk and uncertainty to a more tolerable level, the government has since made enormous efforts to crack down on and/or reform the sector.

3.6 OPENING UP

Domestic reform was carried out simultaneously with the opening up to the world. The domestic reform followed the example of the market economy in developed countries, and the opening up was consistent with the logic of the domestic reform. Therefore, the Chinese economy was opened up to the outside world for the first time since 1949. Knowing that China was far behind the outside world in economic development, the Chinese leadership decided to re-open China's doors to the world in the late 1970s. The most significant event in China's opening up in the period of 1978 to 1989 was the establishment of special economic zones, which were separated from the rest of China and acted as an experiment for market economy and opening up to the outside world.

Changing the Strategy of Economic Development

China followed a strategy of import substitution from 1949 to 1977, by setting up a high import tariff to protect its infant industries. The strategy completely failed, mainly because it prevented technology and management skill transformation coming from the outside world. In many fields in the 1970s, technology developed in the 1930s in developed countries was still used.

The import substitution strategy was adopted by many developing countries during the same period and created many problems. The strategy could not raise productivity because there was insufficient competition and technology transformation. Many countries and regions changed their strategy to an export-orientation strategy in the 1960s and 1970s, which promoted export-oriented manufacturing production, using competition in the international market to raise the productivities of its industries. Japan, South Korea, Taiwan, and Hong Kong adopted this strategy one after another, and created high-speed economic development. This set up an example for mainland China.

At the end of the 1970s, the Chinese government sent large numbers of officials around the world to search for approaches towards economic development. Deng visited Japan in October 1978, Thailand, Malaysia, and Singapore in November 1978, and the United States from 28 January to 5 February 1979. Deng realised that China was far behind the Western developed countries in economic development and made the decision to open up China's borders to the outside world. China followed the example of Taiwan and Hong Kong, adopting an export-orientation strategy from the end of the 1970s.

Reform of Government Foreign Trade Management System

The first thing the reformers did was to change the government-monopolised foreign trade management system. From the late 1970s, the government implemented the reform of the foreign trade management system nationwide. The system was highly concentrated in the central government during the planned period, since most of the production and most of the financial resources were under its control. An American businesswoman told a story of her experience in China in the 1980s. She set up a consultant company in Beijing to help foreign business people who wanted to do business in China but did not know whom he or she should contact. Her job was extremely easy. She asked them, 'What business do you want to do?' If the answer was 'textiles', her answer would be, 'Go to China Textile Import and Export Company'. If the answer was 'machinery', she would say, 'Go to China Machinery Import and Export Company'. There were only 12 companies dealing with exports and imports at that time, all of which were state owned and at the national level (Branstetter and Lardy 2008, p.635).

Starting in 1979, the power of the foreign trade administration and approval authority was delegated from the central government to local governments and to ministries that had not dealt with foreign trade during the planned period. Provinces, autonomous districts, and the cities specifically designated in the state plan opened ports based on their direct foreign trade management authority. Ministries of industries and some large SOEs were given the authority to operate foreign trade businesses. Trading authority for many ordinary commodities was given to local branches of state-owned foreign trade companies and other companies. Foreign-invested companies and private companies were also allowed to trade internationally. Although the government still restricted the right to engage in international trade, the number of domestic firms granted trading rights increased from 12 firms directly controlled by the Ministry of Foreign Trade to 800 firms in 1985 (Branstetter and Lardy 2008, p.635).

The central government relaxed its control of foreign trade in 1985, and stopped the preparation of the export and import plan[12] in 1994 to allow enterprises to make their own decisions of whether and how much to export (Xiao and Sui 2011, p.263). However, as the government stopped the quantitative planning of foreign trade, they became more reliant on tariffs, quotas, and tougher commodity inspection requirements. The import tariffs were 56 per cent in 1982 and 43 per cent from 1985 to 1992 (Branstetter and Lardy 2008, p.634). In February 1988, the State Council published a decision to speed up and deepen the reform of the foreign trade system, which required the provinces and cities specifically designated in the state plan to fully implement foreign trade contract responsibility systems. After turning over the required foreign exchange, the extra foreign exchange would be shared by central and local government. Before this reform, all foreign exchange earned by local government had to be handed over to the central government, therefore the local government had no incentive to promote export. After this reform, the local governments had more incentive to encourage the export of goods, from which they could keep some foreign currency. The local branches of state-owned foreign trade companies were thereafter split off from their parent companies and transferred to the local governments, operating as business corporations (State Council 1988b).

Special Economic Zones and Foreign Investments

Before the reform, severe restrictions on FDI existed, resulting in very little foreign investment in China. Policies were dramatically changed after the beginning of the reform, and foreign firms were allowed to operate in China, with a relaxation on restrictions on foreign trade and foreign investment. Provincial and local governments were given more power to regulate the foreign-invested companies in their jurisdictions.

To overcome resistance nationwide, the leadership set up special economic zones to separate eastern coastal areas from most parts of mainland China. Special policies were tested and implemented first in these special zones. This policy minimised the resistance from inside and outside the Party against the reform and opening up.

Experiments of opening up were first implemented in the provinces of Guangdong and Fujian in Southern China, near Hong Kong. In October 1978, Guangdong province created a plan to set up Baoan county (currently Shenzhen) and Zhuhai county as export bases, using funds and equipment from Hong Kong and Macao, to develop agriculture for export and processing production, as well as trade (Xiao and Sui 2011, p.198). In July 1979, the CCP Central Committee and the State Council decided to implement these special policies and flexible measures first in Shenzhen and Zhuhai, to gain experience, and then consider implementation in Shantou in Guangdong province and Xiamen in Fujian province (Jiang 2008, p.287). In August 1979, the CCP and the State Council set up a national import and export administration committee and a foreign investment administration committee to deal with affairs concerning foreign trade and investment. The State Council published the Measures for the Development of Foreign Processing and Assembly and the Medium and Small Sized Compensation Trade in September 1979 (State Council 1979b). In March 1980, the CCP officially changed the name 'export zones' to 'special economic zones'. In August 1980, the 5th National People's Congress Standing Committee and the State Council approved the proposed special economic zones set up in Shenzhen, Zhuhai, Shantou in Guangdong province, and Xiamen in Fujian province and approved the Guangdong Provincial Economic Zones Regulations. Following these changes, various laws and regulations were developed and passed, including the law on income tax for foreign firms published in 1981 (National People's Congress 1981b) and many local regulations on immigration, labour, and land use by foreign firms published by the Guangdong province government.

Shekou is an area at the southern tip of Shenzhen, facing Hong Kong across Shenzhen Bay. In January 1979, it became officially known as the Shekou Industrial Zone, earlier than the formation of the Shenzhen Special Economic Zone, when Deng drew a circle on the map and donated the area to the industrial zone. The zone was under the leadership of Yuan Geng, the director of China Merchants Steamship Company. Yuan invited many Hong Kong investors to invest in the Shekou Industrial Zone.

In the special economic zones, policies and regulations were different from inland China. 'Double customs' were implemented between foreign countries (or regions not controlled by the Chinese government), special zones, and inland China, and customs duties were exempted when companies imported and exported between special zones and foreign countries. Foreign firms were allowed to set up their enterprises with 100 per cent of their own investments or set up joint ventures with Chinese firms. The tax rates in special zones were lower than that in inland China. Immigration procedure was simplified, and profits and incomes were allowed to be transferred to other countries, after paying taxes.

Processing manufacturing and trade were developed on a large scale in the coastal areas, especially in the special economic zones. Policies and regulations provided incentives for the processing trade. Bonded supervision was implemented on imports for the processing trade, under which dutiable goods could be stored, manipulated, or undergo manufacturing operations without payment of duty. Imports licences and quotas for processing trade were abolished.

The restrictions on FDI were dramatically relaxed at the end of the 1970s. At the beginning of China's opening up, large amounts of investment came from Hong Kong, Macao, and Taiwan. From 1983 to 1986, investments from Hong Kong and Macao, which were concentrated in labour-intensive industries, accounted for 53.6 per cent of total foreign investment. This increased to 72.8 per cent from 1987 to 1992 (Jiang 2008, p.71).

The open-door policy was doubted by some officials and policy makers. People questioned whether the raw material supply of the country could be guaranteed by foreign suppliers. They asked, how could a large country like China rely on exports of labour-intensive products by TVEs? Some people worried that the development of the coastal area would widen the gap between eastern and western areas. In spite of these doubts, Deng and a group of leaders fully supported the open-door policy and the policy was implemented gradually and smoothly.

Deng Xiaoping inspected Shenzhen, Zhuhai, Xiamen, and Baoshan Steel Co. in Shanghai from 24 January to 21 February 1984, affirming and providing support to the reform activities in special economic zones and suggesting the government set up more special zones. In May 1984, the CCP and State Council decided to open up a further 14 coastal cities: Dalan, Qinhuangdao, Tianjin, Yantai, Qingdao, Lianyungang, Nantong, Shanghai, Ningbo, Wenzhou, Fuzhou, Guangzhou, Zhanjiang, and Beihai (CCP Central Committee and State Council 1984). The economic development zones expanded to 288 cities and counties, and Hainan province became the largest special economic zone in 1988 (Jiang 2008, p.291). As special economic zones, these cities and Hainan province were given more autonomy. FIEs in these areas were given special treatment. The government implemented a group of policies to support the economic reforms in these areas. These cities had the right to invite outside investment and set up foreign-invested companies. The approval process of foreign investment projects was relaxed. The local governments' approval authority for production projects was raised to $30 million for Tianjin, Shanghai, and Shenzhen; $10 million for Dalian; and $5 million for other opened-up cities. When a project was approved by the local government, related imports, training abroad, and negotiations were also handled by it. The amounts set for foreign exchange quotas and foreign currency loans were increased for these open areas. Tianjin had a quota of $200 million, while Shanghai had $300 million each year. Joint ventures, cooperative enterprises, and wholly foreign-owned enterprises were given preferential treatments. For technology-intensive projects, after reporting to the Ministry of Finance, income tax was reduced. Imported production equipment, construction equipment, materials, components, parts, and packaging materials; imported vehicles and office supplies that were for the use of foreign firms and not for sale on the Chinese domestic market; and household articles and vehicles for personal use, joint ventures, cooperative ventures, and wholly foreign-owned enterprises, were all exempted from customs duties and consolidated industrial commercial tax. The economic and technological development zones and processing trade were promoted in these open areas. The procedure of entry and exit for foreign personnel was also relaxed in these areas.

A number of laws and regulations on foreign investment and special economic zones were implemented, and several international treaties for protecting foreign investments were negotiated and signed between China and foreign countries in the 1980s. The National People's Congress passed the Law on Chinese-Foreign Equity Joint Ventures in July 1979 (National People's Congress 1979b), the Law on Foreign Investment Enterprise in April 1986 (National People's Congress 1986c), and the Law on Sino-Foreign Cooperative Joint Ventures in April 1988 (National People's Congress 1988c), and the State Council issued detailed rules for the implementation of the law on foreign investment enterprises in 1990 (Xiao and Sui 2011, p.213). The 1979 version of the law on joint ventures provided a basic framework for foreign firms to operate within. The law on foreign investment firms of 1986 represented a major change in FDI regulation applied throughout China, making these firms eligible for reduced business income tax, and relaxing the controls on the retaining of profit in foreign currency. There was a degree of de facto local autonomy in regulating foreign investments.

The cumulated actual use of FDI was $25.1 billion in the period from 1979 to 1991. The foreign investment was mainly in travel, service, food processing, and textile industries in the early 1980s, and moved to light processing industries in the late 1980s (Jiang 2008, p.71).

In the same period, China's foreign trade increased dramatically as a result of the opening-up policy. China's total foreign trade increased from $20.6 billion in 1978 to $115.4 billion in 1990. Exports and imports kept increasing during the 1980s. Exports increased from $9.8 billion in 1978 to $62.1 billion in 1990, while imports increased from $10.9 billion in 1978 to $53.4 billion in 1990 (National Bureau of Statistics 2015, Table 11.2).

3.7 THE GOVERNMENT

With a transitional economy, the government faced great challenges and needed to be reformed. The strategy of the reform in the 1980s was to decentralise power and share the financial resources with local governments. The relationship between the central and the local governments was a 'financial franchising system'.

Decentralisation

At the beginning of the reform, the leadership's strategy in dealing with the relationship between central and local governments was to delegate more power to local governments, which included the provincial and lower-level governments. The direction of the change was decentralisation, which actually followed the principle of power division during the planned economy.

At the beginning of the People's Republic, in the early 1950s, the power was highly concentrated. Then the power began to shift to the local level, in order to reduce supervision costs. After the beginning of the reform in 1978, decentralisation was used by the reformers on a larger scale in many fields. This decentralisation was widely supported by both central and local leaders.

The 1982 version of the Constitution included some principles of central–local government relations. First, the Constitution defined the responsibilities of the local governments in general, compared with previous versions of China's Constitution. It stated that the local government was responsible for managing economic, educational, scientific, cultural, and many other affairs, as well as for appointing and dismissing government officials. Second, it stated that provincial and municipality government directly under the central government could make local laws, if they were not inconsistent with the Constitution and any other national laws. In addition, the central government changed the rule of personnel management in the early 1980s. From the 1950s to the early 1980s, the central government controlled the appointment and promotion of officials at two lower levels of the bureaucratic system, the provincial and prefectural levels. At the beginning of the 1980s, the central government changed the rule to a new system in which the central government only controlled one lower level of officials, partly because the central government could not afford the huge workload of controlling two lower levels of officials. That meant the local governments were given the power to appoint and promote officials at the prefectural level, which was extremely important for provincial governments to form a complete system of governance. The logic behind decentralisation was that, since the political development after Mao's death was a result of the collective efforts by both central and local leaders, everyone should get his or her share.

During the early stages of economic reform, power was moved down from central government to local government. However, the distribution of power among local governments was not equal. The central government adopted a preferential policy for some of the eastern coastal provinces (e.g. Guangdong and Fujian). This policy was based on the fact that these provinces are geographically close to Hong Kong and Taiwan and therefore it is easier to introduce foreign investment into them. It reduced the cost of marketisation when financial resources were extremely limited at the beginning of the economic reform.

Before the reform, provincial planning was included in the national plan, but city planning was not. After the beginning of the reform, in the 1980s, a number of cities were given independent planning status, which meant they were treated as provinces and their planning was included in national planning. These cities thus received provincial-level foreign trade authority, provincial fixed investment examination and approval authority, provincial tax collection authority, and provincial fiscal budget authority. Independent planning status gave the municipal government more authority to develop its local economy without interference from the provincial government. It was also good for the central government to get tax revenues directly from these cities. The independent planning status was ended for most of these cities in the 1990s, because it reduced the revenue of the provincial government and was opposed by many provincial governments.

Tax for Profits reform was carried out in 1983 and 1984. Before the reform, SOEs had to hand over their profits to the Ministry of Finance. After the reform, a large part of the profit was paid to the government as taxes. The enterprises were allowed to keep the remaining profit.

Central–Local Government Relationship: Financial Franchise System

The decentralisation of administrative power was accompanied by the decentralisation of financial resources. China is a large country with a multilevel government system. The financial relationship between central and local governments changed a lot after the founding of the People's Republic in 1949. The pure form of a financial system in the Soviet-style planned economy is a 'unified revenue and expenditure system', which was implemented in China in the early 1950s. Its pure form existed for a short period of time in China. Under this system, government revenue and expenditure was completely controlled by the central government. The local government had to hand over all its revenue to the central government, as well as request approval for its expenditures. The local government had no incentive to provide services to its residents. Meanwhile, it was difficult for the central government to handle all these transactions. Two basic financial forms of the financial franchise system, 'unified revenue and expenditure system' and 'revenue sharing system', were imposed starting in the late 1970s.

To solve the incentive problem, some form of a sharing system was adopted even in the planned period. The pure Soviet-style highly centralised fiscal system was set up when the People's Republic of China was established in 1949. Under this system, all fiscal revenue, including taxes and agricultural tax paid in grain, was concentrated in the hands of the central government, except very limited local tax revenue and local surcharges of agricultural tax, which were left to the local government. All local expenditures had to be approved by the central government. The system was soon revised to a 'division of revenue and expenditure classification management' system. A financial hierarchical management system was set up in 1951, with central, regional, and local being the three levels. All fiscal revenue (taxes and SOE profits) was divided into central revenue, local revenue, and revenue shared by central and local governments. Commodity tax, industrial and commercial tax, stamp tax, transaction tax, and tobacco and alcohol tax were shared by central and local government, and the ratio of sharing for different provinces were dependent on the particular situation of each province. The extra revenue of agricultural tax was also shared by central and local government. The profit from local government-owned industries belonged to the local government and was used for local industrialisation. All fiscal expenditure was divided into central and local expenditure, based on the ownership of the enterprises and institutes. This early adjustment deviated slightly from the purely Soviet system and treated local government as a relatively independent institution. An adjustment was made in 1958, when the previous 'revenue determined by expenditure every year' system changed to 'revenue determined by expenditure every five years'. Under this system, the local revenue included local fixed revenue, local share of the enterprise profit (including that of locally managed enterprises along with the local share of centrally managed enterprises), and readjusted revenue from the central government. Local expenditure included normal expenditure and special expenditure supported by the central government. The system detailed the approach for defining 'local normal expenditure', which was based on the different fiscal situations of the local governments. If the local revenue exceeded expenditure, the local government could keep the balance. The system was soon changed to 'revenue and expenditure delegated to local, plan contracting, regional readjusting, total sharing, and re-setting every year' (*shouzhi xiafang, jihua baogan, diqu tiaoji, zongefencheng, yinian yibian*), under which most of the central revenues and expenditures were transferred to the local government. This change of fiscal management was the most complete downward shift of fiscal power within the centralised financial system. It replaced the principle of 'expenditure determined by revenue' with 'revenue determined by expenditure'. That meant that local governments had some autonomy to plan their economies. The system was adopted during the 'Great Leap Forward' movement, and caused chaos in the economy. The central government abolished the system and took back financial power from the local governments in 1961. The Cultural Revolution saw the adoption of several financial approaches. During the economic meltdown in 1968, the central government re-centralised the fiscal revenue and expenditure. When the economy recovered in 1970, the central government shifted some fiscal resources down to the local governments. From 1971 to 1973, a revenue and expenditure contract system, 'fixed revenue and expenditure, revenue and expenditure contracting, guaranteed turnover or subsidy, balance retaining, and renegotiate every year' (*dingshou dingzhi, shouzhi baogan, baozheng shangjiao (huozhe butie), jieyu liuyong, yinian yiding*), was adopted. Most of the financial revenue of central government was transferred to local governments, and most of the expenditure, except that directly managed by the central government, was transferred to the local governments. Whenever the local revenue exceeded expenditure, the local government had to turn over the amount defined in the contract, and whenever the local revenue was less than its expenditure, the central government gave subsidies based on the amount of deficit as defined by the contract.

After the beginning of the reform, in 1980, a financial franchise system, the 'fiscal responsibility sharing system' (*caizheng baogan*), was adopted. In February 1980, the State Council issued a temporary regulation on implementing a division of revenue and expenditure (between central and local government) classified as a 'contract' fiscal management system (State Council 1980). The reform changed the central–local government relationship, by dividing revenue and expenditure between the central and local governments and using a contract to determine the amount of revenue and expenditure for each province. Under this system, in each period the Ministry of Finance held negotiations with every province to agree and set up the quota the local government had to hand over in the next period. The local government could then keep the remaining part of the revenue and use it for local construction and development. For the provinces in which the revenue was less than the expenditure, a quota of the retained portion was set. If a province retained all revenue but still could not meet its expenses, a quota of subsidy was set by the central government. The policy gave local governments the incentive to create more revenue. Different provinces received different quotas. The central government used the policy to control the direction of local investment. For example, it is well known that Guangdong province received a larger portion of revenue each year than other provinces, because the central government had a special policy for coastal provinces at the beginning of the reform.

The system had various versions. From 1980 to 1984, most provinces adopted a 'division of revenue and expenditure classified contract' (*huafen shouzhi, fenji baogan*) programme, while Guangdong province and Fujian province implemented the 'fixed lump sum for five years' (*huafen shouzhi, dinge shangjie, wunian bubian*) and 'quota subsidies unchanged for five years' (*huafen shouzhi, dinge butie, wunian bubian*) programmes, respectively. For Guangdong and Fujian provinces, a fixed amount of hand-ins or subsidies were determined based on actual revenue and expenditure in 1979. The amount was fixed for five years. The extra revenue was retained by the provincial government.[13]

A tax system reform was implemented in 1983, which changed SOEs' profit handover to taxes. From 1985, adapting to the tax reform, most provinces implemented the 'dividing the tax category classified contract' programme, under which the division of tax revenue was based on tax category, while Guangdong province and Fujian province implemented the 'fixed lump sum profit contract' and 'fixed lump sum subsidy contract', respectively. From 1988, a revised system, the 'greater financial franchise system', was imposed, which included all provinces, as well as cities with independent plans. Guangdong's programme was revised to 'increasing profit contract', under which the handovers of tax revenue increased by 9 per cent annually. Overall, the financial franchise system represented a comprehensive transfer of government responsibilities, financial powers, and personnel management powers from the central government to the local government.

Under the financial responsibility system, or financial franchise system, local governments had incentives to increase their revenue. To do so, they (i) promoted and protected local industries and (ii) worked hard to attract outside investors to start programmes in their jurisdictions. The system gave incentives to local governments and changed the behaviour of the local leaders for several decades following the beginning of the economic reform in the late 1970s. Politically, this system was set up on the back of the reform consensus and the good relations between the central and local leaders after the Cultural Revolution.

Besides the incentive effects, the financial franchise system had a large number of other advantages:

1. The subcontracting of tasks reduced administrative costs. Given the existing communication and management technologies, the financial franchise system was much cheaper than the direct vertical government system, in which the central government let the 'lines' run directly and deeply to the end of the bureaucratic hierarchy. The tax burden had been one reason for peasant revolts in ancient China. To keep society stable, rulers of the past dynasties tried hard to keep government expenditures and tax burdens low. This was also one reason for Chinese leaders' preference for the financial franchise system.

2. The financial franchise system drew a clear line between the responsibilities of central and local governments and also neighbouring local governments. This gave a credible commitment to the local officials so they could use their power in their jurisdictions.
3. The financial franchise system created a checks and balances relationship between the central and the local government. As a contractor, the local officials had to finish the tasks defined in the contract. On the other hand, if the central government changed the rules or asked for more than was defined in the contract, the local leaders could threaten to strike or refuse to perform their duties. Since replacing a local official was usually costly, the central government had some limits when it came to changing local officials (Zhou 2008, pp.69–71).

This system also created disadvantages:

1. The annual negotiations created a huge workload and a transaction cost for the Ministry of Finance and the local governments. It also led to short-term behaviours from the local governments. Because of limited information, it was extremely hard to set a fair share between the central and the local governments.
2. It created an opportunity for corruption between local officials and business firms.
3. Although the original intention of the fiscal franchise system was to reduce supervision costs, it created new supervision costs. Sometimes the central government had to set up special vertical institutions to supervise the behaviour of the local officials, which was costly.
4. Since the contract changed a lot, it could not become a credible promise from the central government. In some cases, the central government revised the terms in the contract and raised its share of profits, which hurt the incentives of local government.
5. The system could not solve the soft budget problem. The less developed provinces continued to ask the central government for extra financial support, which resulted in the central government's budget deficit. The central government had to borrow money from the local governments. In 1983, the central government stopped borrowing from local governments and instead cut the local expenditure defined in the contracts.

The financial franchise system between central and local governments of the 1980s was an extreme form of a franchise/subcontracting system. It was introduced at the beginning of the economic reform, when the local government had no incentives to develop the local economy. The system gave enormous incentives to local leaders, since they could keep a relatively large share of total revenue. The system played an important role in the economic development in the 1980s and early 1990s, and also created tremendous problems. The system was a continuation of the experiments under the planned system. During the planned period, different forms of financial contracts between central and local governments had been experimented with. The idea of fiscal contracting had been the main direction of policy design, focusing on promoting the incentives for local government.

The economic reform also changed the 'unit' system and the 'apanage management' of the local government. Under the planned system, each urban resident belonged to and was managed by a *unit*. The unit is a general term and could be a factory, an office, or a school. In the countryside, the peasants were organised in the People's Communes and production brigades. The local governments, however, were organised by the 'apanage management' principle, which meant the local government was responsible for controlling all citizens living in the locality. The 'unit' system was consistent with 'apanage management' and was actually the lowest level of local government. The movement of people between localities was strictly restricted under the planned system. Economic reform fundamentally changed the 'unit' system and the 'apanage management'. In the 1980s, urban residents began to quit their old jobs to find new ones or start their own businesses. Rural residents began to work in TVEs or move to the cities and find new jobs. The urban food rationing system ended and urban welfare housing was not as important to the families as it had been before. In the countryside, the People's Commune, the lowest level of local government, was abolished. Some of its functions were replaced by the village authority, but the power of the latter was much more limited than the former.

Civil Service Reforms

The management of government officials needed to be reformed along with the government. China's public sector employed 70 million people in 2002, about half of whom worked in government. Another 33 million worked in SOEs. The total number of public employees declined in the late 1990s and the early 21st century, mostly due to the contraction of the SOEs. Of those employed in government departments and other government bodies in 2004, only 4.98 million were formally classified as 'civil servants' (Burns 2007). The Chinese definition of civil servant is both more and less inclusive than definitions of civil service used in other countries, and includes senior politicians and white-collar government employees. According to data from 1998, about 10 per cent of civil servants work at the central level, 11 per cent at the provincial level, 21 per cent at the prefectural level, 41 per cent at the county level, and 17 per cent at the township level.

The CCP plays an extensive role in the management of personnel in public organisations. The CCP Central Committee delegated policy-making and management of the civil service to its Organisation Department. The State Council's Ministry of Personnel implements the policy under the Organisation Department's supervision.

Since the 1980s, the leadership has sought to improve the efficiency and effectiveness of governance through civil service reform. Deng Xiaoping put reform of the leadership system on the Party's agenda. Lifelong tenure for officials was abolished in the early 1980s. In 1982, the revised Constitution of the CCP stated that 'The Party selects its cadres according to the principle that they should possess both political integrity and professional competence, adhere to the practice of appointing people on their merits and oppose favouritism; it exerts genuine efforts to make the ranks of the cadres more revolutionary, younger in average age, better educated and more professionally competent' (CCP 1982, Article 34). In the 1990s, the government took significant steps to reform China's civil service system:

1. Civil service reform had lowered the average age of civil servants. In the early 1980s, the CCP officially adopted a mandatory retirement policy and younger people have been increasingly selected for leadership positions. From 1981 to 1989, the average age of officials of ministerial or bureau rank fell from 63.6 years to 56.9 years (Burns 2007). The CCP Central Committee issued a resolution on cadre retirement in 1982, which provided that, for the officials of central government departments and provincial government, the principal should be forced to retire at age 65, and the deputy should retire at 60. All division chiefs should retire at 60 (CCP Central Committee 1982). The Central Committee proposed in 1992 that the average age of the provincial leaders should be 55, and there should be at least three officials under 50 (Zhou 2008, p.105).
2. Education background has been emphasised more when recruiting new civil servants. A university degree has been a requirement for new civil servants since the mid-1990s.
3. To attract the best people to the civil service system, a selection procedure has been adopted and qualified people are selected through open and competitive means. The CCP Department of Organisation issued a suggestion on cadre assessment, which made specific provisions on the criteria and content of assessment.

This reform of the civil service changed the overall conditions for government officials, and provided a base for government-led economic growth in the 1990s and the first decade of the 21st century.

Formal Laws and Regulations

China experienced a continuing succession of changes in formal law and regulations, which reflected the changes in the society during the process of economic reform. A deeply rooted human desire for fairness was the driving force of the reform of the judicial system. Learned from the lessons of the Cultural Revolution, the society began to regard citizens' rights as a basic premise for the development of a fair society, and the legal system began to be used as a safeguard for these rights. The first stage of the reform created a small but significant opening to the domestic non-state sector and foreign enterprises. The development of formal laws reflected the needs created by the development of these two sectors in urban areas, as well as the development of rural sectors.

Some new regulatory agencies were created, such as the regulatory agencies in the financial sector. But most of the regulatory functions were performed by old government agencies which were reorganised during the reform. The laws and regulations were poorly implemented during the early stages of the economic reform due to inefficiency of the judicial system.

During the earlier stages, many reforms were issued via CCP and State Council documents. There were almost no formal laws regarding the market system at the start of the economic reform. For example, the major rural reforms were regulated in a series of 'Number 1' documents issued by the CCP each year from 1982 to 1986. The first formal law published at the end of the 1970s was the Law on Chinese-Foreign Equity Joint Ventures in 1979, which regulated foreign investment in China and made joint ventures feasible, with restrictions stating that the Chinese parties of the joint ventures must be SOEs (National People's Congress 1979b). During this period, no organisational vehicle was provided by law for larger private enterprises. These private firms had to register as collective enterprises and were subordinate to the local government. In 1981, the Economic Contract Law, the first contract law since 1949, was passed, which only covered contracts between domestic entities other than individuals, and was intended to regulate relations between SOEs (National People's Congress 1981a). The 1982 revision of China's Constitution was passed and published, which declared that the basis of the socialist economic system of the People's Republic of China is socialist public ownership of the means of production. The state economy, according to the 1982 Constitution, is the leading force in the national economy and the individual economy of urban and rural working people is a complement to the socialist public economy (National People's Congress 1982a).

In the second half of the 1980s, a large number of laws were passed to formally accept the principle of market allocation of resources and private ownership. The 13th Congress of the CCP recognised the private sector in 1987, under the guidance, supervision, and control of the state, as a necessary supplement to the state sector (CCP 1987b). The 1988 amendment of the Constitution reflected this change officially, allowing sole proprietorships, partnerships, and limited liability companies to hire eight or more employees. The 1988 Constitution also legitimised land leasing, which was considered to be a key step in the commodification of land (Clarke et al. 2008, p.389). In addition, the General Principles of Civil Law was passed in December 1986, which provided the basic legal principles for the operation of a market economy (National People's Congress 1986a).

Many laws passed in this period dealt with the regulations of various forms on the businesses that emerged in the new market economy, including Patent Law (National People's Congress 1984), Enterprise Bankruptcy Law (National People's Congress 1986b), Provisional Regulations on the Administration of Urban and Township Individual Industrial and Commercial Households (State Council 1987), Technology Contract Law (National People's Congress 1987), Law on Industrial Enterprises Owned by the Whole People (National People's Congress 1988b), and the Provisional Regulations on Private Enterprises (State Council 1988c). Foreigners were kept in a separate legal regime in this period. The Foreign Economic Contract Law was passed in March 1985, covering contracts between Chinese entities and foreign parties (National People's Congress 1985). The Law on Wholly Foreign-Owned Enterprises was passed in April 1986, which was the first time an enterprise wholly owned by foreign investors was allowed (National People's Congress 1986c). The Law on Sino-Foreign Cooperative Joint Ventures was passed in April 1988, and provided more flexible features for Sino-foreign joint ventures (National People's Congress 1988c).

In the field of regulations on government behaviour, the Administrative Litigation Law was passed in April 1989, which established the principle that government agencies must justify their actions by referring to laws and regulations (National People's Congress 1989).

Macroeconomic Control/Adjustment

Macro-control refers to the government policy measures implemented to deal with short-run macroeconomic fluctuations. Market creation and macro-control/adjustment are always alternated during the process of reform.

As the micro-foundation of the Chinese economy changed, the measures government used to control the economy also changed significantly.

The national economy was booming in 1986 and 1987, and fixed investment increased at a speed much higher than before. Price levels increased significantly. The dual pricing system caused rent-seeking and corruption, leading to public discontent. The government implemented a campaign of rectification in 1988 and 1989, by depressing aggregate demand, building market order, and strengthening price supervision.

These kinds of macro-control in the past several decades followed the same pattern. First, the boom caused scarcity of resources. Then the government intervened to redistribute resources using administrative means, through which the SOEs and private enterprises were treated differently. Some of the private firms were crowded out of business. The macro-control maintained the economic order while hurting some economic actors.

3.8 GOVERNMENT VS MARKET

The relationship between the market and the government has been a never-ending topic of debate during China's economic reform. It is involved in every theoretical exploration as well as policy decisions.

Different Views on Market among the Leaders

Although a consensus on reform existed at the beginning, there were divergent views about the target and the approach of the reform among the leadership.

Deng was inclined to use the market approach to solve China's economic problems. He pointed out that socialism does not exclude markets. The planned economy should therefore coordinate with the market economy. As to which should come first, the plan or the market, the answer would depend on the situation (Zhao 2009, p.132).

But Deng had his bottom line. He developed the 'four cardinal principles' in March 1979, which pointed out that bourgeois liberalisation opposed the principles of the leadership of the CCP. The four principles the reformers must follow were (i) adhere to the socialist road, (ii) adhere to the people's democratic dictatorship, (iii) adhere to the Chinese Communist Party's leadership, and (iv) adhere to Marxism–Leninism and Mao Zedong Thought (Deng 1979). The speech was quite inconsistent with the freer atmosphere in China at that time, but it clearly drew the bottom line on the reform.

The main objections to the reform within the leadership came from

Chen Yun, a senior in the circle of CCP leaders. Due to his good relationship with Mao, Chen was the only one who could raise objections against Mao's opinions about economic policies during the planned period. He believed in a conservative way of economic planning. He insisted that 'the leading role of the planned economy [should be] supplemented by the market'. He said that running of the economy was like keeping birds in a cage. You can neither crush the bird nor let the bird fly out of the cage.

Zhao Ziyang, the premier in the mid-1980s and party secretary in the late 1980s, raised several points about the economic reform when preparing documents on economic reform for the 3rd Plenary Session of the 12th Central Committee of the CCP in 1984: (i) the Chinese economy was a planned economy, not a market economy; (ii) the Chinese economy was a commodity economy, not a natural economy; (iii) the plan included a direct plan and an indirect plan, and China needed to reduce the former and increase the latter; and (iv) the indirect plan needed to rely on market adjustment (CCP Central Committee 1984). By 1987, Zhao asserted in the report to the 13th Party Congress that 'the state adjusts the market, and the market leads the enterprises' (Zhao 1987).

The illegal operations of the private sector gave the hardliners an excuse to stop the rapid development of the market. Jinjiang in Fujian province was a base for fake drug production. The government implemented punishments on private business from 1989 to 1992. The government's crackdown made private owners worry about the future of the market. The political weather affected the growth of the private sector. Some private businessmen donated their businesses to the township or village government, and more private business was subordinated to SOEs or TVEs.

As noted by Barry Naughton, in the first stage of reform, the top leadership was fragmented with certain 'veto players'. Deng was the most important leader, but he could not make all the important decisions like Mao did in the planned period. A number of revolutionary elders had the power to veto certain decisions made by Deng, while Deng had a certain degree of trust in the elders. A group of younger leaders, led by Hu Yaobang and Zhao Ziyang, was designated as successors and actually ran the government and the Party. The elders opposed certain reforms and blocked others. Zhao Ziyang lost the confidence of the elders in the late 1980s and completely lost power during the Tiananmen Square events.

The Reform of the Political System

The economic reform since 1978 was led by the leadership within the CCP hierarchy. These leaders had been overthrown during the Cultural Revolution and wanted to reform the system to some degree. The political system had to be reformed, but the ultimate target was for the CCP to retain power.

Deng mentioned political system reform many times in the 1980s. His idea of political system reform in China was basically an administrative reform, to improve the organisation system, working procedure, working style, and operational mode, while keeping the leadership of the Communist Party untouched. He proposed to (i) separate party work from government work, (ii) decentralise and delegate power to the lower levels of government, and (iii) streamline the administration structure of the government. Deng wanted to strengthen vitality and enhance the efficiency of the government. Deng was strongly against the idea of a parliamentary system and the separation of powers.

Deng's speech at the enlarged meetings of the Politburo in August 1980, titled 'The Party and State Leadership System Reform', expressed his ideas about political reform just after the Cultural Revolution. He said that the main drawbacks of the current party- and country-specific systems were a bureaucratic phenomenon, with an excessive concentration of power, and a patriarchal phenomenon, as with the life tenure in leading posts and privileges of all kinds. He believed that the CCP's errors of the past were related by some leaders' thought and working style. Deng said, 'Stalin seriously undermined the socialist legal system. Comrade Mao Zedong said that such incidents cannot happen in western countries such as Britain, France and the United States' (Wu Wei 2014a). While he recognised this, Mao did not actually solve the leadership system's problems, which lead to the Cultural Revolution. This lesson was extremely profound. Deng pointed out that the leadership's organisational problem was more fundamental. He stressed that the timing and conditions were ripe for putting forward reform and implementing the tasks of the party and state leadership system. His generation might not complete this task, but at least had the responsibility to lay a solid foundation for completing it (Wu Wei 2014a).

Deng talked about political democratisation when he met visitors from Yugoslavia in June 1986. He said, since democratisation was a new problem for Chinese leaders, 'we cannot copy the political system of multiparty and separation of powers'. On one occasion he said that there were three governments in the United States, and he did not know which would make the decisions (Zhao 2009, pp.274–275).

Zhao Ziyang held that political system reform was important for the overall reform in China. Without political reform, the economic reform could not go deep enough. Before 1989, Zhao's basic idea of political reform in China was to keep the Communist Party's ruling party position, while changing the form of rule. The changing of the forms of rule included the following components: The decision-making process should be more transparent. The government should open up channels for dialogue. To do that, different kinds of social organisations would be needed. The Party needed to protect the development of these organisations. The election procedure of the People's Congress should reform and allow multiple candidates. Citizens' rights should be protected, with specific laws to protect freedom of assembly, association, demonstration, and strikes. Freedom of speech should be opened up under the leadership of the Party.

After 1989, Zhao changed his point of view, and he believed that the parliamentary system was the best, but not perfect, political system in the current world. He considered that a long transitional period would be needed to realise the political reform in China (Zhao 2009, pp.292–298).

The 13th Party Congress in 1987 listed the tasks of political reform:

1. Separate the Party and the government. The Party's leadership is a political leadership. The main way to implement the Party's political leadership on national affairs would be through legal procedures. A clear line should be drawn between the party organisation and the government.
2. Further decentralisation of power. The general principle is that anything suitable to be dealt with by the lower level of government should be decided and executed by the lower level. The responsibilities of the central and local governments should be clearly defined.
3. Reform of the government institutions. The government institutions should change their functions and the government's management of enterprises should be changed from direct management to indirect management.
4. Reform of the cadre and administrative personnel system. The existing system would be changed to a national civil service system.
5. Establishment of a social dialogue and consultation system. Channels must be established to reflect the demands and voices of the ordinary citizens. Dialogues should be launched at the national, local, and grass-roots levels. The major issues should be publicised and discussed by the people.
6. Improvement of the system of socialist democracy. The function of the People's Congress and Chinese People's Political Consultative Conference (CPPCC) should be improved and the role of the existing other democratic parties should be strengthened (Zhao 1987).

The political reform did not go far after the 13th Party Congress, and stopped in 1989.

3.9 THE END OF THE FIRST STAGE OF THE REFORM

The Tiananmen Square events in 1989 ended the first stage of China's reform.

Corruption was one of the reasons behind the Tiananmen protests of 1989. Corruption was widespread in ancient China, both in the court and among the local elites. The widespread corruption of the Kuomintang (KMT), the Chinese National Party ruling China from the 1920s to the 1940s, is often credited as an important reason for the CCP's victory over the KMT. Corruption existed during the planned period, but the magnitude and depth of corruption was not as significant as that after the planned period, due to the restrictions on market development.

The economic reform that started in the late 1970s created a market and a private sector, coexisting with the government and SOEs. This tempted government officials to misuse their power and propel their sons and daughters, also called the 'princeling's party', into the most profitable positions and generated large personal wealth in business. This aroused the discontent of the masses.

The Tiananmen Square movement was a result of an attack against the existing order. The events were initiated by the death of Hu Yaobang in April 1989, a deposed party leader, and the student protest against the corruption of government officials, which was supported by people from all levels of the society. Some of the reformers, led by the party secretary Zhao Ziyang, and a group of social intellectuals tried to use the student movement to promote political reform. Deng Xiaoping, the actual leader of the Party, took over power and ordered troops to enter Beijing to stop the student movement. Several armies were called, and some of the officers hesitated to shoot the students congregating and protesting in Tiananmen Square. Finally, on 4 June 1989, the troops opened fire and cleared the square. Zhao Ziyang was deposed, and Jiang Zemin became the party secretary. The reformers and intellectuals involved in the movement were purged, and some of them fled overseas.

3.10 A SUMMARY OF THE PASSAGE OF THE REFORM

The reform followed a gradualism strategy because it was led by a group of leaders within the political system who emerged from the planned period. This leadership was hurt by the Cultural Revolution and wanted reform. But they had to make the reform gradual because of the resistance within the political structure.

The reform was started in rural areas, partly because the poverty in rural areas was an urgent problem that needed to be solved, and partly because agriculture was a remote domain and was not as important as the industrial and urban sectors in the economy. The peasants initiated the reform, taking political and economic risks. The leadership, however, did not simply ban the reform; instead, they let the reform continue as an experiment. The rural reform followed a principle of 'separation of the ownership and the user rights'. The government gave the user rights of the land to the peasants, while keeping the collective ownership unchanged. The lesson learned from the rural reform was that a downward shift of power to the lower level of society gives producers the incentive to work.

After the success of the rural reform, the leadership tried to apply the same principle to the urban SOEs at the core of the planned system, but failed. They tried to implement the responsibility system in urban SOEs without changing the ownership. The reforms of SOEs in the 1980s were not successful, because the incentive mechanism of SOEs was much more complex than that of the production teams in the countryside. At the same time, as an auxiliary of the SOE reform, the reformers relaxed the prices of a large portion of products and created a lot of market facilities. China also opened its doors to the outside world in the 1980s.

As Zhao Ziyang said, the reform was implemented in two major areas: a new market economy created outside the planned economy, and a reform within the planned economy. The size of the planned economy was gradually reduced, while a new non-planned economy was created and competed with the planned economy (Zhao 2009, p.140). The growth of the new economy was quite a success, but the reform within the planned economy was not so successful. Reviewing the process of the reform and decisions made during its course, the view that the reform had not followed any plan seems untrue. It seems the decision makers optimised their choices at each critical point of the reform to reach their target.

The Tiananmen Square events ended the first stage of the reform. It was a conflict between different political forces pursuing different targets for the reform. The leadership faced a tough decision as to whether to stop the political reform, which was a logical continuation of the economic reform but could lead to the Party losing power. Deng made the decision to restrain the scope of the reform. The reform of the political system was not allowed. In the three decades after 1989, the reform has adhered to this restriction.

NOTES

1. A good harvest due to the land ownership reform.
2. 1 Mu equals 0.0667 hectares.
3. The peasants could decide what to produce within the restrictions of the state plan, because the state plan was usually a general plan which was not detailed. Peasants could decide what kind of grain or vegetable to produce after completing the planned handover of wheat or rice.
4. 'Big pot' is widely used slang in China describing the lack of responsibilities and incentives to work in SOEs during the planned period.
5. The village government is the lowest level of government in rural areas in China.
6. This will be analysed later in the book.
7. Compensation trade is a form of countertrade in which an incoming investment is repaid from the revenues generated by that investment.
8. The assembly of the Beijing jeep continued after Chrysler purchased AMC. Since its founding in 1984, the company has kept the same Chinese co-owner but has had several foreign co-owners. Now it is a joint venture between Beijing Automobile Production Company and Daimler AG.
9. In the late 1970s and early 1980s, the government raised the price of food in urban areas several times. Each time the price was adjusted, urban consumers were given certain price subsidies.
10. This market was closed by the government in the 2010s, because the Beijing government thought it had a negative impact on the appearance of the city.
11. This included funds from the firm's retained earnings, capital collected from owners, and money borrowed from friends.
12. Before 1985, exports and imports were performed according to the plan. The stopping of the plan was one of the major reforms in the foreign trade area.
13. Jiangsu province adopted a 'fixed ratio contract' system as early as 1977. Five minority autonomous regions, Inner Mongolia, Xinjiang, Tibet, Ningxia, and Guangxi, and three less developed provinces, Yunnan, Qinghai, and Guizhou, adopted a fixed subsidy system.

4. Reform and political coalition: 1990–2003

The economic reform in China restarted in the early 1990s after a clear line on the limit of the reform was drawn in 1989. The Tiananmen Square events ended the dream of a Western-style political reform. The leadership resolved the political crisis and reinitiated the economic reform, though it was subject to narrower political restrictions. The attempts to balance political control and economic development by the government are consistent with the political economy theory of government decision-making in a bureaucratic-market society developed in section 1.2. The clear restrictions on political reform maintained the stability of the society, which was important for economic reform, but also planted the seeds of a bureaucratic-market system, which affected the direction of institutional evolution in the next several decades.

From 18 January to 21 February 1992, Deng Xiaoping made his famous South China tour, inspecting Wuchang, Shenzhen, Zhuhai, and Shanghai. During his trip, Deng made important speeches to promote economic reform. He pointed out that whether to use planning or market forces to promote economic growth is not a fundamental difference between socialism and capitalism. This meant a socialist China could use market forces as a tool to develop its economy. These speeches offered answers to a series of important theoretical and conceptual questions, thus playing a crucial role in guiding and accelerating China's reform and opening up. Deng's southern tour represented the restarting of economic reform, which was temporarily stopped after the events of Tiananmen Square in 1989.

The radical political reform died while the economic reform continued in the second decade of the reform, from 1992 to 2003. State-owned enterprise (SOE) reform and tax reform were the major elements of the reform in this period. Everybody, including government officials and business managers, had lost hope of reviving the SOEs by franchising them to the managers. The incentive-based reform in the 1980s showed that incentive improvement could not be an alternative to the privatisation of the SOEs. The reform in the 1990s was driven partly by the top-down design and partly by the enthusiasm to develop the market economy from the bottom of the society. Deng's inspection trip in South China in 1992 reconfirmed the direction of the economic part of the reform. The reform was largely designed and initiated by the government, supported by a large part of the society. The most important institutional changes were (i) the reform of SOEs, in which the small SOEs were sold to the public, while the large SOEs were kept by the government; (ii) the setting up of the tax-sharing system between the central and local governments, which readjusted the financial source and responsibilities of the central and local governments; and (iii) China's World Trade Organization (WTO) entry, which further opened the door of the Chinese economy to the world. The 3rd Plenary Session of the 14th Central Committee of the Communist Party of China (CCP) passed a resolution on the socialist market economy in November 1993, which confirmed that the Chinese economy is essentially a market economy (CCP Central Committee 1993).

Through further economic reform, especially the ownership reform of the SOEs, the setting up of a primary institutional framework of a government-led market economy was completed by the end of the 20th century. A large private sector had been formed by the end of this period, which became the ownership base of China's market economy. The tax-sharing system redefined the roles of the central and local governments. Based on this system, the local government started to search for new financial resources and play a larger role in local economic development. As the reform went on, the effectiveness of the market, compared with the planned system, attracted more and more people into the market system.

Deng Xiaoping died in 1997. Jiang Zemin and Zhu Rongji were the actual leaders of the economic reform in the 1990s. As the vice-premier in charge of the economy from 1991, and premier from 1998, Zhu Rongji completed many tasks that were unfinished in the 1980s, using his strong governing style. Zhu initiated contractionary policies to reduce aggregate demand when inflation surged in 1993 and 1994. He led a silent revolution to solve the ownership problems of SOEs later.

4.1 A SILENT REVOLUTION: THE OWNERSHIP REFORM OF SOES IN THE 1990S

The SOEs' performance worsened in the 1990s due to the unsuccessful reform of the 1980s. In 1996, 6,232 SOEs went into bankruptcy, more than the sum of bankruptcies in the previous nine years (Wu Xiaobo 2014b, p.93). Two final ways to rescue SOEs in the 1990s were (i) improving the management of SOEs and (ii) listing the SOEs on the stock market. Handan Steel, an SOE in Hebei province, was presented by the National Economic and Commercial Committee in 1992 as a good example of SOE reform that Chinese enterprises nationwide should follow. The company set up an internal price system and a cost target to control the activities of divisions and groups, which was considered a copy of the Taylor system in the United States in the early 20th century. Another way to save the SOEs was to list them on the stock market, where the company's huge debts were sold to the stockholders. Neither approach could stop the bad performance of the SOEs.

The failed reform of SOEs in the 1980s forced the leadership to rethink the solution to the SOEs problem. The conclusion was that incentive improvement could not replace ownership reform. The strategy of SOE reform was changed from franchising or contracting to selling small SOEs. The Communiqué of the 3rd Plenary Session of the 14th Central Committee of the CCP first raised the policy of invigorating large SOEs while relaxing control over small ones, or '*Zhuada Fangxiao*', which focused on the restructuring of major SOEs while leaving minor ones to fend for themselves.

'Fang Xiao' (Selling Small SOEs) and 'Zhua Da'(Improving Large SOEs)

The primary reason for changing the strategy of SOE reform was the failure of the approach using franchising to improve the management of SOEs. The direct driving force of the SOE reform in the late 1990s was the bad financial situations of the SOEs. In 1995, 87,900 independently accounting industrial SOEs existed, including 15,700 large and medium-sized SOEs and 72,200 small ones. In addition, there were more than 500,000 town- and village-owned enterprises (Wu and Ma 2013, p.155). One-third of the SOEs had profits, one-third had explicit losses, and the rest had hidden losses in 1996. The whole SOE sector experienced losses in 1997 (Xiao and Sui 2011, p.250). This was not a sudden deterioration. It was the accumulation of problems in the previous three decades under the planned economy and during the failed reform of SOEs in the 1980s.

As there were already signs of the failure of SOEs, the preparation of the SOE ownership reform started several years earlier. The National People's Congress passed the Corporation Law of the People's Republic of China on 29 December 1993 (National People's Congress 1993a). The 15th CCP Congress defined the areas the state-owned economy must control, including (i) national security-related industries (e.g. defence or currency printing); (ii) natural monopoly industries (e.g. telecommunications, railways, electricity, gas and water); (iii) important public goods and service industries (e.g. large irrigation facilities, environmental protection, urban public transportation, finance and insurance); and (iv) backbone enterprises in core or high-tech industries (e.g. large oil fields, large steel plants, and large auto plants) (Zheng et al. 2009, p.1). The SOEs should gradually retreat from other areas not listed above.

The 15th CCP Congress called for the acceleration of reform of SOEs, '*Zhuada Fangxiao*', or managing large enterprises while adopting more flexible policies towards smaller ones, and implementing the strategic reorganisation of SOEs. According to Jiang Zemin's report to the Congress of the CCP, in order to speed up the pace of SOE reform, the government would reorganise, merge, lease, or sell the problematic SOEs (Jiang 1997). In other words, 'Fang Xiao' meant that most of the small SOEs would be sold or reorganised.

The leadership set the target of resolving the SOE problem within five years. Experiments started in 1997, with the reform implemented nationwide in 1998 and finished in 2003. Small enterprises with low technology and/or poor product quality, as well as those that waste resources and pollute the environment, were closed by the government. In practice, the restructuring of small SOEs followed several forms, including (i) transferring all or part of the property rights to employees, becoming a joint-stock cooperative enterprise and letting the employees own all or part of the stocks; (ii) selling to non-state legal persons or natural persons and becoming private, joint-venture or foreign-invested enterprises; (iii) transferring to limited liability corporations; (iv) merging with other firms; or (v) leasing all or some of the assets of the SOE to other firms or to the management and employees of the SOE (Wu and Ma 2013, p.162). Most of the local governments chose to 'completely withdraw and transfer' when dealing with local SOEs. A survey shows that 25 per cent of the private companies in the sample were transferred from SOEs and TVEs. Sixty per cent of the owners of these firms were former managers of the firms, and 50 per cent of them were party members. From 1998 to 2003, the number of SOEs or state-controlled enterprises reduced by 40 per cent (Wu Xiaobo 2014b, p.153).

For example, Zhucheng Electric Machinery Factory in Weifang, Shandong province, was sold to 'insiders'. To buy the ownership of the factory, 9 factory leaders each paid RMB40,000 ($4,825.2), 20 middle-level managers each paid RMB20,000 ($2,412.6), and workers each paid RMB6,000 ($723.8). The young mayor of Zhucheng, Chen Guang, oversaw the reform, supported by the National Reform Committee. Chen sold all 272 SOEs and TVEs in the area to individuals (Wu Xiaobo 2014a, p.321).

In some cases, the management set up a new company, which bought the stock of the original SOE or TVE. For instance, Midea, a famous TVE set up in 1968 and a producer of household appliances, started its privatisation in 1999. The management set up an investment company in 2001 and it became the largest shareholder of Midea (Midea n.d.).

In other cases, the management of SOEs received shares during the reform. TCL, another producer of home appliances, signed an agreement with the Huizhou government in Guangdong province. According to the agreement, all assets of the company were under the control of the government. Hereafter, under the condition that the return on net assets was no lower than 10 per cent, the management got a certain percentage of the shares each year if the growth rate reached the target. Due to good performance, the management and the union owned over 50 per cent of the shares at the beginning of the 21st century (Xu 2005).

Some foreign investors were involved in the reform of property arrangements. In a meeting with Vice-Premier Zhu Rongji in 1994, Eastman Kodak raised a proposal to buy the entire Chinese film industry for $1 billion and received support from Zhu. By 1998, Kodak had set-up joint ventures with all seven Chinese film producers (He et al. n.d.).

In the process of the reform of small and medium-sized SOEs, some of the managers sold the SOEs to their friends or relatives at low prices. Some of the employees could not get their social insurance back. Some of the state assets were transferred to 'insiders', especially the management of the former SOEs, at prices lower than their market value. In some cases, the manager sold the firm to himself and did not adequately compensate the company's workers. Throughout the whole process, there was no formal legalisation and regulation of the reform in relation to the selling-off of small SOEs. Provincial governments could choose their approaches. It was considered a silent revolution.

Mass layoffs of SOE workers accompanied the closing of a large number of small and medium-sized SOEs. It was estimated that 28 million workers lost their jobs from 1998 to June 2001 (Xiao and Sui 2011, p.250). The CCP and the State Council ordered local governments to set up Re-employment Service Centres to deal with the laid-off SOE workers' unemployment benefits and re-employment. A laid-off SOE worker, who was treated differently from a regular unemployed worker, could stay in the Centre for up to three years, receiving greater unemployment benefits than that of regular unemployed workers. The financial sources of the Re-employment Service Centre came from the fiscal budgets of the central and local governments, enterprise, and the unemployment insurance fund (CCP Central Committee and State Council 1998). The SOE reform and mass layoffs of the 1990s created the first generation of losers from the reform. Privately owned business became the main channel to absorb the laid-off workers. The government took great risks in implementing the reform of the SOEs and in meeting the challenge of mass layoffs.

While closing the small SOEs, the government tried to improve the corporate governance framework of large SOEs. The 15th National Congress of the CCP in 1997 set the target for large SOE reform, deciding that most of the large SOEs should be reorganised into multi-shareholding limited liability companies, with some exceptions (CCP 1997; Wu and Ma 2013, p.165). The state controlled the companies by holding the majority of the shares, but allowed private investors to hold a portion of stock shares. Although the managers of large SOEs gained much greater authority in dealing with the assets of the company, the nomination of the higher-level managers continued to be tightly controlled by the Organisational Department of the CCP.

The reform of SOEs in the 1990s built the microeconomic foundation of the market economy in China.

Social Security System: Complement to SOE Reform

The old social security system could not meet the requirements of a market economy. The ownership reform of SOEs, which created a huge unemployed population, needed a new system of social security, including unemployment insurance, medical insurance, and workers' compensation insurance.

In 1993, the 3rd Plenary Session of the 14th Central Committee of the CCP raised the need 'to set up a multilevel social security system'. The urban worker pension and medical insurance was to be funded by both the '*unit*' and the individuals, through a social pooling account and an individual account (CCP News 1993). In March 1995, the State Council issued a notice on the deepening of the reform of workers' pension insurance (Law Library 1995). In July 1997, the State Council issued a resolution on setting up a unified basic workers' pension insurance and specified the unified formula for the individual payment and a standard for pension benefits. In the long run, according to the original design of the program, a worker needs to pay 11 per cent of his or her salary into an individual account, and 3 per cent should be paid by his or her enterprise.[1] In 1997, the actual payments of the individual were lower than this target, while the enterprise payments were higher. The individual payment should increase gradually to reach this target, while the enterprise payment should reduce gradually (Law Library 1997).

The new system was based on several basic principles, including coverage of the whole society (not only the state sector) and introducing individual accounts. However, from the beginning, the new system had funding problems. Under the old 'pay-as-you-go' system,[2] no individual accounts existed. The low wages of the SOE workers under the planned economy meant the state had withheld the pension payments of the workers. Now the state needed to return these loans to the retired workers.

Most of the SOEs gave the retired workers a one-time payment, based on the years of working and the rank of a worker, which was usually not enough to meet the basic requirements for their remaining life. In 2001, the government decided to reduce the share of the individual account and increase the share of social pooling, which meant a return to the 'pay-as-you-go' system. The obstacle to the pension reform was the funding for the empty individual accounts of the older SOE workers. Using part of the state assets to pay the debt owed to the old SOE workers was one possible solution to the problem.

Medical insurance system reform started in the late 1990s. The State Council issued a resolution to establish a basic medical insurance system for urban workers in 1998. The new system consisted of two parts: social pooling funds and individual accounts. The social pooling fund was used mainly for critical illness and in-hospital care. The individual account was usually used for outpatient services (Central Government of the People's Republic of China 1998).

In 1999, the State Council issued a regulation for urban residents' minimum living insurance, which established the minimum living insurance system in China (State Council 1999). The minimum living insurance came from the local government budget. The minimum living standard was set by the local government. The benefit equalled the gap between the minimum living standard and the average per capita income in a family.

4.2 THE DIVERSITY OF SOLUTIONS IN THE PRIVATE SECTOR

The closing and selling of small and medium-sized SOEs created a large number of non-state-owned small and medium-sized firms in the 1990s. After Deng's inspection trip to the south, another wave of private businesses started in the early 1990s. It is estimated that 100,000 government officials quit their positions and 'jumped into the sea of business' around 1992 (Wu Xiaobo 2014a, p.337). At the end of 2001, 29.3 million small and medium-sized enterprises existed in China, employing 174 million workers and providing 43.2 per cent of the tax revenue (Wu and Ma 2013, p.163). These enterprises developed rapidly nationwide, especially in the eastern coastal area.

Recapitalisation of the Private Companies

By the turn of the century, for enterprises that came originally from SOEs, TVEs, and other sources in China, the most important thing was the clarification of property rights, or changing the ownership from government-owned to some form of private ownership. Many enterprises were originally owned by different levels of government, and many of them were on the verge of bankruptcy when the firms were taken over by private entrepreneurs. Because of the efforts of entrepreneurs who got the opportunity to run the businesses, these enterprises grew rapidly. The entrepreneurs therefore wanted to get their share of the ownership of the enterprises. All large firms in China needed to make this step sooner or later. Entrepreneurs adopted different approaches to solve the ownership problem. Some were successful, while others failed.

To solve the ownership problem, the entrepreneurs had to seize any opportunities that may arise. As early as in 1990, the government initiated a movement to clean up fake TVEs[3] and to promote 'Rural Stockholding Cooperative Enterprises'. Many private investors of TVEs in the eastern coastal area seized the opportunity to change the property rights arrangement and enable private shareholders to own a large share of the enterprises. They tried to enlarge their ownership of former TVEs and change them to private firms, in which they would be collective owners. This became the first attempt of property rights clarification. The towns and villages still held a certain share of the companies after this reform, and much more time was needed for private investors to get rid of this share.

Shenyang Jinbei was the first large SOE that diversified its ownership by adopting the shareholding reform and issued RMB100 million ($26.9 million) in public stock in 1988. Yang Rong, a private investor, bought 40 per cent of Jinbei's stock in 1991 and later increased his share to 51 per cent and seized control of the company. He then set up Brilliance Jinbei in Bermuda, which was 100 per cent controlled by Hainan Huayin, a company owned by a friend of Yang Rong. By Mr Yang's arrangement, Brilliance Jinbei was listed on the New York Stock Exchange (NYSE) in 1992 as the first Chinese firm listed on an overseas stock market. It was also the first case of a stock from a formerly socialist country being listed on the NYSE. Mr Yang took over the control of the production of Jinbei passenger cars and introduced foreign technology and equipment. The first Brilliance car rolled off the production line in December 2000. The party secretary and the mayor of Shenyang, where the main production base of Jinbei is located, were arrested for corruption in 2001. The new leadership of the city had a suspicion that Mr Yang tried to move the investment to other localities in Southern China. The key disputes regarded the ownership of Brilliance. Negotiations between the Shenyang government and Mr Yang broke down in 2002 and the government took over all the properties of Brilliance. Yang Rong lost everything and fled to the United States in 2002 (Xu 2017).

Liu Chuanzhi, the president of Lenovo, knew that gaining equity clarity was an extremely important task for the company. Lenovo was originally established with initial capital given by the Institute of Computing Technology, a state-owned research institute, but the growth of the company in previous years was the result of the work of him and his team. He created a plan for equity distribution in 1994, in which 65 per cent of equity would belong to the Academy of Sciences, the higher authority over the Institute of Computing Technology, and 35 per cent to employees. The plan was approved by the president of the Academy, Zhou Guangzhao, an open-minded scientist (Yu Donghui 2015). This arrangement is not valid today, but the Academy of Sciences is still a partial owner of Lenovo.

Li Jingwei, director of Sanshui County Wine Factory, started the production and promotion of Jianlibao, a sports drink, in 1984. He targeted the Los Angeles Olympics, and the promotion of Jianlibao was pretty successful. Jianlibao became the number one brand of sports drink in China. He considered the property rights problem as early as 1994. He planned to list his company on the Hong Kong Stock Exchange and gave the management a certain portion of the shares. The plan was vetoed by the Sanshui government, the ultimate owner of the company. In 2002, the Sanshui government decided to sell the company to an outside buyer, instead of selling it to Li Jingwei and his team. One day, Li was called upon to attend a banquet, where the mayor told him the government would sell the company to a businessman from Singapore. Li fought against the proposal and tried hard to raise funds to buy back the company. Just before he had collected enough money, the government sold the company to another domestic company. Nine days after the sale, Li suffered from suffusion of blood on the brain and never left the hospital. Later that year, he was removed from the National Congress for corruption (Huashang Taolue n.d.).

Chunlan was the largest air conditioner producer in China, located in Taizhou, Jiangsu province. The company was a county collective enterprise, on the verge of bankruptcy in 1985. Under the leadership of Tao Jianxing, the company grew rapidly. Its total assets increased from RMB2.8 million ($1.0 million) in 1985 to RMB12 billion ($1.4 billion) in 2000. The board of Chunlan announced in 2000 that, without touching state-owned assets, the company would sell 25 per cent of the RMB5 billion ($0.6 billion) collective assets to management and about 10,000 workers. Banks would provide loans for employees to buy the shares. The news of Chunlan's property reform caused a hot debate about whether the arrangement resulted in the loss of state assets, which caught the attention of the government. The reform was halted due to pressure from the public, which thought the reform was a transfer of state-owned public assets to the pockets of individuals (Xiao 2009).

Most of the non-state-owned companies in China today came from SOEs or TVEs. To become modern private shareholding companies, the private investors needed clarification of their property rights, through complicated ownership rearrangements. Most of these SOEs or TVEs experienced bad management and were close to bankruptcy when the private investors took over the operation of the companies. They put tremendous efforts into the operation of the firms and should be paid in return. But the ownership of the firms was not clear; some of them were still partly controlled by the government or collectives. This means the private investors have to change the ownership of the enterprise from state ownership or collective ownership to private ownership through some legal or illegal means. Some of them were successful, while others failed.

Improving Management

Companies, especially privately owned companies, improved their management greatly in the 1990s. Ren Zhengfei, president of Huawei Technologies Co., set up the Basic Law of Huawei, which was the company's strategic plan or bylaw. The 'law' set the long-term targets of Huawei (e.g. to be a world-class telecommunication equipment provider, and to never enter the information service sector). The 'law' secured employees' stock ownership in the company, which would not change in the long run. Huawei also invested a large percentage of its revenue in technical innovation (Zhao and Yan 2010).

Haier, based in Qingdao, Shandong province, had been founded as Qingdao Refrigerator Co. in 1984. Zhang Ruimin, a young assistant city-manager, was hired by the government as the managing director of the company in 1984. In 1985, when a customer returned a faulty refrigerator to the factory, Zhang found the failure rate of his products was 20 per cent. He had 76 dud refrigerators lined up on the floor and ordered the workers to destroy them. He said, 'if we pass these refrigerators for sale, we will be continuing a mistake that will bankrupt our company'. In the following years, Zhang made great efforts to improve the management and quality control of the products of the company. He then established a joint venture with the German producer Liebherr, introduced technology from Germany, and started to produce 'Haier' branded refrigerators (Haier n.d.). The production and sale of 'Haier' refrigerators was very successful and the company became one of the largest household appliances producers in the world.

TVEs: Wenzhou Mode and Southern-Jiangsu Mode

Located near Taiwan, Zhejiang province was not heavily invested in by the state during the planned period and reached only mid-level development among all the provinces in China in the early 1980s. The total industrial output was RMB21 billion ($12.3 billion) in 1980, of which only 0.035 per cent was produced by private companies. However, people in Zhejiang have a tradition of doing private business. Even in the planned period, they made attempts to develop private businesses and were cracked down on by the government again and again. Private small and medium-sized enterprises developed rapidly in the 1980s and 1990s in Zhejiang. By 1985, 264,000 rural enterprises had been set up. Urban and rural private businesses produced 49 per cent of the total output in 2000 (Wu and Ma 2013, pp.163–164).

'Wenzhou mode' is a mode of production and trade based on family industries and specialised markets. Wenzhou mode of development focuses on small products produced by small private firms based on the behaviour of people from Wenzhou, a coastal city in Zhejiang province. At the early stage of economic reform, people in Wenzhou developed the Wenzhou mode, which is different from other development modes in China, especially those developed in Southern Jiangsu province. In 1982, Wenzhou had 100,000 sole proprietorships, one-tenth of those in China, and 300,000 sales people were travelling across the country. The first specialised small-product market, the button market at Qiaotou, Yongjia county, was set up in 1983. The government in Wenzhou adopted a low profile, letting the market operate itself.

What the Wenzhou people achieved in the past 40 years was an economic miracle. It demonstrated the creativity of private firms when they are freed from a planned economy. These former farmers, initially without any raw materials, technology, distribution channels, or skilled labour, occupied the market and beat the SOEs. Most of their equipment was borrowed from the SOEs being phased out, their technology was learned from engineers of SOEs, and their markets were those neglected by the SOEs. Many engineers of the SOEs worked for private firms during the weekends. Many SOEs were taken over by private firms that then learned their technologies. Collective enterprises and urban and rural individual enterprises produced 56.9 per cent of industrial output in 1996 (National Bureau of Statistics 1997).

'Southern-Jiangsu mode' was another development model in China's rural area during the reform years. TVEs in Southern Jiangsu province expanded quickly in the 1970s and 1980s, due to the protection provided by the local government and the financial support from local banks. The mode refers to the approach of developing the economy by using a large number of TVEs. TVEs were called 'Local State Corporations' by some people, since they were actually owned and operated by the town and village governments. The TVEs were developed as early as in the planned period in this area. After the beginning of the economic reform, TVEs expanded rapidly. Based on the credit of the local government, the TVEs could borrow from local banks and got cheap land and labour in the local area. The local government also helped the TVEs to find raw materials out of the national plan, and to sell their products. The situation changed dramatically in the 1990s, and many TVEs encountered similar property rights problems as SOEs. As TVEs grew in size, they were usually franchised to the management and therefore controlled by insiders. Because the ownership was not clear, the managers demonstrated short-term behaviour, which hurt the long-run efficiency of the operation. Because of this short-term vision, the management tended to split the assets of the enterprises, borrowed a large amount of money, and invested the funds in the stock market and real estate instead of focusing on long-term goals. The provincial government hesitated to reform the TVEs at first, but then decided to implement the reform to better define property rights. Most of the TVEs became proprietorships or corporations. By the end of 2002, 93 per cent of the TVEs in Southern Jiangsu province had been restructured to form private companies (Wu Xiaobo 2014b, p.126). After most of the TVEs had changed their ownership structures, the 'Southern-Jiangsu mode', a development mode based on TVEs' performance, ended.

In addition to Zhejiang and Jiangsu, Guangdong province became an experimental area in the 1980s, and a large number of non-SOEs have developed since then, including foreign firms, TVEs, and private firms. The area's connection to the Hong Kong economy helped the outward processing manufacturing TVEs in Guangdong province to rapidly develop during the 1980s and 1990s.

High-Tech Companies

A number of high-tech companies grew from the process of economic reform and development. In the 1980s, the first generation of high-tech companies started in China, including Lianxiang (which later became Lenovo) and many others. The second group of high-tech companies started their operations in the late 1990s. In January 1997, Zhang Chaoyang set up Internet Technologies China (ITC, Aitexin). Ding Lei established Wangyi (163) in Guangzhou in June 1997, with three employees and RMB200,000 ($24,126.0) in capital. Wang Zhidong's RichWin (Sitong Lifang), the first Chinese company to receive foreign venture capital, received $16.5 million in venture capital in October 1997[4] (Chen and Zeng 2011). Three of the largest internet companies, Sina, Netease, and Sohu, were listed on NASDAQ in 2000.

Jack Ma (Ma Yun), a former English teacher and a tour guide, set up Alibaba in 1999 in Hangzhou, Zhejiang province, with a registered capital of RMB500,000 ($60,398.9) and 18 employees. Alibaba is a business-to-business (B2B) electronic commerce (e-commerce) company, providing a playing field for retail and wholesale trade allowing small businesses to compete effectively in the domestic and global markets. After 18 years of development, Alibaba's businesses currently include Taobao Marketplaces, China's premier online shopping destination; Tmall.com, a third-party platform for brands and retailers; and Alibaba.com, a global wholesale platform for small businesses (Alibaba n.d.). Alibaba sought an initial public offering (IPO) in the United States in 2014 after a deal could not be reached with the Hong Kong Stock Exchange. Its market value reached $231 billion at the end of its first day on the New York Stock Exchange. Its stock value traded down and its market value was $212 billion at the end of 2015. Alibaba's websites accounted for over 80 per cent of China's online sales by September 2014 (Alibaba n.d.).

Ma Huateng (Pony Ma) and four of his classmates founded Tencent, one of the largest internet companies in China and in the world, in 1998. The company provides social networks, web portals, e-commerce, and online gaming platforms. It offers the well-known instant messenger Tencent QQ and mobile chat service WeChat. The market value of Tencent exceeded $200 billion on 13 April 2015. Ma was born in Shantou, Guangdong province. He graduated from Shenzhen University in 1993 with a major in computer science. After working with China Motion Telecom Development for several years, he set up his own company. Ma was familiar with the innovations in other countries and tried to adapt them to China. Inspired by the idea of ICQ, the world's first internet instant messaging service, Tencent launched a similar software, with a Chinese interface, OICQ, in 1999. Ma later improved the platform by allowing users to send messages to mobile handsets and changed the name of the software to QQ[5] (Tencent n.d.).

Government–Business Relationship

Under the bureaucratic-market system, it is vital for private firms to maintain a good relationship with the government. Governments, especially local governments, are in a dominant position and have discretionary power to collect taxes and fees selectively and implement preferential policy towards their favoured enterprises, legally or illegally. Administrative approval, favourable tax deduction, financial support, and supervision of illegal activities are basic powers that governments hold. To keep their close relationship with government officials, private firms need government protection and adopt various means including different types of bribery towards government officials.

A lot of the enterprises today in China came from SOEs and TVEs, which were owned by different levels of governments for several decades. After the property reform at the end of the 20th century, most of these firms gained independence. However, the government still has close relationships with these firms, either in support of or periodically intervening in the business activities of these firms. The firms need to pay taxes and social security payments for their workers, to borrow from local banks, and to buy raw materials and sell products, which may also need government support. Every enterprise needs to maintain a good relationship with the government.

The government, especially local government, gave administrative and financial support to the enterprises. In the eastern coastal area, local government sometimes acted as a spokesperson for companies in its jurisdiction and worked like a company to provide a wide variety of services to the firms in the locality. For example, in Shunde, Guangdong province, the local government's support helped the city become one of the largest centres of home electrical equipment production in China.

In some cases, the government's extra support produced zero or negative results, due to the lack of information and wrong incentive mechanism. In 1996, the National Economic and Commercial Committee announced a policy to help some SOEs and private firms to enter the world top 500. Baoshan Steel, Jiangnan Shipyard, North China Pharmaceutical, Beida Fangzheng, and Changhong were on the target list. The government supported these enterprises with large amounts of technical innovation funding. However, most of these firms failed to enter the world top 500 later, which shows the limited impact of the government's industrial policy.

A number of successful entrepreneurs were selected by the government to be members of the central and local People's Congress. In certain cases, the entrepreneurs even entered the local government. For instance, Tao Jianxing, the manager of Chunlan Air Conditioner, a county-owned collective firm, became a member of the local CCP standing committee as a result of the company's excellent performance. Many entrepreneurs used to be, or are currently, local government officials.

Many enterprises in China started as badly performing SOEs or TVEs. It was the entrepreneurs' efforts that allowed these firms to develop. But these efforts were not recognised or reflected in the equity structures of the firms. To get their share the entrepreneurs tried to change the property rights arrangements of the firms, which caused conflicts between government, especially local governments, and enterprises. Some of the entrepreneurs lost their firms when they clashed with the government. Chu Shijian worked as the president of Hongta Tobacco Group, a large SOE in Yunna province, for 17 years, starting in 1979. Under his management, and partly due to the monopoly position given by the government, the firm earned a large amount of profit. In the mid-1990s, the firm earned combined profits and taxes of RMB20 billion ($2.4 billion) each year, or 60 per cent of Yunnan province's fiscal revenue. While the firm earned large amounts of profit, as a manager of SOE, Chu earned, in 1990, a total of RMB1000 ($209.1) per month, including wages and bonuses. Most profits and taxes were handed in to the government. When he learned he would be asked to step down, he secretly embezzled RMB7 million ($0.8 million) and tried to flee from China. He was arrested and sentenced to life in prison in 1997, but was released in 2000. After being released, he and his wife franchised 2,000 Mu of wasteland and produced high-quality oranges (Li 2015).

To protect their business, the entrepreneurs needed to maintain good relationships with the government. Sometimes, they invited former government officials to be advisers or hidden shareholders of their companies. In other cases, they gave financial support to officials' children for their schooling overseas. Because government–enterprise relations have been crucial to the success of many companies, corruption has become a typical way of doing business in China. Various forms of corruption developed, including the improper use of gifts and favours in exchange for personal gain, embezzlement, theft, and fraud.[6]

Macro-Control

Macroeconomic control, or the use of government intervention by the central government to cool down the overheated economy, occurred repeatedly in the history of economic reform in China from the late 1970s. Whenever a new market was created, there would be a follow-up of government control to keep the market in order. After a period of high-speed growth and expansion of money supply, the economy would become overheated; firms would compete for economic resources, which caused inflation. The central government would then intervene, using administrative means to redistribute scarce resources and reduce the scale of production in certain sectors. Vice-Premier Zhu Rongji used strong means to stop the two-digit inflation in 1993 and 1994: limiting monetary supply, eliminating duplicate low-tech industrial projects, cutting interest rates, and many other administrative measures.

The policy usually treated SOEs and private enterprises differently, and local governments usually protected local firms from the central government's interventions. Some industries experienced incredible growth due to expectations of future increases in demand and the protection of local governments. In 2002, steel production increased by 46 per cent, while the production of electrolytic aluminium and cement increased by 93 per cent and 122 per cent, respectively (Wu Xiaobo 2014b). At the end of 2003, the State Council issued documents which required local governments to tighten the control of steel, electrolytic aluminium, and cement production. To overcome resistance from the local governments, the central government sent supervision groups to various regions. Some of the projects were stopped, and some of the firms were closed by governments using administrative force, including the police. Compared with the large SOEs, macro-control often damaged the interests of private firms, because they had less power of negotiation with the government.

The steel plant Tieben, a private enterprise, is an example of how macro-control damaged a private firm. Tieben was operated by Dai Guofang. Dai was born into a farmer's family and started his business by building a factory that recycled ferrous waste iron and steel scraps to make pressured products. In 1996 he set up Jiangsu Tieben Cast Steel Co., Ltd with RMB2 million ($0.2 million) of capital, and by 2000 he had a thousand workers. Considering the large demand for steel, Dai planned to build a bigger steel plant. The plan was supported by the Changzhou city government. To develop their own steel plant had been the dream of the local government and business people in this rapidly growing industrial area. The local government encouraged Dai to increase the scale of his new plant. The capacity was increased to 840,000 tons and the budget was RMB10.6 billion ($1.3 billion) in the final plan. To get the approval of the government, the project was subdivided into seven smaller projects. Tieben became a prime case of making illegal investments, and a large group of supervisors from nine ministries of the central government came to Changzhou. The project was stopped, and Dai was arrested for tax evasion; some of the local government officials were penalised as well (Liu 2015). This illustrates well how macro-control can hurt private companies.

4.3 REFORMS IN SPECIFIC INDUSTRY SECTORS

The economic reform made different levels of progress in different industrial sectors. The regulation of most manufacturing industries was lifted in the 1990s. Government agencies in charge of these industries during the planned period were also reorganised.

Steel and Iron

The steel and iron industry was fully regulated in the planned economy. Investment, production, and product distribution were all controlled by the government. Prices were controlled and all profits were collected by the government.

The Ministry of Metallurgical Industry was removed in 1998, and some of its functions were transferred to the Committee of Development and Reform. The prices of steel products were freed in the 1990s, and by the early 21st century all steel prices were determined by the market. Entry into the market was freed in the 1990s. Investment in the industry was diversified, and some private companies entered into the industry. Reacting to the increase in steel investment, the government tightened the entry requirement in 2004, and all large investments in the industry now have to be approved by the government.

Some of the state-owned steel companies were reorganised in the late 1990s as shareholding corporations. Seventeen of the twenty-one large steel companies (each has over 5 million tons of annual production) were listed on the stock market in 2006. By 2010, most of the steel companies were still state owned. The asset share of the state-owned and state-controlled steel enterprises was about 85 per cent of total assets. The government continues to control most of the shares in the shareholding companies, and heavily intervene in firms' operations.

Automobiles

Before the reform of the late 1970s, the auto industry was regulated and operated by the Bureau of Automobile Industry under the Number 1 Ministry of Machinery.[7] An industry guild was established in 1987, which worked as a government representative. In 1998, the Bureau of Automobile Industry was shut down, and the government supervising function was transferred to the Committee of Development and Reform.

After China joined the WTO in 2001, government supervision was further reformed according to international rules. The price regulation of cars was dropped in the early 21st century, according to WTO rules. The entry restrictions on private companies were relaxed during this period. The regulation of the entry of foreign companies was also relaxed. The ownership structure of the industry was diversified. The big assembly companies have since been listed on the stock market. The parts sector was completely privatised. Fifteen major international automakers have entered the Chinese market. Because of the importance of the industry, the central and local governments are still interfering in the auto industry through industrial policy, financial support, and tax policy.

Despite these reforms, it is still difficult for private firms to enter these key industries. The cases of companies successfully entering the key industries are very limited. China Minsheng Bank (CMSB) was one case of a private bank entering the banking industry.

Social Intermediary Organisations and NGOs

Social intermediary organisations – institutions linking enterprises and the government – and non-governmental organisations (NGOs) developed quickly in the 1990s in China. The social intermediary organisations provide market entities with services including providing information, training, brokerage, legal support, and so on. Most of these institutions are privately owned, though a few of them have a governmental background. An NGO is a not-for-profit organisation that is independent from the state, usually funded by donations or run by volunteers. China had almost none of these institutions during the planned period. Many of them emerged after the reform. According to an estimate, by 2016 there were 7,000 foreign NGOs in China (Buckley 2016). The government tightened its control of these organisations in the early 21st century.

4.4 LOCAL GOVERNMENTS AS ENGINES OF ECONOMIC GROWTH (I)

As a result of the downward shifting of power from the central government, the local governments played a significant role in the economic development in China in the 1990s and the opening years of the 21st century. The local governments showed a great interest in promoting local economic development, which was described as 'local-government enterprise'.

The local governments' key role in China's economic development was a result of institutional designs. The central–local government franchise/subcontracting system and the competition among local officials were the most important institutional drivers behind the role of local governments in economic development.

Franchise/Subcontracting and Local Government Competition

The historical Chinese central–local government relationship was a system of franchise/subcontracting. The administrative power came from the top of the bureaucratic pyramid, the emperor. Power delegation was a step by step process, first from the emperor to provincial officials, then from the provincial officials to the county officials (Zhou 2008). At each lower level of the bureaucratic structure existed a group of government organisations.

Each lower-level organisation had a small structure similar to that of the higher-level government, with departments in charge of different functions. This kind of homogeneous structure that stretched all the way down to the bottom of the society, the villages, has been named a 'cellular' structure (Shue 1988). Similar systems continue to exist everywhere in Chinese society, and even appear in Chinese families or primary school classes. At the village level, before the Communist Revolution in the 20th century, some kind of village autonomy existed, and order was kept by the squires. In this power delegation process, only the lower level of government has the responsibility of implementing the policy.

This franchise/subcontracting system, or financial contracting system, had two major components: (i) the distribution of financial resources to finish the tasks delegated and (ii) the subcontracting of the tasks. In ancient China, when the emperor delegated power to local officials, limited financial resources were attached to this power. The emperor's logic was that power itself meant resources. The local officials were supposed to extract resources from the local people. In ancient China, tax farming was popular, under which the local government handed in a fixed amount of taxes to the central government and kept the remaining amount. With these resources, the local officials were expected to finish the tasks delegated by the higher level of government. The tasks ordered by the central government were focused on results, without detailed descriptions of the methods and procedures to be used to finish the tasks. The local officials had the freedom to choose their approaches to finishing the tasks. The franchise/subcontracting system was a 'management approach without details' that operated on the macro-scale, with no attention to detail. This management system was suited to the outdated transportation and communication technology in ancient China. Under this system, the emperor had the power of appointment and removal of local officials, by which the emperor controlled the whole system, and the officials' promotion depended on their performance. Supervision was the duty of upper-level government. The supervision from the bottom of the society was very weak. If the bureaucratic structure had many levels, most of the officials' work was supervision of the work done by the lower level, except for the lowest level, which was responsible for implementing policy.

Tax System Reform and Task Franchise/Subcontracting

The system of fiscal contracts between central and local governments changed to a 'tax-sharing system' in 1994, which became the framework of the financial system in the government-led market economy in China. Under the planned system from the 1950s to 1970s, China had a highly centralised public finance system, which severely hurt the incentives of the local government and SOEs. The system was changed in 1980 to a financial franchise/subcontracting system, which included two elements: (i) dividing revenue and expenditure between central and local governments and (ii) contracting out the task of raising the revenue that needed to be turned over to the central government to different levels of local governments. Under this contract system, revenue and expenditure were divided between central and local government, based on the revenue and expenditure in the base year. If local revenue was greater than expenditure in the base year, the revenue delivery to the central government would be based on the extra revenue in the base year; if expenditure was greater than revenue in the base year, the central government made lump-sum transfer payments. The local government would keep the extra income after turning over the amount defined by the contract. The financial franchise system transferred some power and resources to the local government, giving more incentives to the local government. After the financial reform in 1994, the government system was formally transformed from a unified system to a multi-unit system, under which the local government became one unit with its own financial interests and had incentives to pursue its own economic activities.

Revenue was unevenly distributed in different localities under the financial franchise system. The system gave local governments benefits and incentives, but also encouraged the local government to build in local protections. The local government built barriers to ban the sales of high-quality products produced in other areas, which resulted in less competition on the local market and provided protection for the fake and shoddy goods produced by the local enterprises. The local governments had incentives to invest in SOEs and to protect their local SOEs. The tax system was too complicated and the local government frequently used tax deduction policies. The financial franchise system and 'apanage management' could not provide inter-provincial public goods, such as nationwide financial services, medical care services, judicial services, and product-quality supervision systems. The financial franchise system dramatically changed the shares of central and local governments in total financial revenue. The share of financial revenue of the central government in gross domestic product (GDP) reduced from 28.4 per cent in 1979 to 12.6 per cent in 1993 (Wu and Ma 2013, p.188). The central government even borrowed money from the local government and never returned the loans. In the early 1990s, Premier Zhu Rongji led a group of officials from the central government to negotiate with the local delegations. This never happened during the planned period. The financial shortage of the central government led to financial reform in 1993.

Tax revenues have been the most important source of fiscal revenue in China since the planned period. There were many types of taxes in the 1990s, but the most important taxes were value-added tax (VAT) and business tax, which were collected from SOEs and other enterprises. Revenues from income tax and property tax were very limited.

In November 1993, the 3rd Plenary Session of the 14th Central Committee of the CCP decided to implement a reform of the public finance and tax system. The contract system was reformed to a tax-sharing system. The target of the reform was to develop a system similar to the fiscal federalism of the United States. Under the tax-sharing system, the tax revenues are divided between the central and local governments, based on the division of the expenditure responsibilities of the central and local governments. The tax-sharing system has several components:

1. The revenue power and expenditure responsibilities are decided based on the characteristics of the financial revenue and expenditure. The responsibilities of the central government include national security, foreign relations, services of the central government agencies, fixed investment managed by the central government, and so on; the local government responsibilities include local police services, fixed investment managed by local governments, city construction, education and health care, and so on.
2. The central–local revenue division was based on taxes. The taxes were divided into three groups: central government taxes (e.g. tariffs, consumption tax, central SOEs' corporate income tax, profits turned over by centrally controlled SOEs, income from banks, railways and other central government-controlled agencies), local government taxes (e.g. business tax, corporate income tax, profit of local enterprises, personal income tax, urban land-use tax, urban construction fees, property tax, vehicle use tax, stamp tax, slaughter tax, agricultural tax, special agricultural product tax, and land value increment tax), and taxes shared by central and local governments (e.g. VAT, resource tax, and securities transactions tax). The revenue from VAT, the largest tax in terms of amount in China, was divided between central and local governments in a ratio of 75 per cent to 25 per cent.
3. The tax revenue was managed by central and local governments separately. A National Tax Bureau was set up and put in charge of collecting central taxes and shared taxes, while the Local Tax Bureau was responsible for local tax collection.[8]
4. The reform simplified categories of taxes. For example, the rate of corporate income tax was unified to 33 per cent and the special treatment to foreign-invested enterprises (FIEs) was removed. Some new taxes,

> such as consumption tax, land value increment tax, and securities transactions tax were added to the tax categories. The central–local revenue share was expected to be 60:40, while the expenditure share was expected to be 40:60. This means that 20 per cent of revenue was collected from rich, developed provinces and transferred to poor areas by the central government.

The forces of resistance to the tax-sharing reform came from the rich provinces, which had a vested interest in the contract system. The central government delegation, led by Premier Zhu Rongji, visited 13 provinces and negotiated heavily with the local governments. The designers of the tax system reform adopted an incremental approach to minimise the income changes of the local governments. The local tax revenues in 1993 were set as the baseline to calculate the level of rebates from the central government. In 1994, central rebates guaranteed that the local revenue would not be lower than that of 1993. For every 1 per cent increase in VAT and consumption tax, 0.3 per cent would go to the local government (CCP News 2016 and Hexun 2008).

The tax-sharing reform ended with the coexistence of a multi-system arrangement and formalised the functions and responsibilities of the central and local governments. The system set up a central government transfer payment programme, which helped to minimise the differences in development among localities. The system also improved the local governments' behaviour in relation to protecting local industries. The establishment of the tax-sharing system ended the annual negotiation between the central and local governments, and therefore eliminated the credible promise problem of the central government. The central government also established its own tax collection agency for the first time in the history of the People's Republic of China.

Besides these advantages, the tax-sharing system created as many problems as it solved. First, the tax-sharing system only divided the revenue between the central and local governments, but did not divide revenue according to responsibilities. This resulted in the imbalance of responsibilities between the central and local governments in the following years. The central government received a larger share of revenue, but did not reduce the responsibilities of the local government. This resulted in the local governments' lack of resources to perform their responsibilities. Second, the central government also ordered the local government to make co-payments for central government projects, which aggravated local governments' financial situations. Third, the new system was only implemented between the central and provincial governments. Under the provincial level, the financial contracting system was still used.

Political Competition and Official Promotion

After the tax-sharing reform of 1993, the pure form of the financial franchise system stopped working. The revenue of the local government depended upon their shares of tax revenue. The local share of some major taxes was small, which resulted in less incentive for the local governments to develop their own industries. The major driver of the local economy shifted to political competition among local governments. Some researchers such as Zhou (2008) called the political competition the championships of the local governments. This section is based on the theory developed by Zhou and others.

Political competition is a performance competition among local government officials. It is correlated with the promotion of local officials, with power to promote officials being held by the central government. The system sets the criteria for officials and monitors the performance of officials. The winners of the competition will be promoted to a higher level position. The competition is based on a promotion procedure within the bureaucratic system. The central government, usually through the Department of Organisation of the CCP, set up the rules of the competition. The performance criteria could be any measurable indicators that affect the behaviour of local officials. This performance standard has been changed from loyalty to the upper-level leaders to economic performance since the 1980s. This was one of the most important changes in the reform. GDP became the most important performance criteria in the 1990s and the first decade of the 21st century. The political competition can be adopted at various bureaucratic levels, from the provincial level to the county level.

This competition gives the local officials large incentives to beat their rivals by developing the economy in their jurisdictions, but at the same time places them under an enormous amount of pressure. It is also beneficial for the top leader to let his or her subordinates compete with each other. The provincial officials will create competition among city or county officials within the province, in order to raise the total output in the province. This chain magnifies the original effect. Therefore, whenever the upper-level government raises a GDP target, the lower-level governments will set up higher targets. For example, when the central government establishes a target of 8 per cent GDP growth, a provincial government may set up a 10 per cent target rate, and the subordinate county government may have a 12 per cent target rate.

Some prerequisites are needed for political competition to be effective:

1. The upper-level government must have a centralised personnel system, which determines the promotion of the lower-level officials.

2. The criteria must be measurable and observable. The performance of the competitors should be separable.
3. The upper-level government (the principal) must make a credible promise to be fair and selfless in supervising the competition and promoting the lower-level officials (the deputy). The principal must not change the rules before the end of the current round of competition.
4. The performance criteria should reflect the effort of the competitor. It must be difficult for the competitors to conspire with each other (Zhou 2008, pp.92–93).

China met most of these requirements. It has a large bureaucratic structure with a centralised government-official promotion system. China has a large number of local governments at each bureaucratic level, most of them with comparable conditions (e.g. similar size and population). Large numbers of local officials compete for a limited number of positions. Economic development has become the most important target for all levels of government since the late 1970s and GDP has become a common measurable indicator in any region in China.

Political competition, combined with a centralised official promotion system, provides strong incentives and creates an incentive-compatible governance structure.[9] Using GDP as the performance criteria, the local officials have great incentives to work hard for economic development, which is exactly the goal of the central government. Usually, an official's incentive towards getting a promotion decreases progressively as his or her age increases. One way to solve this problem in China is reducing the average age of officials by implementing compulsory early retirement. An official exchange system was set up in the 1980s and normalised in the 1990s. A certain percentage of the officials in a locality should be exchanged with those in another locality. Under a challenge system, a new county party secretary or county director cannot accept positions in his or her hometown. These rules and regulations reduce the possibility of cliques and nepotism resulting from long service in the same locality.

Competition creates a restriction on local governments' power. Due to the non-democratic nature of the Chinese political system, the local governments control large amounts of resources without much supervision from the society, while the central government is not capable of fully implementing its duty of supervision. The political competition of local officials also forces the local government to protect property rights and create a good investment environment, working as a temporary substitute for the formal judiciary system. In addition, the competition prevents to some degree the possible capture of the local government by local interest groups.

The political competition among local governments is a temporary institutional setting during the process of economic reform. It cannot replace true financial federalism. Political competition has several defects:

1. The GDP criteria do not necessarily reflect the preference of the local society.
2. Some of the indicators are easy to measure, such as GDP, while others are not. The political competition makes some local officials pursue easy-to-measure targets and ignore indicators that are difficult to measure. Using GDP as a sole measurement of performance makes local officials ignore many other aspects of development such as environmental protection and equality of income. For example, environmental protection was widely ignored in the early stage of reform, since this indicator was not easily measured and was not included in the list of performance criteria.
3. Soft budget constraint problems exist in new forms. Since the local government pursued a target of GDP maximising, the local government will play the role of lender of last resort, which gives the local enterprises incentives to expand their business through extensive borrowing.

4.5 FINANCIAL SYSTEM REFORMS

The financial system is one of the weakest parts of the Chinese economy. It is dominated by a handful of large banks. Even with the entrance of a large number of domestic and foreign banks, this banking system is mainly controlled by the four largest state-owned banks. The small size of two domestic stock markets, the Shanghai Stock Exchange (SHSE) and the Shenzhen Stock Exchange (SZSE), is not comparable to the banking sector, and the markets are highly speculative. The informal financial markets and coalitions among firms, investors, and the local government play an important role in supporting economic development. Urban residents have provided the majority of the bank deposits, while firms are the second most important source of deposits. The majority of bank loans go to SOEs in manufacturing sectors, while most of the 'infrastructure/construction loans' fund government-sponsored projects in the late 1990s and early 21st century (Allen et al. 2008, p.518).

According to Allen et al. (2008), China's banking system is more important than the stock market in terms of its size relative to the stock markets, with its ratio of total bank credits to GDP equalling 1.11 in 2002. However, when considering bank credit issued to the hybrid sector,[10] China's ratio was much lower compared with other countries, suggesting that most of the loans were issued to the state and listed sectors (Allen et al. 2008). At the beginning of the 1990s, capital was still distributed by government instead of the market. The central bank did not have the complete ability to control the economy, and the economy fluctuated dramatically in the early 1990s. The hyperinflation from 1992 to 1994 exposed the efficiency problems in the Chinese financial system.

Starting from the 1990s, the reform strategy was to separate the policy activities and commercial activities of the large state-owned banks and to change the specialised banks into commercial banks. The 3rd Plenary Session of the 14th Central Committee of the CCP decided to start a new wave of reform of the financial system in 1993 (CCP News 2016). The State Council issued the Provisional Regulations on the Administration of Issuance and Trading of Stock in April 1993, which was, in effect, the first law on securities since 1949 (State Council 1993b). The State Council issued a decision on the reform of the financial system in December 1993. According to the decision, the goals of the financial structure reform are (i) to set up a macro-regulatory system of the central bank that implements monetary policy independently under the leadership of the State Council; (ii) to set up a financial organisation system that separates 'policy-based finance' from commercial finance;[11] (iii) to make the state-owned commercial banks the principal part of the banking system and to allow different financial institutions to coexist; and (iv) to build a financial market system which is uniform and open, with orderly competition and strict administration (State Council 1993c).

Banks

The CCP Central Committee decided that the major function of the People's Bank of China is to independently implement monetary policy under the leadership of the State Council. The People's Bank of China became the central bank in the 1980s, separating this function from the operating part, which became one of the four large state-owned banks, the Industrial and Commercial Bank of China. The Monetary Policy Committee of the People's Bank of China, a monetary policy consultant institute set up in 1997 and consisting of department officials and researchers, was responsible for providing opinions on monetary policies. In that respect, the important decisions were made by the State Council. In 1998, to avoid the intervention of local government, 31 provincial-level branches of the People's Bank were dissolved and, following the example of the Federal Reserve in the United States, nine district branches of the central bank were set up.

The financial reform therefore separated commercial banking from policy banking. Three policy banks, the China Development Bank, the Export-Import Bank of China, and the Agricultural Development Bank of China, were set up. The government emphasised that the principles of policy banks were to undertake risks, to operate on a break even basis, and to not compete with commercial banks. These principles guided the policy banks. Since these banks were operating on policy-based projects, they were not active in the market. They would take risks a commercial bank did not want to take, and making profits was not their target.

At the same time, the government redefined the scope and principles of operation for large commercial banks. The four major special banks, the Bank of China, the Agricultural Bank of China, the Industrial and Commercial Bank of China, and China Construction Bank, started commercial operations in the 1980s. But these banks were basically still state-owned special banks, or operating branches of a unified state-owned bank, before the reform in the 1990s, and needed further reforms. A Commercial Bank Law was passed and implemented in 1995 (National People's Congress 1995a). This defined the type of business through which a commercial bank could operate and prescribed that a commercial bank should have a status of 'independent legal person', operate independently and free from any interference by 'units' and individuals, undertake its own risks, assume sole responsibility for its own profits or losses, and be self-restrained. A bank should undertake civil legal liabilities independently with its status as a legal person. A commercial bank should accept the supervision and administration of the People's Bank of China. A state-owned commercial bank should centralise its management, exercising a financial system of unified accounting and fund control. A branch of a commercial bank is not a legal person and has no independent authority for investing. The head office of a state-owned commercial bank has full responsibility for its asset liquidity and solvency. The reform broke the restriction on the fields of operations of special banks that became commercial banks, and they were allowed to operate with other banks in multiple fields. A segregated operation principle was adopted, under which a commercial bank is not allowed to expand its operations to non-financial areas. According to the law, a commercial bank should decide the interest rate of loans in accordance with the upper and lower limits of loan interest set by the People's Bank of China, its capital sufficiency rate[12] should be no less than 8 per cent, and the ratio between the balance of loans and that of deposits should not exceed 75 per cent.

As a result of economic reform that started in 1978, urban credit cooperatives also developed in the late 1970s and 1980s. By the end of 1998, 3,240 urban credit cooperatives existed nationwide, with total assets of RMB267 billion ($32.2 billion). These credit cooperatives were active in supporting local development, but were also risky due to the low quality of their management and personnel. To minimise the risks, the State Council decided to restructure them into urban commercial banks through mergers. Urban commercial banks were supposed to serve local economies and small and medium-sized enterprises. In February 1995, the first urban commercial bank, the Urban Cooperative Bank of Shenzhen, was established. By the end of 1998, 70 urban cooperative banks existed. All urban cooperative banks changed their name to 'urban commercial banks' in 1998.

China's state-owned banking sector, especially the four largest state-owned banks, faced serious performance problems with their loans (hereafter identified as NPLs: non-performing loans) in the 1990s and the beginning of the 21st century, due to poor lending decisions made in relation to SOEs. The four largest commercial banks had serious capital shortages and were technically in a state of bankruptcy. The NPLs reached $269.3 billion in 2000, or 22.5 per cent of GDP (Allen et al. 2008, p.523). This figure does not include the bad loans that had been transferred to four state-owned asset management companies (Li et al. 2009, p.145). The Ministry of Finance issued RMB270 billion ($32.6 billion) of special national bonds to supplement the capital of the four state-owned commercial banks. The capital sufficiency rate of the four largest banks reached 8 per cent after this injection of capital, according to the calculation made at the time. This injection of capital did not solve the problem fundamentally. RMB1.4 trillion ($0.2 trillion) in NPLs of the four banks were stripped out in 1999. Four asset management companies were set up by the State Council to take over the bad loans of the four major state-owned banks. These asset management companies finished the task of disposing of non-performing assets in 2006.

Foreign banks entered more cities and more business areas in the 1990s. The State Council published a Regulation on the Administration of Foreign Funded Financial Institutions in 1994, the first regulation on foreign banks after the economic reform (State Council 1994). The regulation listed the standards of market entry and supervision of foreign banks. Foreign banks were allowed to set up offices in all Chinese cities. The minimum registered capital for a foreign bank was RMB200 million ($23.2 million), of which the paid-up capital should not be lower than 50 per cent. The head office of a foreign bank branch should allocate a working capital of no less than RMB100 million ($11.6 million) to its branches. The business activities of a foreign bank, a foreign bank branch, or an equity joint-venture bank included foreign currency deposit, deposit-taking, lending or bill discounting, foreign exchange investment, import and export settlement, foreign currency dealing and brokerage, exchange of foreign currencies and bills, and foreign currency credit card payment. The deposit and lending rate of a foreign-invested bank was determined by itself in accordance with the relevant rules and regulations of the People's Bank of China. A foreign bank was required to deposit reserves free of interest with a local branch of the People's Bank of China, with a reserve ratio determined by the People's Bank of China. The total assets of a foreign bank should not exceed 20 times the sum of its paid-up capital plus reserves. The loans granted to an enterprise by a foreign bank should not exceed 30 per cent of the sum of its paid-up capital plus reserves. The fixed assets maintained by a foreign bank should not exceed 40 per cent of the sum of its paid-up capital plus reserves. These regulations guarantee the safety of the loans and set restrictions on the size of fixed assets of a foreign bank. In 1996, the People's Bank of China issued interim measures for the operation of RMB business by foreign-funded financial institutions in Pudong, Shanghai (People's Bank of China 1996a), under which RMB business to FIEs and foreigners was opened up to foreign banks. After that, the same kind of business was opened up to foreign banks in Shenzhen. Foreign banks were also allowed to enter the inter-bank loan market to solve the People's Bank's RMB shortage problem.

Non-Banking Financial Institutions

The insurance sectors in China experienced rapid development in the 1990s. In June 1995, the National Congress published the Insurance Law of the People's Republic of China (National People's Congress 1995b). The People's Bank of China issued a number of regulations between 1996 and 1998. The China Insurance Regulatory Commission (CIRC), a government institute directly under the State Council in charge of the supervision of the insurance market, was set up in November 1998. A supervision system in the insurance sector was formed. The insurance law confirmed the principle of the separated management of property insurance and life insurance. Starting from 1995, the insurance companies implemented a reform of separating property insurance and life insurance operations. The China People's Insurance (Group) Company (PICC) was established in 1996 with three subsidiaries: PICC Property and Casualty Insurance Company, PICC Life Insurance Company, and PICC Reinsurance Company of China. The three subsidiaries changed their names to People's Insurance Company of China, China Life Insurance Company Limited, and China Reinsurance Company. China Pacific Insurance Company, Ping An Insurance Company, and other large shareholding insurance companies completed the management segregation reform and set up subsidiaries in accordance with the regulation. At the beginning of the first decade of the 21st century, a competitive insurance market with multiple companies had thus taken shape, with the state-owned and shareholding insurance companies remaining dominant. By the end of 2001, the total number of insurance companies reached 52, including 5 solely state-owned companies, 15 shareholding companies, 19 joint-venture companies, and 13 foreign companies (Li et al. 2009, p.174). A policy insurance company, China Export & Credit Insurance Corporation, was set up in 2001 to support foreign trade and investment. Compared with other countries, China's insurance market was still significantly smaller in 2004 in terms of total assets managed by insurance companies as a percentage of GDP. The insurance industry was also undersized compared with China's banking industry (Allen et al. 2008, p.532).

Three large bank-based securities companies, Hua Xia, Guo Tai, and Southern Securities were also set up in the early 1990s. These securities companies expanded their businesses and networks to the whole country. This process created a large number of illegal operations and NPLs. In 1996, the People's Bank of China implemented a policy of segmenting banking, securities, and insurance operations. The National People's Congress passed the Securities Law of the People's Republic of China in 1998 (National People's Congress 1998). The State Council delegated the responsibility for supervision to the China Securities Regulatory Commission (CSRC) in 1998. To reduce the illegal operations, the CSRC started to rectify the problems in the securities sector at the beginning of the new century by checking the operations of the securities companies, punishing illegal corporations, and closing some of the illegally operated companies.

The development of trust companies, which were actually conducting mixed banking operations, was similarly accompanied with government regulatory activities. In 1995, 146 trust companies were shut down by the regulatory agency; 40 others survived including 4 solely state-owned security companies. The financial leasing companies experienced a rapid growth, with many illegal operations sprouting up. The government finally issued a regulation on financial leasing companies, the Measures for the Administration of Financial Leasing Companies, in 2000 and ended the lawlessness (People's Bank of China 2000).

Stock Exchanges

During the planned period, all shareholding companies were reorganised into public–private partnerships or SOEs. In 1978, some of the TVEs first became shareholding companies. This was followed by transfers of small

SOEs and collective enterprises in urban areas to shareholding companies. Redtory Fushun, in Liaoning province, issued 2.8 million shares of stock to its employees in 1980 with the help of the Fushun branch of the People's Bank. Shanghai Audio Equipment Factory initiated the establishment of Shanghai Feile Audio Company in 1984 and issued stocks to the public, raising a total amount of RMB400,000 ($172,414.0). Facing these new economic activities, local governments issued temporary regulations on shareholding companies and stock issuance.

As the demand for stock trading increased, over-the-counter trading was developed by investors in the 1980s. Shenyang Investment Trust Company first started its securities brokerage business in 1986. The Jing'an securities business department of the Shanghai Investment Trust Company, a subordinate of the Industrial and Commercial Bank of China, provided over-the-counter trading services, selling stocks of two companies in 1986.

A cornerstone event in China's finance history happened at the beginning of the 1990s. Approved by the central government, two stock exchanges, the Shanghai Stock Exchange (SHSE) and the Shenzhen Stock Exchange (SZSE), were set up in 1990 and 1991, respectively, and grew rapidly in the 1990s. In 1991 and 1992, the SHSE issued 41 stocks and the SZSE 33 stocks, raising RMB1.84 billion ($0.3 billion) and RMB1.78 billion ($0.3 billion), respectively. At the beginning, the two exchanges only dealt with the transactions of local companies' stocks. In 1993, they started to deal with the stocks of companies nationwide. Following Shanghai and Shenzhen, the local governments in some big cities (e.g. Tianjin, Wuhan, and Shenyang) set up their own stock exchanges. These exchanges were jointly set up by local branches of the People's Bank, local governments, securities companies, and enterprises. The supervision agency soon closed these exchanges, trying to control the risks, and all stocks were moved to the SHSE and the SZSE.

Before 1992, all financial supervision was implemented by the People's Bank of China. The China Securities Regulatory Commission (CSRC)[13] was established in October 1992, which was the representative of the State Council in charge of the securities market. The State Council delegated the responsibility of supervision over the securities market in China to the CSRC in 1998. The CSRC implemented strict regulation on China's stock market. Stock issuance was placed under an approval system, with a quota system and an administrative approval system. Within the quota, stocks were recommended by the local government and a supervisory body of enterprises. To be listed on the stock market, a company has to get recommendations from the local government and a government branch that regulates the industry. The stock must meet the requirement of capital and performance, and be consistent with the national industrial policy. The issuance quota was controlled each year by the central government and was distributed to central government departments and local governments. During this period, stock issuing was actually subject to two stages of approval: by the local government and by the CSRC. The issuing price was set up by the CSRC, based on profit after tax and a fixed price-to-earnings ratio (P/E ratio).

To attract foreign investment, the Shanghai and Shenzhen branches of the People's Bank established regulations on the issuance of B shares in 1991. The first B shares, Shanghai Zhenkong, were issued in 1991, on the SHSE. B shares were RMB-denominated special stocks, issued by Chinese companies, and traded by foreign investors. H shares were issued later in the 1990s on the Hong Kong Stock Exchange. B shares and H shares were subject to many administrative restrictions in terms of price range and investors' qualifications. The State Council issued the Regulations on Domestic Listing of Foreign-Oriented Stocks by Share-Holding Companies in 1995 (State Council 1995), the first national regulation on B shares, and the Detailed Rules for the Implementation of the Listing of Foreign Shares of Co. Ltd in 1996 (State Council 1996). The two documents regulated the issuance, trading, information disclosure, and auditing of B shares. Starting from 1999, the CSRC adopted additional measures to promote the B share market. The ownership restriction of B share-issuance companies and pre-election were abolished in 1999 to promote more companies to issue B shares. 'A+B' shares were allowed to be issued, and qualified B share companies were allowed to issue A shares. After 1 June 2001, domestic residents were allowed to trade B share stocks, using their foreign exchange already deposited in China. These policy changes made domestic residents the dominant group of investors of B shares. Following the expansion of H shares, which replaced many functions of the B shares, at the turn of the century the B share market shrank. B shares were traded in China mainly by foreign investors, while the H shares were traded in Hong Kong by foreign investors. It was much easier for foreign investors to trade H shares in Hong Kong.

A large number of stock exchanges, without the approval of the CSRC, existed nationwide in the 1990s. During the Asian financial crisis, to reduce risk, the CSRC closed 23 local stock exchanges in 1998. At that time, 41 illegal stock exchanges existed, 520 companies were traded at these exchanges, and these exchanges attracted 3.4 million investors and had a market value of RMB3 billion ($0.4 billion, Li et al. 2009, p.132).

Bond Markets

The central government resumed the issuance of Treasury bonds in 1981 after a prolonged break during the Cultural Revolution. The interest rate was lower than the deposit rate in the banks and the trade of treasury bonds was prohibited initially. The People's Bank of China and the Ministry of Finance allowed the trade of treasury bonds in the late 1980s. An experiment of Treasury bond trading was held in seven large cities, including Shenzhen, Guangzhou, and Wuhan, in 1988. Treasury bonds were traded over-the-counter, in service bureaus and securities companies. The Security Trading Automated Quotations (STAQ) system started formal operations in 1991, and a group of non-banking financial institutions was set up in the early 1990s. The Treasury bond exchange was opened to the public in 1993. In 1994, the Ministry of Finance issued a six-month short-term treasury bill and a book-entry treasury bond for the first time, to promote the dematerialisation of bond issuance. In 1996, the national bond issuing mode started the transition from underwriting by subcontractors to open tendering. More types of bonds were issued by the Ministry of Finance, including three-month and six-month short-term bills and seven-year, nine-year, and ten-year long-term bonds. The Ministry of Finance also issued bonds in international markets. In 1997, more regulations on individuals investing national bonds, bond repurchasing, and risk control were published, and the inter-bank bond market started operation. In 2000, all Treasury bonds traded in inter-bank bond markets were traded through open tendering, most of them under 'Dutch' bidding.

Besides national debt, other financial debt included policy financial bonds and bonds issued by various financial institutions in China. Three policy banks – China Development Bank, the Export-Import Bank of China, and Agricultural Development Bank of China – were set up in the 1990s and issued different kinds of bonds in the inter-bank bond markets. The bonds issued by China Development Bank focused on infrastructure construction, basic industry development, and pillar industry development. They were initially issued through commercial banks, then issued in the inter-bank bond market through open tender. Other policy banks also carried out experiments in issuing bonds in the open market.

Bonds issued by financial institutions included bank bonds and non-bank bonds. The former included subordinated bonds and ordinary bonds. Commercial banks issued bonds for special loans as early as 1985. Non-bank bonds consisted of bonds issued by insurance companies, securities companies, and asset management companies. The Ministry of Finance also issued RMB-denominated bonds sold by a non-Chinese issuer inside China, which were called 'Panda Bonds'.

Enterprise bonds were issued by enterprises for different purposes as early as the 1980s, with various risks. The government regulated the enterprises' bond issuing in the 1990s. The State Council issued a regulation on corporate bonds in August 1993 (State Council 1993a), creating provisions for the issuer's scale of operation, accounting standards, and solvency, and its use of funds. The government therefore intensified the supervision on enterprise bonds. The securities law passed by the National People's Congress in 1998 required the issuance of enterprise bonds to be approved by authorised departments of the State Council, and the trading in the market to be approved by the CSRC (National People's Congress 1998). In reality, the quota was approved by the State Planning Committee, the issuance was approved by the People's Bank of China, and the market trading was approved by the CSRC. Real name book-entry distribution became the major mode of bond issuance in the late 1990s.

Money Market

China's money market started as early as the 1980s, when the specialised banks were split from the unified banking system, including the inter-bank borrowing market and bond repo market.[14]

The inter-bank money market in China was originally started by private financial institutions in the eastern coastal areas. The central bank allowed the commercial banks to borrow money from each other in 1984, and all provinces except Tibet set up their inter-bank money market in 1987. The amount of funds financed through the inter-bank money market increased dramatically in the early 1990s. The market was used as a tool by financial institutions to bypass the supervision of the government and to invest in long-term projects. Due to the large demand for funds, interest rates were often higher than those set by the central bank. A large amount of borrowed funds went into the real-estate market. The central bank therefore introduced strict supervision over this market. A national inter-bank money market was established in 1996. The market included two levels. The first level consisted of the head offices of commercial banks and a provincial financial centre led by the provincial office of the People's Bank. The second level was led by the provincial finance centre and included commercial bank branches and non-banking institutions. Members of the first level traded directly in the market, while the members of the second level traded locally through the local financing centre.

The bond repo market was initially developed by financial institutions, firms, and individual investors. At the beginning of the 1990s, it was difficult to find buyers for Treasury bonds because the bonds could not be resold in the market. To solve this problem, the STAQ system started a national debt repurchase operation in 1991. The bond repo operation was introduced at the Wuhan securities exchange in 1992 and at the SHSE in 1993. Repo became an emergency method of financing and the scale of repo increased in 1993. Trading of repo in stock exchanges and exchange centres amounted to more than RMB400 billion ($47.9 billion) in 1995 (Li et al. 2009, p.249). The boom of the market revealed problems, such as the lower collateral for loans than required by the central bank, non-member trading, and funds from repo being used in the stock market or housing market. Over-the-counter trading was common countrywide. To reduce these illegal behaviours, the People's Bank cleaned up the repo market in 1995. Bond repos increased dramatically in 1996 and 1997.

In the early 1990s, the bond repo was traded in the SHSE and the SZSE, local securities exchange centres, and directly between traders. The monetary authority ordered all state-owned commercial banks and other commercial banks and non-banking financial institutions that attended the first level of the inter-bank money market to retreat from the SHSE and the SZSE, to form a closed inter-bank bond repo market in 1997. In 1997, the China Foreign Exchange Trading Centre and the National Inter-Bank Lending Centre introduced spot trading and collateral repo. The bonds traded included government bonds, central bank bonds, financial bonds, and so on, which were approved by the People's Bank to be used in transactions in the national inter-bank bond market. The term of repurchase includes 1 day, 7 days, 14 days, 21 days, 1 month, 2 months, 3 months, 4 months, 6 months, 9 months, and 1 year. From 2000, trust companies, financial companies, insurance companies, and mutual funds were allowed to enter the inter-bank repo market, and the amount of trading soared.

In a market economy, the bond repo market has multiple functions. Financial companies use the repo market to keep the liquidity, profitability, and safety of their financial assets, while the central bank uses the repo market as a place for its financial policy operations. However, in the early years of the development of the repo market in China, the financial companies tried to use it to raise funds for long-term purposes by bypassing the central bank's regulation. As the central bank's regulation improved and the financial companies' behaviour normalised, the function of the repo market improved. Since 1998, the term of borrowing has become shorter, most being within seven days, and the inter-bank market and repo market have become mechanisms of liquidity management. This was an indicator which showed that the function of the repo market had improved, and that financial institutions used it more for maximising the liquidity of their assets in the short run rather than for long-run fund-raising.

The Underground Financial Sector

Now let us switch topics from formal financial institutions to underground financial institutions, which are an important part of China's financial institutions. Because of the financial needs of small private enterprises, large funds cumulated in the hands of residents, and the strict regulations on the domestic and international flow of funds, the underground financial institutions experienced a dramatic development in China during the years of economic reform from 1978 to the 2010s. According to a survey in 2003 (Li 2006), which covers 20 provinces and 82 cities and counties, the scale of China's underground financial sector ranged between RMB740 to 830 billion ($89.4 to 100.3 billion) in 2003, which was about 28 per cent of the formal financial sector. Farmers' loans from the informal financial sector were 56 per cent of the total loans in 15 provinces.

The underground banks used a large number of small firms, masquerading as clothing stores and fruit shops, to deal in currency exchange. These small underground currency exchanges usually had one or two employees in a small office with a telephone and a calculator. They usually only dealt with regular customers. New customers needed to be introduced by a regular customer. As more and more people started using internet banking, underground banks also began to use internet banking and credit cards more frequently to launder money domestically and internationally.

Underground banking has infiltrated many fields, causing enormous problems and risks. A large amount of hot money entered the housing market through underground banks. The return in the housing market was much higher than that in most other countries in the world, due to the increasing housing prices. One of the reasons for high housing prices is the large amount of hot money from other countries in the world, which entered China's housing market through underground banks and pushed up prices in large cities.

The underground banks introduced hot money[15] into China through illegal activities. When dealing in international trade, some illegal operations cheated by reporting a higher export price and lower import price in order to introduce hot money into China. Others moved money into China under the name of fake trade credits or fake trade contracts. The Chinese government implemented strict foreign exchange control for several decades, but huge amounts of foreign exchange entered China through underground banks, which are illegal banks operating under a forged sign. These underground banks were located in many places in China, especially in eastern coastal areas. A large amount of money was brought into China by individuals carrying cash across the border between Hong Kong and Shenzhen.

Hot money entering into and leaving the stock market was one of the causes of the fluctuation of the stock market in China in the first decade of the 21st century. Investors outside of China moved funds into China through underground banks and used these funds in the stock market to control prices. Large amounts of money moved into or out of China through these banks. The underground banks also moved funds from China to Hong Kong's stock market to seek gains.

Since the formal investment objectives are limited, the funds cumulated in the hands of residents and institutions that entered commodity markets one after another. Coal, cotton, electricity, and even garlic and beans, became speculation objects. Underground banks have played an important role in raising large amounts of funds for speculation.

CASE 4.1: SPECULATIONS BY WENZHOU INVESTORS

People in Wenzhou have a tradition of raising funds from relatives and friends for speculation. Groups of property speculators from Wenzhou were active in housing, coal, garlic, and many other markets.

Groups of real-estate speculators from Wenzhou were common in China in the early 21st century. The first group of Wenzhou investors, which consisted of 157 members, went to Shanghai, the largest city in China, on 18 August 2001. The group bought more than 100 housing units, worth RMB50 million ($6.0 million), in three days. In the next several years, Wenzhou investors threw RMB200 billion ($24.2 billion) into the real-estate market, including RMB100 billion ($12.1 billion) in Beijing and Shanghai. The groups used group purchasing to increase their power of negotiation. The housing developers used phoney sales to raise the price for forward delivery housing, and then the Wenzhou investors retreated from the market and got their money back. These wash sales increased the housing prices and attracted other investors into the market. This kind of activity was not clearly defined as a crime and no specialised supervision agency was in charge of it in China during that period.

When the market was stagnant, the underground banks retreated rapidly, and this had a dramatic impact on the market. The government introduced housing control policies later, and the group of Wenzhou investors retreated from the housing markets in the largest cities. Some of the Wenzhou investors moved their investment into the housing markets in medium-sized cities, while others looked for opportunities in housing markets outside of China.

The Structure of the Financial System

By the 1990s, China had built a financial system which met the preliminary requirement for the operation of a market economy. The system was built mainly by the central government, and supported by local governments and individual investors. The system has been dominated by the banks and supplemented by non-banking institutions and capital markets.

Table 4.1 shows that during the 1980s and 1990s, residents' deposits became the most important source of banks' funds, and government funds

Table 4.1 Structure of deposits and shares of state-owned banks in deposits and loans, %

Year	Deposits		Shares of state-owned banks	
	Enterprises	Residents in urban and rural areas	Deposits	Loans
1980	33.3	16.7	93.7	95.3
1985	38.1	23.2	82.7	85.5
1993	29.0	51.3	78.4	80.3

Source: Li et al. (2009, p.134).

Table 4.2 Financial instruments, China, RMB billion ($ billion)

Year	Deposits	Loans	Treasury bonds	Corporate bonds	Stock
1980	169.0 (99.1)	247.8 (145.3)			
1990	1,394.3 (291.5)	1,751.1 (366.1)			
1993	2,964.6 (514.5)	3,295.6 (572.0)	31.5 (5.5)	23.6 (4.1)	27.6 (4.8)

Note: Data for deposits and loans are amount of stock, while others are amount of new issuance.

Source: Li et al. (2009, p.133).

decreased. This was the result of the increase in personal income and the decrease of the financial resources controlled by the government since the beginning of the economic reform.

Table 4.2 shows that loans exceeded deposits in all three years shown in the table. Actually, from 1952 to 1993, loans exceeded deposits in China's entire banking system. During the planned period, this phenomenon was the result of the SOEs' soft budget constraints. After the beginning of the economic reform, the local governments had incentives to expand fixed investments. During this period, local governments had a large influence on the lower levels of the state-owned banks, and forced the local branches of these banks to provide loans for local development. This was the main reason why loans always exceeded deposits even during the early period of the reform.

At the same time, the banking system, as the main component of the financial system, was dominated by state-owned banks. This is because the financial system was completely controlled by the government before the reform, especially the central government, and the reform in this sector was designed and implemented by the government.

The 1997 financial crisis affected many Asian countries. The RMB had been pegged to the US dollar and there was speculation that China would soon be forced to devalue its currency to protect the competitiveness of its exports. However, that did not happen. While China was relatively unaffected by the crisis compared to some Southeast Asian countries, GDP growth slowed sharply in 1998 and 1999, calling attention to structural problems within China's economy. The government was convinced of the need to resolve the issues of its enormous financial weaknesses, such as having too many NPLs within its banking system.

4.6 FURTHER OPENING UP OF FOREIGN TRADE AND FOREIGN INVESTMENT

Further reforms in the foreign trade system were carried out in the 1990s. The state mandatory planning in foreign trade was replaced by a guidance plan in 1994. Quota control and licence approval were introduced for major export products. The Foreign Trade Law of China was implemented in 1994 (National People's Congress 1994).

Exports and imports kept increasing during the 1990s, as a result of opening up. China's exports increased from $62.1 billion in 1990 to $249.2 billion in 2000, while imports increased from $53.4 billion in 1990 to $225.1 billion in 2000 (National Bureau of Statistics 2015, Table 11.2). The trade deficits in the 1980s turned to trade surpluses in most years in the 1990s. The structure of commodity exports changed during the 1990s, and more manufacturing goods and equipment were exported. The share of manufacturing goods in total commodity export increased to 50.23 per cent in 2000 from 47.88 per cent in 1990 (Jiang and Wang 2008). The share of primary goods decreased during the same period. There was a persistent and growing trade surplus with the United States.

Foreign investment in China increased significantly in the 1990s. The amount of foreign investment actually utilised increased to $59.4 billion in 2000 from $10.3 billion in 1990, including actually utilised direct foreign investment of $40.7 billion in 2000, up from $3.5 billion in 1990. Foreign direct investment (FDI) by large multinational companies increased in the 1990s. By the end of 1997, 360 Fortune 500 companies had invested in China. Of the total actually utilised FDI in 1997, 9.56 per cent came from Japan, 7.16 per cent from the United States, and 9.22 per cent from the European Union (Jiang 2008, p.72). Most of the FDI in China was in the manufacturing sector. A large processing manufacturing and trade sector has been built in China through its economic development. The 1997 Asian financial crisis slowed down the growth in foreign trade and investment for a while, but rapid growth resumed soon after the crisis.

Significant changes in the foreign currency system and taxation of foreign firms took place in the mid-1990s. The National People's Congress published a law on foreign trade in May 1994, defining the foreign trade dealers, the restrictions on trade, and the responsibility of the government (National People's Congress 1994). The government tried to control the structure of foreign investment by publishing a revised 'List of Industries, Products and Techniques Currently Encouraged by the State' (State Planning Commission 1998) and 'Category of Industries Guidelines for Foreign Investment'[16] (State Planning Commission et al. 1997). During this period, the Chinese government continued negotiations with the General Agreement on Tariffs and Trade (GATT) and the WTO. During these negotiations, China agreed to undertake a series of important commitments to open up and liberalise its regime in order to better integrate into the world economy. The Chinese government agreed to lower its average tariff levels and to modify its import registration system according to WTO regulation. China also agreed to relax restrictions on foreign investment including requirements of technology transfer to local partners.

Exchange Rate System

Before the economic reform, the Chinese government maintained an overvalued exchange rate to subsidise the imports of capital goods, which created an excess demand for foreign exchange and necessitated a tight control of foreign currency. In the course of reform, the government relaxed the restrictions and lowered the exchange rate to give firms more incentives to export. The export firms were allowed to retain part of their foreign exchange earnings and to trade them in the foreign exchange market.

Effective from January 1994, China abolished the dual exchange rate system and effectively devalued its currency, Renminbi or RMB, to RMB8.7 per dollar. The dual exchange system, or the coexistence of an official rate and a market rate in the foreign exchange swap market, was replaced by a unified managed floating exchange rate system. A unified inter-bank foreign exchange market was set up. The official exchange rate is announced by the People's Bank every working day, based on the supply and demand in the inter-bank foreign exchange market. Firms' foreign exchange retention was abolished and an exchange settlement system was set up. Under the system, any domestic firm could not keep the foreign currency they earned through selling goods to foreign countries. They have to sell the foreign currency to banks and receive RMB in return. The foreign currency was then sold by the banks in the foreign exchange market, which became the basis of the official exchange rate. The People's Bank published provisions on the sale and payment of foreign exchange settlement, including foreign-invested firms into the exchange settlement system and promising to abolish the remaining restrictions (People's Bank of China 1996c). In December 1996, the Chinese government announced that RMB convertible under current account had been realised (Xiao and Sui 2011, p.265).

The foreign exchange certificate, which foreigners used in China as a currency in lieu of the RMB, was removed from circulation and replaced by the RMB. Effective from 1996, China relaxed foreign exchange control over current account terms. The RMB was convertible for normal business transactions, including payments and receipts for goods and services purchased or sold internationally. But capital account items, including direct investments, loans and debts, and securities investments, were still under government control. The People's Bank issued an Interim Measures for the Administration of the Pilot Operation of RMB Business by Foreign Funded Financial Institutes at Pudong District, Shanghai in December 1996, allowing approved foreign financial institutes to carry out RMB deposit, lending, and other business within the district (People's Bank of China 1996a). The People's Bank issued regulations on the foreign exchange system in the same year (People's Bank of China 1996b), providing that all foreign exchange receipts of domestic entities for current account and capital account transactions shall be repatriated and shall not be deposited abroad. The regulation also relaxed the control of foreign currency held by individuals. According to the regulation, an individual's foreign exchange savings deposit is placed with banks on a voluntary basis, can be withdrawn freely and bears interest, and the purchase of foreign exchange for personal travel abroad and other miscellaneous expenses is granted within the specified limit. The State Administration of Foreign Exchange issued a regulation on the private exchange of foreign exchange in May 1996, abolishing some of the restrictions on individual use of foreign exchange and raising the thresholds of individual purchase of foreign exchange (State Administration of Foreign Exchange 1996).

Investment Incentives

To encourage exports, the Chinese government formulated and implemented a series of policies in the 1990s, of which the export tax rebate is one of the most important. The export tax rebate is not considered by the

WTO as a 'subsidy' so long as the tax rebate does not exceed the amount of tax paid to domestic tax authorities.

China began to implement its export tax rebate policy in April 1985 as a way of enhancing the country's competitiveness in foreign markets by eliminating double taxation[17] on exported goods (Dezan Shira & Associates 2013). The export tax rebate refers to the refund of tax on export products in the actual payment of the product tax, VAT, business tax, and special consumption tax. In 1988, the 'full refund' principle was established. By 1991, the export subsidy, the amount above the export rebate, was abolished. In 1994, the government implemented a major tax system reform, by abolishing the industrial and commercial standard tax (*gong shang tong yi shui*) and introducing a new value-added tax (VAT), with a basic rate of 17 per cent. For export goods, the VAT rate was zero. The export tax rebate increased drastically after the introduction of the VAT due to tax fraud. In 1994 alone, the rebate increased by 150 per cent, which greatly exceeded the export growth. Some firms claimed rebates for goods that were never exported. The central government's export tax rebate obligation was therefore too large to fulfil. Consequently, in 1995 and 1996 the government lacked the revenue to cover rebate taxes and twice reduced the export tax rebate rate to avoid the revenue loss due to the firms' cheating behaviour. The government raised the rebate in 1998 to increase firms' incentive to export during the Asian financial crisis in 1998.

The tax treatments of foreigners and foreign-invested firms were not regulated before the 1980s. As a large number of foreigners and foreign-invested firms entered China, their tax treatments needed to be regulated. The National People's Congress passed the Law on Individual Income Tax in 1980 which applied to foreigners (National People's Congress 1980). The Law on Income Tax for Foreign Invested Firms was passed in 1991 (National People's Congress 1991).

As a result of opening up, China significantly reduced import tariffs in the 1990s. At the end of 1992, the Chinese government cut the import tariff rates for a wide range of commodities, within 3,000 duty catalogues, resulting in a tariff reduction of 7.3 percentage points. At the end of 1993, the tariff was further reduced by 8.8 percentage points. The State Council announced in December 1995 that, starting from 1 April 1996, the tariff rate would be reduced to 23 per cent (Jiang 2008, pp.293–294).

Foreign Investment and Foreign Firms

FDI inflows resumed in the early 1990s, after the brief slowdown due to the Tiananmen incident, and grew thereafter. The FDI inflows diversified as major industrial countries increased their FDIs into China, while investment from Hong Kong and Taiwan still played an important role. Investment in wholly owned FIEs grew faster than that for equity joint ventures.

China built a large processing manufacturing and trade sector, importing raw materials and parts from developed countries and exporting products to major world markets. The exports of the processing trade made up a large share of China's total exports. Three manufacturing centres, the Bohai Rim, the Yangtze River Delta, and the Pearl River Delta, which are home to 35 per cent of China's population, produced over 50 per cent of GDP and over 80 per cent of exports in the 1990s (Wu Xiaobo 2014b, p.250).

The government introduced various economic incentives to attract foreign investments at this stage of the opening up. A number of laws governing economic activities and foreign investments were promulgated, including the Corporation Law, the Foreign Banking Law, the Arbitration Law, and the Securities Law. New accounting standards, introduced by the Ministry of Finance, were implemented in July 1993. The standards, with many similarities to International Accounting Standards, provided a much better framework for the preparation of meaningful financial information needed in a market economy.

FIEs enjoy a number of advantages compared to the local firms. FIEs may import their own raw materials through their own channels without using the state-owned import–export companies. FIEs may retain foreign currency earned from their exports and use the currency for their own purchases. More advantages are available in the free trade zones. Goods imported into the zone from abroad are exempt from customs duties. Products produced in a free trade zone are exempt from customs duty when sold inside the zone or shipped outside of China.

In the 1990s, tax incentives were given to FIEs, including reduced income tax rates and tax exemption and reduction periods. The standard income tax rate payable by FIEs was 30 per cent. A reduced rate of 15 per cent was applied if (i) the FIE was set up in an special economic zone and was engaged in production-oriented activities; or (ii) the FIE was established in an open coastal economic zone, provided that the enterprise was engaged in a technology-intensive project, a project with foreign investment of at least $30 million, or a project in energy, transportation, or harbour construction; or (iii) the FIE was established in a national high- and new-technology industry development zone. FIEs that were scheduled to operate for at least ten years and were engaged in production-oriented activities were entitled to an exemption from income tax for two years, followed by a 50 per cent reduction in the next three years, with some exceptions. A foreign investor that directly reinvested its share of profits derived from an FIE might obtain a refund of 40 per cent of the tax already paid by the FIE on the reinvested amount, subject to the approval of the tax authority. The profits must be reinvested for at least five years. Provincial governments and local governments might waive or reduce the local income tax payable by FIEs.

Setting up a firm in China is a complex process. Foreign investors must obtain multi-department government approvals, including the approval of the Ministry of Foreign Trade and Economic Cooperation (MOFTEC) and that of the ministry responsible for supervising the industry to which the project belongs. Most foreign firms were required to form a joint venture with a local Chinese firm, usually a SOE, in the early years of China's opening up. The requirement for a Sino-foreign joint venture includes two stages: (i) after the foreign investor and the Chinese party have signed a letter of intent, the Chinese party must bring the letter to apply to the relevant local government authorities for permission to continue with the negotiations; (ii) once the two parties have drawn up a contract, the documents must be submitted to the MOFTEC for approval. The joint-venture contract describes the terms of the joint venture agreed by the participants, including the name and address of the joint venture, the scope and scale of the business, the amount of the registered capital, and the ways and means of purchasing raw materials and selling products. The MOFTEC has to decide whether to grant approval within three months. If it is approved, the joint venture must be registered within one month with the State Administration for Industry and Commerce (SAIC) to obtain a licence to start business. The establishment of a wholly foreign-owned enterprise, or a sole FIE, will go through the same procedure, except that no joint-venture contract is involved. In the initial stages of the economic reform, foreign investors were required to form joint ventures with local Chinese firms. This requirement has been relaxed over the years. Foreign investment in tertiary industries was highly restricted until the 1990s (Deloitte Touche Tohmatsu International 1997, pp.25–32).

Urban land in China is owned by the state, while rural land is owned by the collectives (villages) and managed by the Land Administration of the government. A joint venture, upon approval of the contract, needs to file applications with the local land management bureau for the use of land. Land-use rights are granted to the joint venture for a specific time period.

Imports are subject to a complex process of applying for approvals. In the 1990s, Chinese firms were generally required to import through designated foreign trade corporations, while Sino-foreign joint ventures and sole FIEs were permitted to import on their own. Imports were limited to raw materials or semi-finished goods for use in the normal production process and an import licence was required. While it is not entirely free of government regulations, exporting from China has been generally easier than importing into China. However, certain exports are controlled, and an export licence may be required. Although price control of most items was lifted in the early 1990s, it still remains for certain essential items imported or exported.

The negotiation of China's entry into the WTO dramatically expanded the freedom with which the FIEs operated in China. FIEs were allowed to sidestep joint ventures entirely and establish wholly foreign-owned firms at the end of the 1990s (Branstetter and Lardy 2008, p.645).

4.7 LAWS AND REGULATIONS: FURTHER DEVELOPMENTS

A large number of formal laws and regulations were established to cover many vacant areas of legislation during the 1990s, although many of them were not implemented effectively. As theorised by Douglass North, 'Institutions are made up of formal rules, informal constraints and their enforcement characteristics' (North 2003). The economic reform from the late 1970s to the 2010s has been a process of institutional innovation. Many new institutions emerged first as informal institutions, like the contract system created by peasants in the late 1970s, which was illegal at the time. If some of the informal institutions were economically and politically superior to the old institutions, they became formal institutions. The government recognised the informal institutions as formal institutions later by setting up formal laws and regulations, which reduced transaction costs further. This section provides a description of laws and regulations passed in the 1990s and early 2000s which consolidated the results of the reform.

Formal Laws

In October 1992, the 14th Congress of the CCP set up the 'socialist market economy' as the goal of the reform (CCP 1992). The Constitution was amended again in March 1993, which states, 'The state practices the socialist market economy' (National People's Congress 1993b). The Constitution was thereafter amended again in 1999 to sanction a larger role for non-public sectors, calling them major components of the socialist market economy (Article 16, National People's Congress 1999b).

The State Commission of Economic System Reform issued the Normative Opinion on Joint-Stock Companies and Normative Opinion on Limited Liability Companies in May 1992. The document served as the first general corporation law in the reform era, providing an organisational vehicle for enterprises that wished to restructure and be listed on a stock market (State Commission of Economic System Reform 1992). The State Council issued the Provisional Regulations on the Administration of Issuance and Trading of Stock in April 1993 (State Council 1993b, see section 4.5 above). The Law against Unfair Competition was passed in September 1993 and was the first antitrust law in China (National People's Congress 1993c). The law defined unfair competition as counterfeiting registered trademarks or names of commodities and enterprises; restricting trade; abusing administrative powers to restrict trade; bribery; false advertisement; infringing trade secrets; unfair price competition; and tie-in sales. The Law on Individual Proprietorship Enterprises was passed in 1999, which regulated sole proprietorships in China (National People's Congress 1999e). The Law on Promotion of Small- and Medium-Sized Enterprises was passed in 2002, to improve the business environment of the small and medium-sized enterprises. The law announced that, with regard to small and medium-sized enterprises, the state applies the principles of active support, strong guidance, perfect service, and lawful standardisation (National People's Congress 2002).

The existing contract laws[18] did not allow individuals and private enterprises that were not legal persons to enter into a contract (National People's Congress 1993d, 1985). This situation was not changed until the Contract Law of 1999, which allowed individuals to enter into legally enforced contracts.

The Corporation Law, passed in December 1993 and effective from 1994, formalised the legislation on the limited liability company and the joint stock company previously regulated by the 1992 Normative Opinions of the State Commission of Economic System Reform (National People's Congress 1993a). The Securities Law was passed in December 1998 in order to standardise the issuing and trading of securities, and was applicable to the issuing and trading in China of shares, corporate bonds, and other securities (National People's Congress 1998). The Partnership Law, passed in February 1997, was intended to standardise partnership enterprises' activities, and provide an organisational vehicle for small businesses (National People's Congress 1997b). The Price Law was passed in December 1997, with a purpose of reforming the price system. According to the law, the state shall introduce and improve the mechanism of regulation of prices mainly through market forces, and, for most merchandises and services, pricing should be determined in accordance with the law of value (National People's Congress 1997c). The Contract Law was passed in March 1999 to protect the legitimate rights and interests of the parties to contracts and replaced three prior laws, the Economic Contract Law, the Foreign Economic Contract Law, and the Technology Contract Law

(National People's Congress 1999c). The Law on Individual Wholly Owned Enterprises was passed in August 1999. A complement to the Partnership Law, this law provided a sound organisational vehicle for small businesses (National People's Congress 1999d).

The Foreign Trade Law was passed in May 1994. The law defines foreign trade operators as the legal persons or other organisations engaged in the operative activities of foreign trade, and presents the conditions foreign trade operators must satisfy. The state allows the free import and export of goods and technology, according to the law, except as otherwise provided in laws and regulations. At the same time, the state may restrict the trade of goods and technology under certain circumstances (National People's Congress 1994). The Antidumping Regulations and The Antisubsidy Regulations were both passed by the State Council in November 2001, in order to fit WTO requirements (State Council 2001a and 2001b).

The Provisions on the Grant and Transfer of Use Rights in Urban Land were passed in May 1990, with the purpose of reforming the urban state-owned land-use system. According to the provisions, the state shall, in accordance with the principle of separating the land ownership from the land-use rights, implement a system of assignment and transfer of the urban state-owned land-use rights, with certain exceptions. The regulation made the commodification of urban land possible (State Council 1990). The Copyright Law was passed in September 1990 to protect the copyright of authors in their literary, artistic, and scientific works (National People's Congress 1990). The Trust Law was passed in April 2001 to regulate the trust relationship and protect the lawful rights and interests of the parties to a trust (National People's Congress 2001). The Law on Legislation and several regulations were passed in 2000 and 2001 to regulate the law-making process itself (National People's Congress 2000).

To sum up, in the process of economic reform, the establishment of formal laws lagged behind reforms which usually created informal institutions first. The establishment of formal laws legitimised the informal institutions and reduced their transaction costs. Although the law makers made great efforts to fill the loopholes of the system of formal laws, the speed of establishment of formal laws still could not catch up with the creation of informal institutions in the large market economy of the 1990s.

Informal Mechanisms

The administrative branch of the government played an important role in the early stages of the reform. A large number of the reforms grew out of administrative directives. Many old institutions of the planned economy were used to regulate the new market economy.

Many informal mechanisms in the realm of contract existed in the early years of the economic reform, including informal and social sanctions, trusted middlemen, networks, reputation, and self-enforcement arrangements (Clarke et al. 2008, p.404). Informal social ties, *Guanxi*, play an important role in economic activities in China. *Guanxi* links relations among entrepreneurs and between entrepreneurs and government officials. *Guanxi* becomes a basis for trust and cooperation and may even reduce transaction costs.[19] Negotiation directly between the contracting parties and self-enforcement are used extensively in contract dispute resolution, while trade associations, most of them set up by the government, play a smaller role. Economic contract dispute cases increased by 18.8 per cent from 1983 to 2001 and reached 1.16 million cases in 2001 (Clarke et al. 2008).

4.8 THE POLITICAL COALITION

During this stage of reform, Jiang Zemin, the general secretary of the CCP, built a political coalition in which political leaders worked closely with economic elites and intellectual elites. As Barry Naughton pointed out, 'China thus went from "reform without losers" to a reform run by a coalition of winners'. Jiang promulgated a theory of 'Three Represents',[20] which stated that 'the CCP should now represent society's advanced material, ideological and cultural forces, that is, the elites and winners in different spheres' (Naughton 2008, p.128).

At the beginning of the 21st century, the Chinese political system was in a process of changing from a totalitarian state to an authoritarian state, and from a planned economy to a market economy. The government still controlled the public sphere, while the private sphere was liberalised. There was a fundamental change in the relationship between government and different groups in Chinese society in this period. The new elite of the society, the economic elite and the intellectual elite, were rising, while the blue-collar workers and peasants became the new 'losers'. The ideas of intellectuals changed from radical political reform to conservatism. If they had to choose between 'stability' and 'democracy', they would choose the former. The leadership formed a coalition with the elites of the society, which provided a foundation for the stability of the society (Kang 2002). For example, cooperation between the government, developers, and banks could be seen in many urban areas in which the government leases the public-owned land to developers who build and sell housing to consumers. In this process, local governments receive revenue and developers enjoy their profit when the housing market is booming.

The relationship between the government and the market was cooperative during the 1990s. The development of a market needed the support of the government. The normal performance of the market needed the government to protect the order of the market, and especially to protect private ownership. An authoritarian regime needs legitimacy to support its rule, and economic development and improvement of quality of life became the sources of legitimacy the CCP needed during the years of reform. To keep its promise, the government needs continuous economic growth. Therefore, in the development process, the government and the market were incentive-compatible. The experiences of many countries (such as Singapore) show that it is not necessary to establish a democratic political system for the development of a market. Economic freedom coexists with authoritarian government in many countries in the world, especially in some Asian or Southeast Asian countries.

The driving force of reform gradually changed from a reverse movement against the Cultural Revolution to a natural evolution under an authoritarian system. The government could not monopolise all areas of the society and the private areas were liberalised, while the public areas remained under tight control. The society experienced some development in China,[21] but political activities were still dominated by the CCP. Competition between the market system and the remains of the planned system became one driving force of the economic development. Economic development and the improvement of the economic situation of ordinary people became the major source of legitimacy of the state and the Party.

Political leaders cooperated with elites in other fields of the society. Both the political leaders and the elites of the society realised that the stability of the society was important for wealth and growth, and this became a foundation of the political power of the CCP. The Communist Party changed its ideology from class struggle to following the 'Three Represents', that is, the Party should always represent the development needs of China's advanced social productive forces, always represent the onward direction of China's advanced culture, and always represent the fundamental interests of the Chinese people. Most intellectuals changed their beliefs from liberalism to authoritarianism, partly because the experience in Eastern Europe showed that political turmoil[22] is not good for economic development. Some of the private entrepreneurs were invited into the representative institutions of the government. For example, Liu Yonghao and other private entrepreneurs were invited into the Chinese People's Political Consultative Conference (CPPCC) in 1993 (Zhang 2009).

An intimate, and sometimes questionable, relationship developed between government and business. Corruption was created partly because of this close relationship between government officials and business owners. The society was losing its communist ideology and failed to rebuild a new ideology (Kang 2002, p.33). The government's function was changing slightly, and gradually, from controlling the society to providing leadership and support for economic growth. Within the bureaucratic structure, the functions of 'lines' were further reduced and 'blocks' played a larger role. At the same time, the central government began to take back financial power by implementing the tax reform in 1994.

The Chinese society entered a temporarily stable equilibrium in the 1990s. The economic reform raised the living conditions of most ordinary people in the society. Firms obtained favours from government to develop the country's wealth. The development of a market economy needed a stable environment, and the Tiananmen Square events and the changes in former Soviet Union made political and economic elites understand the importance of a stable political environment for a market economy. A new consensus on the need for stability within the society formed.

However, since the political reform was limited, the seeds of social conflicts were planted at the same time. The principle of path dependence still had an influence on the development of the reform.

NOTES

1. In the 2010s, an individual pays 8 per cent and company pays about 20 per cent of the salary for pensions in most areas.
2. Pay as you go is a form of social security payment system used in many countries. Under this system, today's workers pay social security taxes into a programme and money flows back out as monthly income to beneficiaries. A pay-as-you-go system differs from a 'pre-funded' system, in which the money is accumulated in advance so that it will be available to be paid out to today's workers when they retire.
3. Fake TVEs refers to TVEs that did not actually operate.
4. Sitong Lifang and Sinanet merged in 1998 and became Sina.
5. Tencent failed to win a lawsuit in the United States in 1998 in which AOL claimed that QICQ.com was in violation of ICQ's intellectual property rights.
6. For details of corruption see Chapter 7.
7. During the planned period, ministries in charge of different industries were ordered by numbers. The Number 1 Ministry of Machinery was in charge of the machinery industry.
8. The National Tax Bureau and Local Tax Bureau were merged again in 2018.
9. An incentive-compatible governance structure is one in which every participant can achieve the best outcome for him/herself just by acting according to his/her true preferences. Incentive compatibility is an important concept of the theory of mechanism design.
10. The hybrid sector includes privately owned firms and firms partially owned by local governments.
11. The policy-based finance provides funds for building infrastructure, poverty reduction, or support for export. The reformed financial system took the function of policy banking from state-owned commercial banks and passed it to policy banks so that the commercial banks could focus on regular business activities and make profits.

12. This is the minimum capital–assets ratio for a commercial bank required by the central bank.
13. The Securities Commission of the State Council and China Securities Regulatory Commission were established in October 1992. The two commissions merged in 1998.
14. A repo is a sale of securities coupled with an agreement to repurchase the securities at a specified price on a later date.
15. Hot money is money moved either legally or illegally between different markets in search of the best interest rates.
16. First published in 1995 and revised in 1997.
17. Double taxation is the levying of tax by two or more jurisdictions on the same goods, declared income, asset, or financial transaction.
18. The Economic Contract Law was adopted in 1981 and amended in September 1993. The Foreign Economic Contract Law was adopted in 1985.
19. When the formal institutions did not exist, *Guanxi* might solve the problem. For example, when small firms could not get financial support from large banks, a group of relatives might provide funds for that small firm, even though it was illegal and involved risks.
20. The 'Three Represents' is Jiang Zemin's socio-political ideology which stipulates that the CCP should represent advanced social productive forces, advanced culture, and the interests of the overwhelming majority. The ideology attempts to transform the CCP into a ruling party representing the majority of the people as opposed to its old image of a revolutionary party driven by the proletariat.
21. For example, many non-government institutions, such as environmental protection institutions, were set up in this period.
22. Russia and many Eastern European countries experienced radical political reform, which followed the collapse of the economy. This made many Chinese intellectuals believe that a gradual approach to reform is better than radical political reform.

5. Stagnation: 2003–2012

Hu Jintao was elected general secretary of the Communist Party of China (CCP) in 2002, and Wen Jiabao became the premier of the State Council in 2003. This began a new stage of China's institutional development. The rule of 'Hu–Wen' existed from 2003 to 2012. The distinctive features of this period are (i) the unprecedented economic growth as a result of institutional improvements that were started in the previous period, such as state-owned enterprise (SOE) reform and World Trade Organization (WTO) entry, and (ii) the stagnation of marketisation reform due to the social and economic problems produced by the government-led marketisation in the previous period. This was a period of speeding up of economic growth and slowing down of institutional reform. The leadership of the CCP slowed down the market-oriented reform and shifted focus onto reducing the impacts of rapid market development on the society.

After 20 years of economic reform, by the beginning of the new century China had successfully created a sizable market. The political system was also changing from a totalitarian system to an authoritarian one. In the late 20th century, reform was based on the consensus of the whole society, as an anti-Cultural Revolution movement. Now the reform was driven automatically by the logic of the reform's development itself. The coalition between the political elites and the economic elites, set up in the 1990s, ignored the demands of ordinary people and subsequently faced new challenges.

The system created by reforms of the previous years was successful in promoting economic development, but it ignored some socioeconomic problems, such as poverty, income inequality, rising housing prices, and increasing health care costs. The market proved to be a double-edged sword in that it benefited some individuals and institutions while harmed others. The expansion of the market created new contradictions between the political system and the market, and the coalition between the political and economic elites increased the society's polarisation. Corruption was widespread as a result of decentralised government power that lacked strong supervision. The possibilities of instability came from both within and without the CCP, and 'maintaining stability' became a new task of the government (Sun 2002; Kang 2002). The consensus on reform was diluting as a consequence of the unequal distribution of benefits in the process of economic growth. The popular public opinion changed as people turned against the reform. For example, large numbers of middle-aged workers lost their jobs during the SOE reform in the late 1990s and became losers and critics of the reform. The new government realised that there were problems, and in response hesitated to continue the reform on such a large scale, slowed down the marketisation process, and shifted its focus onto social problems. However, these efforts were not totally successful. Redistribution of wealth and resources between different social groups became the first wave of adjustment in the economic reform process.

During this period, the government worked hard to use its power to promote economic growth. The local governments played a more important role than before in economic development. The central–local government relationship changed from a financial franchise system to a performance assessment and competition-based system, in which the central government established a set of performance indicators connected to the promotion of local leaders, and the local government leaders competed with each other for promotions. During this period, marketisation reforms in different fields continued without important breakthroughs.

5.1 INERTIA OF THE REFORM AND DEVELOPMENT

The period enjoyed two-digit economic growth, which was mainly a result of the economic reform and opening up in the previous period.

WTO Entry

The most significant event in China's opening up in the first decade of the 21st century was China joining the WTO. According to Premier Zhu Rongji, WTO membership was an essential element of China's reform strategy and a source of pressure for domestic reform (Branstetter and Lardy 2008, p.650). WTO entry provided an unprecedented opportunity for economic growth and created high-speed growth after the turn of the century, establishing a golden age for the Chinese economy.

China's membership of the WTO was approved at the 4th WTO Ministerial Meeting held in Doha, by representatives from 142 member countries/regions, on 10 November 2001. On 11 December 2001, China formally became the 143rd member of the WTO (World Trade Organization 2001). Before this, the Chinese government made great efforts to negotiate with the General Agreement on Tariffs and Trade (GATT) and the

WTO, as well as with major countries around the world. China signed bilateral agreements with the United States in November 1999 and with the European Union in May 2000. In these negotiations, China agreed to extra market-opening conditions that were more stringent than those under which other countries had acceded.[1] Premier Zhu Rongji and China's chief negotiator Long Yongtu played important roles in China's negotiations for WTO membership. China's leadership's decision to join the WTO was based on two basic premises: (i) deeper involvement in the world economy is necessary for China's economic development, and (ii) greater opening up is necessary to introduce international competition into the domestic economy and is an essential source of pressure for domestic reform.

To meet the WTO's requirements, China revised and improved its laws and regulations regarding foreign trade and economic cooperation before and after joining the WTO. By the end of 2001, relevant ministries of the State Council had revised 2,300 laws and regulations, and a list of 221 administrative regulations annulled by the State Council had been published (China.org 2016). By January 2005, China's average import tariff was reduced to 9.9 per cent (Jiang 2008, pp.299–300). Considering that less than 40 per cent of imports were subjected to tariffs, the actual tariff revenues were much lower than the average statutory rates. Tariff values, as a share of the value of imports, calculated by Branstetter and Lardy (2008), peaked in the 1980s at about 16 per cent and fell steadily thereafter, reaching about 3 per cent by 1994. They increased slightly to 4 per cent in 1999. Leakage[2] of goods and components into the domestic market via the export processing regime also contributed to the reduced tariffs and increased market openness. Before joining the WTO, China regulated foreign direct investment (FDI), including provisions on local content requirements (e.g. requirement of parts etc. that have been made in China rather than imported). Foreign-invested enterprise (FIE) approvals were often contingent on the transfer of technology to domestic firms. In terms of intellectual protection, China passed a patent law as early as 1984, and amended it in 1992, 2000, and 2008 (State Intellectual Property Office 2011), but lack of enforcement continues to be a problem. These measures are precluded by WTO rules, and China agreed to fully enforce the related terms of WTO agreements. Before joining the WTO, China restricted imports of some agricultural products by instituting tariffs and quotas with effective rates of protection that were higher than the 21 per cent average statutory rate. China agreed to reduce the average statutory import tariff rate for agricultural products to 15 per cent (Rosen et al. 2004, pp.8, 41). After reducing the tariff rates, China used health standards more frequently as a non-tariff barrier to agricultural imports by issuing a large number of new quality and health standards for foods. These new barriers blocked or discouraged the imports of meat, citrus products, and wheat from the United States (Branstetter and Lardy 2008, p.654).

China promised to open up its services sector to foreign investment, especially in the distribution, financial service, and banking sectors, as conditions for its accession to the WTO. Some progress has been made, while many restrictions still remain in a large number of areas. Before China entered the WTO, foreign firms were allowed to import inputs directly related to their operations but were restricted from distributing products in China. After entering the WTO, the Chinese government phased out restrictions on wholesaling and retailing, and related services. Some restrictions in banking have since been lifted; for example, the restrictions on the number of cities in which foreign banks could operate were lifted in 2005 and foreign banks were allowed to set up branches in all cities in China (Branstetter and Lardy 2008, p.658 and Li et al. 2009, p.167). The State Council issued regulations on the administration of foreign banks in 2006, and announced that the restrictions regarding location and customers on foreign banks' RMB operations were lifted, and that foreign banks were allowed to deal with RMB operations (People's Bank of China 2006). Although some restrictions have been lifted, the progress has been slow, and many restrictions that apply only to foreign banks are still in place. Although the opening up of the securities industries was restricted in the first decade of the 21st century, a number of joint-venture security firms had been established by large foreign firms. China promised to ease restrictions on foreign investment in the telecommunications sector, but no foreign participation actually developed in the area in the first decade of the 21st century.

Some policy makers worried about the pressure of competition on domestic firms after WTO membership facilitated the entry of foreign firms in certain sectors, such as agriculture, automobiles, and financial services. That pressure was not as great as the policy makers expected before WTO entry. This was because of the hidden barriers to entry and the quick response of Chinese firms to foreign competition.

WTO entry removed some of the major barriers to China's exports. China's exports experienced two-digit growth in the first decade after China's entry into the WTO. China's trade in goods surged to nearly $3 trillion in 2010, from $509.8 billion in 2001, with exports soaring by nearly fivefold and imports up by 470 per cent (National Bureau of Statistics 2015, Tables 11.1, 11.3, and 11.4). Due to the rapid increase in imports from China since that time, more disputes and frictions in many countries have occurred, particularly in the fields of textiles, shoes, auto parts, iron and steel, and chemical products.

The RMB exchange rate became a topic of hot debate between China and the United States. In July 2005, the People's Bank announced a RMB revaluation of 2 per cent as well as the adoption of a managed floating exchange rate system, a new exchange rate regime where the rate is set with reference to a basket of currencies. This announcement marked the end of pegging RMB to the US dollar and the beginning of a new stage of the reform of the RMB exchange rate regime. The new regime increased the flexibility of the RMB exchange rate while preserving enough manoeuvrability to allow the People's Bank of China to maintain the stability of the RMB exchange rate through market intervention. As a result of the enhanced flexibility, the RMB exchange rate increased by more than 20 per cent in the following three years (People's Bank of China 2005).

The National People's Congress published a revised Law on Foreign Trade in July 2004. Compared to the 1994 version, the 2004 revision allowed individuals to engage in foreign trade and abolished the need for government approval of import and export, changing it to a register system (National People's Congress 2004a).

Foreign investors changed their strategies of investment in China following China's entry into the WTO. They moved from consumer products to industrial products, from FDI to financial investments, and from joint ventures to wholly foreign-owned enterprises. Many foreign firms entered deeply into the Chinese service market and met product quality issues, bringing about credibility crises.[3]

Boom of Infrastructure Construction

China's industrial growth was concentrated in the light industrial sectors before the turn of the century; many firms were in processing manufacturing and trade sectors. Entering the 21st century, China experienced a second wave of industrialisation, the development of heavy-chemical industries, which was due mainly to the boom in housing and urban infrastructure construction. Total floor space of buildings completed increased from 251 million square metres in 2000 to 787 million square metres in 2010 (National Bureau of Statistics 2015, Table 15.8). In 2003, the contribution of industries to the growth in gross domestic product (GDP) was 64 per cent, with transportation equipment, electronic equipment, electric power, chemicals, and electric equipment having the highest growth rates. The annual growth rate of heavy industries reached 18.6 per cent, exceeding the growth rate of the light industries, indicating a new wave of industrialisation (Zhao 2010). The huge demand for steel and raw construction materials was due to the institutional changes in residential housing and the amended functions of local governments. Welfare housing from the planned system changed to commercial housing at the end of the 1990s. Most urban residents have to buy houses or apartments through the residential housing market. This created a huge demand for residential housing. At the turn of the century, local governments changed their behaviour from directly managing local enterprises to managing cities, which promoted urbanisation and created a huge demand for raw materials and capital goods. The campaign of city construction required steel, cement, glass, and much more. The construction of housing and highways has created a great demand for concrete and steel tubing. Aluminium, steel, wood, and glass were needed for millions of new windows and doors. This wave of new industrialisation depended on the development of the housing market and urbanisation. In other words, construction on the largest scale in Chinese history has rebuilt the country. However, once development slows down, the huge capacity of industrial production will become a burden on the enterprises, the banks, and the government.

The rapid growth of the housing sector provided opportunities to private developers. The changes in the industrial structure from light industries to heavy industries also gave large SOEs in the producer goods sectors[4] a chance to come back.

5.2 SOCIAL PROBLEMS: HOUSING, HEALTH CARE, AND POLLUTION

As marketisation continued, many social problems emerged in Chinese society. Housing is one of the biggest problems for most urban families. Before the economic reform, urban residential housing was provided and distributed by the government and SOEs, through *Danwei*s or working units (e.g. government offices, factories, or schools). Under this system, housing leases were made for life, rent was extremely low, and housing was under-maintained. Due to the low rent, no state-owned construction companies had any incentive to build apartments, and no working units had any incentive to maintain them. Because of the small amount of new housing that was being built, the living space of urban residents decreased from the 1950s to the 1970s, and young people had to share apartments with their parents or grandparents. The housing reform that was enacted in the late 1990s aimed to end welfare housing, raise rents to the market equilibrium level, and allow individual home ownership. The *Danwei*s were allowed to sell the existing housing units to sitting tenants at a discounted rate. The *Danwei*s would no longer provide housing for new employees; employees now had to buy their houses through the housing market. As a consequence, the residential housing market in China developed rapidly in the first decade of the 21st century. The huge demand for housing caused housing prices to soar. The average selling price for residential buildings nationwide increased from RMB1,948 ($235.3) per square metre in 2000 to RMB4,725 ($698.0) per square metre in 2010. In large cities, housing prices per square metre increased much more (National Bureau of Statistics 2002, 2011). Many families in urban areas, especially young couples, cannot now afford to buy a house of their own, which causes social problems. Young people face cultural pressures to purchase a home. A young male usually cannot marry before buying an apartment. Without the support of their families or banks, they have to work their entire lives to earn enough money to buy an apartment. The housing bubble was partly driven by the government's policy of setting up housing as the pillar industry to accelerate economic growth. Rising income, cheap credit, and developer promotions were other factors that led to rising housing prices. Local government also had incentives to lease state-owned land for residential use to generate more revenue. As the housing bubble grew, the central government imposed housing price controls. This occurred as early as 2006. New curbs, most of which were administrative measures, were imposed on housing prices in 2010 and thereafter. Local governments, under pressure from the central government, put restrictions on second-home purchasing or required second-home buyers to make a larger down payment. Forced demolitions without due process and fair compensation have been another problem in the housing construction process. Many property disputes have occurred due to conflicts of interest among property owners, developers, and local government. The compensation is usually very low. When a property owner does not agree with the compensation and refuses to move, the developer, with support from the local government, uses force to drive the residents out and then demolishes the house. In October 2010, demolition workers broke into a house slated for demolition that belonged to Meng Fugui, a 54-year-old man living in Shanxi province. Meng was pulled from his house and beaten to death, which was widely reported and sparked public outrage (Zhang Shouwen 2014).

Health care is another area under intense criticism. Under the planned system, health care was provided by the government and was essentially free for urban families. Most urban residents were employees of SOEs, and SOEs covered most health care expenses of their employees. The economic reform abandoned the old unit-based free health care system in the 1990s. A universal health care system was set up, covering urban and rural residents separately. Problems in the area included a lack of access to decent services, soaring medical bills, and low medical insurance coverage. All in all, SOE reform in the health care sector has been much slower than in many other sectors. Although most of the major hospitals are still owned by the state, the government has dramatically reduced the health care funding for hospitals. Because hospitals do not have enough money to pay doctors, doctors have to prescribe highly profitable drugs to get commission,[5] in order to maintain their income. Commission is a large part of total profit and a large part of doctors' income. Soaring costs make medical services less affordable to ordinary people, which is one of the reasons for the high saving rates in China. The health care market is dominated by a relatively small number of large state-owned hospitals. Although it is difficult for private hospitals and clinics to obtain permits to enter the market, private hospitals have entered some of the sectors in which the state-owned hospitals are relatively weak. These private hospitals are under weak supervision. A new Rural Cooperative Medical System is developing quickly, covering much of the rural population. The system is organised and promoted by the government. It is funded by individuals, collectives,[6] and government. The system became the basic health insurance system in rural areas in 2009. The leadership realised there were problems with health care and began to change policies to solve these problems (Yu n.d.). Health expenditure has increased dramatically in recent years, due to the aging population and the costs of new techniques. Total health expenditure in China increased to RMB2.4 trillion ($0.37 trillion) in 2011 from RMB0.5 trillion ($0.06 trillion) in 2000, with an annual growth rate of 16.4 per cent (Zhang Fan 2014, p.163). Although there have been some improvements, the overall condition of the sector has not changed.

China's labour migration over the past 30 years is unprecedented in human history. By 2011, the total number of migrant workers in urban areas was estimated to be about 250 million, of which 150 million were living permanently in these areas (National Bureau of Statistics 2012). The rural–urban income gap has been the driving force of this dramatic migration, whereas the major obstacle that has kept peasants in poor rural areas has been the *Hukou* system. *Hukou*, or resident ID, is a resident registration system used by the government to control migration. In this system, a household registration record officially identifies a person as a resident of an area. The modern *Hukou* system in China was established in the 1950s. The system was used to control migration from rural to urban areas during the Great Famine. Under the planned system, having no urban *Hukou* meant that a person was excluded from food rationing in an urban area, meaning that one could not survive there. Money was useless for getting food unless it was accompanied by food coupons. Under these conditions, peasants dreamed of changing their status and becoming urban residents (Zhang Fan 2014).

The economic reform that started in 1978 not only opened China's doors to the world but also opened Chinese cities to rural residents. The

Hukou system still exists today, but its implementation has been relaxed. Rural residents are allowed to apply for temporary urban residency permits to work and live in cities, but these migrant workers still do not have *Hukou*, and therefore cannot enjoy many of the public goods supplied by the government. For example, the children of many migrant workers are not allowed to enter the local primary and high schools. Therefore, when parents moved to the cities, the children were left behind in the countryside. Those children were looked after by their grandparents, and some of them have mental problems because of this. The policy changed in 2010 to encourage local schools to accept children from migrant families. The major reason the central government has not completely removed the *Hukou* system is the explosion of the population in the largest cities. The preference of the central government has therefore been to start the reform of the *Hukou* system in small cities, where the system is mainly the responsibility of local governments. Local governments have hesitated to remove the *Hukou* system because they do not have sufficient financial resources to provide public goods to those migrants.

Rapid economic growth over the past 40 years in China has created serious environmental problems. Poorly regulated industrial emissions have caused severe water and land pollution. China's economic development has made the country one of the world's leading contributors to global warming. Similarly to the United States, the Chinese central government issues fairly strict regulations, but unlike the United States, the actual enforcement is largely undertaken by local governments, which do not have enough incentives to impose the policy and are more interested in economic development. The number of complaints to the environmental authorities increased significantly in the first decade of the 21st century, and the number of mass protests over environmental issues grew dramatically. Resource scarcity and environmental pollution has even provoked violence. The government realised there was a problem and displayed an increased level of concern towards environmental issues. Some of the polluting plants were shut down and some of the subsidies for polluting firms were cancelled. However, these policy measures were not enough to change the overall trend of environmental pollution.

Directly or indirectly, all of these serious social problems were created by rapid economic growth and marketisation. Facing these problems, the CCP leadership changed their reform strategy significantly in the first decade of the 21st century. The pace of reform towards a market economy was slowed down, whereas more focus was placed on social problems and the society's stability. This was the first wave of strategic adjustment in the process of economic and political reforms in China.

5.3 INEQUALITY AND CORRUPTION

Marketisation exacerbated the problems of unequal income and wealth distribution. Corruption, which is widespread in China, damaged the relationship between the government and the public. Efficiency was no longer the only target, nor the only standard for evaluating the reform.

New Class Division

During the planned period, according to the official view, society consisted of three classes: the workers, the peasants, and the intellectuals. In addition, some researchers have pointed out that as early as the 1970s the ruling class[7] in China formed another class: the class of government officials.[8] The class division has changed dramatically since the beginning of the economic reform, becoming much more differentiated and complicated.

Sociologist Lu (2002) proposed a model of class systems in China at the beginning of the 21st century. It consists of ten distinct social groups, which constitute five social classes: (i) the upper class, consisting of high-level government officials, high-level managers of large SOEs, high-level specialists, and owners of large private companies; (ii) the upper-middle class, consisting of middle- and low-level government officials, middle-level managers of large enterprises, managers of small and medium-sized enterprises, middle-level specialists, and owners of middle-level enterprises; (iii) the middle class, consisting of low-level specialists, owners of small enterprises, clerks, high- and middle-level technicians, and rich farmers; (iv) the lower-middle class, consisting of sole proprietors, service-sector workers, blue-collar workers, and farmers; and (v) the lower class, consisting of poor workers and farmers, and unemployed or part-time unemployed workers. Lu (2002) estimated the shares of the ten social groups in the Chinese population, based on official statistics, other statistics, and research data, as shown in Table 5.1.

Table 5.1 shows that the lower class has been shrinking since the 1950s. The percentage of peasants decreased to 44 per cent in 1999 from 84 per cent in 1952. This has been the major driving force of the decline of the lower class in China over the past half century. Within the lower class, the share of blue-collar workers and service workers increased, which changed the composition of the lower class. The middle class has grown rapidly since the late 1970s. This is one of the positive changes that have occurred over the past 30 years in China, and this trend will continue into the near future. At the top of Chinese society, high-rank government officials still control a large portion of power and resources. A small group of large private enterprise owners have entered the upper class, by controlling

Table 5.1 Changes in social group structure, China, %

	1952	1978	1988	1999
Government officials and Society managers	0.50	0.98	1.70	2.1
Enterprise managers	0.14	0.23	0.54	1.5
Owners of private enterprises	0.18	0.00	0.02	0.6
Specialists and Technicians	0.86	3.48	4.76	5.1
Clerks	0.50	1.29	1.65	4.8
Sole proprietors	4.08	0.03	3.12	4.2
Service workers	3.13	2.15	6.35	12.0
Blue-collar workers	6.40	19.83	22.43	22.6
Peasants	84.21	67.41	55.84	44.0
Full- and part-time unemployed workers	–	4.60	3.60	3.1

Note: Estimated by Lu (2002) based on official statistics, other statistics, and research data. The estimates in 1999 are less accurate compared to the other years and hence are only given to one decimal place.

Source: Lu (2002, Table 14).

a relatively large amount of wealth. Chinese society is changing from a pyramid shaped society to an olive shaped society, but the change is far from finished.

The class division in contemporary Chinese society is mainly due to economics, whereas political power is correlated with economic status to some degree. In the first decade of reform, the income of peasants and blue-collar workers, as well as of owners of private enterprises and sole proprietors, far surpassed that of managers and technicians. Then, in the 1990s, the income of managers and technicians also increased. By the beginning of the 21st century, class ranking was more or less consistent with income distribution. The returns on education increased to 6 to 7 per cent of total earnings at the beginning of the 21st century from less than 2 to 3 per cent in the 1980s (Lu 2002, pp.29–30).

Political status still plays an important role in determining a person's class status. Many government officials are party members. Many managers of private enterprises come from the government, and some of them are party members, too. Table 5.2 shows the percentages of the Communist Party members in each social group at the beginning of the 21st century.

The classes of Chinese society can be summarised as political elites, economic elites, the intellectual elites, the masses, and the poor. In the planned period, the only elite group was the party and government officials, which had the power to redistribute products. During the reform, the elite group was enlarged to include the political elite, the economic elite, and the

Table 5.2 Share of party members in social groups in three cities, %

	Shenzhen	Hefei	Hanchuan
Government officials and Society managers	100.0	77.5	100.0
Enterprise managers	35.7	58.8	53.8
Owners of private enterprises	22.2	24.4	9.1
Specialists and Technicians	27.2	25.2	17.8
Clerks	28.2	40.7	54.5
Sole proprietors	13.7	10.4	7.7
Service workers	10.4	7.6	10.6
Blue-collar workers	0.0	13.3	5.9
Peasants	–	–	4.3
Full- and part-time unemployed workers	2.0	9.1	1.8

Note: Shenzhen is a city in Guangdong province. Hefei is the capital of Anhui province. Hanchuan is a county-level city in Hubei province.

Source: Lu (2002, Table 9). Shenzhen's data are from a survey conducted in 2000. The data for Hefei and Hanchuan are from a survey in 1999.

intellectual elite, whereas citizens and peasants constituted the masses (Kang 2002). The reform changed the rules of resource distribution, from redistribution by political power to distribution both by political power and through physical and human capital. Social mobility was enhanced during the reform, too. Large numbers of former peasants entered the city, enjoying some of the benefits previously enjoyed solely by citizens. Conversely, some SOE workers lost their jobs and became part of the poor.

The goal for the economic elites, mainly the owners and managers of private enterprises, is profit. They even might accept autocracy if profit is guaranteed. The government created an environment to facilitate profit-seeking activities by promoting marketisation, developing the economy, banning labour unions, and reducing environmental protection standards (especially in the early years of the reform). The government also made arrangements to invite economic elites into the People's Congress, either at the local level or at the national level. Baum and Shevchenko (1999) proposed four modes of relationship between local political elites and economic elites in China: (i) developmental – the political elite create an environment for local economic development that favours local firms but is not involved in the business of local firms; (ii) entrepreneurial – the local political elites are directly involved in business activities; (iii) clientelist – the political elites are only interested in power–money trading with local firms; and (iv) predatory – the political elites directly plunder the local firms. Kang (2002) added a fifth mode, the political elites help their relatives set up and operate businesses. These different modes were widespread in China at the beginning of the 21st century.

The intellectual elites are the government's natural enemy in most countries. However, the Chinese government established coalitions with intellectuals in the 1990s and 2000s.[9] The coalition between the reformers in the Party and radical intellectuals that existed in the 1980s broke down in 1989, but a new coalition between the government and mainstream intellectuals was established in the 1990s and the early 21st century. The attitude of intellectuals changed dramatically in the 1990s because of the continued economic reform in China and the failure of radical reform in Russia and Eastern European countries. The radical intellectuals of the 1980s were marginalised, and the 'New Left', which argues that authoritarianism is a necessary stage from autocracy to democracy, became an influential ideology among intellectuals.

In the planned period, the masses, which included workers and peasants, were the nominal leading class. Their political status did not change much, and their life improved immensely in the early years of the reform. It was a 'win–win' situation in the 1980s; both elites and the masses improved their situation. In the 1990s and early 21st century, the political status of the masses decreased, and their economic status worsened relatively. Numerous urban workers lost their jobs during the SOE reform. Due to the size of this population, it had considerable influence. To maintain social stability, the government made efforts to improve the situation by implementing a large aid-the-poor programme.

Income Inequality

An important feature correlated with class division in China is income inequality. Before the economic reform started in 1978, China's income distribution pattern was basically egalitarian. Since the late 1970s, virtually all Chinese people have experienced a dramatic improvement in their standards of living. However, as the average income increased, the income and wealth disparity between different groups of citizens increased even faster, and this became the most pressing socioeconomic issue in China in the early 21st century. At the same time, the economic disparities between urban and rural sectors were large. Both sectors had grown since the beginning of the reform, but the urban sector expanded far more robustly. The economic reform substantially redistributed the national income. The measure of income inequality involves three interconnected problems: (i) income inequality among households; (ii) income inequality between urban and rural residents; and (iii) income inequality between eastern, central, and western areas. Within urban residents, the 10 per cent of families with the highest income possessed 45 per cent of the wealth, whereas the 10 per cent of families with the lowest income possessed 1.4 per cent of the total wealth in 2002 (Xiao and Sui 2011, p.287).

The largest income disparity was between urban and rural residents in the planned economy, because of (i) the uneven trade between manufacturing and agricultural products and the biases in the relative prices of agricultural products; and (ii) the resident registration system, which restricted migration from rural to urban areas. The economic reform reduced the income disparity between urban and rural areas at the beginning, but then enlarged the gap thereafter, mainly due to the rapid increase in wealth and its uneven distribution. The income disparity between urban residents and rural residents reduced to 1.82:1 in 1983, due to the rural reform. This disparity increased to 3.23:1 in 2010, with the per capita disposable income of urban households reaching RMB19,109 ($2,822.8) whereas that of rural households stood at RMB5,919 ($874.4. National Bureau of Statistics 2016a).

The shares of GDP in eastern, central, and western areas also enlarged from 1980 to 2010, although these did not change much from 2000 to 2010 (Table 5.3).

According to data from household surveys, there was a dramatic increase in income inequality among households during the first decade of the 21st century, compared with the 1980s and 1990s. Disagreements exist among researchers and policy makers about the seriousness of income inequality. Different researchers have reached different estimates of the income inequality. However, it is no surprise that inequality rose as China moved to a market-oriented economy. The issue is how great inequality has become.

Table 5.3 Shares of GDP in different areas, %

	1980	1990	2000	2010
Eastern	50.2	51.5	57.3	57.3
Central	29.8	28.3	25.6	24.1
Western	20.0	20.2	17.1	18.6

Note: The eastern area includes Beijing, Tianjin, Hebei, Liaoning, Shanghai, Jiangsu, Zhejiang, Fujian, Shandong, Guangdong, and Hainan; the central area includes Heilongjiang, Jilin, Shanxi, Anhui, Jiangxi, Henan, Hubei, and Hunan; the western area includes Inner Mongolia, Guangxi, Chongqing, Sichuan, Guizhou, Yunnan, Tibet, Shaanxi, Gansu, Qinghai, Ningxia, and Xinjiang.

Source: Xiao and Sui (2011, p.287); National Bureau of Statistics (2011).

The National Bureau of Statistics (NBS) estimated that the household Gini coefficient[10] was 0.479 in 2003, 0.491 in 2008, and 0.465 in 2016 (National Bureau of Statistics 2013, 2017). According to the China Household Financial Survey (CHFS), conducted by the South Western University of Finance and Economics, the Gini coefficient for households in both urban and rural areas was 0.61 in 2010, and the Gini coefficient for urban households and rural households were 0.58 and 0.61, respectively. These numbers decreased slightly to 0.60, 0.57, and 0.58, respectively, in 2012. According to the CHFS report, wage/salary accounted for the largest part of household income, and it was the largest contributor to income inequality (CHFS 2013). The huge disparity between the NBS and the CHFS is largely due to the sample of the two surveys. Official estimates of inequality by the NBS are probably too low, because its sample may have missed some high-income households. The CHFS's sample included a larger number of high-income households.

The Institute of Social Science Survey (ISSS) of Peking University issued a report on the living conditions of Chinese households in 2013. Based on a sample of 14,960 households in 25 provinces, the report estimated a Gini coefficient of 0.49, which is lower than the CHFS estimates but higher than that of the NBS. According to the ISSS report, the per capita average annual household income was RMB13,033 ($2,017.9) in the 2010–2012 period, with a median income of RMB8,984 ($1,391.0). The lowest 10 per cent of households accounted for less than 1 per cent of total income, whereas the highest 5 per cent of households earned about one-quarter of the total income. The 5 per cent highest-income rural households earned a per capita income of RMB27,000 ($4,180.3), whereas the lowest-income rural households only have a per capita income of RMB900 ($139.3), so that the former was 30 times greater than the latter. In urban areas, the richest 5 per cent of households had an average per capita income of RMB42,000 ($6,502.8), 35 times greater than the lowest 5 per cent of households, whose average per capita income was RMB1,200 ($185.8, Jiang 2013).

Benjamin et al. (2008) found that overall inequality had risen in China since 1987. The increase in inequality is common to both urban and rural China, but the increase was higher in urban China. The paper used several data sets, including the China Health and Nutrition Study (CHNS), the Research Centre on Rural Economy (RCRE), and the National Bureau of Statistics (NBS). Using NBS data, they found that the Gini coefficient in urban areas increased from 0.22 to 0.34 from 1987 to 2001. The increase in inequality has been quite steady during this period. The spatially deflated Gini coefficient is slightly smaller, but it shows similar growth over this period. Other common measures (such as 20:20 ratio[11]) confirmed the increase in inequality during this period. Benjamin et al. (2008) found that in rural areas, inequality was slightly higher and experienced a slightly smaller increase than it did in urban areas. The Gini coefficient increased from 0.32 in 1987 to 0.37 in 2001 based on RCRE data. To include the effect of the widening gap between urban and rural incomes, Benjamin et al. (2008) pooled the urban and rural samples and found that the Gini coefficient increased from 0.37 to 0.44 from 1991 to 2000, using CHNS data. The authors also pointed out a significant difference in the inequality dynamics between interior and coastal provinces. Inequality rose more rapidly in the interior provinces, which was due to a more rapid increase in rural income inequality and a widening urban–rural income differential. Benjamin et al. (2008)'s results about the effect of the urban–rural distinction on overall income inequality are valid for the 1980s and 1990s. If we include the first decade of the 21st century, the effect may be larger, since the urban–rural gap has been significantly widened during this period.

With regard to wealth distribution, a CHFS study found that the average household assets in China reached RMB919,000 ($147,549.9) in 2015. Housing accounted for 69 per cent of average household assets (CHFS 2016).

To sum up, overall income inequality has risen in China since the 1980s. This increase is common to both urban and rural areas in China. The official estimates of inequality are probably too low. The true overall Gini coefficient is likely in the range of 0.50–0.60 at the end of the first decade of the 21st century.

There are some institutional factors influencing income inequality. In rural areas, the level and growth of inequality is mostly due to the unequal access to non-farm family business income in the early years of the reform. The inequality also depends on the unequal conditions of family members' migrating to cities in more recent years. For wealth distribution, the purchasing of housing assets in the early years of reform is an important factor in making people rich in a booming housing market.

The income and wealth inequality is a natural by-product of China's market-oriented economic reform. In some senses, it has been created by the leaders of the reform. Deng Xiaoping set up the principle 'let some become richer than others' at the beginning of the reform, to create economic incentives for the majority of the population. As the reform went on, the income disparity caused some social conflicts and instabilities, which potentially endangered the stability of the society as well as the legitimacy of the ruling party. To reduce income and wealth inequality in China, government transfer payments must play their part. In this respect, the Chinese government has not been very efficient in redistributing the transfer payments to the poor. The fund has often been held back by various levels of bureaucracy. More supervision may solve this problem, but it is costly.

Migration is a way out of the urban–rural income inequality. Migrants experience hardships when moving from the countryside to cities. Like the migrants in the United States in the early 20th century, described by David Kennedy, the migrant workers in the early 21st century China are 'strangers in a strange land, awkwardly suspended between the world they had left behind and a world where they were not yet fully at home' (Kennedy 1999, p.14). But in cases where this process of migration has been achieved, the migrants have changed their status and economic condition fundamentally.

Corruption

Corruption, not democracy, has been the main concern of ordinary Chinese people. Corruption is basically a product of the bureaucratic-market system. Three types of corruption exist in China: graft, rent-seeking, and prebendalism.[12] Corruption in China can be classified as either structural or non-structural. The latter refers to corruption that can be clearly defined as 'illegal', whereas structural corruption arises from the structure itself. The housing boom, particularly in China, provided government officials more opportunities to engage in corruption. Large-scale governmental construction projects and illegal land grabs by local authorities take place unchecked. Government officials collude with land developers to share the profits while paying little or no compensation to displaced residents. Corruption comes from the innate character of a bureaucratic-market economy, in which temptation exists for the government officials to use their political power in exchange for wealth. Without political support from government officials, the business operations will be extremely difficult in an economy in which many business activities need to be approved by the government. This happens more frequently when political power is not supervised. Some government officials and their sons and daughters use 'white gloves' to hide ill-gotten gains. Companies sometimes give free shares to government officials. These shares are often held in other people's names. These people are often trusted relatives or acquaintances and are called 'white gloves'.

In 2009, 106,000 officials were found guilty of corruption, an increase of 2.5 per cent from the previous year (Sommerville 2009). This widespread corruption was due to two main institutional reasons. First, the state was unable to maintain a disciplined administrative corps, as the power shifted from the central to the local governments. Second, state agencies and local governments were granted regulatory power without institutional constraints. The burden of supervision is always on the shoulders of the higher level of government. Supervisory power was reduced when the power was shifted downward in the bureaucratic structure. Supervision of the same-level officials by the same-level supervision agency is almost impossible in a bureaucratic structure. This is the reason why the supervision committee at the provincial level cannot work effectively in supervising the provincial party secretary (the top leader at the provincial level) in China. The provincial supervision committee works effectively only when the central supervision committee delegates power directly to the provincial committee.

The effects of corruption in China are negative for economic growth and political stability. Bribes lead to a misdirection of resources into wasteful projects. Rent-seeking prevents innovation and creates entry barriers in the market for those without connections. In the long term, corruption has potential consequences of widening income inequality. Corruption became the top concern of the Chinese public in the first decade of the 21st century. A survey conducted by the Central Party School of over 100 officials from 1999 to 2004 showed that corruption was ranked either the most serious or the second most serious social problem (Pei 2007).

In the first decade of the 21st century, the Chinese government has tried a variety of anti-corruption measures, but none of them have proven to be effective. The CCP imposed regulations on officials assuming posts in business and enterprise in 2004 (Transparency International 2006). According to the Anti-Unfair Competition Law, it is prohibited to give or receive bribes when selling or purchasing goods. In cases of misconduct, companies are fined between RMB10,000 ($1,735.5) and RMB200,000 ($34,710.2) (National People's Congress 1993c). The Criminal Law of China prohibits giving and receiving property to obtain an undue benefit (National People's Congress 1997a). However, such measures are largely ineffective, due to the insufficient enforcement of the relevant laws. This is mainly due to the weak position of the legal system in the bureaucratic structure, compared with that of the administrative branch of government. The failure to contain widespread corruption is among the most serious threats to China's future stability.

5.4 OWNERSHIP STRUCTURE OF SOES: AN ERA OF STATE CAPITALISM

The combination of the political power and the large SOEs survived the 1990s reform, characterising the so-called state capitalism of the first decade of the 21st century. These large SOEs are less efficient due to unclear property rights, their monopoly position, and the policy inclination towards them.[13] In some senses, this state capitalism becomes one of the major obstacles of further marketisation and a potential source of corruption. The reform of large SOEs continued during this period. The major idea of the SOE reform was to set up 'modern enterprise' institutional mechanisms inside the SOEs, simulating the institutional framework of a modern, private company while maintaining state ownership (CCP 2007). Following this basic idea of reform, a group of institutions have been established.

State-Owned Assets

The reform of SOEs in the 1990s led to most of the small and medium-sized SOEs being sold off, while government control of the large SOEs was maintained. This left the problem of how to build a principal–deputy relationship and a management system within the SOEs and between the government and the SOEs. According to widely used definitions, state-owned operating assets are defined as valuable assets owned by SOEs, assets owned and used by public institutions, and state-owned natural resources that have been put into the production process (Zheng et al. 2009, p.3).

Even after the selling of a large number of small SOEs in the 1990s, state-owned assets reached RMB35.48 trillion ($4.67 trillion) in 2007, or about 1.3 times the value of GDP at that time (Table 5.4).

The SOEs were spread widely across most sectors. In industries providing important public goods and in natural monopoly industries, SOEs were in a dominant position. In competitive industries, the share of SOEs was relatively small, but these SOEs still existed. The shares of SOEs were smaller in the eastern area than they were in the central and western areas. The number of SOEs controlled by the central government was reduced to 132 in 2009 from 196 in 2003. Each of these existing large SOEs had a large number of subsidiary companies. Although the profit to sales ratio of SOEs improved from 2003 to 2009, poor management of the SOEs still

Table 5.4 Main financial statistics of SOEs

Year	2003	2007
Number of SOEs	149,988	115,087
Total assets (RMB trillion ($ trillion))	19.71 (2.38)	35.48 (4.67)
Sales (RMB trillion ($ trillion))	10.37 (1.25)	20.08 (2.64)
Profits (RMB trillion ($ trillion))	0.50 (0.06)	1.76 (0.23)
Taxes paid (RMB trillion ($ trillion))	0.81 (0.10)	1.77 (0.23)

Source: State-owned Assets Supervision and Administration Commission of the State Council (SASAC) (2009).

resulted in inefficiency problems. Researches show that the growth rates of total productivity of some of the SOE-dominated industries (e.g. railways, water, and electricity) were lower than the average of 37 two-digit SIC code[14] industries from 1997 to 2005 (Wu 2009).

The State-owned Assets Supervision and Administration Commission (SASAC) was set up in 2003 as a special commission under the State Council responsible for managing the remaining SOEs after the SOE reform in the late 1990s, including appointing top executives and approving mergers or sales of stock or assets. The SASAC set up rules and regulations, including Temporary Regulations on the Supervision and Management of the Enterprise State-Owned Assets (issued by the State Council in May 2003, Yang n.d.), and other documents on reform, property rights transfer, asset assessment, and performance evaluation.

Before the establishment of the SASAC in 2003, the administration of the centrally controlled SOEs and other state-owned assets was carried out separately by several government branches. The Ministry of Finance oversaw return on assets; any large investments were implemented by the State Planning Committee; economic reform and technical renovation were managed by the State Economic and Commerce Committee; overseas investments were organised by the Ministry of Foreign Trade; the salaries of employees were controlled by the Ministry of Labour; and top-level managers were nominated and supervised by the Department of Organisation of the CCP. This system had many problems:

1. The property rights and decision rights were not well defined among central and local governments and among different government departments. Because the government would always rescue the SOEs, the SOEs were willing to take greater risks than other firms.
2. Many government departments functioned as both public management agencies and state asset owners, with no clear division between these functions. The government used administrative tools to interfere with the firms' activities.
3. SOEs suffered from weak regulation and supervision, with principal–agent problems. Many of the SOEs were actually controlled by insiders.
4. The reform of the shareholding system had many problems, including a weak shareholders' conference or a weak board, direct control by insiders or government departments, and an unclear division of power among the CCP committee, the labour union, the board, and the supervision committee.
5. Because the managers were nominated by the Department of Organisation of the CCP, the shareholders' meeting or the board were not able to ever fire a manager of a SOE.

The national SASAC was set up in March 2003, and SASAC branches were set up in all provinces and in most Chinese cities.[15] The SASAC made some progress in state-owned assets management, but it did not solve all the problems listed above. The 3rd Plenary Session of the 16th Central Committee of the CCP set out the following plan for the SOE reform: (i) establish a budget system and performance evaluation system; (ii) test effective forms of state-owned asset supervision and operation; (iii) improve the rules for property rights transfers and promote such transfers; and (iv) set up a supervision system for state-owned financial assets, non-operating assets, and natural assets (Zheng et al. 2009, p.45). The state-owned asset management system included three levels of investors: the state, the central government, and the local government. The operation system included the SASAC, the state shareholding companies, and the SOEs. The performance evaluation system for the managers of the centrally controlled SOEs was set up in 2003, and the regulation for salaries of the managers of the centrally controlled SOEs was set up in 2004.

State-Owned Holding Companies

A holding company – a company that owns other companies' stock shares and controls these companies – usually does not produce goods or services itself. A large number of state-owned holding companies had been established in China since the late 1990s, as links between the SASAC and ordinary SOEs. These state-owned holding companies came from the following sources:

1. Former government departments became state-owned holding companies. The subordinate enterprises became subsidiary companies, and the government–administration relationship changed to a relationship between investors and invested companies.
2. Industry-wide parent companies were reformed into holding companies. Numerous industry-wide parent companies had been established since the 1980s in industries such as petrochemicals, ship building, and aeroplane manufacturing, performing several administrative functions. These parent companies were reformed into holding companies.
3. A number of state-owned large corporate groups, such as Dongfeng Automobile Group, were changed into state-owned holding companies.
4. The central and local governments set up some new state-owned holding companies.

In China, state-owned holding companies are usually solely state-owned limited liability companies. According to Article 67 of the 2005 revision of the Corporation Law (National People's Congress 2005b), a solely state-owned company shall not set up a shareholders' conference, and the functions of a shareholders' conference shall be exercised by the SASAC instead. The SASAC may authorise the company's board of directors to exercise some of the functions of a shareholders' conference and to decide on important matters of the company, excluding those that must be decided by the SASAC, such as mergers, split-ups, dissolution of the company, increases or decreases in registered capital, and the issuance of corporate bonds. According to the Corporation Law, a solely state-owned company shall establish a board of directors that shall exercise its functions according to the law. The term of office for the directors shall not exceed three years. The board of directors shall include representatives of the employees. The members of the board of directors shall be designated by the SASAC, but the representatives of the employees on the board shall be elected by the company's employees. The board of directors shall have one chairman and may have a deputy chairman. According to the Corporation Law, a solely state-owned company shall have a manager, who shall be hired or dismissed by the board of directors. Upon consent of the SASAC, the members of the board of directors may concurrently hold the post of manager. The board of supervisors of a solely state-owned company, according to the Corporation Law, shall comprise at least five persons, of whom the employees' representatives shall account for no less than one-third of the board. The members of the board of supervisors shall be appointed by the SASAC.

The state-owned holding companies have many problems, including conflicts between the social targets and the economic targets, holding companies' over-interference in the SOEs, and collusion between holding companies and their subordinate SOEs. The high-level managers of the large holding companies are still nominated by the Department of Organisation of the CCP.

By 2000, 81 per cent (i.e. 2,016 out of 2,473) of large SOEs in the sample of survey by National Bureau of Statistics had set up 'modern enterprise systems'. In 2004, to improve enterprises' governance structure, the SASAC started the experiment of setting up the boards of the solely state-owned, centrally controlled companies, which before this point had no boards of directors (Zheng et al. 2009, p.182). SASAC tried to add external directors to the board. By September 2009, 16 of the 21 enterprises in the experiment had more external directors than internal directors on their board.

The State Council began to send special inspectors to large SOEs in 1998. These inspectors were responsible for auditing the financial condition of these SOEs. Thirty-eight inspectors were sent to 301 large SOEs in 1998. Based on the inspectors' work, the system of having a board of supervisors was set up in 2003. The members of the board of supervisors were appointed by the SASAC to the parent companies, with a term of three years. These board members have the right to meet anyone in the company, to check any document, and to attend any meetings. The tasks of the board of supervisors were centred on accounting supervision. The board of supervisors solved the problems of information asymmetry to some degree, working as a deterrent to the managers of large SOEs.

Numerous state-owned parent companies and subsidiary companies exist in the Chinese economy. These companies come from two sources. First, when a dominant company buys other companies, the latter become subsidiaries of the dominant company. Second, the government administratively deputes power to the parent company to establish a parent–subsidiary relationship. According to the Corporation Law, the company may set up subsidiaries that enjoy the status of an enterprise juridical person and shall bear civil liabilities independently (National People's Congress 1993a). The board of supervisors of the state-owned holding companies implemented supervision of the subsidiaries. From 1998 to 2000, special supervisors did the job, but in 2001 the board of supervisors took over this task. In 2006, the board of supervisors of about 100 state-owned holding companies supervised 1,672 enterprises, including company groups and their second and third levels of subsidiaries. Daily supervision covered both parent companies and important subsidiaries (Zheng et al. 2009, p.248).

Natural Monopoly Industries

Most of the enterprises in natural monopoly industries are SOEs. The entry restrictions make it extremely difficult for solely private-owned firms to enter these areas. Even within the joint-stock enterprises in these industries, the state share always dominates. The managers of these large SOEs are nominated by the Department of Organisation of the CCP, and many of their economic activities are controlled by government departments (Table 5.5).

The current company governance structure of the SOEs in natural monopoly industries includes (i) solely state-owned companies with no shareholders' conferences and with government-nominated boards of directors and boards of supervisors; and (ii) limited-responsibility companies wherein the state is the dominant shareholder. For the solely state-owned companies, the government's nomination of the board of directors, the board of supervisors and the managers results in unifying government functions with business operations. For limited responsibility companies, the state's dominance in decision-making damages the proper function of the shareholders' conference.

Table 5.5 Property rights in major natural monopoly industries in the early 21st century

Industry	Property rights
Postal services	Totally owned by the state, and the operation and government functions are unified in one agency.
Railways	The whole industry is state owned, and the operation and government functions are unified in one agency.
Airlines	Business operations have been separated from government functions, and the three largest company groups have been publicly listed. However, the state shares dominate, and outstanding shares are limited.
Telecommunication	Business operations have been separated from government functions, and several of the largest company groups have been publicly listed. However, the state shares dominate.
Electricity	Business operations have been separated from government functions, and electricity generation is separate from transmission networks. Several large company groups exist in the area of electricity generation. Two large company groups are in charge of the networks in different areas. All the company groups are solely state-owned companies.
Water	Operated locally, owned by government, private firms, or state-owned holding companies in different areas.

Source: Zheng et al. (2009, p.88).

In this section, I present more detailed information about some of the key natural monopoly industries.

Coal

During the planned period, most of the coal mines were SOEs. The government opened up the coal production industry to non-SOEs in the 1980s and reduced entry restrictions. A large number of non-SOEs entered the market, most of which were collectively owned firms.[16] From 1985 to 1996, the share of government investment reduced from 61 per cent to 19 per cent, and the share of village/county coal mines in coal production increased from 29 per cent to 45 per cent (Industrial Economic Research Institute 2008). One main issue of this deregulation is reduced occupational safety due to fewer inspections. In the early 21st century, the government drove numerous non-state-owned businesses out of the industry, for the purposes of tightening control and reducing accidents.

This was called 'the advance of the state vs the retreat of the private firms'.

The government deregulated coal price control in 1994. Currently, most coal prices are determined by the market.

Petroleum

The investment diversification in the petroleum industry started with the entry of foreign investment in offshore drilling in the 1980s. Multinational companies entered the retail market in the late 1990s. However, the market was mainly occupied by big SOEs. A structural reorganisation was performed in 1998, to improve the efficiency of production. The three big petroleum companies, China National Petroleum Corporation (CNPC), Sinopec Group (SINOPEC), and China National Offshore Oil Corporation (CNOOC), became vertically integrated company groups. They have huge profits due to their monopolistic position, the rise in international oil prices, and government pricing and tax policies. During the 1998 restructuring, two large oil companies, CNPC and SINOPEC, split oil extraction and refinement operations on different sides of the Yangtze River. The third SOE, CNOOC, deals mainly with offshore oil. CNPC and SINOPEC competed to occupy most of the retail market and incorporated many small private companies.

Currently, petroleum prices are determined by a system that connects the domestic price to the world price. The crude oil price is set every month by the production firms according to the international price, whereas the government controls the retail price.

Electricity

The price of electricity has been and remains controlled by the government. Because the price of coal is determined by the market, the electricity producer cannot make a normal profit and has no incentive to produce enough electricity.

To deal with the shortage of investment funds, a policy of investment diversity in the electricity industry was implemented in the 1980s, and the non-state share of power generation represented near 50 per cent in 1998 (Industrial Economic Research Institute 2008). Regulatory reform was carried out in 1999 and 2002. In the production area, the state-owned asset was divided and reorganised into five national electricity companies that now compete with one another. The network was divided into two parts that are operated by two independent publicly owned companies. The network system is still regulated. An independent regulatory agency, the State Electricity Regulatory Commission, was set up to oversee the regulatory works in 2003. This was the first and only independent industrial-level regulatory agency in China; it was dissolved later in 2013. The slow development of networks placed a restriction on the amount of power distributed.[17]

Airlines

Civil aviation existed in China before the CCP gained power in 1949. The new government established the aviation authority and operator, the General Administration of Civil Aviation of China, in 1949, which was both a government department and a state-owned airline. The regulatory agency changed its name several times and is now known as the Civil Aviation Administration of China (CAAC).

In 1985, the State Council approved the *Report on Reforming the Management Structure of Civil Aviation*. It ruled that the CAAC's administrative function would be separated from its enterprise function. It was to become primarily an administrative and regulatory agency responsible for formulating aviation policies and development plans, negotiating international air transport agreements, instituting technical standards for airline and airport operations, managing civilian air traffic control, issuing air operator licences, monitoring safety, regulating air fares, coordinating aircraft acquisitions, setting rules on airlines' financial accounting and reporting, and supervising aviation training schools. The CAAC's monopoly was broken up into several airlines based on their existing administrative regions, and regional bureaus were abolished. The airlines were to manage their own operations and be responsible for their own profits and losses. The CAAC would no longer be engaged directly in airline management. Government departments, local authorities, and business enterprises were also permitted to establish new airlines. Except for international and key domestic airports, the CAAC gradually transferred control of airports to local authorities, these airports were to be managed as businesses.

In 1986, the State Council issued provisional regulations on airline licensing to permit the CAAC to act as a regulatory agency. The regulations were subsequently promulgated in the 1995 Civil Aviation Law (National People's Congress 1995c) that also covered aircraft registration and mortgage, airline security, and carriers' liability. Neither the 1995 law nor the 1986 regulations contained provisions dealing specifically with issues of airline competition, such as route allocation and pricing. That left the CAAC with its traditionally broad power over such matters, offering airlines few legal grounds to appeal the CAAC's decisions.

Six major airlines were spun off from the old CAAC between 1987 and 1991. Three of them – Air China, China Eastern, and China Southern – were known collectively as China's 'big three' airlines. They handled half of the passenger traffic carried by all Chinese carriers. The other three major carriers – China Northern, China Northwest, and China Southwest – handled another 26 per cent. Many more carriers have been formed since then. The number of airlines mushroomed to more than 40 in 1994, which put intolerable strains on the aviation infrastructure and raised concerns about airline safety. In response, the CAAC stopped issuing new airline licences in 1994. It also cancelled the licences of several airlines and allowed small airlines to be taken over by larger carriers (e.g. Swan Airlines by China Northern and Fujian Airlines by Xiamen Airlines).

In 1994, the CAAC and the Ministry of Foreign Trade and Economic Cooperation (which licenses foreign investment projects) issued the *Notice on Policies Concerning Foreign Investment in Civil Aviation*. The new policy permitted foreign investors, including foreign air carriers, to establish airline joint ventures with Chinese partners, to buy shares in existing airlines, and to enter cross-equity holdings with Chinese airlines. It excluded foreign airport authorities and aircraft manufacturers from such investments, and it limited foreign investors' holdings to a maximum of 35 per cent of the registered capital and 25 per cent of the voting rights in an airline. Some of the largest airlines were given permission by the government to apply for listing on overseas stock markets. China Eastern and China Southern listed their shares on the New York and Hong Kong stock exchanges.

Currently, China's passenger airline industry is dominated by the three state-owned airline groups (Table 5.6). There is limited competition from

Table 5.6 Market share, airline industry, 2006

	Revenues, main operation (RMB mil. ($ mil.))	Assets (RMB mil. ($ mil.))	Market share (%)
Air China	47,006 (5,896)	87,117 (10,928)	31.6
China Eastern	36,806 (4,617)	60,129 (7,543)	21.8
China South	47,047 (5,902)	76,196 (9,558)	27.7
China Hainan	12,448 (1,561)	35,729 (4,482)	13.0
Shanghai	9,934 (1,246)	11,198 (1,405)	4.1
Xiamen	2,229 (280)	4,421 (555)	1.5
Aokai	NA	300 (38)	0.1
Spring	NA	300 (38)	0.1
Yinglian	NA	300 (38)	0.1

Note: Shandong, Sichuan, and Shenzhen Airlines are not included due to lack of data. The data for Xiamen Airlines is from 2005.

Source: Zheng et al. (2009, p.116).

private operators such as Spring Airlines in the commercial passenger market, but the state-owned operators have the political and financial wherewithal from the central government to lead the market. The CAAC sets domestic air fare prices, but airlines may apply to have their fares changed. The government started pricing policy reform in 2004 to let the carriers have more of a say in determining their fares. For the domestic trunk lines, the government set the baseline prices and included a range of flexibility so that carriers could change the fares within this range. For short routes, the fares are determined by the market. The fare ceilings are 25 per cent of the base fare, and the lowest fare limit is 45 per cent of the base fare. All these policies increased the airlines' autonomy to adjust their prices according to market demand and supply. In 2010, the government announced that first-class and business-class fares would be determined by the market. In 2013, the CAAC removed the upper and lower limits on airfares (Bai and Zhou 2013), thus increasing competition.

Railways

Economic reform in the railway industry is far behind most other industries. The Ministry of Railways is both a government agency and an operating unit, and there have been no major changes in the railway transportation area during the past 30 years.

The Ministry of Railways has control over transportation price. The price has been raised several times since the 1980s, and the price system has been diversified and the decision-making level lowered. There are some degrees of flexibility within the planned prices. The Planning Committee (which was renamed the Committee of Development and Reform) set up a system of hearing procedures about price changes in 2002.

Some researchers calculated the total factor productivity (TFP) of the railway industry and compared it with that of other industries. They found that TFP in the railway industry was significantly lower than it was in other industries (Davis 2017). Wu (2009) found that the growth rate of TFP of China's railway industry from 1997 to 2005 was 2.22 per cent, lower than the average of 37 industries (7.5 per cent) in China during the same period.[18]

Over the years, there have been many different proposals to reform the railway industry. Most of them agreed to separate government administration from the business operations of the Ministry of Railways, but there have also been different ideas about how to set up competition among state-owned railway companies. One proposal is to separate the railway network from the operating companies, whereas others propose to separate companies by geographical area.[19] The government does not have enough incentive to carry out the reform. Because railway reform would impact a large portion of the population and many industrial sectors, the government has been careful in making large reforms. As of early 2017, no reform has been implemented (ZGTLYS 2016).

Telecommunications

Before the 1980s, China's telecommunication industry was monopolised by the Ministry of Posts and Telecommunications (MTP). The industry was fully regulated by the government. Price controls resulted in the industry's low profits, and the lack of funding restricted further development.

Before 1994, the MTP provided telecom services through its operational arm, China Telecom. Pressured by other ministries and dissenting customers, the Chinese government officially started a telecom industry reform in 1994 by introducing a new competitor, China Unicom, which was supported by several government departments, such as the Commission of Economy and Trade, the Ministry of Electricity, and the Ministry of Electronic Engineering. This could be viewed as a rent-seeking process by other interest groups, since numerous government departments were privy to the potential profits from China Unicom. However, considering the size of China Unicom in term of assets, personnel, and customers, it could hardly compete with the giant China Telecom.

In 1998, due to a ministerial reorganisation, the MTP was replaced by the new Ministry of Information Industry (MII). The establishment of the MII split the government functions in telecommunications from the operating functions, so that the operating agencies became independent of the government functions. The MII undertook two large-scale restructuring exercises that targeted the inefficient state monopoly. In 1999, the first restructuring exercise split China Telecom's business into three parts: fixed-line, mobile, and satellite. China Mobile and China Satcom were created to run the mobile and satellite sectors, respectively, but China Telecom continued to keep its monopoly over fixed-line services. The second restructuring exercise in 2002 split China Telecom geographically into North and South: China Telecom-North kept 30 per cent of the network resources and formed China Netcom (CNC); 70 per cent of the resources were retained by China Telecom-South, or simply the new China Telecom. Parallel to this double fission (i.e. two large steps of reform separating operations among companies and splitting China Telecom geographically), the telecommunications division of the Ministry of Railways established a new actor in the industry in 2000: China TieTong. Overall, the second restructuring exercise created six operators in the market: China Telecom, China Unicom, China Mobile, China Satcom, China Netcom, and China TieTong (Table 5.7).

Table 5.7 Market share, telecommunication, 2006

		Sales (RMB bil. ($ bil.))	Assets (RMB bil. ($ bil.))	Market share (%)
Mobile and satellite	China Mobile	295 (37)	635 (80)	78.6
	China Unicom	80 (10)	236 (30)	21.4
Fixed-line	China Telecom	178 (22)	557 (70)	63.7
	China Netcom	85 (11)	277 (35)	30.2
	China TieTong	16 (2)	55 (7)	5.5
	China Satcom	2 (0.3)	NA	0.5

Source: Zheng (2009, p.114).

In May 2008, MII, the National Development and Reform Committee (NDRC), and the Ministry of Finance announced a third restructuring exercise and launched three 3G licences. China Telecom purchased China Unicom's CDMA network, China Unicom merged with China Netcom, China Satcom was incorporated into China Telecom, and China TieTong merged into China Mobile. The third reform combined six main telecom operators into three similar-sized operators – China Telecom, China Unicom, and China Mobile – with the aim of developing 3G business and full telecom services, and avoiding monopolies as well as excessive competition.

To sum up, in the first decade of the new century, the Chinese telecom industry changed from a state-run monopolistic structure to a state-run oligopolistic structure. In other words, a preliminary market competition framework has been established.

Performance of Large SOEs

The Chinese government launched a macro-control campaign in 2004, in which the government used economic and administrative means to balance the economy. Many small companies were closed by the government. After macro-control,[20] the large SOEs strengthened their dominant positions. In the three years after the establishment of the SASAC, the SOEs, directly under the control of central government, improved their performance. From 2003 to 2007, the prime operating revenue of SOEs increased by 17 per cent annually, and the profit increased by 37 per cent annually (Zheng et al. 2009, p.8). This was the result of (i) improvements in the management of large SOEs, and (ii) the monopolised position of large SOEs and the favourable policy treatment they enjoyed.

Because of the jump of the international oil price in the early 21st century, the profits of the three large oil companies, CNPC, SINOPEC, and CNOOC, increased dramatically. The three large SOEs in the telecommunication sector – China Mobile, China Telecom, and China Unicom – were engaged in a fierce price war in the early 21st century. The SASAC therefore rotated the presidents of these companies, which caused concerns that the government was undermining the market principle.

5.5 PRIVATE FIRMS

Private firms, after 20 years of growth since the 1980s, became a sizable force in the Chinese economy in the first decade of the 21st century. The role of private business in economic growth could not be ignored, even though they were still unequally treated in many areas and their size were still much smaller than that of SOEs. In 2006, there were only 74 private firms on the China Top 500 list, and their total capital was less than one-third of China Industrial and Commercial Bank, a large SOE (Wu Xiaobo 2014b, p.375).

Development under Government Regulation

This section is about the success and failures of private firms in a highly regulated economy. By the early 21st century in China, most of the downstream manufacturing industries had been opened up to private firms, but most of the resource-related upstream industries were still monopolised by large SOEs. There was an attempt by private firms to break this glass ceiling to enter into the monopolised industries in the early 21st century, but most of their efforts failed.

China's automotive industry was dominated by large SOEs and multinational manufacturers which had partnerships with domestic manufacturers. Li Shufu and his GEELY auto obtained a car production licence in November 2001 from the State Commission for Economics and Trade. This was a milestone of the development of China's private enterprises. Before this, no private firms could enter the automobile industry. Li is a businessman from Taizhou in Zhejiang province. He bought a motorcycle factory and the licence for motorcycle production in 1996. He then decided to produce automobiles in 1997 and bought an auto factory in Sichuan province. The first GEELY car rolled off the production line in 1998. Li was targeting the lower-income market, so he set the price for a vehicle at RMB58,000 ($7,005.5), which was much lower than that of most other brands, including Volkswagen, Hyundai, Chevrolet, Changan, and Toyota. He did his best to get a licence to produce cars (it was possible to buy the factory without this licence) from the government and finally got it in 2001. To expand its business overseas, GEELY bought Swedish automaker Volvo in 2010. In 2015, GEELY produced more than ten vehicle products and various types of engines, and had 700 retail centres all over China (Zhang 2017).

China's oil sector has been monopolised by three large SOEs since the 1980s. The Great Wall United Oil Company, a coalition of over 100 small private oil companies, was established in 2006, initiated by Gong Jialong, CEO of Tianfa Oil. The company had RMB870 million ($109.1 million) in registered capital and planned to operate in exploration, exploitation, refining, and sales. Although the company got a business licence, it could not get a refined oil wholesale licence, a refined oil retail licence, a refined oil import licence, or a domestic mineral exploration and exploitation licence. Without these licences, Great Wall was not able to conduct business. Mr Gong was soon arrested in 2007 for 'obtaining bank loans by using illegal means'. The attempts made by private enterprises to enter the oil sector failed, and as a result, some of the small private oil firms were sold (Wu Xiaobo 2014b, p.374).

Shanxi is the primary coal mining province in China. The frequent accidents in the coal mines made the Shanxi provincial government decide to close all small coal mines (i.e. mines under 90,000 tons) in 2005. In 2009, the provincial government decided that the whole coal mining industry should be restructured by large state-owned mines, and that the scale of each enterprise should be no less than 3 million tons. This drove almost all private companies, many of which were owned by Wenzhou investors, out of the coal mining sector. This was called 'the advance of the state vs the retreat of the private firms'.

Some of the private firms entered the monopolised sectors successfully, whereas others failed. Overall, the situation of monopolised industries still dominated by large SOEs did not change very much.

Strategic Development

The private enterprises in China experienced rapid growth and engaged in strategic development during this period. The house appliances retail channel dominated production in the new century. Huang Guangyu, the founder of GUME Electric Appliance, opened his first electrical appliance store in Beijing in 1987. In 2004, GUME was listed on the Hong Kong Stock Exchange (SEHK). GUME followed a low-price, high-gross-profit-margin strategy and reduced its purchase costs by improving purchase approaches. In 2013, GUME had 1,063 stores[21] in 256 cities in China. Huang was rated as the richest person in China by the *Hurun Report* in

2005. However, he was arrested for stock price manipulation in 2007 and sentenced to 14 years in prison (Wu Xiaobo 2014b, p.341).

Many Chinese companies adjusted their strategies and started to invest overseas. In May 2005, Lenovo completed the acquisition of IBM's personal computer division, including the ThinkPad laptop and tablet lines. Lenovo paid $1.25 billion for IBM's computer business and assumed an additional $500 million of IBM's debt. Lenovo also bought IBM's Intel-based server lines in 2014. The biggest challenges of the acquisition were the cultural difference[22] and the regulations of the US government (Lenovo n.d.).

A group of high-tech companies burst out around the turn of the century. NetEase, created by Ding Lei in 1987, made its first profit in 2002. The company started 163.com to provide a free webmail service in 1998 and was listed on NASDAQ in 2000. The stock price of NetEase ballooned in 2002, and Ding Lei became the richest person in China in 2003. Baidu, China's largest search engine, was listed on NASDAQ in 2005. The stock price of Baidu reached $120 and broke the record for the largest first-day increase for a foreign company. Liu Chuanzhi, founder of Lenovo, passed the torch of day-to-day operations to two younger entrepreneurs, Yang Yuanqing and Guo Wei, in 2000, and continued to be a key adviser and decision maker. Yang tried to change the company into an internet-based company but failed. In 2004, Lenovo's stock price plunged. Liu and Yang decided to return to the PC market and bought IBM's PC branch for $1.75 billion in 2005 (Lenovo n.d.).

The private companies experienced great development during this period. This development sometimes was supported by the government; at other times, it was stopped due to government control.

5.6 LOCAL GOVERNMENT AS THE ENGINE OF ECONOMIC GROWTH (II)

The local government played an important role in the economic development during this period, as the organiser and manager of local economic activities. The competition between local governments and the official evaluation criteria system gave the local government incentives to accelerate the local economic growth. At the same time, the local governments were more reliant on the land leasing revenues as one of the major sources of finance. This relationship between central and local governments was called 'de facto federalism' by Zheng Yongnian (2013).

During this period, China's local government heavily invested in city infrastructure, including road and subway systems in urban areas, housing for low-income residents, industrial parks, and government buildings.

The regular daily expenditure of local governments included education, social security, and public security. Different from the United States, local government covered most of the social security expenditures.

Extra-Budgetary Revenue and Land Finance

Since the early 1980s, Chinese local governments have collected a significant amount of revenue outside the budgetary system. This extra-budgetary revenue refers to revenues controlled by central government departments, local governments, or SOEs that are not included in the national budget. The reason for needing extra-budgetary revenue was local governments' shortage of budgetary revenue under the existing central–local fiscal arrangements. Extra-budgetary revenue constitutes the only financial resources a local government can plan by itself.

During the planned period, the extra-budgetary revenue was not an important source of local government financial revenue. In 1953, the central government slightly enlarged local governments' financial resources, including local governments' industrial and commercial tax surcharge, toll for highway maintenance, school fees, as well as the SOEs' special fund. Extra-budgetary revenue accounted for 6 to 9 per cent of the national budgetary revenue from 1953 to 1958. This ratio increased to 30 per cent before the economic reform in the 1970s. In 1986, the State Council first defined the term 'Extra-Budgetary' revenue as a self-extracting fund not included in the national budget, which belonged to local governments, central government departments, and other units. From 1989, the central government tried to standardise the management of extra-budgetary revenue, requiring it be saved in a special account set up by the Ministry of Finance. In 1999, 'separation between revenue and expenditure' was adopted, under which all non-tax revenue had to be saved in a special account and all expenditure had to be managed according to an extra-budgetary plan and appropriated from the special account. Local government extra-budgetary revenue has been an important part of local governments' financial resources. The ratio of local extra-budgetary revenue to local budgetary revenue increased from 1982 to 1988 and decreased after 1988. It was still maintained at a high level in the first decade of the 21st century (Table 5.8).

Fiscal shortage is commonly cited as the main reason for needing local extra-budgetary finance.[23] The central government has limited means to standardise the management of local extra-budgetary revenue. Despite the constant calls by the central government to reform and regulate the extra-budgetary system, the centrally issued administrative directives have little impact on local practices. This is mainly because the central government did not want to increase the local governments' share of budgetary

Table 5.8 Local governments' extra-budgetary revenue

Year	Local revenue within budget (A) RMB billion ($ billion)	Local extra-budget revenue (B) RMB billion ($ billion)	B/A	B/central extra-budget revenue
1982	86.5 (45.7)	53.2 (28.1)	0.61	1.97
1985	123.5 (42.1)	89.4 (30.4)	0.72	1.41
1990	194.5 (40.7)	163.5 (34.2)	0.84	1.52
1995	298.6 (35.8)	208.9 (25.0)	0.70	6.58
2000	640.6 (77.4)	357.9 (43.2)	0.56	14.45
2005	1,510.1 (184.3)	514.2 (62.8)	0.34	12.77

Note: No extra-budget revenue data has been published in recent years.

Source: Zhou (2008, pp.180–181); National Bureau of Statistics (2011, Table 8.3, 8.12).

revenue. Therefore, the central government had to allow local governments to solve the financial problem by themselves. The extra-budgetary revenue is necessary for local governments to survive and keep operating in an apanage management system[24] with inadequate financial resources. The logic is that, if the central government does not give local governments enough resources, it has to give local governments the freedom to create resources by themselves. In addition, if the central government cannot keep its promise and change the ratio of the local retained revenues, the local governments may prefer to keep its extra-budgetary funds. This is a credibility problem for the central government.

Land grant premiums and land tax revenues have become two major sources of fiscal revenue for local governments in China in recent years. This type of fiscal revenue strategy for local governments is generally referred to as 'land finance'.

After the tax-sharing reform in 1994, the fiscal relationship between the central and local governments changed dramatically. The central government changed the rules of the game and claimed the stable, easily collected taxes for its own treasury. As a consequence, the central government got a relatively larger share of tax revenue, while its responsibilities for providing public goods were relatively limited.

As shown in Figure 5.1, in most years after 1994, the central government has controlled over 50 per cent of the national fiscal revenues but has covered less than 30 per cent of the expenditures. Considering the inefficiency of the intergovernmental transfers from the central government, the local governments have been responsible for a larger share of the expenditures with a much smaller portion of the revenue. The local governments established

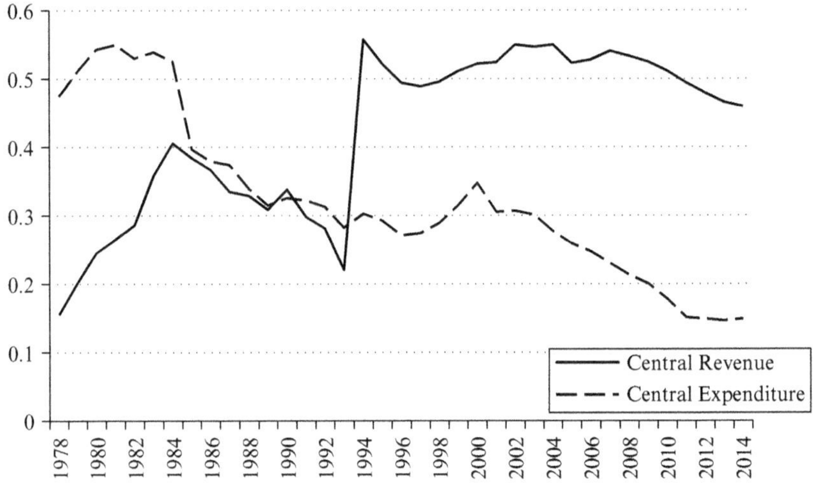

Note: The central government's total revenue exceeded total expenditure after 1994. The gap was supposed to be the transfer payments to the local government.

Source: National Bureau of Statistics (2015).

Figure 5.1 Central government's revenue and expenditure as a proportion of the national total, 1980–2010

'land finance' as an additional revenue source later. Land is a scarce resource in China. According to the 1982 version of China's Constitution, land in the cities is owned by the state. Land in the rural and suburban areas is owned by collectives except for those portions belonging to the state in accordance with the law; house sites and privately farmed plots of cropland and hilly land are also owned by collectives. The state may, in the public's interest, requisition land for its use in accordance with the law. No organisation or individual may appropriate, buy, sell, or lease land or otherwise engage in the transfer of land by unlawful means (National People's Congress 1982a). Only the government can transfer rural land into urban land legally by requisition, which is crucial to the expansion of urban areas and the local public finance. Land grant premiums and land-related tax revenues have become two major sources of fiscal revenue for local governments, especially the city governments. It is not surprising that the local government has chosen land as its source of revenue, because land, unlike capital and labour, is the only immobile asset firmly under the control of municipal government (Lin 2007). Land finance is actually an aspect of public finance through selling the future value of state-owned land (Zhao 2014).

Land finance has been used in Hong Kong for many years. At a meeting with Hong Kong business people in the 1980s, officials from Shenzhen complained that they did not have enough financial resources. As a response to the complaints, Huo Yingdong, a Hong Kong businessman, pointed out a new way to get financial resources by leasing state-owned land. He said, 'how can you have no money if you have land?' (Zhou 2013, p.106). After some years of searching, the local governments found that land requisition and public land leasing are important sources of revenue. They buy land from collectives (villages) in the countryside, paying a low requisition fee, and lease the land to housing developers for a higher-than-market price. The monopoly power in the land market gives the local government extra economic rent.

Local governments also collect various taxes related to land, including (i) taxes collected only from the housing sector – housing property tax, urban land-use tax, land appreciation tax, farmland occupation tax, and deed tax; (ii) taxes related to housing/business – corporate income tax, personal income tax, urban maintenance and construction tax, and stamp tax; (iii) fees, including land management fees, vegetation development funds, public service project development fees, and land-use rights fees.

The total government revenue from land leasing, including revenue directly from land leasing, and related tax collections and fees, has accounted for a large share of local government revenue in recent years. The share of total land leasing revenue in total local government revenue was 16.6 per cent in 2001. The land leasing revenue increased to RMB1.6 trillion ($0.2 trillion) in 2009, 48.8 per cent of the total local government revenue, including both budgetary revenue and extra-budgetary revenue. According to a report from the Research and Development Centre of the State Council, land-related taxes account for 40 per cent of the local governments' budgetary revenue, and land leasing net revenue accounts for 60 per cent of local governments' extra-budgetary revenue (Baike Mingpian n.d.).

The local governments played a major role in the rapid economic growth in the first decade of the 21st century. Policy is designed by the central government and implemented by local governments. This pattern of task-division between central and local government works well in most cases, but also has some problems. When the local government does not have enough incentives, the policy will not be implemented. For example, the local governments were not very active in relation to environmental protection, since they were more interested in GDP growth. The problem is due to the performance criterion set by the central government before 2010, in which GDP growth was the most important measure. It was also a problem of the implementation of policy. The leadership tried to extend authorities for environmental protection to the local level by using a strategy of extending the administrative 'lines' to the lower level of the bureaucratic structure.

Vertical Management and Multiple Criteria

Political competition created enormous incentives for the local governments to drive the rapid economic growth in the late 1990s and the first decade of the 21st century. It also created problems. While focusing on GDP, the local government ignored a number of important aspects of life (e.g. environmental protection, corruption, and public goods provision). To correct these deviations, the central government attempted to implement some changes in the first decade of the 21st century.

As early as in the 1990s, the central government tried to increase the use of 'lines' to solve problems, by setting up extensions of central departments deep into the local level. For example, the central government established local product quality supervision branches that reported directly to the central agency on product quality control. These attempts were not successful, partly because the local government needed these local branches for local development, and partly because the local government, in some cases, provided the funding of the operation of the local branches of these agencies.

A regional structure was adopted in a number of fields, following the example of the Federal Reserve regional-bank system. In 1997, the central government decided to adopt vertical (line) management for the central bank and large state-owned commercial banks. In 1998, the People's Bank of China removed the provincial branches and set up regional branches, which functioned across provinces, to avoid the interference of the provincial government. In 1998, the state decided to implement vertical administration for Commercial Administration agencies under the province level. All funds and personnel of the Commercial Administration under the province level were managed by the provincial Commercial Administration agency (not by the lower-level local government). A similar approach was adopted for Land Administration agencies in 2008. All Land Administration agencies under the provincial level were managed by the provincial Land Administration agency. This was an attempt to reduce the power of local government in the allocation of land resources. Before 2008, the powers of land planning, land examination and approval, and land leasing fee collection were controlled by the local government. Land leasing was actually controlled by city and county governments. The establishment of local branches directly under the central government agencies represents an important shift of power upward. Another fundamental change was the attempt to change the content of official performance criteria. In a political competition, the behaviour of local officials is determined by the performance criteria set by the central government. To correct the bias of over-emphasising GDP while ignoring other development indicators, the performance criteria had to be changed. The central government tried to add two important criteria into the official access standards,[25] as early as the first decade of the 21st century. First, attempts were made to add environmental pollution and energy consumption into the list of criteria. In 2006, the CCP Department of Organisation issued a Proposed Regulation on the Access Procedure of Local Party and Government Leadership (CCP Department of Organisation 2006). The regulation emphasised a change from the GDP-centred official access system to a more comprehensive access system. The new system focused on a group of indicators (e.g. per capita GDP, per capita fiscal revenue, income of the residents in urban and rural areas, and citizen's satisfaction), to reflect the overall economic development of a region. According to the regulation, opinion polls can be conducted through using questionnaire surveys, household surveys, or surveys on the internet. From 2008, the CCP Department of Organisation authorised the National Bureau of Statistics to conduct an opinion survey on the 'organisation work'[26] of 31 provinces, cities and central departments, SOEs, and non-profit public institutions. The main aim of the survey was to get feedback on people's satisfaction with the organisation's work and the official promotion procedure, and it did this by way of a questionnaire, with the sample size being 80,000 (Zhou 2008, p.121). Today, meetings between workers in an office and representatives of the CCP organisation before an official being nominated has become a rule in many 'units'. This is an important change. However, the access procedure needs to be more transparent, fair, and unitary.

5.7 GOVERNMENT ADMINISTRATIVISATION

In the first decade of the new century, the governments at different levels became more formal and routine-focused. This decade saw the implementation of a series of laws and regulations, which covered many fields related to a rule-based market economy and the safety network protecting the people and the society. The development of the market economy has expanded the activities over which courts have jurisdiction.

The Constitution was amended in March 2004. The amendment to Article 11 further legitimised and encouraged the 'non-public owned economy'. The amendment provided further protection for private property (National People's Congress 2004b).

More legal vehicles for business organisations were provided by the People's Congress. The Corporation Law, initially passed in 1993, was revised in 1999 and 2005 (National People's Congress 2005b). The Partnership Law, passed in 1997, was revised in 2006 (National People's Congress 2006b). The Tort Law was adopted in 2009 and implemented in 2010, to protect the legitimate rights and interests of parties in civil law relationships. The civil rights and interests, according to the law, include the rights to life, health, name, reputation, honour, self-image, privacy, marital autonomy, guardianship, ownership, usufruct, security interest, copyright, and patent (National People's Congress 2009a). The Enterprise Bankruptcy Law was passed in 2007. Compared to the previous 1986 Enterprise Bankruptcy Law (provisional), which only applied to state-owned enterprises, the new bankruptcy law covers all business entities (National People's Congress 2006c). The Enterprise State-Owned Assets Law was adopted at the 5th session of the 11th Standing Committee of the National People's Congress in October 2008 and became effective in May 2009. The law, which had been drafted and deliberated for more than ten years, is China's first law addressing state-owned assets, and replaced a set of administrative regulations (National People's Congress 2008a).

A number of laws were adopted to protect the ownership rights of business participants. The Property Law was passed in March 2007. The law covers ownership rights, usufructuary rights, and secured property rights. The law clarifies property ownerships, protecting the property rights of the right holders (National People's Congress 2007d). The Copyright Law, originally implemented in 1990, was revised in 2010 to protect the rights of authors (National People's Congress 2010a). The Patent Law, passed in 1984 and revised in 2000, was revised again in 2008 (National People's Congress 2008b). The Law on the Administration of Urban Real Estate, adopted in 1994 and revised in 2007, was revised in 2009 to regulate land use for development of real estate and real-estate transactions (National People's Congress 2009d). The Regulation on the Expropriation of Buildings on State-Owned Land and Compensation was adopted by the State Council in 2011, to regulate the government expropriation of buildings on state-owned land and compensations for expropriation (State Council 2011). The Law of Land Administration, adopted in 1986 and revised in 1988, was amended in 2004. The 2004 revision differentiated the concept of 'land expropriation' (ownership changes) from 'land requisition' (National People's Congress 2004d). The Law on Land Contract in Rural Areas, adopted in 2002, was revised in 2009 to protect the rural collectives when contracting the land to farmers (National People's Congress 2009e).

An Enterprise Income Tax Law was passed in March 2007 and implemented in January 2008. The new law unified the two corporate income tax systems that were applicable to domestic enterprises, solely foreign enterprises and foreign-invested enterprises, respectively (National People's Congress 2007b). The Individual Income Tax Law, originally passed in 1980 and revised in 1993, 1999, 2005, and 2007, was revised again in 2011. The law raised the minimum taxable income to RMB3,500 ($460.3) per month and changed the tax rates to 3 to 45 per cent (National People's Congress 2007c and 2011b). A group of revisions of regulations was issued by the State Council on value-added tax, consumption tax, and business tax in 2008 (State Council 2008a, 2008b, 2008c).

The Law on Negotiable Instruments, originally passed in 1995, was revised in 2004. The law applied to activities within China involving negotiable instruments, including bills of exchange, promissory notes, and cheques (National People's Congress 2004c). The Banking Supervision Law was passed in 2003 and revised in 2006. According to the law, the banking supervision institution of the State Council is responsible for the supervision of the national financial institutions, including commercial banks, urban credit cooperatives, rural credit cooperatives, and policy banks (National People's Congress 2006d). The Law on the People's Bank of China was passed in 1995 and revised in 2003. According to the law, the People's Bank of China is the central bank of China and the objective of the monetary policy is to maintain the stability of the value of the currency and thereby promote economic growth (National People's Congress 2003).

More efforts have been made to build a safety network for society against possible damage coming from the market. The Trade Union Law, adopted in 1992 and revised in 2001, was revised a second time in 2009 and regulated the organisation, rights, and obligations of the Trade Union (National People's Congress 2009h). The Labour Law, adopted in 1994, was amended in 2009, and covered labour contracts and collective contracts, working hours, wages, labour safety, protection for female and juvenile workers, and labour disputes (National People's Congress 2009i). The Social Insurance Law was adopted in 2010, and covered basic pension insurance, basic medical insurance, work-related injury insurance, and maternity insurance. It also regulated the collection and payment, handling, and supervision of the social insurance (National People's Congress 2010c). The Law on the Protection of Disabled Persons was adopted in 1990 and revised in 2008 (National People's Congress 2008d). The Law on the Protection of Minors, which was adopted in 1991, was then amended in 2012 (National People's Congress 2012a). The Law on the Protection of Rights and Interests of Women, adopted in 1992, was amended in 2005 (National People's Congress 2005c).

The Antitrust Law was passed in 2007. The law was enacted for the purpose of preventing and restraining monopolistic conducts, protecting fair competition in the market, enhancing economic efficiency, and safeguarding the interests of consumers. According to the law, 'monopolistic conduct' is defined as the activities of monopolistic agreements, abuse of dominant market positions, and concentration of undertakings that eliminate competitions. The law specifically defined the administrative monopolies and ordered that governments shall not abuse administrative power in order to limit competition (National People's Congress 2007a).

Environmental protection was raised on the legislative agenda. The Water Pollution Prevention and Control Law, adopted in 1984 and revised in 1996, was revised again in 2008. The law established the standards of water quality, regulated the supervision of water pollution control, and specified the legal consequences of violating the law (National People's Congress 2008c). The Product Quality Law, adopted in 1993 and amended in 2000, was revised a second time in 2009. It covered supervision and control over product quality, liabilities and obligations of producers and sellers, compensation for damage, and penalties administered for poor-quality products (National People's Congress 2009f).

The 2004 revision of the Foreign Trade Law gave individuals the right to engage in foreign trade (National People's Congress 2004a).

The Audit Law, originally adopted in 1994, was revised in 2006. According to the law, the State Council and the local people's governments at or above the county level shall establish auditing organs. The law regulated the functions, responsibilities, and limits of power of auditing organs, audit procedures, and legal liabilities (National People's Congress 2006f). The Statistics Law, adopted in 1983 and revised in 1996, was amended in 2009, and covered the management and publication of statistical data, statistical institutions and personnel, supervision and inspection, and legal responsibility (National People's Congress 2009g).

A number of laws have been passed to regulate the government itself. The Administrative Licensing Law was passed in 2003, to regulate the establishment and implementation of administrative licences. The term 'administrative licensing' as used in this law means the acts by the administrative organs to permit the citizens, legal persons, or other organisations to engage in special activities. The law set up the principle that the licensing of business activities should be justified only by public necessity.[27] The law regulates the establishment and implementation of administrative licensing, to protect the legitimate rights and interests of citizens, legal persons, and other organisations. According to the law, the relevant regulations on an administrative licence shall be announced to the public, the implementation of the administrative licence and the results shall be disclosed, and the regulations shall not make extra requirements for the implementation of the licence set down by the law (State Council 2003).

The Administrative Penalty Law, adopted in 1996, was revised in 2009 to standardise the creation and imposition of the administrative penalty (National People's Congress 2009b). The Administrative Reconsideration Law, originally passed in 1999, was revised in 2009. According to the law, when a citizen, a legal person, or any organisation considers that its lawful rights have been infringed upon by a specific administrative act, it can apply to an administrative organ for administrative reconsideration (National People's Congress 2009c). The Regulations on the Disclosure of Government Information was adopted by the State Council and implemented in 2008. The regulation defined the range of information, most of it related to citizens and organisations, that government should publicly release (State Council 2007). The Administrative Coercion Law was first adopted in 2011 to regulate the implementation of administrative coercion and to supervise the behaviour of the government (National People's Congress 2011a). The Civil Servant Law was adopted in 2005 to regulate the administration of civil servants. Civil servants were defined as personnel who perform public duties, who are state administrative staff, and whose wages are provided by public finance (National People's Congress 2005a). The Administrative Supervision Law, adopted in 1997, was amended in 2010, and strengthened the supervision and guaranteed the smooth implementation of government decrees. According to the law, the supervisory organs shall exercise their functions in accordance with law and shall be subject to no interference from other administrative departments, public organisations, or individuals (National People's Congress 2010b). The Law on the Supervision by the Standing Committee of the People's Congress at Various Levels was passed in August 2006 and implemented in January 2007. It defined the powers of the Standing Committee of the People's Congress on the administration and judicial branches of the government, including listening and discussing the reports of these administrative and judicial parts of the government, examination and approval of the budget, inquiries to the government, investigation of special issues, and dismissing government officials between congress meetings (National People's Congress 2006a).

A number of important areas (e.g. some administrative procedures) still have not been covered in separate single laws (Zhu 2010, p.127). And not all these laws have been implemented effectively. The inefficiency of the implementation of laws was due to the fact that (i) the legal branch of the government was much weaker than the administrative branch, in terms of political power, personnel, and financial support; and (ii) government officials and citizens were not accustomed to following the law. While administrativisation improved the efficiency of governance, it also increased the transaction costs of market activities in many cases when the bureaucratic structure became more rigid. For example, business registration has become very complicated in recent years in China. To register a business, the owner has to spend several months getting licences from different government departments.

5.8 CONTINUATION OF THE FINANCIAL REFORM

The financial sector was one of the major sectors that continued its market-oriented economic reform on a large scale during the first decade of the 21st century in China.

On 11 December 2001, China formally joined the WTO. The expected future competition from foreign financial institutions pushed the government to continue the reform in the financial sector. The Second Financial Work Conference, which was held in 2002, confirmed that the core of the financial reform was the reform of the state-owned commercial banks. The target of this reform is to change the shareholding structure of the state-owned banks in accordance with the properties of modern financial enterprises.

The global financial crisis from 2007 to 2009 had negative impacts on China's economy and significantly reduced the share of exports in GDP. The Chinese government used an expansionary fiscal policy to meet the challenge by spending RMB4 trillion ($0.6 trillion), mainly on infrastructure construction. This in turn raised the government debt dramatically, especially local governments' debt. The experience of financial crisis pushed the Chinese government to speed up the financial reforms to reduce the risks in the financial sector.

The Banking System

At the end of 2003, the Bank of China and the Construction Bank of China were selected to implement shareholding reforms. The Central Huijin Investment Corporation, a state-owned asset management company, injected RMB22.5 billion ($2.7 billion) and RMB20 billion ($2.4 billion) of capital into the Bank of China and the Construction Bank of China, respectively (Baidu Baike n.d.-c). The two banks wrote off asset losses of RMB407 billion ($49.2 billion) and stripped out RMB279 billion ($33.7 billion) in non-performance loans (NPLs), transferring them to asset management companies. The two banks standardised their governance structure and financial structure and in 2004 changed from solely state-owned companies to shareholding companies with limited liability. The Central Huijin Investment Corporation, representing the state, exercises the right of sponsor[28] of the Bank of China and the Construction Bank of China.

China experienced a wave of foreign investment into Chinese banks in the first decade of the 21st century (Table 5.9). In 2005, the Construction Bank of China signed subscription agreements with the Bank of America and Temasek Holdings (Private). The Bank of America and Temasek Holdings would hold 9.0 per cent and 5.1 per cent of the stocks of the Construction Bank of China. The Construction Bank of China had its stocks listed on the Hong Kong Stock Exchange (SEHK) in October 2005.

On 18 August 2005, the Royal Bank of Scotland and Merrill Lynch/Li Ka-shing Fund signed an agreement to buy \$1.6 billion (5.16 per cent) and \$1.5 billion (4.84 per cent) of the Bank of China's stock, respectively. On 31 August 2005, ATF, a wholly owned subsidiary of Temasek, agreed to buy \$3.1 billion, or 10 per cent, of the Bank of China's stock. One month later, on 27 September, Swiss Bank (UBS) announced that it would buy \$500 million of the Bank of China's stock, becoming the third investor in the Bank of China. On 1 June and 5 July 2006, the Bank of China listed on the SEHK and Shanghai Stock Exchange (SHSE), respectively.

The restructuring of the Industrial and Commercial Bank of China started in 2005. The Ministry of Finance kept its original capital of RMB124 billion (\$15.1 billion), while Central Huijin Investment injected RMB15 billion (\$1.8 billion) to dispose of RMB705 billion (\$86.1 billion) in non-performing assets. The bank changed its name to Industrial and Commercial Bank of China Ltd in October 2005. Goldman Sachs investment group announced that it would buy \$3.78 billion, or 10 per cent, of the stock of Industrial and Commercial Bank of China in January 2006. China Social Security Fund Council also invested RMB18 billion (\$2.3 billion) in 2006. On 27 October 2006, A and H shares of the Industrial and Commercial Bank were listed on both the SHSE and SEHK at the same time.

The restructuring of the Agriculture Bank of China lagged behind. The State Council passed the proposal for the shareholding reform of the Agriculture Bank of China in 2008. At the end of 2007, the Agriculture Bank's NPL reached RMB818 billion (\$107.6 billion). The Central Huijin injected RMB130 billion (\$17.1 billion) and held 50 per cent of shares of the Agriculture Bank of China. The Agriculture Bank of China Ltd was established in January 2009, with a registered capital of RMB260 billion (\$38.1 billion), and the Ministry of Finance and Central Huijing each hold 50 per cent of the stock shares.

The financial restructuring and public listing prompted the large commercial banks to begin improving their internal organisation structures, with a board of directors, a board of supervisors, and management teams.

Table 5.9 Major foreign investors of the large commercial banks

	Bank	Foreign investor	Shareholding before listing
June 2005	Construction Bank of China	Bank of America	8.52%
July 2005	Construction Bank of China	Temasek Holdings	5.88%
August 2005	Bank of China	Royal Bank of Scotland	10%
September 2005	Bank of China	Swiss Bank (UBS)	1.61%
October 2005	Bank of China	Asian Development Bank	0.24%
December 2005	Bank of China	Temasek Holdings	10%
December 2005	Industrial and Commercial Bank of China	Goldman Sachs investment group	10%

Source: Li et al. (2009, Table 6.1, p.148).

A preliminary risk control system was set up and the performance of these banks improved. The restructuring did not solve all the problems of these large commercial banks. The internal organisations still need further reforms, the internal incentive mechanism of managers and employees need to be improved, and the NPLs need to be controlled.

In 2007, the central government confirmed that the direction of the reform of policy banks is commercialisation. This means these policy banks will operate like commercial banks, setting up boards of directors and making profits. Central Huijin Investment injected RMB20 billion ($2.6 billion) into China Development Bank in December 2007. The Ministry of Finance and Central Huijin Investment hold 51.3 per cent and 48.7 per cent of total shares, respectively. With total assets of RMB3.8 trillion ($0.5 trillion), China Development Bank became the fourth largest bank in China.

A number of shareholding commercial banks were set up in the 1980s and 1990s by central government departments, local governments, and enterprises. Some of the shareholding commercial banks were established in the first decade of the 21st century (e.g. China Zheshang Bank in 2004, China Bohai Bank in 2005, Huishang Bank in 2005, and Bank of Jiangsu in 2006). Like the four large commercial banks, many of these shareholding commercial banks introduced foreign investors[29] and were listed on the SHSE, SZSE, or SEHK.

Urban commercial banks experienced rapid development in the first decade of the 21st century. The China Banking Regulatory Commission

(CBRC) allowed the cross-regional development of the urban commercial banks in 2005. To reduce risks, many small urban commercial banks merged with other urban commercial banks. For example, six urban commercial banks and seven credit cooperatives merged into Huishang Bank in 2006. The urban commercial banks also introduced foreign investors to raise the quality of their management. International Finance Corporation (IFC), a subsidiary of the World Bank, became a shareholder of Bank of Shanghai in 1998 and many international investors bought shares of China's urban commercial banks. In the first decade of the 21st century, the urban commercial banks started listing their stock on domestic stock markets. Bank of Ningbo, Bank of Nanjing, and Bank of Beijing were listed on domestic stock markets in 2008. By the end of 2008, there were 140 urban commercial banks, with total assets of RMB4.1 trillion ($0.6 trillion), or 6.6 per cent of the total assets of the banking sector (Li et al., 2009, pp.160–161).

The opening up to foreign banks continued after China's entry into the WTO in 2001. The foreign currency business for all customers[30] was opened up to foreign banks. Foreign banks' RMB business was extended gradually from foreign enterprises and foreigners to Chinese enterprises and Chinese citizens. The restriction of the ratio of deposit in China was relaxed gradually. The State Council revised the Regulations on the Administration of Foreign Banks in November 2006 (State Council 2006). The CBRC issued more regulations for the implementation of the policy in the same month (China Banking Regulatory Commission 2006). According to these regulations, the geographical and customer restrictions applied to foreign banks' RMB business were lifted on 11 December 2006.[31] Foreign banks were allowed to take deposits and provide loans in foreign currencies as well as in RMB; foreign bank branches were allowed to take more than RMB1 million ($0.13 million) in fixed-term deposits, the non-prudential restrictions on foreign banks were abolished, and the government promised national treatment to foreign banks.

Non-Banking Institutes

After China's entry into the WTO in 2001, the non-banking industry saw a rapid expansion in China.

The reform of the insurance sector focused on state-owned insurance companies' shareholding reform. In 2002, the national finance working meeting decided that the shareholding reform of insurance companies should stick to the principle of (i) state control, (ii) absorbing foreign and private capital, and (iii) diversification of the ownership structure. In 2003, the Property and Casualty Company (PICC) listed its stock on the

SEHK. After that, China Life Insurance Company listed on both the New York Stock Exchange and the SEHK. More foreign insurance companies entered the Chinese market. By the end of 2007, 43 foreign insurance companies from 15 countries had set up 134 operating institutions in China, occupying 5.97 per cent of the market. By the end of 2008, the total number of insurance companies in China reached 130, with RMB3.3 trillion ($0.48 trillion) in assets, RMB0.98 trillion ($0.14 trillion) premium income, and 3.2 million employees (Li et al. 2009, p.176).

Trust companies boomed in the first decade of the 21st century, offering a large number of financial products, such as real-estate investment trusts and foreign exchange trusts. In 2004 and 2005, the regulatory agencies implemented a 'cross checking' of trust companies by the regulatory agencies of other provinces or cities, to avoid the interference of local governments. The CBRC revised the regulation on financial trust companies in 2007 (China Banking Regulatory Commission 2007). According to the revised regulation, a financial trust company must have a sponsor and fulfil the minimum capital requirement, and only qualified commercial banks, foreign financial leasing companies, large equipment producers, and other institutes approved by the CBRC can be a qualified major sponsor. The CBRC has permitted Industrial and Commercial Bank of China, Construction Bank of China, Bank of Communications, China Minsheng Bank, and China Merchant Bank to set up financial trust companies since 2007. The CBRC revised the regulation on trust companies again in 2014 to tighten control over these companies (China Banking Regulatory Commission 2014).

The Stock and Bond Markets

In the 1990s, the issuance of stocks in China was under an examination and approval system. An enterprise that intended to issue stocks had to be recommended by local government and the government department in charge. The CSRC made an annual plan with a quota of issuance, approved the stock issuance, and decided the price of the stock. This examination and approval system was actually a remnant of the planned system, creating opportunities for rent-seeking and corruption. The examination and approval system for stock issuance was replaced by an approval system in 2000. The planned quota was abandoned. The stock was selected and recommended by the underwriter. The approval process included mandatory information disclosure and compliance audit. A supporting measure of the approval system, the pathway system, was implemented in 2001. Under the pathway system, a securities company set the current year's issuance pathway, based on the previous year. Potential stock issuers waited in line, since the number of issuances was restricted. A sponsor system was introduced in 2004, in which the sponsor's interest was correlated with the quality of his or her listed company. The mode of stock issuing also changed several times during this period. In October 1995, the CSRC changed the policy from limiting the number of application forms that could be sent out to unlimited distribution. Because the unlimited issuance led to high costs, the CSRC changed the issuance method to internet pricing issuance. In 1999, the CSRC adopted internet issuance to individual investors and a placement and sales combination to corporations. Starting from 2005, an inquiry system[32] was implemented in the stock market and became a major stock issuance model.

Before 2005, in China's stock markets, SOEs' shares were divided into state-owned shares, corporate shares, and public shares. The state-owned shares and corporate shares were not allowed to enter the stock market for trading, and the stocks were divided into tradable shares and non-tradable shares. This is called 'equity division' or 'split share structure', and two-thirds of the shares of these SOEs cannot be traded. The original purpose of this policy, due to ideological reasons, was to keep the dominant position of the state and the SOEs. This resulted in conflicts between corporate shareholders and tradable shareholders since the former could easily seize the interest of the latter. To develop fair competition in the stock market, the 'equity division' had to be reformed to allow state-owned shares and corporate shares to enter the market. In 2005, the CSRC published a regulation on the reform of the equity division system, allowing state shares and corporate shares to enter the market for trading (China Security Regulatory Commission 2005). The core of the reform was about compensation for the tradable shareholders. The reform was basically completed in 2007. It represents a cornerstone in the development of the Chinese stock market, resulting in the full circulation[33] of the stocks traded in the market. This is the foundation of equity decentralisation of the Chinese stock market.

The opening up of China's stock markets continued during the first decade of the 21st century. After the B-share markets shrank at the end of the 1990s, the government considered other ways to attract foreign investors. Qualified Foreign Institutional Investor (QFII) status and Qualified Domestic Individual Investor (QDII) status were adopted by the monetary authority in the early 2000s. The CSRC and the People's Bank of China published the Interim Measures on the Administration of Domestic Securities Investment by Qualified Foreign Institutional Investors in 2002 (China Security Regulatory Commission and People's Bank of China 2002). The CSRC revised the regulation in 2006, reducing the entry requirements, allowing QFIIs to open securities accounts, and reducing the fund lock-up period. By August 2007, 87 foreign institutional investors were awarded QFII status. The CSRC relaxed the foreign exchange restrictions on overseas investment by domestic firms in 2006. Qualified domestic banks, fund companies, security companies, and insurance companies were allowed to invest in overseas markets. By the end of 2007, 50 domestic companies were granted QDII status.

To reduce illegal operations, the CSRC started the rectification of the securities sector in 2004, by creating evaluation criteria and checking the risks of securities companies. An information disclosure system was established, as well as risk control and an early warning system. A number of high-quality companies, showing high performance, were listed on domestic stock markets. By the end of 2008, there were 106 securities companies in China's securities sector; they managed RMB4.2 trillion ($0.60 trillion) in client assets, with RMB353 billion ($50.8 billion) in net assets, earning RMB43 billion ($6.2 billion) in net profits (Li et al. 2009, p.179).

The stock market fluctuated dramatically in the first decade of the 21st century. After the stagnant market from 2001 to 2005, China's stock market boomed in 2006 and 2007 due to the fast economic growth and the equity division reform of the stock market. The annual increase in the Shanghai Stock Exchange Composite Index (close) increased from 1,161 in 2005 to 5,261 in 2007 and the Shenzhen Stock Exchange Composite Index (close) increased from 278 to 1,447 during the same period (National Bureau of Statistics 2009b, p.781). The number of investment accounts doubled from 78.1 million at the beginning of 2007 to 138.2 million at the end of the year, which marked the beginning of the era of the 'national stock market'. A large amount of hot money from all over the world entered the Chinese stock market and played an important role in raising stock prices, even though the capital market in China had not been opened up yet. Hot money entered China through QFIIs and the underground banking system. The QFII programme allows, on a selective basis, global institutional investors to invest in China's RMB-denominated capital market. Once licensed, foreign investors are permitted to buy RMB-denominated 'A shares' in China's mainland stock exchanges. China's stock markets experienced another downturn in the years that followed, lasting until 2015, as a result of the global financial crisis and the downturn of the Chinese economy.

The bond market continued its development in the first decade of the 21st century. The scale of the Treasury bond market expanded. Three Treasury bonds with more than 15 years term of redemption were issued in 2001, which improved the term structure of Treasury bonds. In 2002, the People's Bank relaxed the regulations on the qualifications of traders in the inter-bank bond market, and transitioned from an examination and approval system to a record-keeping system. A central operating system for desk trading, the CDC operating system, started operating in the same year. This was linked to the high-value payment system of the People's Bank of China in 2004. Before 2006, the government managed Treasury bond issuance through an annual quota system. As the amount of issuance increased, the government adopted a Treasury bond balance management method in 2006. The Ministry of Finance and the People's Bank of China issued a 'Central Treasury Cash Management Approach' in 2006, which defines the Treasury cash management as a combination of term deposit of commercial banks, Treasury bond purchasing, Treasury bond repurchasing, and reverse repurchase (Ministry of Finance and People's Bank of China 2006). During the first decade of the 21st century, the Treasury bond market expanded and the trading institutions improved.

Corporate bonds saw a rapid growth in the first decade of the 21st century. Many new types of corporate bonds appeared – for example, bonds with options and swaps, and bonds with floating interest rates. The issuance of corporate bonds increased dramatically in 2006 and 2007.

Money Market

The money market expanded in scale in the first decade of the 21st century. Even during the global financial crisis of 2008, China's money market kept growing. The trading volumes of all three subordinate markets – the bond repo market, the inter-bank money market, and the commercial paper market – saw rapid, stable development.

From Table 5.10, we can see a dramatic increase in China's money market. The repo market and inter-bank money market became commercial banks' most important measure of liquidity management. During the same period, the repo market became an important channel for the central bank's open-market operations. The growth of the commercial paper market enriched enterprises' trading means and created the foundations for the central bank's monetary policy.

Table 5.10 Money market trading, in RMB billion ($ billion)

Year	Commercial paper market trading	Inter-bank money market	Bond repo market
1998	868 (105)	198 (24)	1,728 (209)
2003	7,170 (866)	2,222 (268)	17,020 (2,056)
2008	20,611 (2,968)	15,050 (2,167)	58,120 (3,368)

Source: Li et al. (2009, p.231).

One significant change in the structure of China's money market was the decrease in the share of the inter-bank money market and the increase in the share of the bond repo market. The inter-bank money market was the earliest money market to be developed, and it was promoted by non-government forces. In the 1980s, in a less developed financial system, the function of the inter-bank money market was to serve as (i) a means of liquidity management, (ii) a way to avoid government regulation, and (iii) a means to channel savings and investments. The government regulated the inter-bank money market and established an official national inter-bank money market in 1996. The inter-bank money market was no longer a means to raise funds; instead, it functioned solely as a means of liquidity management. After 2000, short-term borrowing for less than seven days became the main trading activity in the inter-bank money market. The early repo market also malfunctioned as a means to avoid government regulation and plan restrictions and to attract savings from residents. As the central bank abolished the credit quota system in 1998, the repo market moved towards more normal functions. As a result, the term-structure of the repo market became shorter, with a dramatic increase in seven-day repurchase, making the central bank's open-market operations possible. In 2007, the People's Bank of China issued the Regulation on Inter-Bank Lending (People's Bank of China 2007a), which regulated the membership of the market, trading, risk control, information disclosure, and supervision of the inter-bank market. Following this new regulation, more financial institutions were allowed to enter the market.

The development of the commercial paper market lagged behind until the end of the 1990s. The situation has changed dramatically since the end of the 20th century, as banks have continued to improve their asset–debt structure. The total amount of commercial papers had increased significantly by 2008. Unlike the inter-bank money market and the repo markets, where the main customers are banks, the commercial paper markets give non-banking enterprises opportunities to circulate funds and manage liquidity. They also provide a foundation for the market determination of interest rates.

Underground Financial System

The underground financial system experienced rapid development in China in the first decade of the 21st century. Li (2006) conducted a survey on underground banks, covering 20 provinces, 82 cities and counties, 206 villages, 110 firms, and 1,203 individuals. The author estimated that the underground financial sector was worth RMB740–830 billion ($92.8–104.1 billion), or 28 per cent of the formal financial sector, in 2003. According to the report, the more underdeveloped the economy is in a region in China, the more the farmers and enterprises use the underground finance system. The loans to farmers from unofficial finance accounted for over 50 per cent of total loans in 15 provinces. Nearly 50 per cent of loans to private enterprises were from the unofficial finance sector in underdeveloped provinces.

The underground banks in China bear many risks and have become a target of government supervision since the beginning of their operations in the 1980s. The underground banks usually adopt family management systems, without strict business procedures, and act based on trust between family members and relatives. This creates a great risk of default, which in turn may cause the breaking of fund chains. The loans are often issued without pledge, which attracts customers but increases the risk of default. When the fund chain breaks, bank owners often escape with the money. Because it is illegal, the rights of lenders and borrowers are not protected by the law, and the disputes cannot be settled by legal procedures.

Some of the underground banks have connections with corruption. For example, the Wu family's underground bank helped a government official, Li Shubin, embezzle public funds of RMB118 million ($17.4 million) for personal gambling in Macau. Mr Li was the director of Housing Fund Management in Chenzhou city, Hunan province (Li Youhuan 2010, p.30). Underground banking often relies on gangs, using violent force to collect delayed debt payments. Large amounts of funds for gambling have flown abroad every year. In 2006, RMB600 billion ($75.3 billion) flew out of China for gambling, 15 times the total issuance of the domestic lottery (CCTV 2010).

Even though the major customers of underground banking are small businesses, some of the large SOEs use underground banks to benefit from illegal trading. On 6 August 2007, the State Administration of Foreign Exchange (SAFE) announced that a large underground bank had been dismantled by SAFE Shenzhen Branch and Shenzhen Police. Six suspects, including Du Ling, the owner, were arrested. About RMB4.2 million ($0.55 million) in 55 accounts were frozen. SAFE revealed on its website that well-known domestic SOEs were involved in the case. Five months later, media reported that the involved SOEs were China National Petroleum Corporation (CNPC) and Sinopec Group (SINOPEC), the two largest state-owned companies in oil exploitation and processing. Shenzhen is adjacent to Hong Kong. Because of differences in taxes, the gasoline price in Shenzhen is much lower than it is in Hong Kong. CNPC and SINOPEC sold large amounts of gasoline to Hong Kong companies to make profits. Because it was beyond their authority, the two companies asked the Hong Kong companies to pay in RMB, whereas the Hong Kong companies preferred to pay in Hong Kong dollars. The Hong Kong party suggested that they use China Hengda, a transfer company controlled by Du's bank, to convert Hong Kong dollars to RMB and settle the dispute. CNPC and SINOPEC agreed. SAFE gave the two state-owned companies a mild punishment (Sina Finance 2007).

According to the current law, underground banking activities are related to three illegal activities: illegally absorbing public deposits, dealing with illegal operations, and money laundering. According to the Law on Commercial Banks, which was passed in 1995, without the approval of the People's Bank of China no unit or individual is allowed to do the business of a commercial bank, such as absorbing public deposits (National People's Congress 1995a). The State Council issued Measures for the Banning of Illegal Financial Institutions and Illegal Financial Business Activities in 1998 (State Council 1998). The document defined an illegal financial institution as any financial institution dealing in attracting deposits, issuing loans, handling settlements, discounting bills, performing trust investment and financial leasing, buying and selling foreign exchange, and many other financial activities, without approval from the People's Bank of China. Any illegal financial institution and activity, according to the document, should be banned by local governments. Whenever illegal banks are discovered, the People's Bank will investigate and ask the police to take over the case. The People's Bank issued a ban on underground banks and usury activities in 2002. The notice stipulated that funds used in lending between individuals should come from the lender's own income; the lender should not use funds borrowed from other individuals for lending. The interest rate in private lending could be negotiated between lenders and borrowers, but it should not be higher than four times the interest rate[34] of the commercial banks, which was set by the People's Bank of China.

According to an amendment to the Criminal Law, without approval it is illegal to sell products monopolised by the state, import and export licences, certificates of import and export, and other licences or document of approval; perform operations involving securities, futures, or insurance; or perform other operations that might disturb the market (National People's Congress 1999a). According to the law, selling and buying foreign currency, one of the underground banks' major businesses, is also illegal. This illegal activity is mainly due to the large demand for foreign exchange and the control of foreign exchange by the government.

Another illegal activity related to underground banking is money laundering. Criminals use underground banks to move their illegal incomes from smuggling and corruption out of China. Following the provisions in the Criminal Law in 1997 and several regulations on money laundering issued by the People's Bank in 2003, the National People's Congress passed an Anti-Money Laundering Law in 2006, setting up basic regulations on money laundering (National People's Congress 2006e). The People's Bank issued Regulations on the Implementation of Anti-Money Laundering Investigation in 2007, defining the task and method of anti-money laundering (People's Bank of China 2007b). The government has made great efforts to crack down on illegal foreign currency trading and money laundering. In 2008, the People's Bank investigated 899 cases of money laundering with the police. The cases included crimes that damaged the stability of the financial market and drug offences. SAFE set up an investigation on illegal foreign exchange that was flown into China in 2010, and it intensified the fight against underground banking and online speculation in foreign currency.

For a long time, China had no legal provisions that applied to private lending companies and activities. As a result, all private lending companies were made illegal. There was no clear-cut boundary to distinguish between legal and illegal private lending activities. The Anti-Monetary Laundering Law of 2006, adopted to prevent money laundering, has limited application to underground banking (National People's Congress 2006e). In addition, there are no government institutions specifically in charge of private lending companies and their activities.

The government recognised the problem of finance for private businesses and tried to legalise the underground financial sector at the end of the 2000s, partly because of the large number of small private firms that collapsed following the financial crisis of 2008. China needs to legalise private lending institutes and activities, because they are an important precondition for the survival of small private businesses. The formal finance sector, which includes, for example, the large state-owned commercial banks, usually focuses on enterprises and projects supported by the government. It is difficult for small private firms and farmers to get financial support from large, state-owned banks. This kind of situation is a natural result of the state monopoly of the financial sector. The commercialisation of the state-owned banks aggravates the problem because state-owned large banks are more profit-seeking, and lending to small businesses creates less profit than lending to large firms. For a long time in China, only law enforcement entities (public security/police) supervised the underground financial sector; no professional government supervision of the underground finance sector existed. Police action cannot replace government supervision. The law should allow the existence for legal private lending under government supervision.

Legal private lending in China has various forms. One form of private lending is small-sum loan companies, which are limited liability companies that deal with small amounts of lending activity without attracting deposits. The source of the registered capital should be all paid-in-money capital and be fully handed in by investors or promoters once and for all, according to a guiding opinion issued in 2008 by the CBRC and the People's Bank of China. Per the guidance, the major sources of funds for small-sum loan companies shall be the capital paid by shareholders, donated capital, and the capital borrowed from at most two banks. The balance of the capital borrowed from banks should not exceed 50 per cent of the net capital, according to the guiding opinions. To apply to establish a small-sum loan company, the applicant should file an application with the appropriate department of the provincial government and, upon approval, should then apply to the local administrative department for industry and commerce that is responsible for handling the registration formalities and issuing the business licence. The applicant is also required to file the relevant material with the local police, the dispatched office of the CBRC, and the branch institute of the People's Bank within five working days. A small-sum loan company operates legally under several restrictions. First, the government encourages the small-sum loan companies to lend to farmers and agricultural-related industries. Second, the small-sum loan companies are not allowed to attract deposits. Third, the interest rate charged by a small-sum loan company should not be higher than four times the official bank rate (China Banking Regulatory Commission and the People's Bank of China 2008).

Since 2005, the government has been active in promoting small financial companies, and the People's Bank of China has started pilot small-sum loan companies in several provinces. The approval of the small-sum loan companies was an important step towards the legalisation of the underground financial institutions. The State Council issued 'Several Opinions of the State Council on Encouraging and Guiding the Healthy Development of Private Investment' in May 2010 (State Council 2010). According to this document, the government encourages private investment in multiple fields, including infrastructure, utilities, health care, education, defence industries, financial services, and many other fields. The document allows private capital to establish financial institutions and relaxes restrictions on the shares of private capital in financial institutions, especially in small-sum loan companies. The People's Bank also drafted a lenders ordinance in 2008 in an effort to legalise the underground financial sector by allowing individuals to register loan businesses (Yu Wentang 2015).

Under the current law, underground banking can be legalised in several ways, including (i) transferring to private equities, which collect funds privately from investors and have existed in China for several years; (ii) transferring to private banks, which are under the supervision of the government; (iii) transferring to hedge funds; and (iv) transferring to foreign currency exchange companies, which need to be approved by the government and can work in certain special areas.

5.9 FINANCIAL CRISIS AND THE SLOWDOWN OF GROWTH

China enjoyed a golden period of economic growth from 2002 to 2008 after joining the WTO in December 2001. The two-digit growth from 2003 to 2007 was led by exports and domestic infrastructure investment. However, the golden years ended around 2010. The global financial crisis came first in 2008, and the shortage of migrant workers occurred in 2010, which led to a domestic economic structural change. A nationwide economic slowdown started in 2012.

Collapse of Part of the Private Export-Oriented Sector

A large number of private businesses experienced serious problems during the 2008 financial crisis. When the global market became stagnant, many domestic problems, such as firms' high tax and social security burdens, were revealed. At the same time, huge government expenditures crowded out many private businesses and helped SOEs bounce back.

In the past 30 years, about 250 million peasants have moved from the countryside to cities. These migrant workers provided a cheap labour force for urban industries. Because this flow of migrant workers from the countryside was exhausted at the end of the first decade of the 21st century, the whole labour-intensive, export-oriented sector faced great difficulties. The labour cost for unskilled workers in the eastern coastal area increased from about RMB1,500 ($221.6) per month in 2010 to RMB2,500–3,000 ($401.4–481.7) or more in 2015. Some inappropriate policies, such as high taxes and strict social security contributions by enterprises for their workers, added extra burdens to the firms. According to the World Bank, China's total tax rate was 68 per cent of commercial profit in 2016 (World Bank n.d.). A firm has to pay an endowment insurance, medical insurance, and other insurances for injury, unemployment, and maternity, as well as a housing provident fund (Dong 2016). These insurances are paid as a percentage of wages.[35] As wages doubled, the insurance payments doubled in a short period. A large number of small domestic private firms closed after the financial crisis and the beginning of the economic structural changes, whereas many foreign-invested firms moved out of China. A part of the export-oriented sector disappeared during the crisis.

It is difficult for small firms to borrow from large state-owned banks. Many small businesses turn to underground usury firms instead, which are illegal under the existing law. It is estimated that about 40 per cent of small businesses in the Pearl River Delta closed during the 2008 financial crisis. As a result, the survivors relied more heavily on usury loans. In Shenzhen city, the loans from large banks to small businesses in the first quarter of 2009 amounted to only RMB30 billion ($4.4 billion), which was much less than the total demand (Li Youhuan 2010). The usury business boomed in major cities in the Pearl River Delta in 2009 due to the financial crisis and the insufficient support offered by the state-owned banking system. Some firms turned to non-state-owned banking to meet the emergent needs for funding. Bonding companies, which work as securities intermediaries, played an important role in these rescue operations, earning interest spread between the bank interest rate and their rate as well as guarantee fees. The usury rate of the bonding companies was between 3 to 20 per cent per month, with the average usually being 5 per cent per month. During the financial crisis, the interest rates increased to 10 per cent or more per month. Pawnshops' business increased dramatically in 2008 in Guangdong province, providing large amounts of loans with high interest rates (Lan 2009).

Government Investments

Once the government realised how serious the crisis was, it took swift and decisive action. In November 2008, Beijing announced plans for a major economic stimulus programme. The government implemented a RMB4 trillion ($0.6 trillion) fiscal expansion programme, investing in projects such as inter-city high-speed railways, urban subways, affordable housing, water and waste-water works, new airports, and SOE plant modernisation. Many of the projects fell into the hands of SOEs. To support the fiscal expansion, M2 growth increased from 17.8 per cent in 2008 to 27.7 per cent in 2009. The central government invested more than RMB1 trillion ($0.14 trillion) in these efforts, and the rest came from local governments. The policy reduced the impact of the financial crisis on China, but it resulted in the real-estate bubble, the crowding out of private firms, and the return of SOEs.

5.10 CONCLUSION

The period 2003–2012 was one of adjustment with relatively slow progress in marketisation reforms. The leadership faced numerous social problems (e.g. inequality) that were created by the market and the bureaucratic-market combination. Inequality, housing, health care, and environmental pollution were among these problems. Urbanisation has brought poverty into the cities. Corruption became a major concern of government and ordinary citizens. The marketisation reform was slowed down, and focus was put on solving these social problems instead.

This was a 'golden age' of economic growth, but the unprecedented economic growth during this period was mainly a result of institutional improvement started in the previous period, such as SOE reform and WTO entry. There has been progress in economic reforms. Although reform continued in many sectors, no major breakthroughs have been achieved during this period. There have been signs of social instability and some of the next generation of leaders are worried about the stability of the regime. New approaches were tested in some local areas. Bo Xilai, a member of the politburo and party secretary in Chongqing, tried to go back to some of the traditions of the CCP and reintroduce some of the old approaches that had been used in the planned period. He ran into political problems and was arrested before the change of leadership in 2012.

Lessons can be learned from this period. First, the marketisation reform followed its own timing and was path dependent. If a major reform, such as the SOE reform, could not finish on time, it may never have a chance to be fully implemented. Second, the marketisation reform raised the efficiency of the Chinese economy, but at the same time created inequality and had other side effects, which resulted in a loss of consensus on reform. The leadership of the CCP reacted rationally to these social problems. These changes in focus unfortunately delayed the marketisation reform.

To sum up, the marketisation reform created many social problems that hurt the interests of different groups of people in the society. The leadership of the CCP adjusted the strategy of reform during the first decade of the 21st century, changing the focus to social problems, which resulted in the stagnation of the marketisation reform. Many policies implemented in this period, such as anti-corruption and reducing inequality, were not market-oriented reform. They were policies created to mitigate damages created by marketisation. Although there was some minor progress in economic reform, mainly in the financial sector, there was no major breakthrough in marketisation reform like the rural land reform of the 1980s and the large-scale privatisation of SOEs of the 1990s.

NOTES

1. For example, China agreed to significant liberalisation of its agricultural markets by reducing the average import tariff for agricultural products from 21 to 15 per cent (Branstetter and Lardy 2008), while many other countries' agricultural markets were still protected.
2. Under existing regulations before China joined the WTO, goods and components of the processing trade were not allowed to be sold on the domestic market, but some of them illegally entered the domestic market.
3. For example, Kentucky Fried Chicken experienced quality problems with its raw materials (chicken meat), which was criticised by the Chinese media (Flower 2013).

4. Goods manufactured and used in further manufacturing, processing, or re-sale.
5. The producers give commission to doctors according to the prescription written by doctors, so doctors have incentives to prescribe highly profitable drugs to get more commission, whether or not the patient can afford it. The management of hospitals allow doctors to do this, because it could solve doctors' low income problem.
6. In a village, peasants are organised as a collective, which is in charge of village affairs, such as the distribution of land, and provides certain benefits to villagers. Collectives are also the lowest level of government in rural areas.
7. There have been some changes with the ruling class since the reform started in the late 1970s.
8. A group of middle school graduates, led by Fan Dongsheng, including Wang Jiguang, Yin Hongbiao, Wang Dayong, and me, created a theory of the class of government officials as early as 1972.
9. The leadership set up these relationships by inviting some intellectuals to enter the government and the People's Congress at the central and local levels. Intellectuals were given some freedom to express their opinions and give suggestions.
10. The Gini coefficient is a measure of statistical dispersion intended to represent the income or wealth distribution of a nation's residents, and is the most commonly used measure of inequality. A Gini coefficient of zero expresses perfect equality, while a Gini coefficient of 1 (or 100%) expresses maximal inequality.
11. It compares, for a given population, how much richer the top 20 per cent are compared with the bottom 20 per cent.
12. Graft refers to bribery, illicit kickbacks, and embezzlement, involving money and gifts being given to, and accepted by, public officials for illegal purposes. Rent-seeking is an attempt to increase one's share of existing wealth by manipulating the social or political environment in which economic activities occur, rather than by creating new wealth. In the case of corruption, it mainly refers to the government officials using monopoly power to grant licences to clients. Prebendalism refers to the fact that incumbents of government office get privileges through that office.
13. For example, large SOEs sometimes received favourable tax treatments compared to privately owned companies.
14. The Standard Industrial Classification (SIC) system is a hierarchical coding structure developed by the US government and used widely in government and private-sector data. It attempts to classify all forms of economic activity – including government and non-profit entities – in order to provide a common statistical and conceptual framework for data collection and analysis.
15. SASAC controls operating state-owned assets, while some other government agencies, such as the Ministry of Finance, control a small portion of other SOEs.
16. These firms are owned by urban and rural communities.
17. The industry has three parts: production, electricity distribution, and wholesale/retail. Production had become unrestricted and increased rapidly, but the networks for electricity distribution were still regulated and had limited capacity, and thus became a restriction for electricity distribution.
18. Compared with other countries, the operation of China's railways was relatively more efficient in the early 21st century in terms of passenger turnover and cargo delivery, mainly due to the large number of passengers and large volume of cargo, without considering investment costs of infrastructure (Li Lanbing 2010).
19. In the United Kingdom, the network is separated from the transportation companies and operated by a national network company. In the United States, the network and transportation along one railway line are operated by one company, and the competition is carried out among similar lines. In Japan, regional companies compete with each other.
20. Macro-controls are the Chinese government's controls to prevent the economy overheating by way of administrative measures.
21. GUME also had 542 non-listed stores in 2013.

22. Lenovo used the IBM PC management team and retained all old employees, instead of bringing over Chinese employees, and therefore had to adjust to the American work culture. The company decided to use English as the working language and Mr Yang himself permanently works at the company's US headquarters.
23. However, a panel data analysis on provincial extra-budgetary practices by Jiang and Xu (2013) suggests that extra-budgetary finance exists in China not as a strategy for local fiscal survival, but rather because local bureaucracies can conveniently exploit their administrative power to extract revenue from the local economy.
24. An apanage management system is a system under which the central government delegates the power to local governments and sets up the targets of local governments but does not give sufficient financial resources to them. The local governments are allowed to use its power to generate its own financial resources. This system has existed since ancient China.
25. Official access standards are standards used by governments to evaluate the performance of government officials. It affects the behaviour of government officials.
26. 'Organisation work' is an official expression used by the CCP, referring to the management of officials of the party and the government, including promotion, nomination, and personnel record keeping.
27. This means the government cannot license business activities if they are not for public necessity.
28. The Central Huijin Investment Corporation is a state-owned investment company, which is one of the major stockholders of the Bank of China and the Construction Bank of China. It represents the state to exercise the right of sponsor, including the rights of supervising the operation of the two banks and receiving investment income.
29. These banks sold part of their stocks to foreign investors, which was previously not allowed.
30. Before this reform, foreign banks could only do foreign currency business with foreign customers. Following the reform, they are now allowed to do foreign currency business with Chinese citizens.
31. This means that after this date, foreign banks were allowed to do RMB business with all customers (both foreign and domestic customers) in any place in China.
32. Under this system, the stock issuer asks potential institutional investors about the price investors want to pay. The issuing price of the stock will be based on this inquiry.
33. This means all stocks are circulated in the market.
34. This reflects the big gap between interest rates charged by banks and underground financial institutions.
35. Endowment insurance is 28 per cent of wages (firms pay 20 per cent) and medical insurance is 8 per cent of wages (firms pay 6 per cent). There are also other insurances for injury (0.8 per cent), unemployment (3 per cent, of which firms pay 2 per cent), and maternity (1 per cent paid by firms), along with a housing provident fund (no less than 10 per cent, of which firms pay 5 per cent).

6. The post-reform period: 2012–present

Xi Jinping became the general secretary of the Communist Party of China (CCP) in November 2012 and the president of the People's Republic in March 2013,[1] which opened a new era of Chinese modern history. Xi focused on changing the government ruling structure and fighting against corruption in the Party and in the government.

Before Xi got into power, some members of the leadership group and their advisers had re-thought the experience of China's economic and political reforms, comparing it with that in Russia. They worried that the CCP may lose control in facing the rapid expansion of the market and social problems created by the market, and thought that it was necessary to change the ruling strategy, using more administrative tools and reverting to certain elements of Mao's legacy. The first thing the new leadership needed to do was to re-establish authority over the Party, especially over the local officials.

In this period, the consensus on market-oriented economic reform has been diluted further, and reform in the direction of marketisation has not made much progress. In the previous 30 years, the government had still controlled the political and public spheres, but the private sphere had since been opened. The reform broke with the traditional ideology of the planned economy, promoting the benefit of market economy and allowing a small group of people in the society to become richer first. This created contradictions with socialist ideology, which emphasises the equality of economic benefits for ordinary people. Confronting these contradictions, the leadership started the second wave of adjustments since 1978, concentrating on discipline within the Communist Party, control of the bureaucratic system, and the rebuilding of the social ideology. The adjustment of the system has focused on the restructuring of power within the government and restraining the behaviour of government officials. This is an adjustment following the logic of government rule, which focuses on the control over the bureaucratic system and the society, instead of the logic of market expansion. One of the key targets of the adjustment is corruption, the main concern of the society.

6.1 THE RE-CONCENTRATION OF POWER

Since the late 1970s, the Chinese central government has been trading part of its power for local government incentives. The incentives of local governments have been important for economic growth under the existing institutional arrangement, and economic growth has been an important source of legitimacy for the rule of CCP since the beginning of economic reform. As pointed out by Naughton, the authoritarian system relies for its legitimacy on short-run economic performance (Naughton 2008, p.127). Compared with the local government, the central government in China has less ability and fewer means to implement policies. In the process of economic reform, the central government lost more power to implement its policies, which is something the new leadership was worried about. Therefore, the thing they wanted to do was re-concentrate power to the central government. To realise this target, they needed a tool to do the job. This is the role of the anti-corruption campaign, a policy supported by most people in Chinese society. To support a radical version of this policy, the leadership argued that the situation required strong medicine, or abnormal means to solve the problem.

At the same time, the government tightened its control of both the ideology sphere and influence from the outside world. The government started enforcing a new cybersecurity law in 2017 to tighten its grip on the content of network platforms.

In order to concentrate the power in the hands of the central government, more administrative means have been used. The central government has tried to use an official accountability system to improve the efficiency of the bureaucratic system, which is a shift from the previous policy of incentives for local officials. A modern version of the official accountability system was created in Hong Kong and introduced to mainland China. In January 2015, Wang Qishan, the head of the Central Commission for Discipline Inspection (CCDI), raised the issue of implementing the main responsibility and strengthening accountability in a working report to the CCDI. In June 2015, Xi Jinping said at a political study session of the Politburo that a sound accountability mechanism should be established, combining supervision and target assessment (Hao 2016). Additionally, the Central Committee of the CCP issued an Accountability Ordinance in 2016, strengthening and standardising the accountability work (Xinhua News Agency commentator 2016).

The leadership also implemented several structural changes to the bureaucratic system to enhance the control of central government branches and the local governments. The management of government officials has become strict, with stringent regulations and clear responsibilities. Issues on candidate nomination and examinations have been discussed, and new procedures have been designed to close the loopholes in the promotion system. The daily management of government officials has been strengthening. Officials who break the rules are punished in large numbers, creating a shock and awe effect. These measures changed the de facto federalism back to a standard bureaucratic system. Regarding the top leadership of the CCP, reform of the structure of the Politburo and the procedure of succession for the top leaders is in progress.

Anti-Corruption Movement

The new leadership has made the campaign against corruption a centrepiece of its governing agenda, and this has been successful to a certain degree. To fight against corruption, the leadership used an old institution and gave it extreme power in the bureaucratic system.

The CCDI of the Central Committee of the CCP, the highest internal-control institution of the CCP, is tasked with enforcing internal rules and regulations as well as combating corruption and malfeasance in the Party. It has played an extremely important role in the past several years. In practice, the CCDI was also the top anti-corruption body in the Chinese government. The modern CCDI was established at the 3rd Plenary Session of the 11th Central Committee of the CCP in 1978. Beginning with Hu Jintao, as the general secretary of the CCP in 2002, and especially following Xi Jinping's accession to the party leadership in 2012, the CCDI has been more independent of party operations and is actually directly below the top leader of the Party. A campaign against corruption was launched shortly after Xi came to power. Wang Qishan headed the CCDI as the secretary until 2017.

The duties and responsibilities of the current CCDI include the following:

1. Inner-party supervision. The power of supervision within the Party was defined by the Internal Supervision Regulation (ISR) in 2004. The ISR separated the central inspection teams from decision-making institutions and confirmed the power of the CCDI. Every party member, especially the leaders, is subject to the supervision of the CCDI. The ISR defines three forms of inner-party supervision: top-to-bottom, bottom-to-top, and peer-to-peer. For top-to-bottom supervision, the central leadership should regularly send central inspection teams to regions, state organisations, and SOEs. The bottom-to-top supervision is less institutionalised. The peer-to-peer supervision is through regular 'democratic life meetings', at which party members self-criticise or criticise each other.

2. Jurisdiction. The CCDI does not have the power to prosecute officials. It transfers cases to the Supreme People's Procuratorate or to the Supreme People's Court.
3. The CCDI at every level has the authority to issue and interpret regulations on the internal activities of the CCP. In recent years, the CCDI has issued several regulations on behalf of the Central Committee (Gong 2008).

The secretary is the head of the CCDI. The secretary, deputy secretary, and secretary-general are elected at the 1st Plenary Session, after the National Congress of the Party. Since 1997, the head of the CCDI has been required to serve concurrently on the Politburo Standing Committee (PSC) of the CCP. The CCDI's Standing Committee is the highest decision-making body of the CCDI. At the central level, the CCDI has more than 20 bureaus and offices (Guo 2014). Below the central level, several commissions for discipline inspection (CDI) exist. The establishment of CDIs is decided by the upper-level party committee. CDI officials were often appointed to the position within the institutions they were tasked to supervise, and it was sometimes difficult for them to carry out their duties. Since 2004, the independence of the CDIs from the same level of the party committee has been increased. In 2013, the 3rd Plenary Session of the 18th Central Committee of the CCP reformed the CCDI's structure, with each CDI directly reporting to the CCDI (Li 2014). The CCDI also sends inspection teams throughout the country to help the local CDIs.

The CCP reported that it investigated nearly 36,911 cases and punished 33,966 officials in 2015, including 37 high-level officials managed by the Central Organisation Department of the CCP[2] (CCP News 2016). Many high-profile political figures have been jailed. There are almost daily reports in the state media of officials being investigated or punished (BBC 2016). Bo Xilai, a former member of the Politburo, was found guilty of accepting bribes and abuse of power, and sentenced to life imprisonment in September 2013. In 2015, Zhou Yongkang, a former member of the Standing Committee of the Politburo, was found guilty of bribery, abuse of power, and sharing state secrets. A northern China court sentenced him to life in prison. Ling Jihua, the top aid of the former president and Communist Party chief Hu Jintao, was sentenced to life in prison for corruption in July 2016. According to state news media, Ling was found guilty of taking bribes, abuse of power, and illegally obtaining state secrets (Wang 2016). Many cases involved administrative examination and approval. The pipeline of investigations promises a steady flow of pending prosecutions. The anti-corruption movement significantly reduced activities such as enjoying banquets at public expense.

As the Party's anti-graft watchdog, the CCDI lacks judicial authority and is limited to investigating corruption. The anti-corruption movement has been using an 'illegal' agency, an agency that lacks formal legal authority, that is directly under the chief leader, and it has achieved great success. But the movement cannot end corruption completely, and its side effects have been serious. When an official is investigated, he or she does not have many legal rights to defend himself or herself. The leaders have been in an awkward situation. Without abnormal means, the corruption within the government cannot be cleaned; with abnormal means, the rights of officials are not protected and the incentives of officials are quashed.

In the long run, the anti-corruption rules and agencies need to be institutionalised and made transparent. A national inspection system should be established and the anti-corruption procedure should be standardised. Related laws should be passed and implemented. Public tip-offs should be lawful and the rights of officials should be protected. The party leaders have said several times that the current anti-corruption approaches are just temporary ones; long-term measures and institutions need to be developed. To formalise the anti-corruption agencies, a pilot experiment of national inspection system reform was carried out in Beijing, Shandong, and Zhejiang in 2016 and 2017 (Zhong 2017).[3] A national Anti-Corruption Law is also needed to normalise anti-corruption in the bureaucratic structure.

The Incentives of Officials and Administrative Omission

The direct cost of the re-concentration of power is the loss of incentives for government officials, especially local government officials. Fears about falling victim to the anti-corruption movement are discouraging bureaucrats from doing extra work.[4] The sin of an official's administrative omission was criticised by the leadership, but it cannot be judged as criminal. The prevalence of administrative omission has damaged to some degree the local government-led economic development which had prevailed in the last 20 years.

The central government has tried to re-establish authority by using specific rules and an official accountability system to solve the incentive problem. In the last 30 years in China, the local government has acted as the leader of the local economy rather than the subordinate of the central government. The relationship between the central and the local governments was 'de facto federalism' to some degree. The introduction of the accountability system means a fundamental change of the bureaucratic system. The system will be much more centralised and power will be shifted up in the bureaucratic structure.

The official accountability system used in China is an administrative system, not a political accountability system. In this administrative system, the lower-level government officials are actually responsible to the higher level of government. The accountability is realised through the administrative system, under common standards of good governance. What the central government is currently doing is setting up clearly defined responsibility standards for government officials, with the aim of using these standards to supervise the officials' performance. Officials who do not follow the standards will be punished according to the rules. The system has already been applied first in certain fields, such as production safety, but much more work has to be done to set up and implement the system in most major fields.

For large SOEs, the State Council will formulate an accountability system to punish SOE managers' illegal business operations, according to a report from August 2016. Managers could be fined or sued for mistakes made in operations (Xinhua 2016).

The adoption of an accountability system is a good example of the changes following the logic of government. The anti-corruption campaign created the concept of officials' administrative omissions. To fight against this, a means of further administrative control must be adopted.

The Further Standardisation of Governance and the Improvement of Law Coverage

The period also saw an effort to further standardise governance functions while power was concentrated into the central government. A large number of laws were passed or revised to regulate the government officials, as well as the market and the society. The focus has been on the standardisation of the administration of different levels of government, by following laws and rules, which makes the implementation of central government's policies more efficient and reliable. It has also emphasised the elimination of the overlapping functions of government departments, using the higher-level government's coordination and supervision. However, this only means the administration ruled by law, not the rule of law. The CCP is still in charge of the design, establishment, and implementation of laws. The CCP has emphasised that their leadership is the fundamental guarantee of the governance by law. The borderlines of law establishment between government agencies should be clearly defined and the legalisation of the special interests of government departments and local governments should be prevented, according to the leadership (Xi 2014).

At the beginning of the economic reform in the late 1970s, China had very few laws for citizens and firms to follow. The creation of a market economy needed the establishment of laws in many fields. The government made a tremendous effort to cover loopholes in the system of laws. These laws standardised the behaviour of market participants. As China's market economy grew, a large number of formal laws were revised, and some new laws have been adopted during the period since 2012. The following is a list of laws related to market and government administration that have been passed or amended since 2012. This system of laws covers many fields of the new market economy created in the process of economic reform. The list of laws provided below shows the wide scope of formal laws established during the economic reform.

Many of these laws define the basic organisations and rules of a market economy. The Corporation Law, originally adopted in 1993 and revised in 1999, 2004, and 2005, was last revised in 2013. The latest revision relaxed the requirement for establishing a company, removed the minimum capital requirement, and simplified the registration process (National People's Congress 2013b). The Labour Contract Law, adopted in 2007, was amended in 2012 and regulates the formation of labour contracts, fulfilment and change of labour contracts, dissolution and termination of labour contracts, supervision and inspection of labour contracts, and legal liabilities (National People's Congress 2012b). Other revised laws concerning the general rules of a market economy include the Trademark Law (National People's Congress 2013a), the Auction Law (National People's Congress 2015b), the Anti-Money Laundering Law (National People's Congress 2006e), and the Charity Law (National People's Congress 2016f).

Other laws revised in this period concerned some special fields or organisations in a market economy. The Insurance Law, originally passed in 1995 and revised in 2002, 2009, and 2014, was revised again in 2015. The amendment deleted the articles about the pre-administration examination and approval of insurance practitioners (National People's Congress 2015c). The Law on Commercial Banks, adopted in 1995 and revised in 2003, was amended in 2015, and defines the business commercial banks were allowed to conduct, such as attracting deposits and issuing loans (National People's Congress 2015d). The Securities Law, passed in 1998 and revised in 2004 and 2013, was revised again in 2014, covering the issuance and transactions of shares, company bonds, and other securities within China's territory. The amendments emphasised disclosure rather than trying to ensure the quality of investments (National People's Congress 2014a). The Securities Investment Fund Law, passed in 2003 and revised in 2012, was amended in 2015, to regulate security investment fund activities and protect the rights of investors (National People's Congress 2015e).

Foreign-invested business was a new type of business in China after its opening up to the world. These businesses needed to be regulated by laws, which were established in the early stage of economic reform and needed to be revised as the situation changed. The Law on Sino-Foreign Equity Joint Ventures, originally passed in 1979 and revised in 1990 and 2001, was revised again in 2016, to regulate joint ventures and promote cooperation with foreign enterprises (National People's Congress 2016a). The Wholly Foreign-Owned Enterprise Law, passed in 1986 and revised in 2000, was revised a second time in 2016. According to the new revisions, the requirement that 'a foreign-owned enterprise should report its business plan to the competent government department' was deleted, and 'raw materials and fuel needed by a foreign-owned enterprise should be pre-empted in China' was changed to 'can be bought either in China or internationally' (National People's Congress 2016b). The Foreign Trade Law, adopted in 1994 and revised in 2004, was revised again in 2016, with minor revisions (National People's Congress 2016e).

Another group of laws concerned the migration of peasants and urbanisation. The Interim Regulations on Residence Permits was adopted in 2015, to facilitate and regulate the residence statuses of rural migrants to urban areas. According to the regulation, a citizen who resides in a city for more than half a year and meets certain requirements on employment, residence, and children's education can apply for a residence permit (State Council 2015). The Population and Family Planning Law, originally passed in 2001, was amended in 2015. The law changed the policy of advocating 'one child per couple' in urban areas to 'two children per couple' to cope with the crisis of the reducing growth of population (National People's Congress 2015i).

A large number of laws regulated the safety of consumer goods, working conditions, and environmental protection. The Food Safety Law, adopted in 2009 and revised in 2015, covers food production and food distribution services, food additives, packing materials, food storage and transportation, and safety management. According to the law, food producers or traders who violate the law should be subject to a fine of RMB2,000 to 50,000 ($321.1 to $8,027.7) if the total value of the commodity is less than RMB10,000 ($1,605.5) or 10 to 20 times of the total value when the commodity exceeds RMB10,000 ($1,605.5; National People's Congress 2015f). The Pharmaceutical Administration Law, adopted in 1984 and revised in 2001 and 2013, was revised again in 2015, to strengthen drug control and administration, ensure the quality of drugs, and guarantee safe drug use (National People's Congress 2015h). The Work Safety Law, adopted in 2002 and amended in 2009, was amended for a second time in 2014, covering work safety within business entities, as well as rights and obligations of employees, supervision, and emergency management (National People's Congress 2014e). The Environmental Protection Law, adopted in

1989, was revised in 2014. The revision was considered the most restrictive environmental regulation in China's history. According to the law, the local government should be responsible for the environmental quality of their own administrative areas (National People's Congress 2014b). The Law on the Prevention and Control of Atmospheric Pollution, adopted in 1987 and revised in 2000, was revised for a second time in 2015. The revision covered the control of more atmospheric pollutants, such as particulates; strengthened the responsibility of the local governments in the prevention of air pollution; allowed the local government to set local standards of air quality; and emphasised joint prevention between different areas (National People's Congress 2015j). The Law on the Protection of Wildlife, first adopted in 1988 and revised in 2004 and 2009, was amended again in 2016. The law added terms on the protection of wildlife habitat, and made punishments more stringent (National People's Congress 2016c).

The last group of laws are related to the government administration. The Law on the Administration of Tax Collection, adopted in 1992 and revised in 1995 and 2013, was revised once again in 2015. According to the law, the imposition of tax, the cessation there of, tax reduction, tax exemption, refund of tax, and payment of delinquent tax shall be governed by the provisions of relevant laws (National People's Congress 2015k). This means some of the current taxes are illegal. The Budget Law, adopted in 1994, was amended in 2014. The law regulated the powers of budget management, the scope of revenue and expenditure, the compilation, examination, approval, adjustment, and implementation of the budget. According to the law, the National People's Congress has the power to change any inappropriate resolutions made by the Standing Committee of the National People's Congress on budget and final accounts. Local governments are allowed to issue local government debt within the quota set by the State Council (National People's Congress 2014c). The Government Procurement Law, adopted in 2002, was revised in 2014 and regulated the procedure, contract, supervision, and queries and complaints involving government procurement (National People's Congress 2014d). The Legislation Law was revised by the National People's Congress in March 2015. According to the revision, legislation should be conducted according to statutory power and procedure, on the basis of the overall interests of the state, and to maintain the unity and dignity of the socialist legal system. The law listed the matters that shall only be governed by laws. In the case of matters for which laws have not been developed but that require some sort of legal framework, the Congress may empower the State Council to first develop administrative regulations except for certain matters (National People's Congress 2015a). The National Securities Law was first passed in 2015, stipulating the national security system and the responsibilities of state security organs

(National People's Congress 2015l). The Cybersecurity Law was passed in 2016, to regulate the construction, operation, maintenance and use of the network, and the supervision and administration of cybersecurity (National People's Congress 2016d). The Electoral Law for the National People's Congress and Local People's Congress, originally passed in 1982, was revised in 1986, 1995, 2004, 2010, and 2015. The law confirmed that the deputies to the National People's Congress and to the People's Congresses of provinces shall be elected by the People's Congress at the next lower level. Deputies to the People's Congress of cities not divided into districts, municipal districts, counties, or townships, shall be elected directly by their constituencies (National People's Congress 2015g).

The standardisation of government administration ensures that the different levels of government and officials follow the law and rules. This may raise the administrative efficiency of the government. However, it may also encourage bureaucracy and increase the inconvenience of businesses and individuals doing business with the government. For example, the recent government-led movement of demolishing illegal buildings in large cities eliminated illegal constructions, but at the same time drove some small businesses and migrant workers out of the large cities. Even though a large number of laws and regulations have been adopted, the implementation of the laws is still a big problem, especially at the lower level of the legislative structure. The leadership noticed the problem and tried to use accountability to improve the implementation of the laws. The current situation of the legislative system is mainly due to its weak position in the bureaucratic system. The extremely strong position of the administrative branch of the government squeezes out the power of the judicial branch at the same level. To change the situation, the powers of government branches need to be rebalanced.

6.2 THE CONTINUED MARKETISATION UNDER GOVERNMENT CONTROL

After nearly 40 years of economic growth, the Chinese economy has become enormous, and many large firms have appeared on the market. One-hundred and fifteen Chinese firms are now listed in the Fortune 500 in 2017 (Fortune 2017). The large consumer market has fostered technical innovation in many sectors. Services based on internet technology are growing dramatically. Economy of scale in both the demand and the supply sides has become one source of economic development.

Market-oriented reform was continued, but without strong momentum after 2012. The 3rd Plenary Session of the 18th Central Committee of the CCP, held in November 2013, approved a Decision on Major Issues Concerning Comprehensively Deepening Reforms. According to the Decision, economic reform is the key, and the core solution lies in the proper relationship between the government and the market, leaving the market to play the decisive role in the allocation of resources while letting the government play a better role in economic development (CCP Central Committee 2013). However, in reality, since 2013 government has set stability as its main goal, rather than economic reform. According to data I collected, due to forces of inertia, the marketisation process is continuing but with a diminishing growth rate (see section 7.4 of this book).

The Reform of SOEs and SOE-Dominated Sectors

The reform of SOEs and SOE-dominated sectors has not made significant progress since the CCP published the decision on economic reform in 2013. The governance structure of the SOEs has been continuously improving, but no significant progress has been accomplished in relation to the scope of SOEs operations and the number of major SOEs. As a result of improved operations and continued exploitation of economic rents, the large SOEs have become stronger in the competition with private companies.

According to a survey by the National Bureau of Statistics from 2006, there were no SOEs in entertainment, computer services, and construction decoration at that time; SOEs occupied less than 10 per cent of the market in wood processing, apparels, and construction installation; less than one-third of the market in textiles, agricultural products processing, plastic products, and chemical fibre manufacturing; but more than 90 per cent of the market in electricity, thermal production and supply, transportation, and transportation equipment; and almost 100 per cent of the market in oil and gas extraction and telecommunication (Wu Xiaobo 2014a, p.368). Not much has changed since then, and the SOEs still dominate the upstream resource-intensive sectors as well as industries considered as strategic. The total value of state-owned assets reached about RMB140 trillion ($22.5 trillion) in the mid-2010s, and 98 national-level SOEs are controlled by the national State-owned Assets Supervision and Administration Commission (SASAC).

The 3rd Plenary Session of the 18th Central Committee of the CCP in 2013 decided to improve the management of state-owned assets and SOEs. The goal was to make the SOEs more efficient and responsive to market forces, while keeping SOEs embedded in the foundations of China's economy. SOE privatisation was not on the menu, and SOEs needed to carry more of the load for China's future growth. In 2014, six big SOEs were selected to pilot reforms in ownership, management, and supervision, including selectively setting up state-owned assets investment companies and a 'board of directors' system[5] (Houwang n.d.). In 2016, more SOEs were selected to pilot reforms, including seven SOEs to pilot reforms of state-owned capital investment companies, four to pilot board reforms, and several other to pilot other reforms (Bestychen n.d.). The 2016 Central Economic Work Conference, the government's annual general economic meeting, pointed out that mixed-ownership reform will be the selling point of the reform of SOEs,[6] and that the reform of state-owned investment companies and operating companies should be accelerated (Jian 2016). The mixed-ownership reform allows private businesses and SOE employees to hold certain shares of SOEs in sectors monopolised by SOEs. The government has been promoting an overhaul of SOEs to revitalise the public sector of the economy, piloting mixed-ownership reform, while opening up some industrial sectors to private capital.

It seems that the strategy of the government has changed from reducing the scope of SOE operations in the late 1990s to keeping the current scope of SOE operations, improving SOE performance, and using large SOEs as one of the key tools for controlling the economy. The domination of SOEs in the upstream resource-intensive sectors will not be changed.

From the governance point of view, there is a possibility to re-use large SOEs as tools of control. The 'lines' and 'blocks' were two major control tools used in the planned economy. During the reform, blocks were used extensively while the role of lines was reduced dramatically. Some of the large SOEs today are actually legacies of the 'lines' industrial ministries from the planned period. The re-concentration of power into central government refreshes the possibility of re-using large SOEs as a tool of macro-control.

The Financial Reform and Opening Up

The market-oriented reforms continued in the financial sector and foreign trade/investment sector after 2013.

Interest rate marketisation[7] started in 2004. The interest rates charged by financial institutions were completely controlled by the central bank before then. The reform followed an order (e.g. loans first, deposits second; large amounts first, small amounts second; foreign currency operation first, RMB operation second). The reform made some progress, but was suspended in 2008 due to the financial crisis. However, it started again after the crisis. By 2015, loan rates had been completely freed. Other interest rates, like interest rates for bonds, had also been freed. The People's Bank announced in October 2015 that the floating ceilings on interest rates for deposits, the last control measure on interest rates, had been lifted (Chen 2015).

In 1996, China achieved current account convertibility, and announced it would seek to achieve capital account convertibility. The process was delayed by the Asian financial crisis and because of domestic objections and unfavourable domestic economic conditions. In 2005, China adopted a managed exchange rate system within which the exchange rate was determined by market supply and demand, but under government control. China has gradually relaxed the control on the exchange rate since then. The floating range of RMB to US dollar was widened in 2007, 2012, and 2014. China has promoted the internationalisation of RMB in recent years, by continuously deepening bilateral monetary cooperation, with over 30 bilateral local currency swap agreements signed. The government has also promoted the steady development of offshore RMB markets, and established RMB clearing banks in many countries and regions. Capital account convertibility has made some progress. The RMB has largely become convertible for foreign direct investment (FDI) and outward direct investment (ODI). In 2014, the Shanghai–Hong Kong Stock Connect was set up, through which Chinese mainland investors can invest in Hong Kong's stock market, while foreign investors can invest in China's domestic stock market. However, due to the fluctuation of the RMB exchange rate since 2015, the central bank has made interventions in the exchange rate market several times and tightened the control of international capital flow (e.g. tightening restrictions on money outflows and re-anchoring RMB to the US dollar), backtracking on the effort to make RMB more market-oriented.

Problems remain in the stock market. The non-accountable actions of the managers of listed companies damage the interests of shareholders, through the misuse of information or through conducting transactions favourable to the managers themselves. The monitoring agencies have limited power to supervise listed companies. The stock exchanges, as branches of government monitoring agencies, do not have the power to set standards for listing and delisting. Civil litigation also has little effect on the behaviour of listed companies, and the monitoring by non-government agencies, such as auditing firms, is weak (Clarke et al. 2008, p.419). A recent stock market turbulence began with the popping of the stock market bubble on 12 June 2015 and ended in early February 2016. A third of the value of A-shares on the Shanghai Stock Exchange was lost within one month. The crash was due to the relaxation of several related financial regulations by the China Securities Regulatory Commission (CSRC), which regulated the act of selling short, speculation in borrowing and selling stock, and trading on margin, or trading with debt. These regulation changes led to significant increases in borrowing for the purpose of trading, and short selling became the most popular investing strategy among traders. It turns out that the stock market turbulence in 2015 was initiated for political purposes by a coalition of some high-level regulation officials and several large bankers. The officials and bankers tried to put pressure on the government by attempting to control stock prices. The CSRC has been tightening the regulation on the stock market ever since. In July 2016, the CSRC announced its decision to delist a company from the stock market following fraud during its initial public offering (IPO), the first time authorities have taken such action in the history of China's modern stock market. In 2017, a large portion of companies applying for an IPO were rejected, and more illegal operations were punished. The CSRC issued a total of 218 penalty notices in 2016, up 21 per cent year on year, and confiscated RMB4.28 billion ($0.64 billion), nearly triple the amount of the previous year (Ying 2017). In July 2017, the National Financial Work Conference established a unified financial supervision commission under the State Council, combining some functions of several existing financial supervision agencies. The function of the agency is limited to meeting regularly to discuss financial stability issues (Bradsher 2017).[8] In August 2017, the government moved to curb overseas investment, through excessive domestic borrowing, by domestic companies and conglomerates in sectors from entertainment and sport clubs to hotels, reflecting the government's worries about capital outflow (Wee 2017).

As part of the anti-corruption campaign, in June and July 2017 the leadership launched a crackdown on some large companies with close government connections. Some of the executives were arrested; others were put under great official pressure to hold their investment overseas.

China has replaced all business tax with a value-added tax (VAT) after extending the policy to cover the construction, real-estate, finance, and consumer services sectors in 2016. The reform does not change the overall tax burden of the firms much, but it might change the tax burden of specific enterprises. One criticism of this tax reform is that it has encouraged investments in housing-related sectors while discouraging those in manufacturing sectors, by reducing the tax burden of the former.

China has opened its doors to the outside world over the last 30 years, but more opening up is still needed. China lowered its average tariff levels on industrial products after joining the World Trade Organization (WTO). However, China still retains the state monopoly on foreign trade for a number of imports (e.g. crude oil, refined petroleum products, grain, and vegetable oil) and exports (e.g. tea, silk, and fossil fuel) (Branstetter and Lardy 2008, p.651). A big step in further opening up the Chinese economy during this period has been the creation of a pilot free trade zone in

Shanghai. The Shanghai Free-Trade Zone (Shanghai FTZ), launched on 29 September 2013 with the backing of Chinese premier Li Keqiang, is a testing ground for a number of economic and social reforms. Commodities entering the zone are not subject to duties or customs clearance, and the zone removes a number of financial requirements for setting up a company in China. The FTZ also introduces a simplified procedure for foreign investors to establish a company in China. The FTZ permits RMB convertibility and unrestricted foreign currency exchange, and there is tax-free period of ten years for businesses in the zone. The State Council published a list of 18 service industries eligible to receive more relaxed policies in the zone, which is the basis for China's future negative list of foreign investment for negotiating with other countries.[9] The experiment with free trade zones was expanded to other areas. In April 2015, the Tianjin FTZ and the Fujian FTZ were founded. If successful, the reform is expected to expand nationwide.

Private Firms and Urbanisation

Private firms, especially small private firms, have been facing tremendous difficulties since the financial crisis in 2008. A large number of small private firms closed and some foreign firms moved out of China for economic and political reasons. I visited a large number of firms in the eastern coastal area in 2015 and 2016 and observed the conditions of small and medium-sized firms. Labour costs doubled from 2010 to 2015, and the labour-intensive sectors (e.g. shoe manufacturing) are shrinking and moving out of China. Tax burdens are high, and the social security payments the firms have to pay for their workers are about 30 per cent of workers' wages. It is difficult for many firms to obtain new loans to cover old ones, and some of them have to borrow at usurers' rates. Firms also face a complicated procedure of business registration. When collecting taxes, the local government has significant discretionary power, which has resulted in large differences in tax burdens among different firms. Recently, under government pressure, some large private companies have reduced their loans by selling their domestic assets. The government has also tightened the control of private firms' overseas investment to prevent capital flight.

The greater involvement of government in the economy has significantly increased the transaction costs of doing business in China. It may have self-enhancement effects and make the government use more administrative means, due to the rule of path dependence. To solve the problem of registration procedure, the central government started a 'reform of the business system' intended to streamline administrative approval procedures. The State Administration for Industry and Commerce (SAIC) loosened regulations over market access. The new regulation cancelled several requirements, including the minimum amount of registered capital, initial paid-in capital, as well as subscription time limitation. The SAIC has been collaborating with relevant ministries to progressively transform the system of 'Approval Certificate before Business Licence' to one of 'Approval Certificate after Business Licence'. The SAIC is promoting the reform of 'three certificates/licences to one', that is, merging the business licence, the certificate of organisation code, and the tax registration certificate into one licence or certificate (SAIC 2015). This reform is a good attempt to reduce the burden of firms. However, as pointed out by some business people, the speed of simplifying the procedure sometimes could not match the speed at which new requirements were being added to the procedure by the government agencies. I visited a local government agency in Dongguan, Guangdong province. The reform of the business registration system finished in 2015, and the time needed to complete the registration procedure was reduced from one month to two–four working days for domestic firms, and from two–six months to three–four working days for foreign firms. The number of certificates has been reduced from over 200 to 13, and the required capital has reduced from RMB300,000 ($48,166.5) to RMB1 ($0.16). The number of businesses registered increased in the area dramatically after the reform.

Private firms have been a driving force of the economic growth in China. Urbanisation has been another engine of economic growth in China since the economic reform started in 1978, and has continued after 2013. The government implemented differentiated policies for large and small cities. Resident registration is still strictly controlled in large cities, while the *Hukou* system in small and medium-sized cities is relaxing. The setting up of a unified urban–rural resident registration system and a resident permit system has been planned. According to the new regulations, a migrant worker who has lived in an urban area for a certain amount of time can apply for a resident permit and enjoy the public services enjoyed by urban residents, such as education for their children and health care services. In large cities with populations of five million and more, the application process is still strictly controlled, using a points system for household registration. Migrants cumulate their points according to years of permanent residency and years paying social security payments (State Council 2014). The migrant workers issue has been one of the social problems that have arisen during the process of reform (this problem was mentioned in Chapter 5). The great migration increased tremendously the income of these migrants, but also brought poverty into the cities. Solving these problems will be a big challenge for the Chinese government in the near future.[10]

The economic reforms in certain areas have continued, but no breakthrough has been made during this period. Officials at all levels, who were educated during the reform period, played an important role in this continuing economic reform.

6.3 THE SLOWDOWN OF GROWTH

Nearly three decades of punctuated economic growth capped by unprecedented prosperity contributed to the 'mood' of the society, creating an air of confidence for the future. However, the surplus labour in the countryside was finally used up around 2010, after over 250 million rural residents had moved out of their home villages. The weak global economy after the financial crisis of 2008 also reduced the demand for Chinese exports. The Chinese economy moved into a downturn and the growth rate slowed down from 10.6 per cent in 2010 to 6.7 per cent in 2016. Export-oriented labour-intensive manufacturing industries are shrinking, due to the weakness of the global economy and the high administrative burden on enterprises. Some coastal towns are emptying due to the closing of firms. Besides labour costs, overall transaction costs are extremely high, due to the non-transferrable farmland, the resources controlled by the large SOEs, and the complicated procedures of the bureaucratic agencies.

This is a period of transition from high-speed growth to slower but stable growth. Several structural problems have to be solved before achieving a stable long-run growth, including (i) transferring from a labour-intensive manufacturing economy to a middle-level capital/knowledge-intensive economy; (ii) reducing the real-estate bubble created by monetary expansion; and (iii) solving the local government debt problem created by fiscal expansions. The government has tried different approaches to solving these problems. They first tried Keynesian policies. After a period of hesitation, in 2015 the government eased fiscal policy to ensure the growth rate target could be met. Since the demand-side approach did not work, the government changed its focus at the end of 2015 to supply-side macroeconomic policies, by reducing the overcapacity of production. The policies of reducing excess manufacturing capacity were precipitated by years of anxiety about overcapacity[11] and cut-throat competition, the very issues that had so disrupted the US economy in the 20th century. The slowdown of the economy appeared to signal a downturn of an economy that had been beset for a decade by overproduction.

Housing prices in many cities increased dramatically in the 2010s due to the government's propagation of measures to promote housing sales in order to improve the macroeconomic situation, as well as the monetary expansion. The government's policies had an impact on the housing market, especially in large cities. Housing prices have risen dramatically in first and second tier cities in recent years.[12] In 2016, if a homebuyer in Beijing were to spend an entire year's worth of wages, he or she could only afford a 0.94 square metre apartment (Daxue Consulting 2017). The government unveiled comprehensive regulations on housing, from both the demand side and the supply side, to curb the sky-high prices of housing in early 2017. Municipal governments in different cities set up their own policies following the guidelines of the central government. For example, according to the new regulation, in Beijing the down payment for a second house should not be lower than 60 per cent of the total value of the house. This kind of policy has reduced the demand for housing significantly in the short term, because potential residents cannot afford the large down payment. But in the long run the policy might not be sustainable.

Debt is another problem in the current Chinese economy. The economic growth in China after the financial crisis of 2008 has been partly due to fiscal expansion and the amount of debt issued, which will be paid by future generations. The main debt problem is with the local government and firms. Local governments were not allowed to issue debt during the first decade of the new century. Therefore, they used non-transparent and risky platforms to issue large amounts of business debt in order to finance local construction. A platform is a financial vehicle which conceals its relationship with the real owner. To solve the problem of platform debt, since 2015 the central government has banned platforms and regulated the issuance of local debt. According to the new regulation, the central government will issue bonds for local governments. The local governments have to transfer their maturing platform debt to local debt in accordance with quotas set by the central government. The quotas were too limited to cover the maturing debt at first, and the central government expanded the quotas later. Chinese firms also have serious debt problems. Some of the smaller firms have closed in the last few years as they have not been able to pay the interest rates, while others continue to operate with a heavy debt burden. The slowdown of the economy has made the debt problems very serious. Large SOEs also have heavy debt burdens, because they are able to borrow cheap loans from state-owned banks.

At the time this book was wrapped up, in 2017, there were some good signs in the economy. The growth rate of gross domestic product (GDP) in 2017 was 6.9 per cent, slightly higher than that in 2016. GDP growth in 2018 is expected to be 6.5 to 6.3 per cent due to the more restricted regulation on housing and financial markets. But much more work has to be done to solve structural problems before China can enter a new long-run growth cycle.

This period of institutional evolution has not reached an end. Some of the expectations of future development are not clear and further observation is needed. However, it is clear that this period has been a turning point in the process of China's reform. Two logics have dominated China's historical movement since the late 1970s: the logic of bureaucracy and the logic of market. The two logics have often conflicted with each other during the reform. At this time the logic of bureaucracy is winning. The government has begun using more bureaucratic approaches to control the current situation and to solve economic and social problems, as predicted by the theory of government decision-making developed in Chapter 1, section 1.2. This has improved the efficiency of governance but created the danger of over-expansion of the government and of excess bureaucratic pressure on markets.

NOTES

1. Li Keqiang became the premier of the central government in 2013.
2. The promotion, retirement, and personal records of these officials are managed by the Central Organisation Department of the CCP.
3. A State Supervision Committee was set up in March 2018.
4. If an official does extra work, he or she has more chance of making mistakes, and has a higher chance of becoming a target of the anti-corruption campaign.
5. A state-owned assets investment company is a company using state-owned assets to invest in SOEs by holding their stocks. Some large SOEs did not have a board of directors. The pilot reforms set up boards of directors in these SOEs to modernise their governance.
6. A mixed-ownership reform of SOEs would attract private investors to invest in SOEs, and this would diversify the ownership of SOEs.
7. Interest rate marketisation is a process in which the government-controlled interest rate changed to an interest rate determined by supply and demand on the free market.
8. In March 2018, China's banking regulator (CBRC) and insurance regulator (CIRC) were merged, and the head of this body China Banking and Insurance Regulatory Commission (CBIRC), along with the head of the China Securities Regulatory Commission (CSRC) and the People's Bank of China, will be governed by the special cabinet level committee set up in 2017 to coordinate regulation called the Financial Supervision and Development Committee.
9. A negative list provides an outline of the sectors in which foreign investment is restrained. For all industries not listed in this document, foreign investors will receive equal treatment to domestic companies. It is widely used in international investment negotiations.
10. In November 2017, some migrant workers who lived in illegal housing were driven out of Beijing by the local government.
11. Buyers could not be found for large amounts of steel and coal, and the prices of these products have been low. From 2013 to 2017, the government reduced steel production capacities by about 150 million tons and coal production capacities by 800 million tons through closing factories or production lines (Jin 2018).
12. Cities in China were grouped into several tiers; the first tier includes the largest cities.

7. Lessons learned and long-term expectations

Institutional evolution has been the major source of economic development in China in the past 40 years. Because of the fruitful marriage between institutional reform and the development of mass markets, production and living standards have grown rapidly since the late 1970s. Great progress has been made, yet problems have also accumulated. Chinese society and the leadership have faced complicated issues in the late 20th century and early 21st century. This chapter will draw lessons from past experiences and predict the future of China's institutional evolution.

7.1 ROLES OF GOVERNMENT AND MARKET IN A BUREAUCRATIC-MARKET SYSTEM

A basic fact is that the Chinese government has played a more significant role in economic development in the past several decades than other governments in regular market economies.

Achievements and Weakness of the Bureaucratic-Market System

What did the government do during the reform? What was successful and what was not? The government allowed the market to play an important role, while maintaining order in the market:

1. The government relaxed a large number of regulations that had been set up in the planned economy.
2. The government relaxed its control of prices in competitive market sectors.
3. The government built different kinds of markets and set up new regulations for a market economy.
4. The government actively cracked down on illegal activities by carrying out campaigns of macro-control.

Most of these government interventions, especially those interventions during the early years of the reform, were within the boundaries of government intervention set by economic theory. The theory argues that the market fails to reach efficiency when several conditions exist, including (i) asymmetric information, (ii) externalities, (iii) natural monopoly, (iv) absences of markets, and (v) poorly defined property rights. Under these situations, the market cannot operate efficiently. When these market failures occur, there is a potential rationale for government intervention (e.g. creating commodity and financial markets, and distributing property rights to producers. See section 1.2 in this book).

Institutional evolution greatly reduced transaction costs and increased the productivity of the Chinese economy. The reform redistributing farmland to households changed the mode of agricultural production fundamentally from collective production to individual family production. This incentivised production by farmers, and the gross outputs of farming, forestry, animal husbandry, and fishery increased 130 per cent from 1978 to 1984 (National Bureau of Statistics 1999). The privatisation of small state-owned enterprises (SOEs) in the late 1990s solved the inefficiency problem of SOEs and raised the real gross output of secondary industry by 53.8 per cent from 1997 to 2002 (National Bureau of Statistics 2016b, Table 3.5).

The government did more than intervene as defined by economic theory of government intervention:

1. The central government controlled the macroeconomic situation through economic and administrative measures, and used a formal evaluation system to control the local governments and large SOEs.
2. The local government worked as the leader of local economies, by improving infrastructure and the environment for local investment.

These interventions were basically reasonable, considering the institutional background in China, especially the weak market institutions and the weak society.[1] Even though the scope of government intervention in China has been reduced during the past four decades, it is still much greater than that in a true market economy (see, for example, the SOEs' direct involvement in economic activities, as developed in the previous chapters).

In other cases during the reform, the government did not function within the boundaries set by the economic theory of government intervention and over-intervened in the market. For example, the macro-controls following each boom usually hurt small private businesses. Some of them were closed by the government for economic or non-economic reasons. For example, Tieben was a case of how macro-control damaged a private firm, as mentioned in section 4.2 in this book. The RMB4 trillion government investment after the 2008 financial crisis crowded out many small businesses and resulted in SOEs' dominance in many industries. The coal mining industry was a case of 'the advance of the state vs the retreat of the private firms', as mentioned in section 5.5 in this book.

The nature of the bureaucratic-market system fostered corruption among government officials and business executives. The reform years were golden times for private businesses. However, the unprecedented progress made by many large private businesses was due to their relationships with the government. Any successful business people in a bureaucratic market like China must have managed their relationship with government well. The initial wealth cumulated by most successful private businesses involved bribing government officials, which in turn means evidence held in government's hands for future punishment. This is one reason why private firms are not fully protected by the government and why some private firms tried to move their assets overseas. The private firms have extraordinary opportunities compared to an ordinary market economy due to the government's support, but face greater risks should the connected government officials be arrested or government policies changed.

The main problem for SOEs' reform is government intervention. SOEs have close historical relationships with the government. The main issue of SOE reform in the past 30 years has been preventing government from intervening in the operations of SOEs. This has not been totally successful, and the SOEs have become stronger and monopolised many sectors. The protection and support from the government has made SOEs less efficient, and this may have a long-term influence on the Chinese economy.

The reform has actually been a process of adjusting the scope of government and market functions. Up to the early 21st century, the main trend for several decades was the shrinking role of government. According to the economic theory of government intervention developed in section 1.2, this was due to the heavy weight put on economic performance in the government's utility function in the early years of the reform. The reform created corruption and loosened the control on government officials. This is to say that government authority did not extend beyond the Zhongnanhai, the location of the central government. In response to this situation, the government has moved in the opposite direction. The government has increased its control beyond the boundaries of government intervention developed by economic theory (see section 1.2) in recent years. The government increased its role further in the economy, through large amounts of infrastructure investment that was controlled and approved by the central government. This reflects the shift of government's priority in its benefit function and a bureaucratic solution to many market-created problems. This kind of adjustment is sometimes necessary if assessed by the logic of government control, but it might be costly and risky in the long run.

In general, the government's over-intervention is fundamentally a phenomenon of a government-led economy with insufficient restrictions on government decisions. The reasons for this include the following: (i) the government does not have enough relevant information when making decisions; (ii) in a bureaucratic-market economy, government officials are occasionally captured by business firms through bribery and other activities; and (iii) the government is rational, but its considerations are multiple and its preferences are sometimes different from that of the society. To reduce the mistakes in government intervention, the government needs to know its limitations in relation to information and decision-making, and government power needs to be restricted through strengthening supervision from various channels, including the legal system.

Weakness of the Legal System

Many changes have been experienced in China's formal legal system over the past 40 years. There have been enormous efforts to build a legal system that covers the tremendous amounts of activity in a market economy and regulates the operation of the government to some degree. Part of the rule-making process has shifted from the Communist Party of China (CCP) and the State Council to the National People's Congress. The role of legal institutions has been expanded to cover increasing numbers of areas in the economy.

However, there have been gaps in China's legal system governing market and government activities. Although many laws have been established in the past 40 years, gaps still exist. For example, when different laws or regulations overlap, no procedure can currently be followed to solve the conflict.

Enforcement of laws is a problem that has existed for decades. Many formal laws are not enforced or followed by different government branches and by ordinary citizens. Although benchmarks have been set by the constitution, there is no effective system for solving conflicts between different rules made by different branches of the government. Many rules are enacted by ministries, and local governments and legislative bodies at the national level are not able to overturn an administrative or local regulation.

Formal legal institutions do not provide a completely secure system of property rights and contract rights, partly because different government bodies have the power to make overlapping rules and no authoritative body exists to resolve conflicts. During the reform process, the administrative branches of the government, especially the local governments, have served as alternatives to the formal legal system in providing security to private investors. Under the official evaluation system and fiscal contracting system, the local government protects the property rights over the assets of the private investors to attract investors and promote local economic growth.

The courts are weak in the political system, and the decisions of the courts are often ignored by the government agencies. The local courts depend on local governments, and the power of appointment of high-ranking judiciary officials is controlled by the CCP Department of Organisation, while the finance and welfare of court officials are controlled by the administrative body of the government. The fundamental problem is the relationship between the law, the administrative branch of the government, and the CCP. In an idealised model of a nation subject to the rule of law, the law should preside over everything else. China is far from this ideal situation. As a first step towards such a nation, the law could be under the top leader of the CCP but over everything else. This is a situation in which the CCP uses law to rule the Chinese society. It is better than the situation in which the ruler rules the society according to his or her own personal opinion, which happened in China during the Cultural Revolution and resulted in tremendous disasters in Chinese society.

Informal rules play an important role when a formal law does not exist or is unfair. In the planned period, peasants peacefully resisted the heavy burden of grain turnover by concealing the size of farmland and output for many years. When a government policy is not reliable, ordinary people usually do not directly go against the policy, but resist the policy softly. During the reform years, small enterprises avoided the heavy tax burden by using similar methods. When a rule is not reasonable, it will not be implemented fully. Most Chinese people, government officials as well as common citizens, lack the concept of rule of law. Most laws in China are theoretical and need to be more specific and detailed for implementation.

Overall, the weak judiciary system comes from the overly strong administration within the bureaucratic structure. With a weak legal system, the market has developed under the protection and regulation of the administrative branch of the government, especially that of local governments. This situation is not sustainable in the long term. Development of the legal system is one way to balance the power of government branches and provide reliable protections for the market in the future.

Checks and Balances: A Challenge

Checks and balances of government power are vital in a bureaucratic-market system. In my political economy theory of government decision-making in a bureaucratic-market system developed in section 1.2, economic performance played an important role as a restriction in the early years of the reform, yet ironically, the excellent performance of the economy has reduced the restrictions on government in recent years.

China is a society composed of nucleus cells (Sun 2015). Different levels of government, units, and families have a similar structure, with a leader at the centre and a group of followers surrounding. The leader is both the decision maker and the highest judge/lawgiver. Checks and balances are not satisfactorily offered in such organisations.

China developed a strong administrative branch of the government 2,000 years ago; however, other branches of the government have been weak, and the society is less developed. Under these circumstances, the administrative branch of the central government works as an alternative institute to perform the function of checks and balances (Fukuyama 2011). The higher-level government plays an important role in checking the power of the lower-level government and individual government officials, as in the case of the current anti-corruption movement, and balances power among local governments. But in many other cases, its effects are limited. The group of retired leaders also plays an informal role as a restriction on the current leadership.

Some of the policy makers believe that the one ruling party can constrain the use of power by itself, through discipline and criticism between party members and self-criticism by the party members (Liu 2014). The positive role of the selection procedure of officials is a strong argument for the current political system in China. The selection procedure moves competition among candidates prior to the actual governance to ensure the most experienced person becomes the government leader. Some researchers consider the current Chinese political system to be a political meritocracy, which selects the political elites as the leaders of the government through an official selection system. It was a Chinese tradition that the emperors used civil-service examination systems to select officials; the system was relatively fair to all candidates irrespective of family background. One problem of this system is how to restrict the officials' abuse of power once they have passed the selection procedure, and how to restrict the abuse of power by the top leaders. Another problem concerns how to explain the legitimacy of power to the outsiders in the society. To make the selection work, the standards of selection must be correct, and the procedure must be transparent.

In recent years in China, the highest level of government has played a more important role in providing checks and balances on the power of lower-level government, including (i) supervising lower-level government officials; and (ii) balancing the relationship between government and ordinary citizens. Recent attempts to improve supervision within the government involve several aspects summarised in the Decision on Major Issues Pertaining to Comprehensively Promoting the Rule of Law, which was passed by the 4th Plenary Session of the 18th Central Committee of the CCP in October 2014. These include (i) standardising the procedure of using and supervising administrative power; (ii) improving accountability mechanisms; and (iii) completing the auditing system[2] (CCP Central Committee 2014). As mentioned above, the anti-corruption movement was initiated and enforced exclusively by top leadership. It is an effective restriction on local governments. In recent times, the accountability system has been used intensively in the bureaucracy to check the power of lower-level government. Inspectors or teams of inspectors are often sent by the supervising agencies to lower-level government agencies to check their behaviour. Inspectors are also widely used in the supervision of SOEs and, recently, in anti-corruption inspections.

The leadership tried to improve the appeal system that has been used since the planned period, which has been a way for ordinary citizens to appeal to the higher authorities for help when they encounter unfair treatment by their local government. Petitioning bureaus (state and local bureaus of letters and calls) work as a communication channel between the government and the ordinary citizenry. The system receives letters, calls, and visits from individuals or groups regarding suggestions and complaints. The officers then channel the issues to the appropriate departments of central or local governments and monitor the progress of settlements. Petitioners may begin their attempts at the local level with letters and calls to local offices. If unsatisfied, they can move up the government hierarchy to provincial-level offices and, at the highest level, the State Bureau for Letters and Visits in Beijing. The number of petitioners has increased since the 1990s, reflecting the intensification of problems in the society. Petition offices annually handled around ten million inquiries and complaints from petitioners from 2003 to 2007. To prevent citizens from appealing in Beijing, which may damage the image of the government, local governments hire people in Beijing to abduct petitioners who have travelled from their areas and force them to go back home (Li and Zhou 2007; Fang 2009). The State Council issued a regulation on letters and calls as early as January 2005 (State Council 2005). The CCP Office and the State Council issued a suggestion on the reform of the letters and calls system in February 2014 to standardise the system and improve the service (CCP Central Committee Office and State Council 2014). While using the system to check the behaviour of local officials, the central government did not want to encourage citizens to appeal and worried that doing so might damage social stability.

Without an effective judicial system and surveillance of the voters, checks and balances are a challenge in a bureaucratic system, especially when the economic constraints get weaker.[3] Although the administrative branch of the government has functioned as an alternative inspector, more formal institutions and mechanism need to be established. The supervision from the bottom of society should be institutionalised and the role of the legal system should be strengthened. Above all, the rules for selecting the successor of the top leadership should be more formalised and transparent.

Rule of Law vs Administrating by Law

Despite great progress in the construction of a legal system, it is difficult to make the case that the formal legal system has played an important role in the economic reform. The gaps in the legal system still exist, and some of them are critical (e.g. lack of an efficient system of rural land ownership, especially the right of transferring rights over land). The absence of dispute resolution institutions is another critical problem. The solution to these problems lies far beyond the legal system itself. Overall, the fundamental problem of China's legislative system is its subordinate position under the administrative branch of the government.

Many Chinese people, including government officials and average citizens, typically lack the basic concepts of the rule of law. This is a result of China's long history of rule by leaders instead of rule by law. To establish a law-based government in China, a serious commitment must be made to some basic concepts of law-based government, including (i) the concept that the authority of the government derives from laws; (ii) that the government, including the central government, cannot define its own powers and cannot relieve itself of its duties; and (iii) that, in the absence of a legal foundation, the government may not impose duties on administrative subjects (Zhu 2010, p.135).

What the Chinese government is actually trying to do is to implement the principle of 'administrating by law' rather than 'rule of law'. The former means that the government rules the society according to law, under the leadership of the CCP. It is better to administrate by law than administrate by person, which had happened in the planned period and had serious consequences. However, the long-run target of a civil society should be 'rule of law'.

In China, there is a lack of coordination of laws, regulations, and other rules. The only organic laws currently in effect are the 1982 State Council Law and the revision of Local Government Law, and the 2005 Civil Servant Law (National People's Congress 1982b, 1982c, and 2005a). China needs more organic laws to cover more fields of different levels of government.

The laws that standardise administrative conduct do not cover some of the important areas, such as administrative coercion and administrative inspection. The enforcement of law in the past several decades has gradually changed from being based on government documents to being based on legal standards. The main aim of administrative law enforcement is to change from controlling society to providing services to society, but this is far from complete. Some administrative law enforcement bodies are organised in a confusing fashion, with two entities covering the same field (Zhu 2010, p.143). Some of the current laws cover only the execution of laws, not the rule-making process. To further reform administrative law enforcement, the government's role needs to change from controlling to providing services. The government needs to publish more information to make the administration transparent and make the administrative review system independent. Law enforcement procedures need to be standardised. The rights of private business and individuals need to be protected by law.

7.2 A BEHAVIOURAL FOUNDATION OF INSTITUTIONAL ADVANTAGES AND DEFECTS IN CHINA

China's most serious problems in the long run are institutional, not economic. The achievements so far in the evolution of China's political-economic system are mainly rooted in China's institutions. The institutional problem partly originated from the behaviour of the Chinese people under the long reign of government in the past 2,000 years.

Human Values and Attitudes of the Chinese People under the Rule of Government

The Chinese people are smart and hardworking. The experience of poverty during the planned economy has caused recent generations of Chinese people, those who have lived during the late 20th century and early 21st century, to make income and wealth a priority. They worked extremely hard to improve their economic position and many of them improved their lives dramatically. For example, it was a common informal rule that factory workers worked for 10–12 hours every day in the east coastal provinces, despite provisions of the formal laws and regulations which mandate they should work 8 hours. To improve their economic circumstances, more than 250 million rural people had the courage to leave their hometowns and travel to other towns, provinces, or foreign countries. To improve their economic situation, in a society without a complete judicial system, they took tremendous risks, and some of them lost their freedom or their lives in the process of achieving their goals.

However, the level of honesty and credibility in Chinese society has been relatively low during the reform years. Counterfeit and shoddy products have proliferated in China during the reform. The falsifying of documents is a common practice. This is partly because of a lack of compliance and partly because of a lack of legislation. At the beginning of the reform, there were many gaps in legislation. Even if a law existed, enforcement was often inadequate. Many laws were outdated and unfit for the new situation after the reform. Many reforms were actually illegal at the beginning. For example, Xiao Gang village's contracting of farmland to households was illegal and the leaders of the reform were facing the risk of being imprisoned. Connections are an alternative to abiding with the law. Some citizens use connections to attain goals that cannot be reached legally.

Historically, China has had a strong government and a weak society, with the government being suspicious of NGOs that could challenge its authority. The war and revolution in the 20th century further destroyed the civil society, whereas the planned economy further developed government power. Today in China, there are not many self-help and voluntary organisations. Instead, some of the functions traditionally provided by society are provided by government agencies. For example, the management of a resident community is in the hands of the lowest level of government – the neighbourhood committee. Sometimes no one pays attention to the sanitation of a community area unless a higher level of government orders the neighbourhood committee to improve it. The government's control of society has increased the burden of the government itself and damaged the incentive of ordinary citizens to solve problems by themselves, resulting in weak non-governmental institutions and a weak civil society.

These defects should not be considered as the nature of Chinese people but as habits cultivated under the strict government rules for generations. These defects create difficulties for the rule of government and may be used as justifications for further strict government control.

Bribes and Corruption: 'Standard Modes' of Doing Business

Many firms pay bribes or give gifts to government officials to operate their businesses, which is an unspoken rule in a bureaucratic-market economy. Business deals often involve participation in corruption, a problem in traditional Chinese society. Reform-era China has experienced increasing levels of corruption because of its combination of bureaucracy and the market. Corruption in China is correlated with the coexistence of a widespread, strong bureaucratic system with weak restrictions and a market without much regulation. The emergence of the market economy within a bureaucratic framework has tempted government officials to misuse their power for their own benefit. Structural and non-structural corruptions exist in China. The latter refers to corruption that can be clearly defined as illegal, while the former arises from the political and economic system itself and is difficult to root out without system reform.

'*Guandao*' (official speculation in business) was a structural corruption spread widely in the 1980s, when a dual-track pricing system existed in different sectors and different regions. People with government backgrounds were able to acquire planned products, usually with lower prices, to sell at higher prices in the free market. This was one of the typical methods of primitive accumulation of capital. The 'princelings party', the sons and daughters of government officials, became rich in business by using their parents' political powers. Corruption also stems from disloyal employees, who make money for themselves and their business partners. The lack of a regulation and supervisory structure has also allowed large-scale corruption.

Failure to contain corruption is among the most serious threats to China's political stability. It is a natural result of the bureaucratic-market system and is one of the top concerns for the public as well as for the leadership. The principal way to eliminate corruption is to draw a clear line between the government and the market and put restrictions on government officials.

Classes and Social Mobility

China is a bureaucratic hierarchical society. Different levels of government have bureaucratic rankings, which are also applied to other social organisations. For example, the universities have bureaucratic rankings, and the professors have ranks that are compared with government officials.

During the planned period, rural residents were a lower-ranked group in the society and enjoyed fewer government-provided benefits than did urban residents. These rural residents could not change their status, which was controlled by the resident identification system, except by joining the army or becoming a college student.[4] During the reform, the situation changed and rural residents were allowed to move to the cities and become city residents as migrant workers.

It is extremely important to China's future to maintain social mobility and form a middle class. A possible danger is the reduction of social mobility for the purpose of temporarily maintaining stability. Social stability is determined by internal factors such as the size of the middle class, which is important for China to avoid the middle-income trap.

7.3 AN UNFINISHED REFORM

Currently, China's marketisation reform was halfway to completion. A lot of reforms have been completed, but many other reforms have not been achieved. The stagnation of the reform is fundamentally due to the resistance to the reform and the changing priority of the government as a result of the country's good economic performance, which reduces the role of economic development in government's benefit function, according to the political theory of government decision-making developed in section 1.2 of this book. This has created an imbalance in the reform in different sectors.

Product Markets and Factor Markets

Although most of the goods markets have been freed from government control, many production factor markets are still controlled by the government. Measuring the degree of marketisation, which is the degree of freedom of exchanges, the product market is much more market-oriented, while the production factor market is much less market-oriented. The prices in many factor markets, such as different energy prices, are controlled by the government. The price of land and interest rates in some areas are still controlled by the government, too.

The coal mining sector had been marketised as early as the 1990s, and a large number of private investors entered the market in the early 2000s. Shangxi province is a major coal producer in China. To reduce the costs of production, the private firms did not install safety facilities, and accidents occurred frequently. To reduce the number of accidents, the National Safety Supervision Bureau and Shanxi province government announced a plan to close a large number of small mines in 2005, and the private investors retreated from the sector completely. This was widely described as 'the state advances as the private sector retreats'.

The marketised and non-marketised sectors conflicted with each other. The price of coal has been freed and determined by the market, whereas the price of electricity is still controlled by the state. The result is that most firms producing electricity from coal have a deficit due to the gap between the planned electricity price (output price) and the market-determined coal price (input price). To solve the problem, three alternative approaches could be used. The plan solution would put the coal price back under the government's control; the market solution would free the electricity price, which might affect the final users of electricity; and a temporary solution would set up a 'mechanism of coal–electricity price linkage' by administrative measures. When the coal prices increase, the electricity price would follow. The government chose the third solution in 2015 to avoid pressure by interest groups; however, it cannot solve the problem completely because this administrative measure cannot be flexible enough to keep up with the frequent changes of demand and supply (National Development and Reform Commission 2015).

Since the early 2000s, private enterprises have attempted to enter fields monopolised by SOEs. Forty private enterprises applied to enter the vehicle assembly sector in Zhejiang province in 2003, and some of them were successful. Fifty private enterprises, led by Gong Jialong, tried to enter the oil industry in 2003 but failed. Overall, it is still very difficult for private enterprises to enter the upstream sectors monopolised by SOEs.

Reform of SOEs

In 1997, the 15th Congress of the CCP confirmed the two parts of the reforms of the state-owned economy: reform of internal governance of SOEs and the retreat of the state-owned economy from competitive fields. The 4th Plenary Session of the 15th Central Committee of the CCP further defined the key areas that the state-owned economy must dominate as follows: sectors related to national security, sectors of natural monopoly, sectors providing important public goods and services, and backbone enterprises in pillar industries and high-tech industries. This redesign of the national economy slowed down in the 2000s. The State-owned Assets Supervision and Administration Commission (SASAC) issued a Guiding Opinion on Carrying Forward the Adjustment of the State-Owned Capital and the Restructuring of the SOEs, broadening the scope of the key areas the state-owned economy should dominate (SASAC 2006). According to the SASAC, the state-owned economy and centrally controlled SOEs should absolutely control defence, the electricity network, oil and petrochemical industries, telecommunications, coal mining, airlines, and ship transportation, and the state-owned economy should maintain strong control in equipment manufacturing, automobile production, electronics and information, construction, steel, non-ferrous metal, the chemical industry, mineral exploration, and science and technology.

For internal governance, all large SOEs are to construct 'modern corporate structures', with boards of directors holding the authority to make major decisions. The reform of the large SOEs was slowed down in the early 2000s. A large part of the first-level SOEs, the group companies or holding companies, did not finish corporate restructuring, while the second-level SOEs, the listed companies, could not become independent legal entities because they were subordinates of state-authorised investment institutions. Because most group companies were still wholly state-owned, some sectors were being monopolised by several companies owned by the same holding company, and the high-level officials of these companies rotated their positions. Most of the listed companies had defects in internal governance, and no checks and balances system existed between the owners and managers.

With the financial crisis of 2008, the Chinese government implemented a huge government investment plan of RMB4 trillion ($0.6 trillion) in 2009. Most of the investment projects were given to the SOEs, especially centrally controlled large SOEs, which resulted, once again, in 'the state advances as the private sector retreats'. Many SOEs entered the local economy on a large scale during this period, resulting in an economy in which the SOEs occupied many important fields. The large SOEs have formed interest groups, which have strongly resisted further reform. Overall, the current reforms are creating stronger SOEs, further cementing the government's control.

Currently, the government's strategy of SOE reform has changed from reducing the scope of SOE operations to keeping the current scope of SOE operations, while improving SOE governance structures and introducing private investment to improve SOEs' management.

Land Administration and Property Market

The reform of property rights, the foundation of a market economy, is far from achieved. In the countryside, the reform in the late 1970s gave the user rights of farmland to the peasants, which improved the enthusiasm for production enormously. But the peasants do not have the permanent user rights of the land, even though the government has repeatedly promised that the use of land is permanent. The land is actually owned by the collectives (villages), and, in the early stages of the reform, it was frequently redistributed among villagers when populations changed.[5] The villages are actually controlled by groups of low-ranked government officials. According to current law, the farmland and homestead cannot be transferred, rented, or used as a mortgage. This has reduced peasants' incentives to protect, improve, and invest in the land. As a result of rapid urbanisation since the 1990s, much farmland has been transferred to urban construction land. Many illegal transactions are in progress, but according to current law, only government expropriation can transfer rural land to urban use.

Land has been a vital factor in the process of China's institutional changes in the past several decades, connecting economic development with government finance, housing, and the property of ordinary people. Rapid urban expansion needs large amounts of land. According to

China's Constitution, land in the cities is owned by the state, whereas land in rural areas is owned by collectives. Only the government can transfer rural land into urban land by requisition. Land requisition has created an important source of revenue for local governments. Local governments' monopolies in land requisition have caused housing prices to rise. The large gap between governments' purchase price from the villages and rental price to developers has encouraged local government to buy and release large areas of land to increase its revenue. Land rights, therefore, have become a problem connecting rural landowners, housing developers, local governments, and urban residents. Land finance by local government is actually a one-time financing for urban public services by selling the future value of state-owned land (Zhao 2016). To solve these problems, the local government monopoly of the land market needs to end and the transfer rights of land should be given to farmers or collectives.[6] This reform has been discussed for a long time, but its implementation has been delayed because of complicated relations among the farmers, collectives, developers, residents, and local governments. Because of the crucial role of land to local government revenue, the local governments have no incentives to distribute the transfer rights of land to farmers.

Marketisation reform has done much but is far from achieved, and the momentum to achieve these reforms is diminishing. SOEs occupy half of the market, particularly the upstream resource-intensive sectors, whereas private firms are active in other parts of the market.

7.4 MEASURING THE RELATIVE INFLUENCE OF THE GOVERNMENT AND THE MARKET: AN INDEX OF MARKETISATION

To illustrate the relative influence of the government and the market during economic reform, I have created an index of marketisation in China.[7] Based on data availability, the index reflects the following aspects:

1. The government's share of revenue and expenditure in GDP, which measures the economic size of the government in the economy, as compared to the size of the non-government sector. The government revenue/expenditure is further divided into central and local government revenue/expenditure.
2. The development of state-owned and non-state-owned firms, which uses data of output/sales, fixed investments, and numbers of employees in the economy.

3. The development of the product market and factor market, which uses the output share of products that have their prices controlled by the government and the reform of state-monopolised sectors.[8]

The index is based on the data of ten time series variables, some of which come from publicly available data, others of which are calculated by me based on publicly available information. The data were processed through a principal component analysis to find the weight of each variable in the index.

More precisely, the data consist of ten time series variables from 1978 to 2014, including the share of the number of employees of state-owned units in total urban employed persons (EMPLSOE, National Bureau of Statistics 1984, 1999, and 2015), the share of fiscal revenue in GDP (FISREVGDP, National Bureau of Statistics 2015), the share of revenues of the central government in total government revenue (CENTREV, including extra-budgetary revenue, National Bureau of Statistics 2015), the share of expenditures of the central government in total government expenditure (CENTEXP, including extra-budgetary expenditure, National Bureau of Statistics 2015), the central government's share in fixed investment (CENTFIXINV, National Bureau of Statistics 2015, 1997), the state economy's share in fixed investment (STATFIXINV, National Bureau of Statistics 2015, 1997), the output share of regulation reform (REG, calculated by me based on facts of regulation reform and weighted by the sector share of GDP), the output share of reform of the pricing system (PRICE, calculated by me based on facts of pricing system reforms and weighted by the sector share of GDP), the SOE's share in value added in the industrial sector (SOEIND, current prices, National Bureau of Statistics 2015), and the share of SOEs and joint-stock companies in the business revenue of the top 100 companies in China (SOE100, China Enterprise Confederation and China Entrepreneur Association (2001–2013), people.com (n.d.), and China Business System (2017)). These variables can be put into the following groups: (i) SOEs' share in employees, fixed investments, the industrial sector, and the top 100 firms (EMPLSOE, CENTFIXINV, STATFIXINV, SOEIND and SOE100); (ii) fiscal decentralisation (FISREVGDP, CENTREV, and CENTEXP); and (iii) reforms in pricing decisions and in monopoly industries (REG and PRICE).

The principal component analysis is a statistical method that uses an orthogonal transformation to transfer a group of possibly correlated variables into a set of linearly uncorrelated variables or principal components.

Technically, the process is as outlined below. The original data matrix V_{onp} includes n=37 periods and p=10 variables. Standardise the data using equation:

$$v_{ij} = \frac{v_{oij} - \overline{V}_{oi}}{S_{oi}},\ i = 1,\dots, n, j = 1,\dots, p$$

Where $\overline{V}_{oi}$ and S_{oi} are mean and sample standard deviation of i.

The principal component F_j is a transformation of V_i:

$$\mathrm{F}_j = \sum_{i=1}^{P} a_{ij} V_i,\ j = 1,\dots, p$$

The index is built by the following mapping:

$$f(F_j) = k_j F_j + b_j,\ j = 1,\dots, p$$

k_j and b_j are found to let $\{f(F_{jmin}), f(F_{jmax})\} = \{0,100\}$, where 0 indicates the situation without market and 100 indicates the ideal situation of a market without government intervention.

After standardisation of the data, my team ran the principal component analysis and derived the loadings that map each row vector of the data matrix to a new vector of the principal component scores. The first principal component has a high correlation with most of the variables (Table 7.1). (Principal components analysis focuses on explaining the terms that sit on the diagonal of the correlation matrix.) After a linear transformation, the first principal component becomes the index of marketisation (Figures 7.1 and 7.2). The index of the second principal component, which is highly correlated with the share of fiscal revenue in GDP, shows a U-shaped curve from 1978 to 2014 (Figure 7.3 and Table 7.1). This shows that the central government relaxed its control in the early stage of the reform and re-concentrated financial resources after the mid-1990s. Based on the first principal component and a linear transformation, I created an index of marketisation.

From the analysis, I reached two conclusions:

1. The index of marketisation shows that there has been continuous progress in the share of the market, compared with the government, due to the continuous expansion of non-state sectors.
2. The government's financial power initially decreased, until the mid-1990s, and then has increased, which shows the change in government control during the economic reform.

The index of marketisation shows that there has been a continuous progress in marketisation in the economy.

The changes in the marketisation index show that the gains of marketisation every five years have been positive but decreased.

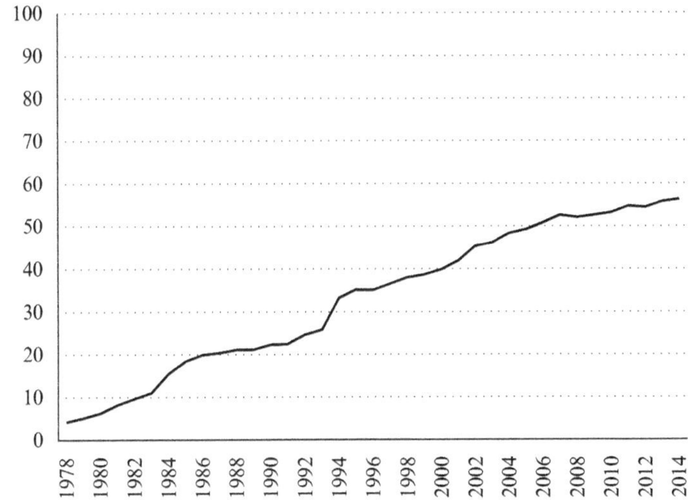

Note: 100 represents a complete marketisation process. Non-marketisation is represented by 0.

Figure 7.1 Index of marketisation, China, 1978–2014

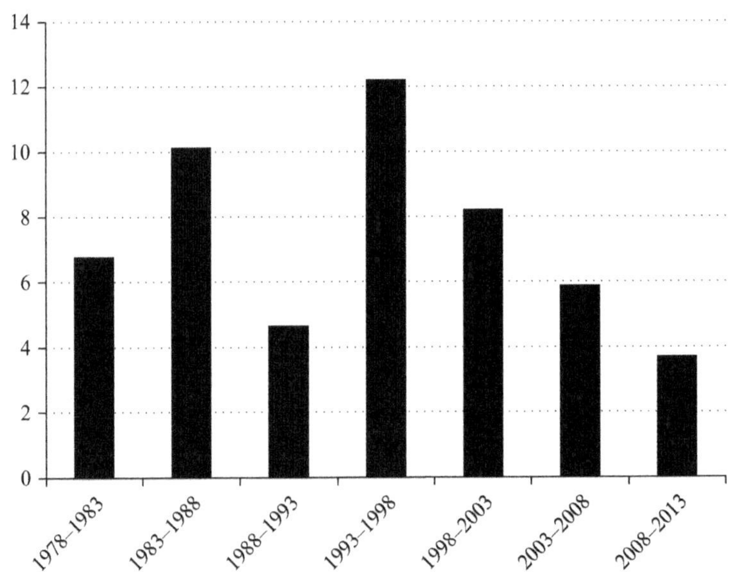

Figure 7.2 Changes in marketisation index, every five years, China, 1978–2013

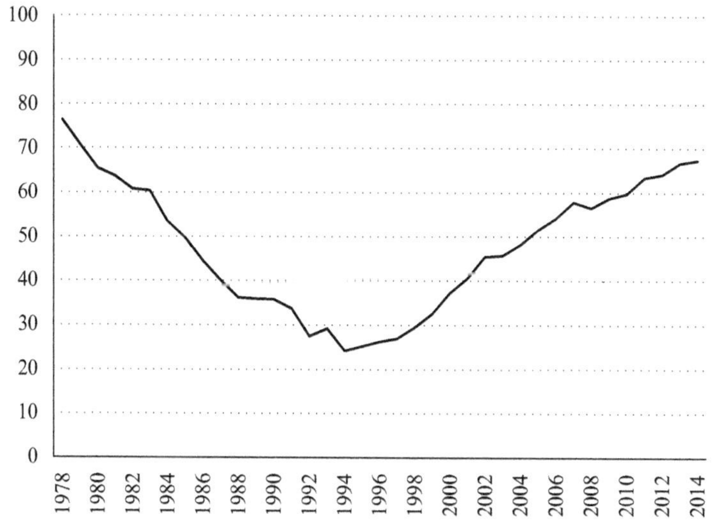

Note: 0 represents no government control and 100 represents fully government control.

Figure 7.3 Second principal components, 1978–2014

The second principal components show that the government's power decreased until the mid-1990s, and has increased thereafter. This shows the central government relaxed control in the early stage of reform, and regained fiscal and other control later on in the economic reform.

To show the robustness of the analysis, different combinations of variables were chosen in doing the principal component analysis. The resulting correlations between the original variables and the first two principal components in three principal component analyses show that the correlations do not change much when the original variables change (Table 7.1).

7.5 LESSONS LEARNED AND LONG-RUN EXPECTATIONS

We are losing it. We are less versed in the facts of history, not only of other countries but of our own.
Peggy Noonan[9]

Reviewing history is important for us to avoid repeating our past mistakes, so as to not lose our memories of reform over the past 40 years. Knowing the history of China's reform will help us better understand the present situation.

Table 7.1 Correlations of the original variables with the principal components

Model	I		II		III	
Variable/Principal Components	F1	F2	F1	F2	F1	F2
EMPLSOE	0.97484	–0.15356	0.977418	–0.1411	0.982788	–0.13462
FISREVGDP	0.319541	0.933288	0.308695	0.937481	0.30666	0.942778
CENTREV	–0.86594	–0.09559				
CENTEXP	0.941534	0.167336	0.948034	0.184878		
CENTFIXINV	0.96734	–0.11241	0.973886	–0.09691	0.978856	–0.09295
STATFIXINV	0.970026	–0.16956	0.966967	–0.16124		
REG	0.951968	–0.21662	0.958207	–0.20244	0.964164	–0.19564
PRICE	0.858256	0.468497	0.852733	0.479183	0.847911	0.478554
SOEIND	0.995646	–0.00512	0.99463	0.006411	0.995827	0.011149
SOE100	0.910549	–0.33653	0.915092	–0.32506	0.908805	–0.32357

Note: F1 is the first principal component, F2 is the second principal component. The robustness of the result can be seen by comparing the correlations of variables in different models.

China has experienced tremendous institutional changes since the late 1970s, when the current economic reform started. This history is in large measure a history of the changing relationship between the government and the market. A market economy and a sizable private sector have been created through the joint efforts of government and society. This is a tremendous achievement, which has brought, and will continue to bring, benefits to Chinese people, both current and future generations. The reform built institutional scaffolding designed to provide unprecedented stability and prosperity in the reform decades. The entire period of economic reform since the late 1970s has seen the economic consequences of China's institutional changes. These changes have reduced transaction costs and given incentives to local governments, private enterprises, and ordinary people. Real GDP increased by a factor of 30.3 (9.4 per cent annually) from 1978 to 2015 (National Bureau of Statistics 2016b, Table 3.4). Not all of the reforms were successful, not all of them were destined to last, but overall the reform significantly changed the condition of the country. Above all, the reform gave countless Chinese people an enormous improvement in their living conditions. From this perspective, the economic reform can be understood as a period of democratic learning and adjustment, even though Chinese society has yet to fully absorb the dreadful lessons of the Cultural Revolution while the effort to find a democratic and truly Chinese solution to the problem has not yet been achieved. How did China manage to keep its high growth rate for more than 30 years? To whom should the main credit be attributed, the market or the government? The market has been the fundamental source of the economic growth, whereas the government cleared obstacles to the development of the market at the early stage of the reform.

The government played a crucial role in the process of economic reform, in a society where the non-governmental institutions have been underdeveloped. The government is the organiser of the economic development, playing a vital role in the new bureaucratic-market economy. The government established markets and maintained order on these markets; sold small SOEs to private business owners and reformed the large SOEs; built the social security net for the market economy; and opened the domestic market to the outside world. The relaxation of regulation and the clarification of property rights greatly reduced the transaction costs of market activities. The government has played many of the roles normally carried out by non-governmental institutions in other societies, working as an alternative to some market institutions. This is an institutional invention in China's economic reform. The government retreated from many fields and let the market play a role in the early years of reform.

While playing a positive role in many cases, the government overly regulated the market in other cases. What is the appropriate role of the government in economic development? To draw a boundary between the government and the market theoretically and practically, two rules have to be followed:

1. According to the theory of economics, government intervention is appropriate if several conditions exist, including asymmetric information, externalities, natural monopoly, non-existence of markets, and absence of property rights.
2. Considering the institutional background, government intervention in certain fields such as reforming institutions will be legitimate if the market is imperfect and some of the functions of the market are absent.

The government should function within these boundaries.

A framework of a political economy theory of government decision-making in a bureaucratic-market economy was developed in section 1.2 to explain why government conducts more or fewer interventions than it would under the rule of appropriate intervention set by economic theory. The target of the government may deviate from maximising social welfare and can be described by a benefit function with two basic components: social stability and economic growth. Economic performance has been an important source of legitimacy for the regime, whereas social stability has been the main target and foundation for the existence of the government. There are two basic types of policy options – economic policy and social stability policy – from which a government in a bureaucratic-market economy like China may choose. Economic policy promotes economic growth and marketisation, whereas social stability policy maintains social stability and the existence of the government itself. The two policies are sometimes contradictory, so the government has to make decisions on how the two kinds of policy mix with each other. Although favourable to economic growth, the economic policy may create political instability and social inequality, whereas social stability policy focuses on the control of the society but could be unfavourable to economic development. The weight of the two policies varies over time, determined by the political and economic environment. The government's behaviour in the system is subject to two major constraints: social instability and economic decline. During the early years of China's reform, most government interventions were either within the boundaries set by economic theory or consistent with the era's institutional background. Economic performance worked as a source of legitimacy and a major constraint in the decision-making process of the leadership.

Despite great economic achievements, China's basic political institutions have not deviated much from their traditional forms. Although many minor changes have been made, including the changing relations between central and local governments, the changing role of local governments in economic development, and the changing government functions from control of the society towards providing public service, China's economic reform has been an experiment within the framework of the existing political infrastructure. The revival of the planned economy has been experienced at different levels of government in the process of reform. The remains of the planned system, the bureaucratic hierarchy, combined with the emerging market formed a dual bureaucratic-market system. This system has played an important role in economic development and seems, in the short term, to be in a kind of unstable equilibrium.

Historically, the economic reform was a direct result of the Cultural Revolution, which was a tragedy for government officials, as well as for ordinary people, and fed a consensus on the need for reform. The government-led and no-balanced-political-counterpart nature of the reform created a bureaucratic-market system, which fostered corruption and loosened the government's control over society and officials. A radical response of the government to corruption and the decree barrier[10] was made through administrative means, which might make the system further centralised and hurt the long-term vitality of the Chinese economy. Although many improvements have been made, the economic reform was a somewhat temporary deviation from the trend – 'a black swan event'. Without the Cultural Revolution, an economic reform with the depth and breadth of the one experienced in the late 20th century would never have happened. And a reform with a similar scale and depth is not likely to happen again in the short and medium term without another large-scale social crisis.

The reform is not finished and contains several fatal flaws:

1. The administrative branch of the government has not been effectively constrained, partly due to its role in the economic reform and partly due to the delay of the political reform.
2. The market reform has not been completed. The upstream resource-intensive sectors are still controlled by the state.
3. Large SOEs still dominate several key sectors, whereas private firms face high tax burdens and strict regulations.
4. Farmers do not have full property rights over land and local governments monopolise the transfer of rural land to urban uses, which causes soaring urban housing prices as well as inefficiencies in agriculture.

5. The nature of the bureaucratic-market system has fostered corruption among government officials and business executives. Many business leaders gained their initial wealth by using their connections with political power, and many officials received benefits from business people by using their political power. This kind of systematic corruption has damaged social equity and justice. To prevent systematic corruption, government power should be reduced and clearly defined, a checks and balances mechanism should be created by institutional constructions, and supervision from the society should be reinforced.

Economic reform without a balanced political counterpart and the government-led nature of the reform reduced the difficulty of the economic reform during the early years of reform, but at the same time left the bureaucratic system largely untouched, which has become a source of anti-marketisation in the subsequent stages of reform. As the government expands without restriction, the market might be further squeezed out by political power. The stagnation of the reform is a fundamental result of the changing priority of the government, which is, paradoxically, a result of the improving economic situation and loosening of social control.

Lessons may be learned from the experience of the reform:

1. The socioeconomic circumstances determine the means used in reform. China's use of government as a major means of the reform is inevitable, considering the institutional environment at the beginning of the reform. The government had to play many functions when the non-governmental institutions in the society were underdeveloped.
2. Path dependence affects the following steps of the reform once the first step has been chosen. The reform reduced transaction costs in the early years of reform due to the reduced size of the government. But in recent years, the society's reliance on the government has led to its enlargement again, and increased the transaction costs of economic activities.
3. Consensus on reform will be weakened when the reform is intensified and affects different groups of people.[11]
4. Checks and balances are crucial when designing a system in which the government and the market coexist and interact.

In the short run, any major change of policy can alter the relative share of the government and the market but cannot completely discard the market from the system. With the Cultural Revolution not being a remote historical event but being continuously present in popular and elite historical memory, it would be difficult to completely deviate from the path of reform. With economic development still being a heavy weight in terms of providing legitimacy to the regime, the market will likely keep functioning under government supervision. The main risks in China today are that the unrestricted government power might further squeeze out the private market and further reduce the sphere and share of the private sector, which will lead to a more government-controlled market economy and a shrunken private sector. The key issue is how to check the power of different levels of government. Economic development and social stability function as constraints on governments' behaviour in the long run; more binding constraints need to be set up by institutional constructions.

The equilibrium in the long run is not stable because the situation could move in different directions under different rules of evolution. Following the logic of the market, the marketisation process must be completed. It is not complete when the upstream sectors are still monopolised by the SOEs, causing distortion of the pricing system and requiring further marketisation. However, following the logic of government, government power must expand to guarantee that government decrees are followed by officials and the society, which requires increasingly more power to be concentrated in the government. Any external factors, which the government might treat as a wartime situation, such as a stock market crash or debt crisis, could break the equilibrium. Therefore, the road of reform has been and remains a process of balancing and rebalancing the interests of different groups of people.

In which direction should China go? The experience in many East Asian countries shows that a market economy could coexist with an authoritarian government for many years. But the contrast of this kind of political system with liberal democracy is profound. In the longer term, it is questionable whether the freedom in the private sphere could protect the market from the invasion of the authoritarian government. If democratisation cannot be implemented in China as a major reform in the political system, an improved, efficient, restricted, and fair administrative government could be a second-best solution. It is quite possible that a combination of a strong, impersonal, and efficient government with a market under control will exist in China in the short run. This system can maintain a large mobilisation of forces to reach many of its targets.[12] At the same time, as a result of government power expansion, the enthusiasm of the market may be more restricted and that may have negative long-run effects.

In the long run, China should move towards an improved government–market system, combining an efficient, restricted, and fair government and a free market. First, this kind of government–market combination is consistent with the traditional Chinese political system and the rule of path dependence. Second, this government–market combination must be improved, absorbing the advantages of the political system in other countries as well as the experience of the traditional Chinese political system. To establish such a system, the following has to be done.

First, with respect to economic reform, the market-oriented reform should proceed into many fields currently still monopolised by non-market forces. The government should retreat from direct interventions in the market and focus on building a safe and fair market environment. Compared with most countries in the world, the Chinese government intervenes much more in the market, even after 40 years of reform. Further retreat from direct intervention does not mean eliminating all government interventions. The government needs to function as a protector of the property rights and other rights of ordinary citizens in a fair society. Second, with respect to political reform, a multi-branch government with improved mechanisms of checks and balances must be developed. The scope of the government's authority should be clarified and the relations between the government and the market should be clearly defined. A judicial system should be established to constrain the government's power. The government also needs to further open up the political system. Other foundations of a civil society (e.g. free media and bottom-up participation in politics) should be developed along with a modernised administration. The central government needs to improve its relationships with local governments to maintain a rational, efficient, and persistent relationship. Third, the government should help to cultivate an active civil society. The theory of class struggle should be abandoned. An ideology needs to be established for the society, which has to be accepted by most people in China. Government control should be combined with the market's self-restrictions and the incentives of ordinary people to create a better life, as the basis of the development of a harmonious society.

NOTES

1. Although there have been some developments in the creation of non-government organisations (NGOs), the civil society remains less developed in China. Many functions of society do not exist or are played by the government. For example, community autonomy does not exist, and most communities are ruled by the lowest level of government.
2. The government will protect the independence of auditing agencies. Auditing will cover public funds, state-owned resources, and government officials.
3. When the economic constraints are tightened, the government is more likely to obey the laws of economy. For example, when the economy was on the verge of collapse at the end of the 1970s, the government made the decision to reform and introduced the market into the system.

4. It was extremely difficult for a rural youth to be admitted as a college student.
5. Population changes were the result of migration of peasants to cities and the rate of birth of children.
6. The rights should be transferred to individual farmers or collectives of farmers.
7. Fan Gang, Wang Xiaolu, and Yu Jingwen have already calculated an Index of Marketisation (Fan et al. 2017), but I include a different group of variables and use a different method.
8. The development is measured by the share of state-monopolised sectors in gross national product of these sectors.
9. Peggy Noonan. 'Why History Will Repay Your Love'. *The Wall Street Journal*, 27–28 May 2017, A13.
10. 'Decree barrier' is an expression that Chinese officials often use. It means that the orders of the central government cannot be fully implemented by a lower level of government due to the inefficiency of the bureaucratic system.
11. Many people became losers from the reform and do not support the reform anymore. For example, many SOE workers lost their jobs.
12. When this book was at the final stage of editing, in October 2017, the 19th Congress of the CCP was being held. Xi Jinping was re-elected as the general secretary of the CCP. In his speech, Xi announced the targets of China's future development and major policies to achieve those targets. In March 2018, the National People's Congress approved an amendment to the Constitution to abolish the term limit on the presidency.

References

Acemoglu, Dam and James A. Robinson (2012). *Why Nations Fail: The Origins of Power, Prosperity, and Poverty*. New York: Crown Business.

Alibaba (n.d.). About Us. Retrieved August 2017 at http://www.alibabagroup.com/cn/about/leadership.

Allen, Franklin, Jun Qian, and Meijun Qian (2008). China's Financial System: Past, Present, and Future. In Loren Brandt and Thomas G. Rawski (eds), *China's Great Economic Transformation*. Cambridge, UK: Cambridge University Press, pp.506–568.

Alston, Lee, J., Thrainn Eggertsson, and Douglass C. North (1996). *Empirical Studies in Institutional Change*. Cambridge, UK: The Press Syndicate of the University of Cambridge.

Aoki, Masahiko, Hyung-ki Kim, and Masahiro Okuno-Fujiwara (eds) (1996). *The Role of Government in East Asian Economic Development: Comparative Institutional Analysis*. Oxford, UK: Oxford University Press.

Bai, Tianling and Qinghua Zhou (2013). CAAC Removed the Limits of Air Fare. People's Net, 6 November 2013. Retrieved June 2017 at http://news.ifeng.com/mainland/detail_2013_11/06/30990583_0.shtml.

Bai, Yongxiu and Songji Wang (2013). Restructuring the Core of Chinese Economic System Reform: The Relation between Government and Market. *Reform*, 2013(7), pp.14–21.

Baidu Baike (n.d.-a). Fixing Farm Output Quotas for Each Household (*Bao Chan Dao Hu*). Retrieved January 2016 at http://baike.baidu.com/view/811109.htm.

Baidu Baike (n.d.-b). Dazhong Agricultural Products Wholesale Market. Retrieved January 2017 at http://baike.baidu.com/view/9463314.htm.

Baidu Baike (n.d.-c). Central Huijin Investment Corporation Limited. Retrieved August 2016 at http://baike.baidu.com/link?url=ZO32MPp9Zg-lH10_oLS8-WreoFETFpe-2h7uqnvwYGehXF985H7m4cyeKTQhXNJl-CokaRDHPD8zY_TESXqEE2K.

Baidu Baike (n.d.-d). Nanyang Commercial Bank. Retrieved August 2016 at http://baike.baidu.com/link?url=wZLeihZ-GdBH4mmJIVFlw3eJm6QhsPA_NzHGMK5Z27XRT5Lr9-8-4WRdQzFnDawUsei_OIWxg15avGg5GkOFJq.

Baike Mingpian (n.d.). Land Finance. Retrieved December 2013 at http//:baike.baidu.com/view/2104332.htm.

Bank of Communications (n.d.). Introduction of Bank of Communications. Retrieved August 2017 at http://www.bankcomm.com/BankCommSite/shtml/jyjr/cn/7804/16356/list.shtml?channelId=7804.

Baum, Richard and Alexei Shevchenko (1999). The 'State of State'. In Merle Goldman and Roderick Macfarquhar (eds), *The Paradox of China's Post-Mao Reforms*. Cambridge, MA: Harvard University Press, pp.344–351.

BBC (2016). China Corruption Crackdown 'Netted 300,000 in 2015'. 7 March. Retrieved August 2016 at http://www.bbc.com/news/world-asia-china-35741357.

Bell, Daniel A. (2016). *The China Model: Political Meritocracy and the Limits of Democracy*. Beijing, China: China CITIC Press.

Benjamin, Dwayne, Loren Brandt, John Giles, and Sangui Wang (2008). Income Inequality during China's Economic Transition. In Loren Brandt and Thomas G. Rawski (eds), *China's Great Economic Transformation*. New York: Cambridge University Press, pp.729–775.

Berkowitz, Daniel and Wei Li (2000). Decentralization in Transition Economies: A Tragedy of the Commons? *Journal of Public Economics*, 76(3), pp.369–397.

Bestychen (n.d.). SASAC: SOE Pilot Reforms Fully Swing. Tencent Finance. Retrieved January 2017 at http://finance.qq.com/a/20160714/043597.htm.

Bradsher, Keith (2017). Chinese Financial Meeting Yields Meagre Results. *New York Times*, 16 July.

Brandt, Loren and Thomas G. Rawski (eds) (2008). *China's Great Economic Transformation*. Cambridge, UK: Cambridge University Press.

Branstetter, Lee and Nicholas Lardy (2008). China's Embrace of Globalization. In Loren Brandt and Thomas G. Rawski (eds), *China's Great Economic Transformation*. New York: Cambridge University Press, pp.633–682.

Bremmer, Ian (2010). *The End of the Free Market: Who Wins the War between States and Corporations*. New York: Portfolio.

Browne, Andrew (2016). Mao Now. *Wall Street Journal*, 14–15 May.

Buckley, Chris (2016). New Legal Hurdles Rattle Foreign Non-Profits in China. *New York Times*, 31 December.

Burns, John P. (2007). Civil Service Reform in China. *OECD Journal of Budgeting*, 7(1), pp.1–26. Retrieved July 2016 at http://www1.oecd.org/governance/budgeting/44526166.pdf.

Cai, Fang, Dewen Wang and Yang Du (2008). *Reform and Evolution of Chinese Rural Area: 30 Year Process and Experience*. Shanghai, China: Gezhi Press.

Cai, Hongbin, Hanming Fang, and Lixin Colin Xu (2011). Eat, Drink, Firms,

Government: An Investigation of Corruption from Entertainment and Travel Costs of Chinese Firms. *Journal of Law and Economics*, 54, pp.55–78.

CASS Institute of Law (1980). *Selected Economic Laws of the People's Republic of China (II)*. Beijing, China: China Finance and Economics Press.

CCP (1981a). A Number of Provisions on Solving the Problem of Urban Employment. 17 October. Retrieved February 2016 at http://CCP.people.com.cn/GB/64162/64165/70486/70503/4867379.html.

CCP (1981b). On a Number of Historical Issues since the Founding of the People's Republic. Retrieved November 2017 at http://www.360doc.com/content/14/0914/10/8533258_409341062.shtml.

CCP (1982). Constitution of the Communist Party of China. Retrieved July 2016 at http://fuwu.12371.cn/2012/09/27/ARTI1348715767823434_9.shtml.

CCP (1984). Notice on the Rural Work in 1984. Retrieved January 2017 at http://CCP.people.com.cn/GB/64162/135439/8134254.html.

CCP (1987a). Memorabilia Communist Party of China in 1987. Retrieved February 2016 at http://CCP.people.com.cn/GB/64162/64164/4416137.html.

CCP (1987b). The Thirteenth Congress of the Communist Party of China. Retrieved December 2016 at http://CCP.people.com.cn/GB/64162/64168/64566/index.html.

CCP (1992). The Fourteenth Congress of the Communist Party of China. Retrieved February 2017 at http://www.chinatoday.com/org/CCP/CCP_14th_congress_standing_polibureau.htm.

CCP (1997). The Fifteenth Congress of the Communist Party of China. Retrieved January 2017 at http://www.chinatoday.com/org/CCP/CCP_15th_congress_standing_polibureau.htm and http://CCP.people.com.cn/GB/64162/64168/64568/65445/4526289.html.

CCP (2007). Constitution of the Communist Party of China (English). Retrieved July 2016 at http://dx.chzu.edu.cn/s/52/t/508/36/5b/info13915.htm.

CCP Central Committee (1982). Resolution on Establishing Old Cadres Retirement System. Retrieved July 2016 at http://CCP.people.com.cn/GB/64162/71380/71387/71591/4854975.html.

CCP Central Committee (1983). Current Problems in Rural Economic Policies. Retrieved February 2016 at http://CCP.people.com.cn/GB/64162/135439/8134114.html.

CCP Central Committee (1984). Resolutions on Economic Reform. 20 October. Retrieved February 2016 at http://CCP.people.com.cn/GB/64162/64168/64565/65378/4429522.html.

CCP Central Committee (1993). The Resolution on the Socialist Market Economy. 14 November. Retrieved December 2016 at http://jg.bucea.edu.cn/llyd/45038.htm.

CCP Central Committee (2013). Major Issues Concerning Comprehensively Deepening Reforms. November. Retrieved January 2017 at http://english.cntv.com/20131112/105054.shtml.

CCP Central Committee (2014). Decisions of the CCP Central Committee on Major Issues Pertaining to Comprehensively Promoting the Rule of Law. October. Retrieved January 2017 at http://www.pkulaw.cn/fulltext_form.aspx?Gid=237344&is_inbook=1500773837392239.

CCP Central Committee and State Council (1983). On the Establishment of Separate Administrative Agency of the Township Government. 12 October. Retrieved February 2016 at http://CCP.people.com.cn/GB/64184/64186/66701/4495412.html.

CCP Central Committee and State Council (1984). Notice by the CCP Central Committee and the State Council on Forward 'Minutes of the Seminars of Some Coastal Cities'. 4 May. Retrieved February 2016 at http://CCP.people.com.cn/GB/64184/64186/66678/4493873.html.

CCP Central Committee and State Council (1998). Notice on Basic Life Allowance and Re-employment of Job-Lost SOE Workers. 9 June. Retrieved March 2016 at http://CCP.people.com.cn/GB/64162/71380/71382/71481/4854303.html.

CCP Central Committee Office and State Council (2014). A Suggestion on Innovation of Approaches of Mass Works to Solve the Significant Problems in Letters and Calls. 25 February. Retrieved January 2017 at http://www.gov.cn/jrzg/2014-02/25/content_2621605.htm.

CCP Department of Organisation (2006). A Proposed Regulation on Access Procedure of Local Party and Government Leadership Reflecting Scientific Development Concept. Retrieved July 2016 at http://wenku.baidu.com/link?url=llMoci6GxcQF6Mg6RqJdqGFsQe8YwteQfHbLngozNN8wZbURVffrYxrYa7nTjEdx3_uSYSMsyw-5Ryp6DDS9WzFi8fjebeOETloCeug_1U.

CCP News (1993). The 3rd Plenary Session of the 14th CCP Central Committee. Retrieved April 2016 at http://CCP.people.com.cn/GB/64162/134580/137920/.

CCP News (2016). 2015 Anti-Corruption Data. People Net, 13 January 2016. Retrieved June 2017 at http://fanfu.people.com.cn/n1/2016/0113/c64371-28047862.html.

CCTV (2010). Focus Talk. 11 June. In Li, Youhuan. *Demystify Underground Banks*. Beijing, China: Economic Daily Press, p.91.

Cendrowski, Scott (2014). Opening Happiness: An Oral History of Coca-Cola in China. *Fortune*, 12 September. Retrieved August 2017 at http://fortune.com/2014/09/11/opening-happiness-an-oral-history-of-coca-cola-in-china/.

Central Government of the People's Republic of China (1998). State Council's Resolution on Establishing Basic Medical Insurance for Urban Workers. Retrieved April 2016 at http://www.gov.cn/banshi/2005-08/04/content_20256.htm.

Che, Jiahua and Yingyi Qian (1998). Insecure Property Rights and Government Ownership of Firms. *Quarterly Journal of Economics*, 113(2), pp.467–496.

Chen Chunxian Studio (n.d.). Professor Chen Chunxian. Retrieved January 2017 at http://chenchunxian.com/career.htm.

Chen, Guidi and Tao Chun (2009). *Story of Xiaogang Village*. Beijing, China: Huawen Press. Retrieved May 2017 at http://lz.book.sohu.com/serialize-id-14205.html.

Chen, Lifen (n.d.). Thirty Years of China's Rural Circulation System Reform: Retrospect and Prospect. Retrieved January 2016 at http://www.ecm.com.cn/past/NewsView.asp?id=695.

Chen, Tong and Xiangxue Zeng (2011). From Sitong Lifang to Sina. Fujian Renmin Press. Retrieved August 2017 at http://book.51cto.com/art/201105/262866.htm.

Chen, Yizi (1985). Dawn in Rural Area, Hope in China. In Research Group of Rural Development in China (ed.), *Rural Area, Economy, and Society*. Beijing, China: Zhishi Press, pp.33–53.

Chen, Yueshi (2015). China Formerly Relax the Interest Rate Control. Pengpai, 24 October. Retrieved June 2017 at http://bank.hexun.com/2015-10-24/180071238.html.

Chen, Yun (1990). Secretary of Commerce Was Fooled When Buying Shoes. Retrieved December 2016 at http://news.xinhuanet.com/newmedia/2006-11/01/content_5277237.htm.

Cheng, Siwei (2013). Deepening Economic System Reform and Deal with the Relationship between Government and Market. *China Circulation Economy*, 27(4), pp.4–7.

CHFS (2013). *China Income Disparity Report 2013*. South Western University of Finance and Economics. Retrieved January 2017 at http://3y.uu456.com/bp_4jnu12amer2r4yi9c260_1.html.

CHFS (2016). 2015 Average Household Assets Reached RMB9.1 Billion. *Chengdu Business News*. Retrieved June 2017 at http://finance.qq.com/a/20151130/017944.htm.

China Banking Regulatory Commission (2006). Detailed Rules for the Implementation of the Regulations on the Administration of Foreign Banks. November. Retrieved August 2016 at http://www.pkulaw.cn/fulltext_form.aspx?Gid=81859.

China Banking Regulatory Commission (2007). Measures for the Administration of Finance Leasing Companies. Retrieved August 2016 at http://www.pkulaw.cn/fulltext_form.aspx?Gid=83589.

China Banking Regulatory Commission (2014). Measures for the Administration of Finance Leasing Companies. Retrieved August 2016 at http://pkulaw.cn/fulltext_form.aspx?Db=chl&Gid=220995.

China Banking Regulatory Commission and the People's Bank of China (2008). Guiding Opinions of the China Banking Regulatory Commission and the People's Bank of China on the Pilot Operation of Small-Sum Loan Companies. Retrieved October 2016 at http://www.docin.com/p-589272566.html.

China Business System (2017). Ownership of Chinese Enterprises. Retrieved April 2017 at http://www.gsxt.gov.cn/index.html.

China Enterprise Confederation and China Entrepreneur Association (2001–2013). Notice on Publishing Top 500 Chinese Enterprises. Retrieved March 2017 at http://www.cec1979.org.cn/c500/chinese/.

China.org (2016). China and WTO. Retrieved July 2016 at http://www.china.org.cn/english/features/38185.htm.

China Security Regulatory Commission (2005). Regulation on Corporation Equity Division System Reform. Retrieved August 2016 at http://www.csai.cn/gupiao/735793.html.

China Security Regulatory Commission and People's Bank of China (2002). Interim Measures on the Administration of Domestic Securities Investment by Qualified Foreign Institutional Investors. Retrieved August 2016 at http://www.pkulaw.cn/fulltext_form.aspx?Gid=43210.

Chuang, Steven N.S. (1968). Private Property Rights and Sharecropping. *Journal of Political Economy*, 76(6), pp.1107–1122.

Claessens, S., E. Feijen, and L. Laeven (2008). Political Connections and Preferential Access to Finance: The Role of Campaign Contributions. *Journal of Financial Economics*, 88, pp.554–580.

Clarke, Donald, Peter Murrell, and Susan Whiting (2008). The Role of Law in China's Economic Development. In Loren Brandt and Thomas G. Rawski (eds), *China's Great Economic Transformation*. Cambridge, UK: Cambridge University Press, pp.375–428.

Coase, Ronald H. (1937). The Nature of the Firm. *Economica*, 4(16), pp.386–405.

Csanadi, M. (2004). A Comparative Model of Party-States: The Structural Reasons behind Similarities and Differences in Self-Reproduction, Reforms and Transformation. Institute of Economics Hungarian Academy of Sciences. KTK/IE Discussion Papers 2004/7. Retrieved May 2017 at http://xueshu.baidu.com/s?wd=paperuri:(37d3af86ad54482bc144fe6b819db070)&filter=sc_long_sign&sc_ks_para=q%3DA+comparative+model+of

+party-states%3A+the+structural+reasons+behind+similarities+and+differences+in+self-reproduction%2C+reforms+and+transformation&tn=SE_baiduxueshu_c1gjeupa&ie=utf-8&sc_us=6064759805912087944.

Cull, Robert and Lixin Colin Xu (2005). Institutions, Ownership, and Finance: The Determinants of Investment among Chinese Firms. *Journal of Financial Economics*, 77, pp.117–146.

Culture.Pl (n.d.). Beijing 798 Art District. Retrieved August 2017 at http://asia.culture.pl/zh-hans/place/bei-jing-798yi-zhu-qu.

Datta-Chaudhuri, Mrinal (1990). Market Failure and Government Failure. *Journal of Economic Perspectives*, 4(3), pp.25–39.

Davis, Joseph (2017). SOE Reform Is the Only Route to Raise Productivity in China. Caixin Net, 26 July. Retrieved August 2017 at http://opinion.caixin.com/2017-07-26/101122251.html.

Daxue Consulting (2017). How Will Strict Government Regulation Affect Real Estate in China? daxueconsulting.com, 15 May. Retrieved June 2017 at http://daxueconsulting.com/real-estate-in-china/.

Deloitte Touche Tohmatsu International (1997). *International Tax and Business Guide: People's Republic of China*. New York: Deloitte Touche Tohmatsu International.

Deng, Xiaoping (1979). Four Cardinal Principles. Retrieved August 2017 at http://cpc.people.com.cn/GB/64156/64157/4509599.html.

Dezan Shira & Associates (2013). Export Tax Rebate in China. China Briefing, 22 March. Retrieved October 2016 at http://www.china-briefing.com/news/2013/03/22/export-tax-rebates-in-china.html.

Dong, Qian (2016). Bai Yansong: Few Countries Have Higher Social Security Costs than China. Sina, 18 March. Retrieved June 2017 at http://news.sina.com.cn/2016-03-18/doc-ifxqnskh0939441.shtml.

Du, Julan and Chenggang Xu (2005). Market Socialism or Capitalism? Evidence from Chinese Financial Market Development. IEA 2005 Round Table on Market and Socialism.

Du, Renhuai (2006). On the Boundary of the Effect of the Relation of Government and Market. *Modern Economic Research*, 2006(4), pp.67–70.

Faccio, M. (2006). Politically Connected Firms. *American Economic Review*, 96(1), pp.369–386.

Fan, Gang, Xiaolu Wang, and Jingwen Yu (2017). *Index of Marketization in China by Provinces: 2016*. Beijing, China: Social Science Press.

Fang, Qiang (2009). China's Current Mail-and-Visit System and Its Fundamental Predicament. *Modern China Studies*, 2009(4). Retrieved August 2017 at http://www.modernchinastudies.org/cn/issues/past-issues/106-mcs-2009-issue-4/1113-chinas-current-mail-and-visit-system-and-its-fundamental-predicament.html.

Fenghua (2012). Nian Guangjiu: Fool Melon Seeds' Founder. Finance iFeng, 13 February. Retrieved August 2017 at http://finance.ifeng.com/news/people/20120213/5568471.shtml.

Fenghuang (2012). Wang Shi's Family History. Wenxuecity, 29 October. Retrieved August 2017 at http://www.wenxuecity.com/news/2012/10/29/2053686.html.

Fisman, R. (2001). Estimating the Value of Political Connections. *American Economic Review*, 91(4), pp.1095–1102.

Flower (ed.) (2013). Kentucky Chicken's Five Quality Problems in Eight Years. Vivijk. Retrieved November 2017 at http://bgt.vivijk.com/hsp/201301/329498_2.html.

Fortune (2017). Fortune 500. Retrieved December 2017 at http://fortune.com/fortune500/list.

Fukuyama, Francis (2011). *The Origins of Political Order: From Prehuman Times to the French Revolution*. New York: Farrar, Straus and Giroux.

Gong, Ting (2008). The Party Discipline Inspection in China: Its Evolving Trajectory and Embedded Dilemmas. *Crime, Law and Social Changes*, 49(2), pp.139–152.

Guo, Xuezhi (2014). Controlling Corruption in the Party: China's Central Discipline Inspection Commission. *The China Quarterly*, 29, pp.597–624.

Haier (n.d.). Introduction of CEO. Retrieved August 2017 at http://www.haier.net/cn/about_haier/ceo/introduction/.

Hale, Galina and Cherry Long (2012). *Foreign Direct Investment in China: Winners and Losers*. Singapore: World Scientific Publishing Co.

Hao, Long (2016). The Central Committee Repeated Order to Strengthen Accountability System. *Jinghua Times*, 29 June. Retrieved June 2017 at http://news.sohu.com/20160629/n456807608.shtml.

He, Miao, Tao Luo, Honghui Liu, Zhengwei Cai, and Fuxiang Zhou (n.d.). Case of Domestic Photographic Industry Acquisition by Kodak. Retrieved January 2017 at http://wenku.baidu.com/link?url=RS6D74yOY1In8EuLMBaOTm9O6cB9VzJju9mITQZtZspbe1dsE9BMBT_UthC0fafOSI5Wkd29oYMFcVQYbD50wwThZR733-1rZuF8MnizQTK.

Hexun (2008). Tax-Sharing System 1994. Retrieved April 2016 at http://news.hexun.com/2008/1994fszgg/.

Houwang (n.d.). Six SOEs Were Selected as the First Group of Pilot Reform. Phenix Net. Retrieved January 2017 at http://finance.ifeng.com/a/20140715/12725018_0.shtml.

Huang, Zhangkai, Lixing Li, Guangrong Ma, and Colin L. Xu (2015). Hayek, Local Information, and the Decentralisation of State-Owned Enterprises in China. The World Bank, Documents and Reports. Retrieved July 2017 at http://documents.worldbank.org/curated/en/454351468188658819/Hay

ek-local-information-and-the-decentralisation-of-state-owned-enterprises-in-China.

Huang, Zhihong (2012). First Private Banks in China. *Wenzhou Daily*, 31 May. Retrieved August 2017 at http://news.66wz.com/system/2012/05/31/103196672.shtml.

Huashang Taolue (n.d.). How Was Jianlibao Brought Down? Huxiao, 18 September. Retrieved August 2017 at https://www.huxiu.com/article/164080.html.

Industrial Economic Research Institute (2008). *Chinese Industry Development Report*. Beijing, China: Economy & Management Publishing House.

Jian, Cong (2016). 2016 Central Economic Work Conference. Yjbys.com. Retrieved January 2017 at http://www.yjbys.com/news/492567.html.

Jiang, Kezhong and Yanhong Xu (2013). Fiscal Decentralisation, Extra-Budgetary Income Expansion and Public Goods Supply – A Panel Data Analysis Based on Data from China. *Journal of Gansu Institute of Public Administration*, 5, pp.98–108.

Jiang, Lingling (2013). Survey Shows Serious Polarization in Household Income. Caixin Net, 19 July. Retrieved July 2016 at http://economy.caixin.com/2013-07-19/100557990.html.

Jiang, Xiaojuan (ed.) (2008). *Thirty Years of China's Opening-Up: Growth, Structure, and Institutional Changes*. Beijing, China: People's Press.

Jiang, Xiaojuan and Jun Wang (2008). The Development of Foreign Trade and Economic Development. In Xiaojuan Jiang (ed.), *Thirty Years of China's Opening-Up: Growth, Structure, and Institutional Changes*. Beijing, China: People's Press, pp.31–68.

Jiang, Zemin (1997). *Report to the 15th National Congress of the Communist Party of China*. Retrieved February 2016 at http://CCP.people.com.cn/GB/64162/64168/64568/index.html.

Jin, Yinzhu (2018). Reducing Steel Capacity: Into Deep Water. *21st Century Report*, 9 March. Retrieved May 2018 at http://futures.hexun.com/2018-03-09/192587140.html.

Joskow, Paul L. and Roger G. Noll (1981). Regulation in Theory and Practice: An Overview. In Gary Fromm (ed.), *Studies in Public Regulation*. Cambridge, MA: MIT Press, pp.1–65.

Kang, Xiaoguang (2002). China: Political Development and Political Stability in Reform Times. *Modern China Studies*, 78, pp.29–59.

Kennedy, David, M. (1999). *Freedom from Fear*. New York: Oxford University Press.

Lan, Zhu (2009). Small and Medium Firms' Financing Difficulties: Deteriorate Financing Environment. *Huaxia Times*, 10 July. In Li, Youhuan. *Demystify Underground Banks*. Beijing, China: Economic Daily Press, 2010, pp.99–101.

Landai Gongzhu (2012). Red Capitalist Rong Yiren. 360doc, 4 October. Retrieved August 2017 at http://www.360doc.com/content/14/1004/10/2831026_414298072.shtml.

Law Library (1951). Labour Insurance Regulation. Retrieved April 2016 at http://www.law-lib.com/law/law_view.asp?id=686.

Law Library (1995). State Council's Notice on Deepening of Workers' Pension Insurance Reform. Retrieved April 2016 at http://www.law-lib.com/law/law_view.asp?id=11169.

Law Library (1997). The State Council's Decision on the Reform of a Unified Worker's Pension Insurance System. Retrieved May 2016 at http://www.law-lib.com/law/law_view.asp?id=13389.

Lenovo (n.d.). Our History. Retrieved August 2017 at http://www.lenovo.com/lenovo/us/en/company-history.shtml.

Li, Chunhui (2015). Chu Shijian: I Have Willingly Done All These. China's Entrepreneurs, 8 January. Retrieved August 2017 at http://www.iceo.com.cn/mag2013/2015/0108/298634.shtml.

Li, David (1996). A Theory of Ambiguous Property Rights in Transition Economics. *Journal of Comparative Economics*, 23(1), pp.1–19.

Li, David (1998). Changing Incentives of the Chinese Bureaucracy. *American Economic Review*, 88(2), pp.393–397.

Li, Eric (2014). Party of the Century: How China is Reorganizing for the Future. *Foreign Affairs*, 10 January.

Li, Hongbin and Li-An Zhou (2005). Political Turnover and Economic Performance: The Incentive Role of Personnel Control in China. *Journal of Public Economics*, 89, pp.1743–1762.

Li, Huizi and Erjie Zhou (2007). China's Public Complaint Department Busiest Office in Beijing. *Xinhua News Agency*, 2 September. Retrieved June 2017 at http://www.chinadaily.com.cn/china/2007-09/02/content_6142475.htm.

Li, Jianjun (2006). *Report on Underground Financial System in China*. Shanghai: Shanghai People Press.

Li, Lanbing (2010). Empirical Study of China's Railroad Efficiency. *Nankai Economic Studies*, 2010(5), pp.58–63.

Li, Ping and Wen Hu (2010). The Relationship between Government and Market in Rural and Urban Development: Case of Chengdu. *Reform*, 2010(1), pp.86–92.

Li, Yang, Jianfeng Yin, Xingyun Peng, Weibin Yu, Gang Zeng, Zhihao Hu, and Liping Zhou (2009). *China's Finance in Sixty Years*. Beijing, China: China Press of Finance and Economics.

Li, Yankai and Tingchun Han (2009). Institutional Evolution and China's Economic Growth: Empirical Analysis Based on Central Cities' Data. *Economy and Management Research*, 2009(6), pp.26–33.

Li, Youhuan (2010). *Demystify Underground Banks*. Beijing, China: Economic Daily Press.

Lin, G.C.S. (2007). Reproducing Spaces of Chinese Urbanisation: New City-Based and Land-Centred Urban Transformation. *Urban Studies*, 44, pp.1827–1855.

Lin, Justin Yifu, Fang Cai, and Zhou Li (2003). *The China Miracle: Development Strategy and Economic Reform*, Revised edition. Hong Kong: The Chinese University Press. Retrieved June 2016 at https://books.google.com/books?hl=zh-CN&lr=&id=_OEwbLZ2vYwC&oi=fnd&pg=PR19&dq=development+strategy+china+1950&ots=0Amy-33Y-U&sig=wvY3uF2cJgk3YWQUl5t29TlSFF4#v=onepage&q=development%20strategy%20china%201950&f=false.

Lin, Justin Yifu and Weiying Zhang (2017). Debate on Industrial Policy. Retrieved April 2017 at http://mt.sohu.com/20161110/n472863504.shtml.

Lingnanhui Laowang (n.d.). How to Evaluate Zhang Ruimin, the CEO of Haier? Zhihu. Retrieved August 2017 at https://www.zhihu.com/question/25971488.

Lipset, Seymour Martin (1960). *Political Man: The Social Bases of Politics*. Garden City, NY: Anchor Books.

Liu, Yuan (2014). Clear the Morally Corrupt People out of the Party. *China News Net*, 2 July. Retrieved January 2017 at http://news.21cn.com/webfocus/a/214/0702/09/27716026.shtml.

Liu, Zhaopu (2015). Dai Guofang, Tieben's Former Boss, Comeback. *China Economic Weekly*, 15 December. Retrieved August 2017 at http://news.sohu.com/20151215/n431278812.shtml.

Long, Chery (2010). Does the Rights Hypothesis Apply to China? *Journal of Law and Economics*, 53(4), pp.629–650.

Lu, Xueyi (ed.) (2002). *Research Report on Social Classes in Contemporary China*. Beijing, China: Social Science Document Pressing House.

Ma, Yong (2001). Pawnshops: Cry up Wine and Sell Vinegar. *Yangcheng Evening News*, 13 November. In Li Youhuan. *Demystify Underground Banks*. Beijing, China: Economic Daily Press, 2010, pp.47–48.

MacFarquhar, Roderick and Michael Schoenhals (2006). *Mao's Last Revolution*. Cambridge, MA: Harvard University Press.

Mann, Jim (1997). *Beijing Jeep: A Case Study of Western Business in China*. Boulder, CO: Westview Press.

Mao, Zedong (1956). On Ten Major Relationships. In *Selected Works of Mao Zedong*, 1977 edition. Beijing, China: Renmin Press, pp.267–288.

Mao, Zedong (1966). A Letter to Jiang Qing. Tianya Luntan. Retrieved August 2017 at http://bbs.tianya.cn/post-books-124114-1.shtml.

Marx, Karl (1867). Capital: a Critique of Political Economy, Vol. I. Hamburg: Verlag von Otto Meissner. First published in German.

Megginson, W.L. and J.M. Netter (2001). From State to Market: A Survey of Empirical Studies on Privatisation. *Journal of Economic Literature*, 39(2), pp.321–389.

Midea (n.d.). Midea's History. Retrieved August 2017 at http://www.midea.com/cn/about_midea/history.shtml.

Ministry of Agriculture Bureau of Policy and Law (1999). *Fifty Years of China's Rural Areas*. Zhongyuan Farmers Press.

Ministry of Finance and the People's Bank of China (2006). Central Treasury Cash Management Approach. Retrieved August 2016 at http://wenku.baidu.com/link?url=K937XjRt0c5F-CdAMD-Srt8pFFRkgKroB0zjgV_4gXBaDWrY4vRc1LQPVEWpAB_sNwkb3TLS7T-yyuH1aRVRYcZAH_L38_n-zeL7lYCART7.

National Bureau of Statistics (1984). *China Statistical Yearbook of Fixed Asset Investment*. Beijing, China: China Statistics Press.

National Bureau of Statistics (1997). *China Statistical Yearbook of Fixed Asset Investment*. Beijing, China: China Statistics Press.

National Bureau of Statistics (1999). *Comprehensive Statistical Data and Materials on 50 Years of New China*. Beijing, China: China Statistics Press.

National Bureau of Statistics (2002). *China Statistical Yearbook 2002*. Beijing, China: China Statistics Press.

National Bureau of Statistics (2009a). *China Trade and External Economic Statistical Book 2009*. Beijing, China: China Statistics Press.

National Bureau of Statistics of China (2009b). *China Statistical Yearbook 2009*. Beijing, China: China Statistics Press.

National Bureau of Statistics (2011). *China Statistical Yearbook 2011*. Beijing, China: China Statistics Press.

National Bureau of Statistics (2012). Report of a Survey on China Migrant Workers. Retrieved March 2013 at http://www.stats.gov.cn/tifx/fxbg/t20120427_402801903.htm.

National Bureau of Statistics (2013). 2003–2012 Jini Coefficients. People.com. Retrieved June 2017 at http://politics.people.com.cn/n/2013/0118/c1001-20253603.html.

National Bureau of Statistics (2015). *China Statistical Yearbook 2015*. Beijing, China: China Statistics Press.

National Bureau of Statistics (2016a). Urban and Rural Family Income and Engel Index. Retrieved May 2016 at http://data.stats.gov.cn/easyquery.htm?cn=C01.

National Bureau of Statistics (2016b). *China Statistical Yearbook 2016*. Beijing, China: China Statistics Press. Retrieved July 2017 at http://www.stats.gov.cn/tjsj/ndsj/2016/indexch.htm.

National Bureau of Statistics (2017). Gini Coefficients. Money.163.com.

Retrieved June 2017 at http://money.163.com/17/0120/14/CB7T3AFJ002 581PP.html.
National Development and Reform Commission (2015). Notice on Improving the Mechanism of Coal–Electricity Price Linkage. 31 December. Retrieved July 2017 at http://www.ndrc.gov.cn/gzdt/201512/ t20151231_770461.html.
National People's Congress (1979a). The Law of the People's Republic of China on Chinese–Foreign Contractual Joint Ventures. April. Retrieved October 2016 at http://wenku.baidu.com/link?url=fewY210i5BFEXjNXL3S8D8 6eDCGSoDYNCmFurYigeSfNw_QgeJImSPgyRBprDKaF6DcuAAE 0T7l6dVGDvC2uuzCqv_ZSnZmq8QC--mwm-nK.
National People's Congress (1979b). The Law of the People's Republic of China on Chinese-Foreign Equity Joint Ventures. July. Retrieved October 2016 at http://www.360doc.com/content/14/0211/11/15754013 _351577630.shtml.
National People's Congress (1980). Individual Income Tax Law of the People's Republic of China. Retrieved June 2017 at http://www.asianlii. org/cn/legis/cen/laws/rftiotiitl560/.
National People's Congress (1981a). Economic Contract Law of the People's Republic of China. 13 December. Retrieved December 2016 at http://www.lawinfochina.com/display.aspx?lib=law&id=18&CGid=.
National People's Congress (1981b). The Law of the People's Republic of China on Income Tax for Foreign Firms. 13 December. Retrieved October 2016 at http://www.law-lib.com/law/law_view.asp?id=44822.
National People's Congress (1982a). Constitution of the People's Republic of China. Retrieved July 2016 at http://www.npc.gov.cn/wxzl/wxzl/2000-12/06/content_4421.htm and http://china.usc.edu/constitution-peoples-republic-china-1982.
National People's Congress (1982b). Organic Law of the State Council of the People's Republic of China. Retrieved January 2017 at http://www. china.org.cn/government/laws/2007-04/16/content_1207259.htm.
National People's Congress (1982c). Revision of Organic Law on the Local People's Congress and Local Government. Retrieved January 2017 at https://zh.wikisource.org/wiki/%E7%AC%AC%E4%BA%94%E5%B1% 8A%E5%85%A8%E5%9B%BD%E4%BA%BA%E6%B0%91%E4%BB %A3%E8%A1%A8%E5%A4%A7%E4%BC%9A%E7%AC%AC%E4% BA%94%E6%AC%A1%E4%BC%9A%E8%AE%AE%E5%85%B3%E 4%BA%8E%E4%BF%AE%E6%94%B9%E3%80%8A%E4%B8%AD% E5%8D%8E%E4%BA%BA%E6%B0%91%E5%85%B1%E5%92%8C% E5%9B%BD%E5%9C%B0%E6%96%B9%E5%90%84%E7%BA%A7% E4%BA%BA%E6%B0%91%E4%BB%A3%E8%A1%A8%E5%A4%A 7%E4%BC%9A%E5%92%8C%E5%9C%B0%E6%96%B9%E5%90%8

4%E7%BA%A7%E4%BA%BA%E6%B0%91%E6%94%BF%E5%BA%9C%E7%BB%84%E7%BB%87%E6%B3%95%E3%80%8B%E7%9A%84%E8%8B%A5%E5%B9%B2%E8%A7%84%E5%AE%9A%E7%9A%84%E5%86%B3%E8%AE%AE.

National People's Congress (1984). Parent Law. March. Retrieved February 2017 at http://english.sipo.gov.cn/laws/lawsregulations/201101/t20110119_566244.html.

National People's Congress (1985). Foreign Economic Contract Law. March. Retrieved February 2017 at http://english.enorth.com.cn/system/2001/05/29/000002093.shtml.

National People's Congress (1986a). General Principles of the Civil Law of the People's Republic of China. Retrieved December 2016 at http://www.npc.gov.cn/englishnpc/Law/2007-12/12/content_1383941.htm.

National People's Congress (1986b). Enterprise Bankruptcy Law of the People's Republic of China. Retrieved December 2016 at http://baike.baidu.com/link?url=8jE7xO3eloO12B8_vMo8_eRjm-xmMdwBQBwSqAXtRZP4ezY3Lnc8cdHm9ro6kIaf0aKgnyzHlYTauflPgqFFXq.

National People's Congress (1986c). Law on Foreign Invested Enterprises. April. Retrieved February 2017 at http://www.ccpitqd.org/law/?type=detail&id=29.

National People's Congress (1987). Technology Contract Law. June. Retrieved February 2017 at www.law-lib.com/law/law_view.asp?id=48413.

National People's Congress (1988a). Amendment to the Constitution of the People's Republic of China. Retrieved June 2017 at http://www.npc.gov.cn/wxzl/wxzl/2000-12/05/content_4498.htm.

National People's Congress (1988b). Law on Industrial Enterprises Owned by the Whole People. 13 April. Retrieved February 2016 at http://www.npc.gov.cn/wxzl/gongbao/2000-12/05/content_5004501.htm. And http://www.asianlii.org/cn/legis/cen/laws/tlotprocoieobtwp833/.

National People's Congress (1988c). Law on Sino-Foreign Cooperative Joint Ventures. April. Retrieved February 2017 at http://english.mofcom.gov.cn/article/lawsdata/chineselaw/200301/20030100065891.shtml.

National People's Congress (1989). Administrative Litigation Law. Retrieved February 2017 at http://www.china.org.cn/english/g.

National People's Congress (1990). Copyright Law of the People's Republic of China. Retrieved February 2017 at http://www.chinaconsulatesf.org/eng/kj/wjfg/t43948.htm.

National People's Congress (1991). Law of the People's Republic of China on Income Tax of Foreign Invested Firms and Foreign Firms. Retrieved October 2016 at http://www.yingyu.com/e/20141121/546e7196d98c2.shtml.

National People's Congress (1993a). Corporation Law of the People's

Republic of China. 29 December. Retrieved March 2016 at http://www.doc88.com/p-370433329697.html and http://www.chinalawedu.com/new/23223a23228a2010/20101222shangf112139.shtml.
National People's Congress (1993b). Amendment of the Constitution of 1993. Retrieved February 2017 at http://www.asianlii.org/kh/legis/laws/aotco1993315/.
National People's Congress (1993c). Law against Unfair Competition. September. Retrieved February 2017 at http://www.lehmanlaw.com/resource-centre/laws-and-regulations/intellectual-property/law-of-the-peoples-republic-of-china-against-unfair-competition-1993.html.
National People's Congress (1993d). Economic Contract Law of the People's Republic of China (1993 Amendment). Retrieved February 2017 at http://en.pkulaw.cn/display.aspx?cgid=1136&lib=law.
National People's Congress (1994). Law of the People's Republic of China on Foreign Trade. Retrieved October 2016 at http://www.law-lib.com/law/law_view.asp?id=10417.
National People's Congress (1995a). Law of the People's Republic of China on Commercial Banks. Retrieved August 2016 at http://www.chinalawedu.com/new/23223a23228a2010/20101223shangf113149.shtml.
National People's Congress (1995b). Insurance Law of the People's Republic of China. Retrieved August 2016 at http://wenku.baidu.com/link?url=ChktfIIiqu4DnAq0xw0gKTXMDJ2TE1mKMjTMMTBAmA9KHC3XT_V_oXWmopPm2eKJF1kivQkh814v2T-LU8j6ZoQo8vl-0nyy404uyjxzxAMO.
National People's Congress (1995c). Civil Aviation Law of the People's Republic of China. Retrieved August 2016 at http://www.lawinfochina.com/display.aspx?lib=law&id=491&CGid=.
National People's Congress (1997a). Criminal Law of the People's Republic of China. Retrieved October 2016 at http://wenku.baidu.com/link?url=C1LyIcQwfUUjKELcJ8nAEseMGcUK8J_bGV0cjA6X3drooN_ESaG53-WKWTger6F7FHWNuyepPT_bNxYE4fIg-ZAl435RPIQeQqMqby-HOY3K.
National People's Congress (1997b). Law of the People's Republic of China on Partnership Enterprises. February. Retrieved February 2017 at http://www.fdi.gov.cn/1800000121_39_2931_0_7.html.
National People's Congress (1997c). Price Law of the People's Republic of China. December. Retrieved February 2017 at http://www.newsgd.com/business/laws/200305140333.htm.
National People's Congress (1998). Securities Law of the People's Republic of China. Retrieved August 2016 at http://www.pkulaw.cn/fulltext_form.aspx?Gid=21319 and http://www.lawinfochina.com/Display.aspx?lib=law&ID=1084.

National People's Congress (1999a). Amendment to the Criminal Law of the People's Republic of China. Retrieved October 2016 at http://www.pkulaw.cn/fulltext_form.aspx?Gid=24095.

National People's Congress (1999b). Constitution Amendment. March. Retrieved February 2017 at www.law-lib.com/law/law_view.asp?id=433.

National People's Congress (1999c). Contract Law of the People's Republic of China. March. Retrieved February 2017 at blog.sina.com.cn/s/blog_92b5622a0101rubd.html.

National People's Congress (1999d). Law on Individual Wholly Owned Enterprises. August. Retrieved February 2017 at www.t262.com/read/134076.html.

National People's Congress (1999e). Law of the People's Republic of China on Individual Proprietorship Enterprise. Retrieved March 2017 at http://www.pkulaw.cn/fulltext_form.aspx?Gid=23175.

National People's Congress (2000). Legislation Law of the People's Republic of China. March. Retrieved February 2017 at www.china.org.cn/english/government/207420.htm.

National People's Congress (2001). Trust Law of the People's Republic of China. April. Retrieved February 2017 at www.chinalawedu.com/falvyingyu/yingwenfagui/yi20131111446289397 2016.shtml.

National People's Congress (2002). Law of the People's Republic of China on Promotion of Small and Medium-Sized Enterprises. Retrieved March 2017 at http://www.eduzhai.net/yingyu/615/763/yingyu_244938.html.

National People's Congress (2003). The Law of the People's Republic of China on the People's Bank of China, 2003 amendment. Retrieved March 2017 at http://www.docin.com/p-428354746.html.

National People's Congress (2004a). Law of the People's Republic of China on Foreign Trade (revised). Retrieved October 2016 at http://wenku.baidu.com/link?url=T1OPBNEKlZ6nlg_AT5UiEHdCQRejRWhdI1FRHh1dohcr-lHgCUYEBkuFnSXYxddEUwelMAtsgyfke8r6jUXT6j7AmVjmmMGNN2BEIC6889W.

National People's Congress (2004b). Constitution of the People's Republic of China, 2004 amendment. Retrieved February 2017 at http://www.npc.gov.cn/npc/zt/qt/gjxfz/2014-12/03/content_1888091.htm.

National People's Congress (2004c). Law of the People's Republic of China on Negotiable Instruments, 2004 amendment. Retrieved March 2017 at http://www.chinalawedu.com/new/23223a23228a2010/20101217shangf12153.shtml.

National People's Congress (2004d). The Law of Land Administration of the People's Republic of China, 2004 amendment. Retrieved March 2017 at http://www.chinalawedu.com/new/23223a23228a2010/20101219shangf165932.shtml.

National People's Congress (2005a). Civil Servant Law of People's Republic of China. Retrieved January 2017 at http://www.asianlii.org/cn/legis/cen/laws/tcslotproc462/.
National People's Congress (2005b). Corporation Law of the People's Republic of China, 2nd revision. Retrieved March 2017 at http://www.chinaacc.com/new/63/73/157/2005/12/xi0768962916221500238 97-0.htm.
National People's Congress (2005c). Law of the People's Republic of China on the Protection of the Rights and Interests of Women, 2005 amendment. Retrieved March 2017 at http://www.chinalawedu.com/new/23223a23228a2010/20101214shangf135830.shtml.
National People's Congress (2006a). The Law on the Supervision by the Standing Committee of the People's Congress at Various Levels. Retrieved March 2017 at http://www.npc.gov.cn/wxzl/wxzl/2006-09/26/content_354987.htm.
National People's Congress (2006b). Partnership Law of the People's Republic of China, 2006 revision. Retrieved March 2017 at http://www.chinalawedu.com/new/23223a23228a2010/20101217shangf114549.shtml.
National People's Congress (2006c). Enterprise Bankruptcy Law. Retrieved March 2017 at http://www.niubb.net/a/2015/11-19/991038.html.
National People's Congress (2006d). Banking Supervision Law of the People's Republic of China, 2006 amendment. Retrieved March 2017 at http://www.docin.com/p-109351085.html&endPro=true.
National People's Congress (2006e). Anti-Money Laundering Law of the People's Republic of China. Retrieved March 2017 at http://www.for68.com/new/2007/2/wa72122641511127002210 22-0.htm.
National People's Congress (2006f). Audit Law of People's Republic of China, 2006 amendment. Retrieved March 2017 at http://en.pkulaw.cn/display.aspx?cgid=75164&lib=law.
National People's Congress (2007a). Antitrust Law of the People's Republic of China. Retrieved March 2017 at http://www.tradelawchina.com/falvfagui/HTML/186.html.
National People's Congress (2007b). Enterprise Income Tax Law of the People's Republic of China. Retrieved March 2017 at http://www.fdi.gov.cn/1800000121_39_3339_0_7.html.
National People's Congress (2007c). Individual Income Tax Law of the People's Republic of China, December 2007 revision. Retrieved March 2017 at http://www.chinaacc.com/new/63/67/81/2008/1/wa68853181112180027033-0.htm.
National People's Congress (2007d). Property Law of the People's Republic of China. Retrieved March 2017 at http://www.zzdzx.com/info_show.asp?news_id=36091.
National People's Congress (2008a). Enterprise State Owned Assets Law of

the People's Republic of China. Retrieved March 2017 at http://hk.lexiscn.com/law/enterprise-state-owned-assets-law-of-the-peoples-republic-of-china.html.

National People's Congress (2008b). Patent Law of the People's Republic of China, 2008 revision. Retrieved March 2017 at http://www.docin.com/p-990058356.html.

National People's Congress (2008c). Water Pollution Prevention and Control Law of the People's Republic of China, 2008 amendment. Retrieved March 2017 at http://www.pkulaw.cn/fulltext_form.aspx?a06a411d-1e2c-4343-823d-e3557aacad0f=1448434032394&Gid=2007.

National People's Congress (2008d). Law of the People's Republic of China on the Protection of Disabled Persons, 2008 amendment. Retrieved March 2017 at http://en.pkulaw.cn/display.aspx?cgid=4924&lib=law.

National People's Congress (2009a). The Tort Law of the People's Republic of China. Retrieved March 2017 at http://wenku.baidu.com/view/f4c25b8783d049649b.

National People's Congress (2009b). Administrative Penalty Law of the People's Republic of China, 2009 amendment. Retrieved March 2017 at http://www.chinalawedu.com/new/23223a23228a2010/20101216shangfl53641.shtml.

National People's Congress (2009c). Administrative Reconsideration Law of the People's Republic of China, 2009 amendment. Retrieved March 2017 at http://www.docin.com/p-390347965.html.

National People's Congress (2009d). Law of the People's Republic of China on the Administration of the Urban Real Estate, 2009 amendment. Retrieved March 2017 at http://wenku.baidu.com/link?url=sHJqwulm3Uc6kIO6e0KIpAX6p_NyedmIe4khwGgAWXsBOFPpOH64th0vpYZvyLjQyC_aTMGhHeO2_GlMfFzweFfnQ2xZF_h0mLhZ55PWuam.

National People's Congress (2009e). Law of the People's Republic of China on the Contracting of Rural Land, 2009 amendment. Retrieved March 2017 at http://en.pkulaw.cn/display.aspx?cgid=167194&lib=law.

National People's Congress (2009f). Product Quality Law of the People's Republic of China, 2009 amendment. Retrieved March 2009 at http://wenku.baidu.com/link?url=oPO7hW72YA2dQnXQ0erD7d3A__LAZWtDdYjyZaGgITUNIISB-tNdoi-tJp65J-_DU03uWa44iRVWwEdwOiJK74ojbTMpGFIZj5poG45vYne.

National People's Congress (2009g). Statistics Law of the People's Republic of China, 2009 amendment. Retrieved March 2017 at http://en.pkulaw.cn/display.aspx?cgid=118404&lib=law.

National People's Congress (2009h). The Trade Union Law of the People's Republic of China, 2009 amendment. Retrieved March 2017 at http://

www.chinalawedu.com/new/23223a23228a2010/20101214shangf13446.shtml.

National People's Congress (2009i). Labour Law of the People's Republic of China, 2009 amendment. Retrieved March 2017 at http://en.pkulaw.cn/display.aspx?cgid=9587&lib=law.

National People's Congress (2010a). Copyright Law of the People's Republic of China, 2010 revision. Retrieved March 2017 at http://wenku.baidu.com/link?url=NoFXt7eZ8oEWYe3gTjxGcCHi2SMGWL5630wtYdhN4pz2Qb305adl1T2XX01VJGVVee0d92kpaYUZVKFnnGLH9Iiqpkvb408RtgeHPf77Txa.

National People's Congress (2010b). Administrative Supervision Law of the People's Republic of China, 2010 amendment. Retrieved March 2017 at http://www.doc88.com/p-8079992180060.html.

National People's Congress (2010c). Social Insurance Law of the People's Republic of China. Retrieved March 2017 at https://wenku.baidu.com/view/d0d07ed44028915f814dc204.html.

National People's Congress (2011a). Administrative Coercion Law of the People's Republic of China. Retrieved March 2017 at http://www.doc88.com/p-662123386533.html.

National People's Congress (2011b). Individual Income Tax Law of the People's Republic of China, 2011 amendment. Retrieved August 2017 at http://www.npc.gov.cn/npc/xinwen/2011-07/01/content_1662341.htm.

National People's Congress (2012a). Law of the People's Republic of China on the Protection of Minors, 2012 amendment. Retrieved March 2017 at http://en.pkulaw.cn/display.aspx?cgid=5369&lib=law.

National People's Congress (2012b). Labour Contract Law of the People's Republic of China, 2012 amendment. Retrieved March 2017 at https://wenku.baidu.com/view/9363824876eeaeaad0f3303c.html.

National People's Congress (2013a). Trademark Law of the People's Republic of China, 2013 revision. Retrieved March 2017 at http://www.shenlantm.com/news/20141024639.html.

National People's Congress (2013b). Corporation Law of the People's Republic of China, 2013 revision. Retrieved March 2017 at http://wenku.baidu.com/link?url=OMrR-rBSyJl2AUMjwvGCx35JBPzDfTq1dtNtTCeZwWfGx8_yNmJMx6zcAPKeRIGY19I0lAb9GKUHQMV6DxKVp-S3cJYwVf0TD-eM-N4wt2eG.

National People's Congress (2014a). The Securities Law of the People's Republic of China, 2014 amendment. Retrieved March 2017 at http://www.chinalawedu.com/new/23223a23228a2010/20101214shangf14746.shtml.

National People's Congress (2014b). Environmental Protection Law of the

People's Republic of China, 2014 amendment. Retrieved March 2017 at http://wenku.baidu.com/link?url=eGaHkbmEoCCPXrnK9u8GTxS1B0JdhMC4euIeotmH1Rtu48mEVOFoF16YYrFnz1CWvLAESXVvb2ZGt3CDoAYJDPg07ZNFPFYEfabLEmBgqcu.
National People's Congress (2014c). Budget Law of the People's Republic of China, 2014 amendment. Retrieved March 2017 at http://www.pkulaw.cn/fulltext_form.aspx?Gid=233287.
National People's Congress (2014d). Government Procurement Law of the People's Republic of China, 2014 amendment. Retrieved March 2017 at http://en.pkulaw.cn/display.aspx?cgid=233283&lib=law.
National People's Congress (2014e). Work Safety Law of the People's Republic of China, 2014 amendment. Retrieved March 2017 at http://www.safehoo.com/Laws/Interpretation/201502/384140.shtml.
National People's Congress (2015a). Legislation Law of the People's Republic of China, 2015 revision. Retrieved March 2017 at http://en.pkulaw.cn/display.aspx?cgid=245693&lib=law and http://wenwen.sogou.com/z/q729772256.htm.
National People's Congress (2015b). Auction Law of the People's Republic of China, 2015 amendment. Retrieved March 2017 at http://www.pkulaw.cn/fulltext_form.aspx?gid=252607.
National People's Congress (2015c). Insurance Law of the People's Republic of China, 2015 amendment. Retrieved March 2016 at http://wenku.baidu.com/link?url=TdWKSA5zRyBSCchreqNlV8kfh0ZWtDUt-aYtK_oTIj8FcQ2IniqChllLsiavjJWz_idiwevvsTp35OY1LDJjMEb_iqs1tv7cx-_d1P2GLUW and http://qu.weixinyidu.com/e_3071497.
National People's Congress (2015d). The Law of the People's Republic of China on Commercial Banks, 2015 amendment. Retrieved March 2017 at http://max.book118.com/html/2016/1206/68685783.shtm.
National People's Congress (2015e). Security Investment Fund Law of the People's Republic of China, 2015 amendment. Retrieved March 2017 at http://www.pkulaw.cn/fulltext_form.aspx?24523fea-4f39-4c31-b60e-f02ccf13941b=1448002496234&Gid=252604.
National People's Congress (2015f). Food Safety Law of the People's Republic of China, 2015 amendment. Retrieved March 2015 at http://wenku.baidu.com/view/b2fac4b2eefdc8d377ee3263.html.
National People's Congress (2015g). Electoral Law of the People's Republic of China. Retrieved March 2017 at http://www.docin.com/p-1469519114.html.
National People's Congress (2015h). Pharmaceutical Administration Law of the People's Republic of China, 2015 amendment. Retrieved March 2017 at http://www.pkulaw.cn/fulltext_form.aspx?Gid=252632.
National People's Congress (2015i). Population and Family Planning Law

of the People's Republic of China, 2015 amendment. Retrieved March 2017 at http://www.pkulaw.cn/fulltext_form.aspx/pay/fulltext_form.aspx?Db=chl&Gid=261790.

National People's Congress (2015j). Atmospheric Pollution Prevention and Control Law of the People's Republic of China, 2015 revision. Retrieved March 2017 at http://www.pkulaw.cn/fulltext_form.aspx?Gid=256292&jiamizi=SUrXf4epKmkI7qqNs0hBgqTy/0xVJdkl and http://3g.en8848.com.cn/fanyi/law-translation/fagui/297699.html.

National People's Congress (2015k). The Law of the People's Republic of China on the Administration of Tax Collection, 2015 amendment. Retrieved March 2017 at http://wenku.baidu.com/link?url=Y9DtwBG-VUQio8rgnI6HiShwB0bfhBbmMfUOf29qAsOjxK11bJEylnBafwmziG6N8zpmyUgwjtXHkNugaZawhY3-TGni4rG7XZd6NQk_77oC.

National People's Congress (2015l). National Securities Law of the People's Republic of China. Retrieved July 2017 at http://www.chinalawtranslate.com/2015nsl/.

National People's Congress (2016a). The Law of the People's Republic of China on Sino-Foreign Equity Joint Ventures, 2016 revision. Retrieved March 2016 at pkulaw.cn/fulltext_form.aspx?Db=chl&Gid=279350&keyword=&Search_Mode=.

National People's Congress (2016b). Law of the People's Republic of China on Wholly Foreign-Owned Enterprises, 2016 amendment. Retrieved March 2017 at https://zhidao.baidu.com/question/8853285.html?fr=iks&word=%CD%E2%D7%CA%C6%F3%D2%B5%B7%A82016+%D3%A2%CE%C4&ie=gbk and https://zhidao.baidu.com/question/684555209488637972.html?fr=iks&word=%CD%E2%D7%CA%C6%F3%D2%B5%B7%A82016+%D3%A2%CE%C4&ie=gbk.

National People's Congress (2016c). The Law of the People's Republic of China on the Protection of Wildlife, 2016 amendment. Retrieved March 2017 at http://www.law-lib.com/law/law_view.asp?id=5353.

National People's Congress (2016d). Cybersecurity Law of the People's Republic of China. Retrieved March 2016 at http://en.pkulaw.cn/display.aspx?cgid=283838&lib=law.

National People's Congress (2016e). Foreign Trade Law of the People's Republic of China, 2016 revision. Retrieved March 2017 at http://www.docin.com/p-1357946739.html and http://wenku.baidu.com/link?url=VvYsphzHCZfBPjX0GzE0VGwSzCJB3OstzYzduqEf6giLZHm9SeC2GNJ3j0BGAFwZiVonXk2fZFOf7KwoanRVdtD7gvbEreefPk1Jr7vgsiUY1xKiOVEnRl1adiLRoSgG.

National People's Congress (2016f). Charity Law of the People's Republic of China. Retrieved March 2016 at http://en.pkulaw.cn/display.aspx?cgid=266755&lib=law.

Naughton, Barry (2007). *The Chinese Economy: Transitions and Growth*. Cambridge, MA: MIT Press.

Naughton, Barry (2008). A Political Economy of China's Economic Transition. In Loren Brandt and Thomas G. Rawski (eds), *China's Great Economic Transformation*. Cambridge, UK: Cambridge University Press, pp.91–135.

Nee, Victor (1992). Organisational Dynamics of Market Transition: Hybrid Forms, Property Rights, and Mixed Economy in China. *Administrative Science Quarterly*, 37(1), pp.1–27.

New Hope Group (n.d.). Introduction. Retrieved August 2017 at http://www.newhopegroup.com/jtjj/index.html.

Newsgd (2014). History of White Swan Hotel. Retrieved August 2017 at http://www.newsgd.com/gdnews/content/2014-09/15/content_108529832.htm.

North, Douglass (1981). *Structure and Change in Economic History*. New York: W.W. Norton.

North, Douglass (1990). A Transaction Cost Theory of Politics. *Journal of Theoretical Politics*, 2(4), pp.355–367. Retrieved December 2017 at https://ideas.repec.org/p/fth/waslbp/144.html.

North, Douglass (1991). Institutions. *Journal of Economic Perspectives*, 5(1), pp.97–112.

North, Douglass (2003). The Role of Institutions in Economic Development. UN Discussion Paper Series, No. 2003.2. Retrieved November 2003 at http://www.unece.org/fileadmin/DAM/oes/disc_papers/ECE_DP_2003-2.pdf.

North, Douglass, John Wallis, and Barry Weingast (2009). *Violence and Social Orders*. New York: Cambridge University Press.

Page, John (1994). The East Asian Miracle: Four Lessons for Development Policy. *NBER Macroeconomics Annual*, 9, pp.219–282.

Pei, Minxin (2007). Corruption Threatens China's Future. Carnegie Endowment for International Peace, Policy Brief No. 55, October.

Peltzman, Sam (1976). Toward a More General Theory of Regulation. *Journal of Law and Economics*, 19(2), pp.211–240.

people.com (n.d.). Top 500 Enterprises in 2014. Retrieved August 2016 at http://gx.people.com.cn/n/2015/0822/c179430-26083935.html.

People's Bank of China (1996a). Interim Measures for the Operation of RMB Business by Foreign Funded Financial Institutions in Pudong, Shanghai. Retrieved August 2016 at http://www.mofcom.gov.cn/article/b/f/200207/20020700031092.shtml.

People's Bank of China (1996b). Regulations on the Foreign Exchange System of the People's Republic of China. Retrieved November 2016 at http://www.chinalawedu.com/new/23223a23228a2010/20101221shangf115514.shtml.

People's Bank of China (1996c). Provisions on the Settlement and Sale of and Payment in Foreign Exchange. June. Retrieved November 2016 at http://www.law-lib.com/law/law_view.asp?id=287.

People's Bank of China (2000). Measures for the Administration of Financial Leasing Companies. Retrieved August 2016 at http://govinfo.nlc.gov.cn/gtfz/zfgb/gwygb/2001042011/201010/t20101011_452991.html?classid=363.

People's Bank of China (2005). Announcement of RMB Exchange Rate Regime. Retrieved October 2016 at https://www.jisilu.cn/question/39500.

People's Bank of China (2006). Regulation of the People's Republic of China on the Administration of Foreign-Funded Banks. Retrieved December 2016 at http://en.unionpay.com/merchantService/regulation/file_4420339.html.

People's Bank of China (2007a). Regulation on Inter-Bank Lending. Retrieved July 2017 at http://e-chaupak.net/database/Legal_Work_Manual/2007/bmgz/mh04.htm.

People's Bank of China (2007b). Regulations of the People's Bank of China on the Implementation of Anti-Money Laundering Investigation. Retrieved October 2016 at http://wenku.baidu.com/link?url=K3zh6vFtyyC-lqx30nS-mTUXVxZpTyLFmrxcgKLlpaIeh0dZnmDd4dtU6MbzQoW4QKeSV4MFoHy-19DBDPEijuTVqNBQuE8EoQ3fWX2Q-FwS.

Polanyi, Karl (1957 [1944]). *The Great Transformation: The Political and Economic Origins of Our Time*. Boston, MA: Beacon Press.

Popov, Vladimir (2007). Lessons from the Transition Economies: Putting the Success Stories of the Postcommunist World into a Broader Perspective. WIDER Working Paper Series 015, World Institute for Development Economic Research (UNU-WIDER).

Przeworski, Adam (2003). *States and Markets: A Primer in Political Economy*. Cambridge, UK: Cambridge University Press.

Qian, Yingyi, Gerard Roland, and Chenggang Xu (1999). Why Is China Different from Eastern Europe? Perspectives from Organisation Theory. *European Economic Review*, 43(4–6), pp.1085–1094.

Qian, Yingyi and Chenggang Xu (1993). Why China's Economic Reform Differ: The M-Form Hierarchy and Entry/Expansion of the Non-State Sector. *Economics of Transition*, 1, pp.135–170.

Rosen, Daniel, Scott Rozelle, and Jikun Huang (2004). *Roots of Competitiveness: China's Evolving Agriculture Interests*. Washington, DC: Institute for International Economics.

SAIC (2015). Background Material of Business System Reform. 27 February. Retrieved June 2017 at http://www.china.com.cn/zhibo/zhuanti/ch-xinwen/2015-02/27/content_34903439.htm.

SASAC (2006). Guiding Opinion on Carrying Forward the Adjustment of the State-Owned Capital and the Restructuring of the SOEs. Retrieved October 2016 at http://baike.baidu.com/link?url=Nvqlgqr-jN5aYdR6qPC8n-Z4hU3RVPo57gmbhw5c6wCsm39YTPBZYPgx_Ezu69BCXJicGLWC7kiZpOa_U7hOXq.

SASAC (2009). *Review of the Five Years of SASAC*. January. In Zheng, Haihang, Ludong Qi, and Dongmei Wu (2009). State-Owned Asset Management System and State-Owned Holding Companies. Beijing, China: Economic and Management Press, p. 8.

Sha, Yinhua (2010). China's Social Security System – Present Status and Issues. *Baidu Wenku*. 2010. Retrieved November 2017 at https://wenku.baidu.com/view/ba9a1336f111f18583d05a21.html.

Shambaugh, David (2016). *China's Future*. Cambridge, UK: Policy Press.

Sheng, Hong (2017). On Concept of Law in Hayek's Theory. *Zhongping Weekly*, no. 28.

Shleifer, Andrei and Robert Vishny (1994). Politicians and Firms. *Quarterly Journal Economics*, 109(4), pp.995–1025.

Shue, Vivienne (1988). *The Reach of the State: Sketches of the Chinese Body Politic*. Stanford, CA: Stanford University Press.

Sina Finance (2007). PetroChina and Sinopec Involved in the Case of Du's Underground Bank. Retrieved October 2016 at http://finance.sina.com.cn/blank/dushiqianzh.shtml.

Sommerville, Quentin (2009). Corruption up among China Government Officials, BBC, 9 January.

State Administration of Foreign Exchange (1996). Approach of Private Exchange of Foreign Exchange. May. Retrieved November 2016 at http://www.law-lib.com/law/law_view.asp?id=12409.

State Commission of Economic System Reform (1992). Normative Opinion on Limited Liability Companies. Retrieved February 2017 at http://www.51wf.com/print-law?id=1152668.

State Council (1977). Regulations on Reorganisation and Enhancing Banking Activities (Draft). 28 November. Retrieved August 2016 at http://www.lawyee.net/Act/Act_Display.asp?RID=183466.

State Council (1979a). Provisions on Several Issues of the Development of Commune and Brigade Run Enterprises. July. Retrieved December 2016 at http://law1.law-star.com/law?fn=chl003s113.txt.

State Council (1979b). Measures for the Development of Foreign Processing and Assembly and the Medium and Small Sized Compensation Trade. Retrieved October 2016 at http://hk.lexiscn.com/law/law-chinese-1-3426.html.

State Council (1980). A Temporary Regulation on Implementing 'Division of Revenue and Expenditure Classified Contract' Fiscal Management System. February 1980. Retrieved July 2016 at http://fgk.chinalaw.gov.cn/article/xzfg/198002/19800200268001.shtml.

State Council (1982). A Notice on the Status of the Bank of China. 31 August. Retrieved August 2016 at http://www.kuaiji.com/fagui/1440603?utm_source=fagui&utm_content=zx_right.

State Council (1984a). Improvement to the Committee of Economic Reform, the Ministry of Commerce, and the Ministry of Agriculture's 'Report on Further Improving Rural Commodity Circulation'. 19 July. Retrieved February 2016 at http://CCP.people.com.cn/GB/64184/64186/66701/4495406.html.

State Council (1984b). Interim Provision of the State Council on the Further Expansion of the Autonomy of the State-Owned Industrial Enterprises. 10 May. Retrieved June 2017 at http://news.xinhuanet.com/ziliao/2005-02/07/content_2558234.htm.

State Council (1985). Interim Provisions on Strengthening Vitality of Large and Medium-Sized SOEs. 11 September. Retrieved February 2016 at https://translate.google.com/translate?hl=en&sl=zh-CN&u=http://news.xinhuanet.com/ziliao/2005-02/06/content_2554639.htm&prev=search.

State Council (1986a). Regulations on Deepening the Enterprises Reform and Enhancing the Vitality of Enterprises. 5 December. Retrieved February 2016 at http://www.gov.cn/zhengce/content/2012-09/21/content_3893.htm.

State Council (1986b). Provisional Regulations of the People's Republic on the Control of Banks Management. Retrieved August 2016 at http://www.pkulaw.cn/fulltext_form.aspx?Gid=2657.

State Council (1987). Provisional Regulations on the Administration of Urban and Township Individual Industrial and Commercial Households. September. Retrieved December 2016 at http://baike.baidu.com/link?url=F-qVe-LhxD_DFNc3Ii0pM0xiyPD8FXEJkaHoPvx6kGgo3I8pgWib69hP8zhiyj-9gj4tlUeryem9brvu6eT2HHAR1jwej-iTBLUVjo92dNLqI2mndUPOhg2lIj7-AsPn1I4Oe91dlA6554Rw_S5_9PFtnqiRYmSE9FS7MUbIR2-Kf1ovqudulTGMIV8ED4P-Wfh7yOcAcKrg0vk1FroamEvG_xJRfj3F3CfwnHzXG3u.

State Council (1988a). Provisional Regulations on SOEs' Contract Responsibility System. Retrieved February 2016 at https://www.google.com/webhp?sourceid=chrome-instant&ion=1&espv=2&ie=UTF-8#q=1988%E5%B9%B4%E5%85%A8%E6%B0%91%E6%89%80%E6%9C%89%E5%88%B6%E4%BC%81%E4%B8%9A%E6%89%BF%E5%8C%85%E7%BB%8F%E8%90%A5%E8%B4%A3%E4%BB%BB%E5%88%B6%E6%9D%A1%E4%BE%8B.

State Council (1988b). Decision to Speed Up and Deepen the Reform of Foreign Trade System Reform. Retrieved October 2016 at http://baike.baidu.com/link?url=eq5vqKmA85xp0qae3DAsSTkZzXgoleqdnxjn3vh2aklrTYXiZvZbXzI10OykX2rCNgmknwT6E0wYoc1ZaA9pmkdyOmTLM7CYZOtRvk64u5zKQgw-iYHDdFU5wkyi9bPJbdVs2QyUhlFeLz020yow64qFKW1xVV8i251Yfw_2lHc5wu3cWJWGF-p8g_HVv2W3MSojDs5DOHELdua6i6wI8iaqhd6JNVnxxDcabQx7cge7UcgaUu-nU3mV8kDBLvGAb9YT3_EbBu5mjf9SWJj5oTfX7n4QtO-0wxPFfw5a_yenZUZsUeo5Wm8LUF_Z0X9OOmb60UOHGRBsGG1wTZ-UJJstSawZHJxc3v9Guhqk0W47lAqQZI-JitS9Locoju64.

State Council (1988c). Provisional Regulations of the People's Republic of China on Private Enterprises. June. Retrieved February 2017 at http://en.pkulaw.cn/display.aspx?id=1286&lib=law.

State Council (1990). Provisional Regulations of the People's Republic of China on Assigning and Transferring the Urban State-Owned Land-Use Right – 1990. 19 May. Retrieved June 2017 at http://www.mlr.gov.cn/zwgk/flfg/tdglflfg/200601/t20060119_642175.htm and http://www.lehmanlaw.com/resource-centre/laws-and-regulations/real-estate/provisional-regulations-of-the-peoples-republic-of-china-on-assigning-and-transferring-the-urban-state-owned-land-use-right-1990.html.

State Council (1993a). Corporate Bond Management Regulations. August. Retrieved August 2016 at https://translate.google.com/translate?hl=en&sl=zh-CN&u=http://www.gov.cn/gongbao/content/2011/content_1860733.htm&prev=search and http://www.gov.cn/gongbao/content/2011/content_1860733.htm.

State Council (1993b). Provisional Regulations on the Administration of Issuance and Trading of Stock. April. Retrieved February 2017 at http://wenku.baidu.com/link?url=dbGgJs2e7a5mqkfbIabwWuQ8Z31F-KVPtrWTnGzjEkJqPxU7ccUmwluuiwOrBcNcEAsIBX1w27-YONdv2zgBOQjW-C-jT5bC2HfcB8raYdWW.

State Council (1993c). Decision of the State Council on Reform of the Financial System. 25 December. Retrieved August 2016 at http://www.lawinfochina.com/display.aspx?lib=law&id=6265&CGid= and https://translate.google.com/translate?hl=en&sl=zh-CN&u=http://www.lawinfochina.com/law/display.asp%3FID%3D6265%26DB%3D1&prev=search.

State Council (1994). Regulations on the Administration of Foreign Funded Financial Institutions. Retrieved August 2016 at http://www.law-lib.com/law/law_view.asp?id=10238.

State Council (1995). Regulations of the State Council on Domestic Listing of Foreign-Oriented Stocks by Share-Holding Companies. Retrieved August 2016 at http://www.pkulaw.cn/fulltext_form.aspx?Gid=13485.

State Council (1996). Detailed Rules for the Implementation of the Listing of Foreign Shares of Co. Ltd. Retrieved May 2017 at http://baike.baidu.com/link?url=_uGmmEPXVjj9zTLxFLPx8OnRRAvim38cty-7nmOr8sXf2GSd8CanmTfhUEZS3y3edwh9_vyUzQddXovmoZBRprVcMzNFiplhLv-VIB5qCZrvO-JOsPsNzBgcSHzvmpxfgJNoTE7ZxOWQrAvTwTjuin6WXrYdxMFp7HvQMqR6sn4GHfAhfAb9uNTAtuirnwXEPGIeTIzk6DeyS-mJJmxcbe_2oOJMJAaXsYkJQCaQubkN0ht0EraoXYeQWBmqoSmR5-YhDN1Zuf3HO4uTpr06XcngYofMzb9x-kJFmZRioqXR2Cd_JIB039bHVgif_dzEN.
State Council (1998). Measures for the Banning of Illegal Financial Institutions and Illegal Financial Business Activities. 13 July. Retrieved September 2016 at http://www.gov.cn/gongbao/content/2011/content_1860858.htm.
State Council (1999). Regulations on Urban Residents' Minimum Living Insurance. Retrieved April 2016 at www.gov.cn/banshi/2005-08/04/content_20243.htm.
State Council (2001a). Antidumping Regulations of the People's Republic of China. November. Retrieved February 2017 at http://china.findlaw.cn/info/jingjifa/fanqingxiaofa/fqx/qxtl/1062132.html.
State Council (2001b). Antisubsidy Regulations of the People's Republic of China. November. Retrieved February 2017 at http://baike.baidu.com/link?url=_P293xonZH3Us6PHfYcfNcPe4xtg4EvmYJWzKD8c6gDDZbM0hQy8IbYxQUpsMU5im2jZs9pySpNbaKVxMxqRXCRzSwYVjp3ViohvjSSZtAZqirNABqkRkDAWfkvfUKxWri-X9eONxwjQ0t4qS-a_IqoSKexmbTs3Wigc-wBLLVE7Xm9dal8vthAtDHXM-0BbAreZ3LBlXICtp0aX3i3idYXMDqGWTtOlwa3U4lauevGi.
State Council (2003). Administrative Licence Law of the People's Republic of China. August. Retrieved February 2017 at http://www.lehmanlaw.com/resource-centre/laws-and-regulations/administration/administrative-license-law-of-the-peoples-republic-of-china-2003.html.
State Council (2005). Regulation on Letters and Visits. Retrieved December 2016 at http://wenku.baidu.com/link?url=p830Ou3LluYxPuOcKb_U9vM8EKUMD-TBxvGTI1nHg1Ocphtx3PColq7mKrZc8WsD_wtoe0uEOqAMWHCEhjhtXkP_K4zpP1DvWKJsG8PPwDK.
State Council (2006). Regulations on the Administration of Foreign Banks. Retrieved August 2016 at http://www.360doc.com/content/14/1031/17/6936776_421487626.shtml.
State Council (2007). The Regulations on the Disclosure of Government Information. 5 April. Retrieved June 2017 at http://en.pkulaw.cn/display.aspx?cgid=90387&lib=law.
State Council (2008a). Provisional Regulations of the People's Republic of China on Value-Added Tax, 2008 revision. Retrieved March 2017

at http://wenku.baidu.com/link?url=Mx84UAxV1Arlp-UKWmiiUHHRICl1mID-_xDEpCKdqxp8l6u1bB5n3hm0HkFNLSpybci0__kh64rGHO2yfsUvsjM9twJKn0wQ4yFTTm4nf31K.

State Council (2008b). Provisional Regulations of the People's Republic of China on Consumption Tax, 2008 revision. Retrieved March 2017 at http://www.pkulaw.cn/fulltext_form.aspx?gid=110550 and http://www.yingyu.com/e/20141121/546e71adbbab2_2.shtml.

State Council (2008c). Provision Regulations of the People's Republic of China on Business Tax, 2008 revision. Retrieved March 2017 at http://www.pkulaw.cn/fulltext_form.aspx?Gid=110548.

State Council (2010). Several Opinions of the State Council on Encouraging and Guiding the Healthy Development of Private Investment. Retrieved October 2016 at http://www.pkulaw.cn/fulltext_form.aspx?Gid=130117&b995b783-d178-4870-8de0-2637e235c3b5=1448022259989.

State Council (2011). Regulations on the Expropriation of Buildings on State-Owned Land and Compensation. Retrieved March 2017 at http://www.pkulaw.cn/fulltext_form.aspx?Gid=144434.

State Council (2014). Opinions on the Reform of Resident Registration System. No. 25. 24 July. Retrieved July 2017 at http://www.gov.cn/zhengce/content/2014-07/30/content_8944.htm.

State Council (2015). Interim Regulation on Residence Permits. Retrieved March 2017 at http://pkulaw.cn/fulltext_form.aspx?Gid=261267&Db=chl.

State Intellectual Property Office (2011). Patent Law of the People's Republic of China. Retrieved November 2016 at http://english.sipo.gov.cn/laws/lawsregulations/201101/t20110119_566244.html.

State Planning Commission (1998). List of Industries, Products and Techniques Currently Encouraged by the State. Retrieved October 2016 at http://xueshu.baidu.com/s?wd=paperuri:(7552525eca41ceb749b01a2e38a37bc3)&filter=sc_long_sign&sc_ks_para=q%3D%E3%80%8A%E5%BD%93%E5%89%8D%E5%9B%BD%E5%AE%B6%E9%87%8D%E7%82%B9%E9%BC%93%E5%8A%B1%E5%8F%91%E5%B1%95%E7%9A%84%E4%BA%A7%E4%B8%9A%E3%80%81%E4%BA%A7%E5%93%81%E5%92%8C%E6%8A%80%E6%9C%AF%E7%9B%AE%E5%BD%95%E3%80%8B%E9%A2%81%E5%B8%83&tn=SE_baiduxueshu_c1gjeupa&ie=utf-8&sc_us=17064965281743078144.

State Planning Commission, State Economic and Trade Commission, and Ministry of Foreign Trade and Economic Co-operations (1997). Category of Industries Guidelines for Foreign Investment. Retrieved October 2016 at http://www.pkulaw.cn/fulltext_form.aspx?Gid=19679.

Stigler, George J. (1971). Theory of Economic Regulation. *Bell Journal of Economics and Management Science*, 2(1), pp.3–21.

Stiglitz, Joseph (1996). Some Lessons from the East Asian Miracle. *The World Bank Research Observer*, 11(2), pp.151–177.

Stiglitz, Joseph (2003). Globalization and the Economic Role of the State in the New Millennium. *Industrial and Corporate Change*, 12(1), pp.3–26.

Stiglitz, Joseph (2016). The State, the Market, and Development. WIDER Working Paper Series 001, World Institute for Development Economic Research (UNU-WIDER).

Sun, Liping (2002). New Trend of China's Social Structure since Mid-1990s. *Modern China Studies*, 78, pp.5–28.

Sun, Longji (2015). *The Deep Structure of the Chinese Culture*. Beijing, China: China CITIC Press.

Tencent (n.d.). About Tencent. Retrieved August 2017 at https://www.tencent.com/en-us/abouttencent.html.

Tian, Guoqiang and Xudong Chen (2015). The Key of the Fast Growth of the Chinese Economy: Letting the Market Play a Decisive Role. Youmenghuizhou. Retrieved May 2017 at http://www.360doc.com/content/15/0827/15/26899349_495191193.shtml.

Transparency International (2006). *Chinese National Integrity System Study 2006*. 7 December, p.13. Retrieved July 2017 at https://www.transparency.org/files/content/nis/NISVietnam20061.pdf.

Viscusi, W. Kip, Joseph E. Harrington, Jr, and John M. Vernon (2005). *Economics of Regulation and Antitrust*, 4th edition. Cambridge, MA: MIT Press.

Wade, Robert (1990). *Governing the Market: Economic Theory and the Role of Government in East Asian Industrialization*. Princeton, NJ: Princeton University Press.

Wang, Aiyun (2013). The Forming and Impacts of China's Identity Society in the Area of Mao. Fenghuang Network, 4 December. Retrieved January 2016 at http://news.ifeng.com/history/zhongguoxiandaishi/special/maozedongshidaishouru/detail_2013_12/04/31801720_0.shtml.

Wang, Edward (2016). Ling Jihua, Ex-Presidential Aid in China, Gets Life Sentence for Corruption. *New York Times*, 4 July. Retrieved August 2016 at http://www.nytimes.com/2016/07/05/world/asia/china-ling-jihua-sentence.html?_r=0.

Wee, Sui-Lee (2017). China Vows Punishment for Deals Overseas. *New York Times*, 19 August.

Wen, James G. (2006). An Economic Geographical Research on China's Long Peasants Based Society. In M. Hua (ed.), *Institutional Change and Long-Term Economic Development: A Comparative Historical Analysis on the Differences in Market Expansion and Economic Dynamic Development between Pre-modern Europe and China*. Shanghai: Fudan University Press, pp.191–236.

World Bank (n.d.). Total Tax Rate. Retrieved June 2017 at http://data.worldbank.org/indicator/IC.TAX.TOTAL.CP.ZS.

World Trade Organization (2001). Accession of the People's Republic of China. Retrieved October 2016 at http://wenku.baidu.com/link?url=sV-bP8mLpg7lM7oQCDGitmAGOLorzBwJzmuK89rssGK2zMKWUM-DqDnkG3E1Pt9dFxeiDS2y4sDVZcXnBoYFVbLEblC4aNrsNHtJIQbsN19ia.

Wu, Jinglian and Guochuan Ma (2013). *Restarting the Reform Agenda.* Beijing, China: SDX Joint Publishing.

Wu, Wei (2014a). Deng Xiaoping's Speech 'The Party and State Leadership System Reform'. *New York Times* (Chinese version), 21 January. Retrieved February 2016 at http://cn.nytimes.com/china/20140121/cc21wuwei/.

Wu, Wei (2014b). 'Price Breaking through the Barrier' Ended and Overthought Zhao in Beijing. *New York Times* (Chinese version), 3 November. Retrieved February 2016 at https://cn.nytimes.com/china/20141103/cc03wuwei35/?mcubz=1.

Wu, Xiaobo (2014a). *Surging in 30 Years I.* Beijing, China: China CITIC Press.

Wu, Xiaobo (2014b). *Surging in 30 Years II.* Beijing, China: China CITIC Press.

Wu, Zhenqiu (2009). Policy Suggestions on Economic Efficiency of Natural Monopoly Industries in Regulation Re-structuring. In Junhao Wang (ed.), *Antitrust and Government Regulation: Theory and Policy.* Beijing, China: Economy and Management Publishing House, pp.298–311.

Xi, Jinping (2014). Explanation about 'CCP Central Commission's Decision on Several Important Problems about a Comprehensive Ruling by Law'. 20 October. China Copyright and Media. Retrieved July 2017 at https://chinacopyrightandmedia.wordpress.com/2014/10/29/explanation-concerning-the-ccp-central-committee-decision-concerning-some-major-questions-in-comprehensively-moving-governing-the-country-according-to-the-law-forward/.

Xiao, Fengbo (2009). Lessons from Chunlan Group Diversification Failure. People's University Thesis. Retrieved August 2017 at http://www.3mbang.com/p-28.html.

Xiao, Gongqin (2012). *Beyond Left and Right Radicalism.* Hangzhou, China: Zhejiang University Press.

Xiao, Guoliang and Fumin Sui (2011). *Economic History of the People's Republic of China.* Beijing, China: Peking University Press.

Xinhua (2016). China to Formulate Accountability System for SOE Managers. Sohu, 24 August. Retrieved June 2017 at http://www.sohu.com/a/111752984_161402.

Xinhua News Agency commentator (2016). Tightening the Cage of an All-Out Effort to Enforce Strict Party Discipline. *Xinhua Daily Telegraph*, 18 July. Retrieved June 2017 at http://news.xinhuanet.com/mrdx/2016-07/18/c_135520343.htm.

Xu, Chenggang (2011). The Fundamental Institutions of China's Reforms and Development. *Journal of Economic Literature*, 49, pp.1076–1151.

Xu, Hongcai (2005). *China Capital Operation Cases: Innovation*. Tsinghua University Press. Retrieved August 2017 at https://books.google.com/books?id=WlE05_3Oa2MC&pg=PA108&lpg=PA108&dq=TCL+%E6%94%B9%E9%9D%A9&source=bl&ots=CyRRSgiwdP&sig=6Ck116YBR_mHR19ktXPiOwyGDJk&hl=en&sa=X&ved=0ahUKEwj_rdTcsfrVAhUI5oMKHadtBfAQ6AEIMzAC#v=onepage&q=TCL%20%E6%94%B9%E9%9D%A9&f=false.

Xu, Zhijin (2017). Yang Rong Come Back. Sina, 22 February. Retrieved August 2017 at http://auto.sina.com.cn/news/ct/2017-02-22/detail-ifyarrcf5381698.shtml.

Yang, Bibo (n.d.). The Approval of State Owned Asset Transfer by SASAC. Retrieved August 2017 at https://www.zhihu.com/question/20915697.

Yang, Decai (2006). Institutional Evolution and China's Transfer of Surplus Agricultural Labour Force in China. *Modern Economic Research*, 2006(12), pp.49–52.

Yang, Long (2009). Secret of the Underground Banks in Ordos: RMB5 Million Operating Funds. *China News Weekly*, 27 May. In Li, Youhuan. *Demystify Underground Banks*. Beijing, China: Economic Daily Press, 2010, pp.85–87.

Yang, Xiaokai (2004). Curse to the Late Comer. *New Finance and Economics*, 2004(8), pp.120–122.

Yao, Zhongqiu (2013). *Outline of Chinese History*. Haikou, China: Hainan Press.

Ying (2017). Economic Watch: Securities Watchdog Stresses Strict Supervision. *Xinhua*, 18 February. Retrieved June 2017 at http://news.xinhuanet.com/english/2017-02/18/c_136066374.htm.

Yu, Donghui (2015). Feelings on Entrepreneurship. *China Business News*, 2 January. Retrieved August 2017 at http://finance.sina.com.cn/leadership/crz/20150102/222021214387.shtml.

Yu, Shaoxiang (n.d.). New Rural Cooperative Medical Insurance System. Retrieved August 2017 at http://www.iolaw.org.cn/showNews.asp?id=22842.

Yu, Wentang (2015). Lenders Ordinance. 360doc, 19 April. Retrieved October 2016 at http://www.360doc.com/content/15/0419/02/819919_464261425.shtml.

ZGTLYS (2016). Proposal of Railroad Reform 2017. *Sohu News*, 27

September. Retrieved August 2017 at http://www.zgdlys.cn/yslw/2016/0927/24519.html.

Zhang, Chaohua (ed.) (2016). China's Richest Man Mu Qizhong Released from Prison and Plan to Re-start His Experiment. *New Beijing News*, 28 September. Retrieved August 2017 at http://news.xinhuanet.com/finance/2016-09/28/c_129302818_2.htm.

Zhang, Fan (2014). *China's Urbanisation and the World Economy*. Cheltenham, UK and Northampton, MA, USA: Edward Elgar Publishing.

Zhang, Jumei, Anna Shi, and Shasha Shi (2008). An Empirical Research on Institutional Evolution and the Expansion of Natural Monopoly Industries: A Case of Water, Electricity and Gas Supply Sectors. *Industrial Technology Economics*, 27(7), pp.95–97.

Zhang, Jun (2014). *Market, Government Governance, and the Economic Transition in China*. Shanghai, China: Truth and Wisdom Press.

Zhang, Qianfan (2012). *State Sovereign and Local Autonomy*. Beijing, China: China Democracy and Law Press.

Zhang, Shouwen (2014). Legal Adjustments of the Relation between Government and the Market. *China Legal Science*, 2014(5), pp.60–74.

Zhang, Tingzhi (2009). *Liu Yonghao: A Biography*. Beijing, China: Enterprise Management Press. Retrieved August 2017 at http://www.99lib.net/book/8037/index.htm.

Zhang, Weiying (2014). *Market vs. Government: The Key Game of China's Reform*. Xian, China: North-West University Press.

Zhang, Wenjun (2017). Private Firms' Auto Production: Hardships. Sina, 5 May. Retrieved August 2017 at http://auto.sina.com.cn/news/hy/2017-05-05/detail-ifyeycfp9270210.shtml.

Zhang, Yan and Liutang Gong (2005). Tax Sharing Reform, Fiscal Decentralisation, and China's Economic Growth. *Economics*, 2005(04), pp.75–108.

Zhao, Fanyu and Jun Yan (2010). *Ren Zhengfei*. Wuhan, China: Huazhong Science University Press. Retrieved August 2017 at https://books.google.com/books?id=KfgBDgAAQBAJ&pg=PT279&lpg=PT279&dq=%E4%BB%BB%E6%AD%A3%E9%9D%9E+%E5%8D%8E%E4%B8%BA%E5%9F%BA%E6%9C%AC%E6%B3%95&source=bl&ots=BZUa75JwCQ&sig=YOwoF3rG-TKqDEQVJrXGrpiyG84&hl=en&sa=X&ved=0ahUKEwjXjtzZufrVAhWL6IMKHWE9BdgQ6AEITjAE#v=onepage&q=%E4%BB%BB%E6%AD%A3%E9%9D%9E%20%E5%8D%8E%E4%B8%BA%E5%9F%BA%E6%9C%AC%E6%B3%95&f=false.

Zhao, Xiao (2010). Can China Bypass the Heavy-Chemical Industry Stage? *New Wealth*, 11 March. Retrieved July 2016 at http://www.xcf.cn/ztlb/201003/t20100311_78554.htm.

Zhao, Yanjing (2014). Land Finance: History, Logic and Choices. *Baidu Wenku*. Retrieved June 2017 at https://wenku.baidu.com/view/8d2045c4aaea998fcd220ee7.html.
Zhao, Yanjing (2016). Local Government Official on Land Financing. *First Finance Economics Daily*, 9 October.
Zhao, Ziyang (1987). Report of the 13th National Congress of the Communist Party of China. 25 October. Retrieved February 2016 at http://CCP.people.com.cn/GB/64162/64168/64566/.
Zhao, Ziyang (2009). *The Secret Journal of Zhao Ziyang*. Hong Kong: New Century Press of Hong Kong.
Zheng, Haihang, Ludong Qi, and Dongmei Wu (2009). *State-Owned Asset Management System and State-Owned Holding Companies*. Beijing, China: Economic and Management Press.
Zheng, Lixin (2013). The Relationship between Government and Market: Core Issue of the Economic System Reform. *Qiushi*, 2013(2), pp.18–20.
Zheng, Yongnian (2013). *De Facto Federalism in China: Reforms and Dynamics of Central–Local Relations*. Beijing, China: Oriental Press.
Zheng, Yongnian (2016). *A Route Map of China's Reform*. Beijing, China: Oriental Press.
Zhong, Qinghui (ed.) (2017). 2016 Inner-Party Supervision Coverage and National Supervision System Reform Report. People's Net, 6 January. Retrieved June 2017 at http://news.sohu.com/20170106/n477976630.shtml.
Zhou, Junsheng (2014). Why Ma Shengli's Contracting Failed? *Changjiang Business News*, 10 February. Retrieved August 2017 at http://finance.sina.com.cn/review/jcgc/20140210/074518160458.shtml.
Zhou, Li'an (2008). *Local Government in Transition: Official Incentives and Governance*. Shanghai, China: Truth & Wisdom Press.
Zhou, Qiren (2004). *Property Rights and Institutional Changes: Empirical Studies of China's Economic Reform*. Beijing, China: Peking University Press.
Zhou, Qiren (2013). *Urban and Rural China*. Beijing, China: China CITIC Press.
Zhu, Weijiu (2010). Towards Governance by Rule of Law. In Cai Dingjian and Wang Chenguang (eds), *China's Journey toward the Rule of Law: Legal Reform, 1978–2008*. Lieden: Koninklijke Brill NV and Beijing, China: Social Sciences Academic Press, pp.101–154. Retrieved January 2017 at https://books.google.com/books?id=nj-EjS0xyN4C&pg=PA429&lpg=PA429&dq=Rules+and+Anti-rule+Behavior+in+china&source=bl&ots=aNiw6o9RHA&sig=lBco-Km_kub4tskBVO5AGL_r4ZU&hl=en&sa=X&ved=0ahUKEwifoIDbgerRAhUJJCYKHRvDCRUQ6AEIIzAC#v=onepage&q=Rules%20and%20Anti-rule%20Behavior%20in%20china&f=false.

Index